Koo Koo Land

Koo Koo Land

a memoir

GLORIA NORRIS

Regan Arts.

NEW YORK

Regan Arts.

65 Bleecker Street

New York, NY 10012

First Regan Arts hardcover edition, January 2016.

Library of Congress Control Number: 2015930624

ISBN 978-1-941393-60-4

Names and identifying details of some of the people portrayed in this book have been changed.

Interior design by Nancy Singer
Jacket design by Catherine Casalino

Printed in the United States of America

10 9 8 7 6 5 4 3 2 1

The stone's been cast and blood's
thicker than water.
And the sins of the family fall
on the daughter . . .

—P. F. Sloan, 1965

For Shirley, Virginia, Susan & Doris
And for James

Blood Feast

It was so hot you could die.

It was summer vacation 1963 and we were going to the drive-in to see a slice-and-dice called *Blood Feast*.

We lived in Manchester, the so-called Queen City of New Hampshire. The drive-in was in the boonies, in nowheresville. We had a drive ahead of us.

My father, Jimmy Norris, herded us into his Pontiac Chieftain. He wanted to get there early. Normally, Jimmy never got anywhere early. Waiting was for jerkos. He preferred to let the other guy wait for him. But tonight was special.

"It's the hour of reckoning, little girls," he cackled in his scary, Boris Karloff voice as he took the corner leading out of the projects at a speed fast enough to make the wheels emit a sharp squeal.

"Jim," protested my mother, Shirley, clutching the paper bag with our supper so it wouldn't go flying. The word seemed to evaporate the moment it left her shimmery pink lips.

Jimmy crooked his right hand into a claw. There was dark hair growing on the knuckles, and mysterious grime under the nails. I had seen that hand rip out the still-warm guts of dead animals ten times my size. I knew what it was capable of.

Jimmy drove with his left hand and swiped the clawed hand behind him into the backseat. The Hairy Claw was going for any part of us it could get.

Virginia, my fourteen-year-old half sister, buried her head under her arms as she'd been taught to do in school to ward off a nuclear blast.

I was five years younger but I took on the Hairy Claw.

As it groped for a fistful of flesh, I grabbed it with both hands. It escaped and clamped down hard on one of my spindly wrists. My fingers with their gnawed-on fingernails wriggled helplessly like earthworms trapped in a Skippy peanut butter jar.

I tried to pry the Hairy Claw off, but it squeezed harder. I pictured my hand snapping off and my stumpy arm pumping blood all over the car. I thought how mad Jimmy'd be if I bled on the upholstery. I'd thrown up a butterscotch-dip

1

ice cream cone in his last car and he'd threatened to brain me one. Blood would be harder to wash out. It seeped right in and you could always see the stain no matter how many times you ran whatever bloody thing it was through the wringer.

My only hope was a sneak attack. Jimmy had taught me that that was the best way to get the jump on somebody in the schoolyard or on a battlefield. I lunged forward and chomped down hard on the Hairy Claw. The taste of sweat and pine sap filled my mouth. I was hoping for a taste of blood, but my chompers just weren't up to the job. A couple of baby teeth were wobbly and the others were pockmarked with cavities.

Besides, Jimmy's skin was tough as a moose carcass. He'd once had a two-inch hunk of wood embedded in his hand for weeks and didn't even know it.

The thing was, I'd never seen him in any pain. Not even when he dug out that hunk of wood with a bowie knife.

Jimmy laughed at me as I gnawed away.

"Dirty fighter, dirty fighter. If you were in the ring, we'd have to disqualify you."

Jimmy often compared life situations to boxing. His father, my Papou Nick, had been a boxing manager and Jimmy had been his cut man from the time he was six. Jimmy could stop a bloody lip from bleeding faster than a guy could scream "Get back in there, you bum."

"Get a loada that kid. She's got a lotta frickin' moxie for a nine-year-old," he said to Shirley.

Shirley nodded, her mouth stuck between a smile and a frown. She quickly lit a Lucky Strike. Her long fingers holding the match shook. She blew some smoke over in Jimmy's direction.

"Hey, gimme that cancer stick, Olive Oyl," he said. He called her that 'cause she was tall and skinny like Popeye's girlfriend.

He gave my wrist one last, extra-hard squeeze and finally let it go. I fell back into my corner, sweaty and breathing hard.

Shirley passed her lipstick-smeared cigarette to Jimmy and lit another for herself.

Jimmy drove faster. The wind from his open window blew smoke back into my kisser. It mixed with the rotten-fish smell from the bucket on the floor next to my Keds. I remembered that butterscotch-dip and felt my stomach start to crawl up my throat.

I tried to get my mind off the fishy smoke by playing a game. I peered into the cars whooshing by in the opposite direction and picked out the one with the blondest family. I pictured myself a part of that family. I was on my way to the Ice Capades. My name was Kelly Swan. I had hair the color of just-churned butter and eyes like bright blue tiddledywinks. I had patent leather Mary Janes so shiny I could see my perfect teeth in them. My daddy was a doctor who saved people's lives on a daily basis. He made Dr. Kildare look frickin' sick. We lived in a big, white house. I had my own bedroom, all purple, with a window seat where I could read my Nancy Drews. Whenever there was a crime in my neighborhood, I solved it like Nancy. On Sundays, I went to church and sat beside Daddy. Sometimes he'd tickle me with his lifesaving hands. After church, we had churchy people over. We had banana splits in real banana split dishes. Never mind one cherry on top, we could put on as many as we wanted. It was frickin' maraschino cherry heaven.

Bam! Jimmy hit the brakes. A fishing pole that had been on the back window ledge flew into my lap. Its rusty hook slid around on my bare thigh. Virginia was fending off a pair of muddy trimming shears.

Jimmy's Pontiac had pulled up behind a creamy white Cadillac. An old lady was behind the wheel. I imagined she was on her way to bingo or a baked bean supper. She was not going Jimmy's speed. He drove an inch from her bumper, trying to get her to go faster.

"Come on, move that jalopy, you old bat."

He looked over at Shirley. "What'd I tell you? Never get behind a Caddy. You could turn into Rip Van Frickin' Winkle before you get to where you're goin.'"

Shirley was already bracing herself against the dashboard.

Jimmy floored it and swerved around the jalopy.

As we passed, I caught a glimpse of the lady's watery blue eyes. She was scared shitless, I could see that.

An oncoming truck driver blew his horn and braked hard to avoid plowing into us. Jimmy scooted back into his lane.

"Chicken Little!" Jimmy called out to the passing truckie. *"Pluck pluck pluck!"*

The truckie flipped Jimmy the bird and barreled away faster to show he was no frickin' Chicken Little.

"See what I mean about women drivers?" Jimmy said to Shirley, jerking his head back toward the lady in the Cadillac, who was fast becoming a white speck. Shirley nodded, shooting a reassuring smile into the backseat that we didn't buy for a second.

The thing was, Jimmy didn't think women should be behind the wheel. He said their hormones prevented them from making smart decisions. They didn't have hair-trigger reflexes like men had from firing guns. It was for my mother's own good and the safety of others that he had put the kibosh on her driving.

Recently, though, she had tried to change his mind. She came up with an angle she thought might win him over. Getting her license would free him up, she had insisted. He wouldn't have to drive her to work or the A&P. He'd have more time to hang out at the bookie joint.

"You'd cream us all," Jimmy had laughed. "You'd cream your own kids. *Splat!* Sayonara, brats. A car is like a gun. Unless a person knows how to handle it, they better not monkey around with it."

"But what if I didn't go all the way to the A&P?" Shirley had tried to bargain. "What if I just went to the Temple Market and back?"

Jimmy nearly split a gut. "With your sense of direction, you'd end up in KooKooLand." KooKooLand was what he called California, his least favorite of the fifty states 'cause all the people out there were surfing ding-dongs.

Shirley's doe-brown eyes flickered with doubt. "I guess you're right," she'd said. "I don't want to endanger the kids."

And that was that. Sayonara, driving, for Shirley.

The road was all Jimmy's now. I watched the needle of the speedometer glide over ninety on its way to ninety-five. I wondered what happened when the needle reached the end of the numbers. Maybe it exploded like in a Road Runner cartoon. *Meep! Meep! Kaboom!*

Jimmy switched on the radio. Louis Armstrong's "Stardust" filled the car. Jimmy turned it way up so we could hear it above the roar of the wind coming through the windows.

"Hey, brats, listen up. This music is so damn beautiful, it'll break your heart and put it back together again."

Jimmy made trumpet sounds along with the song, dueting with Satchmo. He sounded pretty good, if you liked that sort of music, which I didn't. I wished I could switch the dial to Radio 1250, WKBR, where they might be playing "Let's Turkey Trot" or "It's My Party." Talk about a song that would break your heart. Poor Lesley Gore got dumped by her boyfriend for a two-face named Judy. At her birthday party, no less.

Life was like that. Sometimes it just sucker punched you.

Jimmy took a drag off his cigarette and went back to making trumpet sounds, letting the smoke seep out from between his puckered lips. He had wanted to be a trumpet player when he was twelve, but had quit after two lessons 'cause he stunk up the joint. If you couldn't be great at something, he insisted, there was no point in killing yourself. He decided to stick to hunting and fishing, since he could clobber anybody in Manchester, in all of New Hampshire even, at those things.

Bonk. My head smacked against the window.

Jimmy had swerved to avoid a squished muskrat or possum or chipmunk. It was hard to tell which it might have been.

"Poor bastard," Jimmy said. "Frickin' civilization."

I stared out the window. I didn't see any frickin' civilization. Just a lotta frickin' trees. And ditches on the side of the road where some maniac could dump a dead body if he was so inclined. I sure hoped we didn't break down or anything. I sure hoped Jimmy's Pontiac didn't blow a frickin' gasket.

Finally a sign for the drive-in appeared. Jimmy pinched out the butt of his cancer stick and tossed it out the window. We took the turnoff and barreled down the winding dirt road toward the ratty-looking white rectangle that had been plopped down in the middle of a paved-over field.

Jimmy turned to Shirley. "Gimme a fin."

Shirley dug into her purse, trying to hurry it up. Jimmy didn't like it when stuff took too long. He never failed to remind us that in the merchant marine he had made his bed in under a minute, no wrinkles, and corners folded so sharp you could cut your keister on them.

"C'mon, c'mon, make it snappy," Jimmy barked, as Shirley fumbled with her red vinyl wallet.

We had reached the booth. A skinny man stood there eating a sub, waiting for the money.

Shirley finally got her wallet open and handed Jimmy a fin and Jimmy forked it over. The sub-eating guy went to give Jimmy his change and Jimmy recoiled.

"A two-dollar bill? Forget it, Clyde."

Two-dollar bills were bad luck. Everybody knew that. Except maybe people out here in the boonies didn't know. Or maybe the guy was just trying to fob off some bad luck on an unsuspecting family.

"I got enough bad luck already," Jimmy told the guy. "I got Norris Luck. You know what Norris Luck is? It's when a two-to-one shot pops an ankle half a stride from the finish line. So don't gimme any goddamn two-dollar bills."

The guy shrugged and gave Jimmy two greasy singles instead.

Jimmy gunned it, kicking up a cloud of dust all over the booth. He sped onto the paved area and snaked between the posts that held the hissing speakers. There were mounded areas on the pavement that you were supposed to park on to get a better view of the screen. Jimmy swerved into a spot dead center and kept shifting the car from drive to reverse to get the best angle. The second the car stopped moving, Shirley jumped out. She Windexed the dead bugs off the windshield until every streak of their guts was gone and it passed Jimmy's inspection.

Then Jimmy yanked the speaker off the post, hooked it onto the window, and adjusted the volume. The sound was muffled and crackly, as if some kid had poured a Pepsi into it.

Jimmy whapped it with his fist.

"Mickey Frickin' Mouse Incorporated musta made these speakers," he said. "And that screen looks like it was a hooker's sheet in a flophouse. Remember, kids, the drive-in's OK for a slice-and-dice, but for a quality picture like *Lawrence of Arabia* you gotta go to the indoor joints."

A happy man's voice was tinkling out of the speaker. ". . . Only twenty minutes till showtime. Visit our snack bar for a juicy hot dog, tasty hamburger, or pipin' hot pizza. And don't forget your popcorn, soda, and candy. Mmm-mmm."

An animated hot dog and hamburger were doing the twist across the screen with a fat bag of popcorn and a smiling soda cup. A worried-looking clock showed there were only twenty minutes left till showtime.

I watched people all around us stampede for the snack bar. I wished I was going to the snack bar too. I could picture those giant boxes of Milk Duds and Junior Mints stacked behind the glass counter. Unfortunately, Jimmy thought snack bars were for ding-dongs.

"Look at all the ding-dongs about to get soaked for a rubber hot dog," he crowed, as he pulled a fifth of Schenley out from under the seat. I always worried he'd cut his hand on the butcher knife he had stashed under there, but, nope, he never did.

Shirley popped open a bottle of Canada Dry ginger ale and mixed up some highballs in the plastic tumblers that Jimmy had gotten from Charlie, the gas station owner. Normally a person had to buy gas to get the glasses, but Jimmy had gotten them for free. He'd given Charlie a tip on a horse that was being hopped up and it won and Charlie came through with a tank of gas and the tumblers.

"It's too bad I couldn't get poor Hank to come," Jimmy said as he slugged the highball. "It woulda been better for him than mopin' around over that no-account ex-wife of his."

I forgot all about the snack bar and leaned closer to the front seat.

Whenever Hank's name was mentioned, I was all ears. Hank Piasecny was one of Jimmy's best friends and he sure as hell wasn't poor. He was a big shot who owned a North End store that, according to Jimmy, had enough guns to kill every dummkopf in the rotten world. He also sold every kind of ammo, and fancy fishing poles to catch giant fish you could hang on your wall if you were a blowhard, and boats and motors that I figured millionaires bought. Hank and his knockout wife, Doris—well, ex-wife as of a few months back—both drove Cadillacs and Doris had a fur coat and jewelry that Shirley said was the real McCoy, so I figured Hank must be a millionaire too. It made me feel like a big shot that my dad was friends with a millionaire. None of the other kids in the projects had even met a millionaire, much less had a father who went hunting and boozing around and to the fights with one.

Jimmy said Hank was a man's man. A man's man was a guy who didn't get all nervous when a copper stopped him. A guy who would belt any palooka who looked at him sideways. Hank had a bulbous nose that had been broken a bunch of times 'cause guys were always looking at him the wrong way. I myself never looked him in the eye so I wouldn't get clocked.

Hank and Doris had a daughter, Susan, and more than anything I wanted to be her best friend. She was in college and I was only going into fourth grade, but I figured once I got into high school I'd be old enough and cool enough to win her over.

According to Jimmy, Susan could do anything. Supposedly all of Manchester and even some people outside of New Hampshire felt the same way.

"Anything that kid touches turns to gold," Jimmy insisted. "She's a real brain, a regular egghead. She's really going places."

I wanted to go places too. I wanted to go where Susan was going.

Jimmy said Susan was going to be a doctor. I'd never seen a lady doctor. I wondered if they got to wear high heels or if they clomped around in those ugly nurses' shoes that looked like the orthopedic ones I got stuck wearing until I was seven so I wouldn't trip over my own feet. I figured they must have lady doctors in KooKooLand. Doris had just come back from there. She must have been scoping things out for Susan.

I'd already made up my mind I was going to be a lady doctor too. That is, when I wasn't writing mystery stories. Or making movies that would scare Jimmy to death. Or flying around the world free of charge as an airline stewardess. Being a stewardess sounded like a real blast. I'd just learned the ins and outs of it from a book I'd stolen from the library. I'd already begun my training by gliding around my bedroom holding one of Jimmy's Louis Armstrong album covers as a tray and repeating, "Coffee, tea, or juice?"

I figured if Susan could do lots of things, why not me?

Susan wrote poems that won awards and she could draw and play the clarinet and ski and ride horses and play basketball and was in school plays and on prom committees and ran a newspaper.

I sure hoped Susan didn't already have a best friend.

I sure hoped Doris didn't drag her off to goddamn KooKooLand.

"Who the hell does that Doris think she is anyway, the goddamn Queen of Sheba?" Jimmy was asking Shirley. "Who the hell does she think she's gonna find better than Hank? The poor sap bought her a new Caddy every time she batted her phony eyelashes. What more did she want? Blood? Hank shoulda booted her ass out instead of the other way around."

"Maybe we could introduce Hank to Shirley," Shirley suggested. Shirley was the sister of Shirley's best friend. Her husband had died and she was desperate to find another one even though the one who'd died had been a no-good drunk.

"She's a little dippy, but her legs are sound. Maybe Hank can ride her around the track a few times," Jimmy said. "I'll go talk to him tomorrow. I gotta get the poor sap out of himself. He's not livin'. And with all that dough, he oughta be livin' the life of Riley."

Shirley gave Jimmy a peck on the cheek, leaving a pink smear, pleased he was aiding in her matchmaking efforts. She dug into the brown bag on her lap and passed out sandwiches, Fritos, and sweet-and-sour pickles. The sandwich was my favorite, pimento loaf, which was like bologna but with olives stuck in it. I wondered how they got the olives into the meat, but I was glad somebody had figured it out. Virginia hated olives and began to pick them out and hide them in the tinfoil wrapping.

As soon as I took a bite of the pimento loaf I realized I wasn't hungry. A knob of fear was lodged in my gullet like a big, fat olive. I felt like that worried-looking cartoon clock on the screen that was now starting to sweat. There were only three minutes left. Three minutes till *Blood Feast*.

I had a pretty good idea of what I was in for.

One Sunday, a few weeks back, we had come upon a movie theater in Boston where *Blood Feast* was playing. The theater was located in the part of town known as the Combat Zone. The area was crawling with girls in skintight skirts who had eyes like sleepy raccoons and guys hawking "genuine Bulova watches" that were phony as a three-dollar bill. Jimmy told us we were lucky he was showing us around the big, bad city. Other families just got to go camping in the boonies and have their keisters chewed by fire ants. Or maybe to

Disneyland, which was for patsies. Well, screw that. Jimmy wanted us to see the watering holes and strip joints he had frequented when he was in the merchant marine. He wanted us to see the real world, baby.

"How else you gonna write the Great American Novel?" he had asked me.

I didn't answer him.

I'd just laid eyes on a giant poster of a half-naked lady dripping blood. The poster was outside the theater playing *Blood Feast*.

Jimmy saw the poster and let out a whistle.

Shirley's hand holding mine tightened.

Virginia stared down at some garbage.

Jimmy sauntered up to the ticket booth. The punk in the booth was reading a magazine. I caught a glimpse of a picture of a woman with breasts like pink birthday balloons stuck to her chest by static electricity.

"What's the lowdown?" asked Jimmy. "Just how rough is this picture?"

"Oh, it's rough, man. Real bloody. Like nothin' you ever seen." The guy suddenly noticed us. His mouth dropped open. "You can't bring kids in here."

Jimmy didn't like the sound of that.

"Oh no? Who says I can't?"

"Read my sign," the punk said.

He pointed to a handwritten sign taped to the glass that said ADDULTS ONLY. I could see he wasn't much of a speller.

"Frick you and frick your frickin' sign," said Jimmy. "My brats love a good slice-and-dice, the bloodier the better. Don't you, brats?"

Virginia and I nodded, doing our best to look eager.

The bad speller wasn't convinced. "Look, this ain't like any other horror movie. It's eighteen and over. That's it, over and out."

Jimmy's tanned face grew a shade darker. He tore into the punk. He said he'd seen a lotta phony-baloney movies in his life. Ones where some hooker dressed like a nurse stood in the lobby to take your blood pressure afterwards but the blood in the movie looked like Karo syrup and he knew what he was talkin' about 'cause he'd seen a lotta blood, for Chrissake, he'd been in World War II when the guy was crawlin' around in diapers. So he wasn't buyin' that this one was so bad. He was goin' in to judge for himself and we were comin' with him. It was a free country, and no little pip-squeak in some rinky-dink booth was gonna tell him where to go. He would tell the pip-squeak where to go first.

Finally, the guy hissed at him, softly so we wouldn't hear, but we did. "Beat it or I'm callin' the fuzz. You want your kids to see you get pinched?"

Jimmy's right fist clenched into a knot. I watched the eagle tattoo on his biceps fill with blood and look like it was about to fly away.

Just then, a big cop lumbered by. He was carrying a large box of pastry. I recognized the box. It was from a bakery in the North End where we often stopped for boozy rum cakes and cannoli after we left the Combat Zone. The Dago Joint, Jimmy called it, 'cause of it being Italian.

"Daddy, can we go to the Dago Joint?" I pleaded, hoping to distract him from knocking the guy's block off.

The cop overheard me and chuckled. Jimmy glared at him. He didn't like cops. Not any cops. They were mostly Micks, he said. McMurphys, McMullens, and McMeatheads. You never saw a Greek cop, 'cause the Micks had it all sewn up. They acted like big shots, but they were really just a bunch of four-flushers in uniform. I didn't know what four-flushers were, but they didn't sound like very nice people. They sounded mean for not letting any Greeks like us work with them.

Not that any Greeks would want to be cops anyway. They were too smart for that, Jimmy explained. Who the hell would want to be pounding the pavement in the dead of winter freezing your keister off when you could be in a café drinking ouzo or shooting the baloney at the bookie joint?

The cop disappeared into a pizza joint.

"Look at that lard-ass go," Jimmy laughed.

The cop did have a fat ass, but it didn't seem right to point it out. Maybe he couldn't help having a fat ass. It might be a glandular thing. Like my friend Tina, she had a glandular thing.

"No wonder they can't finger the Boston Strangler if that's what they got for USDA prime fuzz around here," Jimmy said.

The ticket taker cracked up. He said he'd been sayin' the same frickin' thing himself. Then he leaned forward and gave Jimmy the lowdown.

"Look, save your dough. This picture stinks," he whispered. "Not enough bazookas."

"I love Bazooka," I chimed in. "I can fit six in my mouth at once."

The guy laughed and said, "Hey, kid, me too."

Jimmy told the guy to quit making fun of his kid or he'd golf him one. Then he said never mind the frickin' movie, he'd take his business elsewhere, that he wouldn't be caught dead in that fleabag joint anyway. He might get bitten by a rat and have to sue them for every red cent they had.

Then he turned away from the window and threw his muscley arms around the three of us.

"I'm taking my dolls to the Dago Joint."

And off we went. We stuffed ourselves silly with rum cakes. Jimmy gave me the maraschino cherry on his. Then he took us to see *Modern Times* and we laughed ourselves silly. Charlie Chaplin played a poor working stiff in a factory, just like Shirley. Except Charlie made machine parts and Shirley made Foster Grant sunglasses, which were mostly shipped to KooKooLand 'cause that's where all the sunshine was anyway.

It was late when we headed back to the car, which was still parked in the Combat Zone. Everything looked scuzzier, but I wasn't afraid. Not even of the Boston Strangler. I knew Jimmy, unlike that lard-ass cop, could take him. Take him blindfolded with one hand tied behind his back and on one foot. Knock him six ways to Sunday and still get home in time for supper. None of my friends in the projects had a father who could do that. Heck, most of them didn't even have a father that I'd ever seen. If they found themselves face-to-face with the Boston Strangler they'd be sliced and diced like that lady in *Blood Feast*.

I must've looked tired 'cause Jimmy suddenly lifted me up like I was no heavier than a skinned rabbit. He slung me on his back and I buried my face in the back of his sinewy neck. I didn't even mind that his Wildroot was greasing up my forehead. A piggyback ride through the Combat Zone was a lot of fun. The raccoon ladies thought so too; they smiled and stepped aside. I was asleep by the time we got back to the car.

Over the next few weeks, Jimmy checked the newspaper to see if *Blood Feast* was playing in our neck of the woods. Finally, he saw an ad that said CALL THEATER FOR FILM TITLE. The paper had a policy against printing the name of any movie it didn't think people oughta be seeing. Usually it was a dirty movie. The paper let you know there was something smutty playing, but what exactly the smut was, you had to get off your lard-ass and find out for yourself.

Jimmy picked up the phone and called. Sure enough, his hunch was right.

"It's coming," he teased us. "*Blood Feast* is coming."

For the next few nights he scratched at our closed bedroom door, pretending to be a maniac.

"We know it's you, Daddy!" I would shout.

"Cut it out," Virginia would add for good measure.

He never let on it was him. He just growled and drifted away, leaving us to stare wide-eyed into the darkness, listening to our hamster, Squirmy, as his toenails clicked frantically on his hamster wheel.

But now, the wait was over. *Blood Feast* was finally here.

The cartoon clock on the drive-in screen was jumping up and down. Its alarm had just gone off. It ran off the edge of the screen and into the darkness.

Shirley reached into the backseat and sprayed us with bug repellent. The mosquitoes were starting to come out.

I peered between my parents' heads. My heart was bumping against my rib cage like it wanted to follow that cartoon clock wherever it was headed.

It couldn't be that bad, I told myself. I had made it through *Psycho*, *Homicidal*, and *The Sadist*. Sure, I got scared, but then everything turned out OK. The bad guys got caught, shot, or, like Charlie in *The Sadist*, fell into a pit of poisonous snakes. The killers got what was coming to them and that made you feel happy. The worse they got it, the happier you felt. Happiness was always waiting for you at the end.

That's what I told myself, anyway.

The movie began with some organ music that sounded like what they played at the ice-skating rink. I relaxed a little. Maybe there'd be some ice-skating in the movie. Maybe it'd be like the Ice Capades with a little blood thrown in.

But there was no ice-skating. No flouncy skirts or bouncy ponytails. Just a blond lady coming home from work to an apartment kinda like ours. The lady took off all her clothes and got into a bathtub. Before long, a man appeared out of nowhere. He began stabbing the lady over and over with a carving knife that looked about a foot long. He stabbed her in the eye, pulling the eye right out of its socket and impaling it like a morsel of Greek shish kebab on a stick. Then he sawed off the bottom of her leg and cut out her heart.

The lady's heart filled the whole screen. It was a huge, drippy hunk cradled in the man's hands like a kitten.

I told myself it must be a deer's heart or maybe a moose's. But I didn't know how they could make it look like it came out of the lady's chest. And the blood looked real and sticky.

"Wow," said Jimmy. "This makes *Psycho* look like a Sunday school picnic with a bunch of frickin' penguins." By penguins he meant nuns.

Virginia started to wail and slid onto the car floor.

Shirley turned away from the screen, making a face like she was sucking on a sour ball. Her left arm flailed into the backseat, trying to locate Virginia. She patted her on the head.

"Jim, maybe this one's too much for them."

"Oh, c'mon, it's just a movie."

He called back to Virginia, "It's just a cow's heart covered in Karo syrup. Don't be a crybaby. Your sister's five years younger, and she's not blubbering."

On the screen, they were showing the dead lady's face with one empty eye socket the size of a hole you'd dig to play marbles.

"But, hell, they're doing a pretty good job with the realism," he said.

He turned back to get my opinion. "What do you think, kiddo?"

I agreed they were doing a pretty good job with the realism and said it was the best slice-and-dice ever.

"See," Jimmy told Shirley. "Don't be a killjoy. Some of us have a movie to watch."

I kept my eyeballs glued to the screen, determined to prove I could take whatever the movie dished out.

Virginia stopped crying but stayed on the floor where she couldn't see anything. Sometimes she would put her hands over her ears if there were screams or if the ice rink music got a little louder.

Now and then, Shirley would glance into the backseat to see if we were OK. Virginia would mumble that she was fine and I acted like I was too wrapped up in the movie to even notice her.

It turned out the killer was an Egyptian caterer with a gimpy leg named Fuad Ramses. Fuad was cooking up a big feast for a party and he planned to serve humans, not hamburgers and hot dogs.

Fuad had to collect a lot of body parts for the feast. After slicing and dicing the lady in the bathtub, he went after a girl making out with a guy on the beach. He cut out the girl's brain but didn't bother with the guy's. I figured the guy's brain must not be as tender and said so.

"That's right," Jimmy said. "Men's brains are tough and women's are all soft and squishy and little Greek girls' brains are the softest of all. They're the best for eating, like a baby lamb at Greek Easter. So you better hold on to your head from now on or some maniac might try to snatch it."

"No maniac's getting my head," I snapped. "I'll stab them in the eye first."

"That's my girl," he laughed.

The next lady got her tongue ripped out, roots and all.

"Aw, it's just a cow's tongue," Jimmy said, sounding disappointed. "A human tongue would be a lot smaller." Jimmy knew everything there was to know about body parts 'cause when he was my age he'd worked after school for Yanco the Macedonian Butcher.

Finally, Fuad kidnapped a lady and brought her back to his place. He hung her up by her arms and whipped her until her back was a bloody mess. He didn't seem to want any of her body parts. I figured he was just mad. Or maybe he wanted her blood for gravy.

After that, the lard-ass cops were onto Fuad and chased him down. Like a numbskull he hid in the back of a garbage truck. The truck ground him up like a giant wad of hamburger meat. You'd never even know he was a person. He just became gunk like the muskratpossumchipmunk I'd seen on the road.

It was the perfect ending.

But something was wrong. I didn't feel happy at all.

I knew I'd never look at garbage trucks the same way. I'd steer clear of them so I wouldn't trip and fall in or maybe get pushed in by some kids who were just goofing around.

I knew every time I played marbles I'd see that lady's eye socket in the marble hole.

I knew from then on I'd be checking my bedroom closet for psychos every night and sleeping with scissors under my pillow.

Jimmy winked at me in the rearview mirror.

"Man, that was a kick in the chops, wasn't it?"

"Yeah, Daddy. I wish we could see it again."

"That wasn't really him in the garbage truck, you know. He pushed in one of the coppers instead and got away."

"He did not. He got all squished up. I saw it."

"No, he got away. You musta got all scared like a girl and closed your eyes for a second. He's still out there. And guess who he's coming for next?"

"You!" I blurted out. "He's coming for you."

He grabbed me around the neck. For a second, I couldn't breathe.

"No, he's coming for you, little girl. He's coming for you."

A Hearty Breakfast

The next morning, Jimmy was going over to talk to Hank Piasecny, the millionaire, about setting him up with Shirley's friend, the miserable, husbandless Shirley. I begged him to take me along. Hank's daughter, Susan, often worked at Hank's Sports Center in the summer, and I was hoping to make some headway on our friendship. Or at least get some Good & Plenty. Susan had once given me a box of those licorice nuggets and I had never forgotten it.

Jimmy said I could come along to Hank's if I hurried the hell up. I forced down the rest of my Rice Krispies that had long ago lost their snap, crackle, and pop. I drank every last drop of the sludgy sugar milk at the bottom of the bowl 'cause you didn't waste food. Not when kids with big bellies that looked like they ate too much were actually starving to death.

Jimmy's plate had only the faintest smear of egg yolk left on it. He had just finished the mess of food Shirley had made him, everything just the way he liked it. Three fried eggs—the yolks nice and runny, the whites hard, none of that goddamn slimy stuff in them—and six strips of bacon, not too crisp, but not too raw either, they should bend not break—and home fries with butter, onions, and green pepper—but not too much, not overdone or anything—and homemade bread—all warm and fluffy, not goddamn Wonder Bread like most lazy American broads slapped down in front of their husbands, but real bread like Greek wives made back in the old country, and the butter soft, not right out of the Frigidaire, where it would tear the bread if you tried to spread it, and coffee—strong but not too bitter, with two teaspoons of sugar, rounded teaspoons, and a little milk but not a drop too much.

Shirley picked up Jimmy's clean plate and exhaled.

"I barely need to wash this," she trilled, before plopping it into a sink full of steamy bubbles, the water scalding hot the way Jimmy liked it, the way it had been in the merchant marine.

I brought my cereal bowl over to the sink and Shirley leaned down and gave me a sudsy hug. I breathed in her scent—lemon Joy and Johnson's Baby Powder. Her soft curls, the color of Hershey's cocoa, tickled my cheek. I hugged her waist, feeling her rib cage through her white summer blouse.

I wished she could come to Hank's with us. I didn't like being alone in the car with Jimmy. If I was going to die in a fiery car crash I wanted my mother with me.

But Shirley couldn't come. She had to finish doing the dishes, wash some clothes, yank 'em through the wringer, hang 'em on the line, fry up a mess of mackerel, mash some potatoes, make a peach pie for Jimmy's dinner, and then go to bed. She needed a few hours of sleep before she went off to make sunglasses at eleven that night.

If she was lucky, she might be able to sneak in a few innings of the Red Sox game while Jimmy was gone. Shirley had grown up in a baseball-loving family but under Jimmy's roof only boxing and horse racing—the sport of kings—were allowed. Baseball was the sport of lard-asses and the Red Sox were a bunch of bums.

Jimmy grabbed his pack of smokes, stuck a toothpick in his mouth, and headed for the door.

He frowned at Virginia, who was sitting there pushing some home fries around her plate. She looked sulky and pale-faced, like she hadn't recovered from the night before.

"Hurry up and finish your breakfast and go out and play," he told her. "You look kinda sickly. You need some sun."

Jimmy was always telling us we needed some sun. Sun was the Greek cure-all. Greek penicillin, he called it. If you had a chest cold, get some sun on it. If you had a cut from a boning knife, sun would do the trick. When a Greek lady was having a baby, ship her back to Greece for some real Greek sunshine. That's where YaYa Kally had gone when she was in the family way with Jimmy. The Greek sun was supposed to be good for sons. I don't know about daughters.

"I gotta polish off these home fries first," Virginia said with a slight smirk, which Jimmy didn't pick up on. "I don't wanna leave a morsel when there are starving Greek kids on the planet."

"Go ride your bike," he ordered her. "Your old lady paid good money for that bike and it's not being used."

Virginia had been avoiding that bike like the plague. She didn't want to look like a frickin' idiot riding a kiddie bike minus the training wheels around the neighborhood.

"Plentya kids would kill for a bike," Jimmy insisted. "I woulda when I was your age."

Virginia and I shared a look. We knew the Bike Story was coming. And, sure enough, he launched into it.

"When I was a pip-squeak, we had one bike. One bike for three boys! We got ten minutes each. Papou timed us with his stopwatch, just like he timed his boxers' workouts. 'Cept your uncle Billy cheated and kept riding around the goddamn block. If I'd done that, Papou woulda golfed me. But Billy got away with it 'cause he was the baby. Lemme tell you, being the oldest, you get the shaft."

Virginia would agree with that. She hadn't been allowed to cross the street until last year, when she turned thirteen, but I was already doing it at nine.

"A bike ride sounds super-duper," Virginia cooed.

I knew she'd just take the bike out and run the tires through the mud to dirty them up and then put the bike back in the shed. Then she'd lock herself in our bedroom and play "Mashed Potato Time" and "Johnny B. Goode" and some other 45s that had been passed down to us by YaYa and Papou when they changed the records in the jukebox at their beer joint, Nick's Ringside Cafe. On Virginia's last birthday, YaYa had given her a pink record player to play the 45s on. Jimmy wasn't too keen on us having our own record player, but he said we could keep it as long as we didn't play any goddamn nigger music.

That had got me all confused.

What about Louis Armstrong? I had asked. He was a colored person, wasn't he? That was different, Jimmy explained. Nigger music was rock and roll, where people shrieked and jumped around like baboons. Nigger music, get it?

Yes, I'd said, still confused.

I didn't like that word *nigger*. Shirley said *colored person* and my third-grade teacher, Miss Rogers, said *colored person*, so that's what I said even though I wanted to be like Jimmy most of the time. Maybe only ladies said *colored person* and men said *nigger*. I'd heard most of Jimmy's friends say the word. Hank the millionaire said it all the time. I figured it was like the difference between *damn* and *darn*. One was a swearword and one wasn't and men swore and ladies didn't.

The first time I realized there was something bad about the word was when Jimmy said it in the checkout line at the A&P and the woman in front of us turned around and told him he should use nicer language, especially around a child. He told her to mind her own damn business, it was just a word like *Mick* or *greaseball* or *Polack*. He said that he had known plenty of niggers in the merchant marine, had drunk out of the same bottle of whiskey with them. He asked her if she would drink from the same bottle of whiskey as a nigger. She nearly choked on her own spit. She paid for her groceries and beat it. Jimmy said the old battle-ax had probably never even seen a nigger in her whole life since there were only ten in the whole goddamn state.

It was true I had seen only two colored people in Manchester that I could remember. In Boston, it was a whole different story. Like this one time Jimmy got lost coming home from the Combat Zone after he'd had too many high-balls in the car. Usually he could find his way out of any place. Stick him in the woods drunk, blindfolded, and without a compass and he'd still make it home in time for supper—that's what Hank once said. But this time we ended up in Roxbury—Spooktown, Jimmy called it—and all we saw were colored people. I suddenly thought about the two colored people I'd seen in Manchester and how they must feel. I'd never seen them again, so maybe they just up and moved away.

Shirley looked scared to be finding herself in Spooktown, but Jimmy said nobody or nothin' scared him. He pulled over and asked some colored guys where the hell we were. Told them he was half-lit and asked did they want a drink. The guys took a slug and Jimmy shot the baloney. He told them he'd take booze over weed any goddamn day. He'd had some weed in the merchant marine and it didn't do shit. The guys laughed and said maybe somebody'd been messin' with him and gave him tobacco instead. Jimmy said hell no, it was the good stuff he'd gotten from a crazy Jamaican named Alboy. Then he gave the guys another slug of whiskey, got some directions, and we headed home.

"Nice niggers, huh?" Jimmy asked, as we snaked through the back alleys of Spooktown.

There was an icy silence. I watched Shirley's jaw tighten.

"I don't care for that word," Shirley finally mumbled like she had a mouth full of cotton.

"Oh yeah? Whaddaya want me to call 'em? Spooks? Jigaboos? Coons? Spear chuckers?" Jimmy asked, trying to get a rise out of her.

Shirley turned and stared out into the darkness. She looked like she didn't know where she was or how she was going to get out of there.

Finally, she grabbed the bottle those guys had just slugged from and poured herself a drink. A double.

I piped up from the backseat.

"Well, I think they were very nice colored people."

North and South

We were running late as usual because after Jimmy told the Bike Story the phone rang and it was some guy looking to see if Jimmy had some new merchandise. Jimmy had to shoot the baloney with the guy for a while before he told him yes, he did have some new merchandise and to stop by later and check it out for himself.

Jimmy hung up the phone and rapped me on the head with the *Daily Racing Form*.

"Shake a leg, dum-dum," he said. Dum-dum was one of his many nicknames for me. He'd taken to calling me that since I started pulling down straight As in school.

"Race you to the car!" he shouted.

Ever since I could walk he'd been making me race him.

"Ready, set, go!"

I tore out the door. He gave me a head start and then charged after me.

I lost. I always lost.

He reached the car first and beeped the horn to celebrate his victory. I collapsed onto the front seat beside him.

"And the winner, by six furlongs, Jimmy the Greek," he announced. "And, in second place, dum-dum."

I will beat you, I vowed to myself. I will beat you someday. I will. I will. I will.

He started up the car and I turned to wave good-bye to Shirley. I knew she'd be standing there in the doorway. Just like Jimmy was superstitious about two-dollar bills and I was superstitious about stepping on cracks and possibly breaking my mother's back, Shirley was superstitious about me leaving. She had to watch until I was clear outta sight or she figured something terrible would happen to me and it would be all her fault 'cause she'd turned her head away a split second too soon. I always put on a big smile to convince her I wasn't going to die and waved until I couldn't see her anymore.

Jimmy cruised through the projects, one eye on the road, one eye on the

Racing Form. He took a Lucky Strike from behind his ear and punched in the car's lighter.

"Your old man's got a college education in horse racing, kiddo," he said.

I nodded like it was news, even though I'd heard it a million times before.

"Handicapping's harder than any straight job, but nobody gives you any credit for it. People call you a bum, but you gotta be a genius to make any dough from it. As much as Einstein knows about the theory of relativity, which is his racket, is what I know about horses."

He pronounced horses *hosses.* Like the name of the fat brother on *Bonanza,* Hoss Cartwright.

He lit his cancer stick and went back to studying the *Racing Form.*

I stared out the window at our neighborhood. The place was called Elmwood Gardens, but there weren't any elm trees or gardens around. The elms had all died of some disease and the gardens, well, I figured that was just a con job to make you think you were living in some kind of paradise like the people at the North End.

The North End was the ritzy part of town, where Hank's store was, where we were headed right now. Jimmy did some landscaping up there when his luck wasn't running so good at the track. Shirley cleaned houses there when she wasn't doing piecework at the sunglass factory. Mansions, Shirley called those North End houses. She made the insides look nice so the rich people would never have to see a bathtub ring or a greasy stove or a dusty tennis trophy. Jimmy took care of the outsides so they wouldn't trip over a twig or step in dog shit or have to shovel any frickin' snow.

We lived in the South End, in what my sister had told me was poor people housing. The poor people housing consisted of a bunch of pink, blue, or pus-green two-story buildings that, rumor had it, were going to be repainted but never were. Our place had a kitchen and living room downstairs, and two bedrooms and a bathroom upstairs. There were also bigger apartments, where the Catholics with nine or eleven or thirteen kids lived. I figured Catholics must like sex more than other people 'cause they had so many kids, but my friend Tina, a major Catholic, got PO'd when I said that and shouted they did not, they liked it less.

It felt like it was a million degrees in the car. I tried to roll down the window but something was broken and it would only go halfway down.

In the summer Manchester got frickin' hot. Jimmy said it was because we were in the frickin' Merrimack Valley and all the hot air got trapped there like in a hot-air balloon except nobody was goin' anywhere. The few people who

could afford a fan would plunk themselves down in front of it and just stare
into the blur of spinning blades. Everybody else would hose themselves down
like the seals at Benson's Wild Animal Farm. At night you had to leave the windows wide open, but then you couldn't sleep 'cause the sound of gypsy moths
against the screen made you think somebody might be breaking in.

That wasn't a far-fetched idea. It's just what had happened a few weeks
before. Somebody had broken in and stolen all our fancy Christmas ornaments. Shirley had brought those ornaments all the way down from Nova Scotia, where she grew up. Had hand-carried them on the Bluenose ferry 'cause
they once belonged to her grammy and were made of glass and painted with
cozy Christmas scenes. They were frickin' antiques, Jimmy had said. He said
he would've shot the punks who stole them right between the eyes if only he
had woken up. If only the fan in his bedroom hadn't been so goddamn loud he
didn't hear the bastards. I wondered what the punks wanted with our Christmas ornaments in the broiling-hot summer. Maybe they had seen our beautiful
tree the Christmas before and had been thinking about those pretty, North
End–looking ornaments ever since. I vowed to peek in every window of every
apartment next Christmas and track them down, just like Nancy Drew would.
Even if I had to freeze my frickin' keister off.

Because in the winter, that's what you did. Froze your keister. It got so cold
you could never believe it had been so hot. People would hang their laundry out
front—that is, if some punk hadn't torn down their clothesline already—and
the clothes would swing on the lines all stiff like paper doll clothes and the
ice on the sheets would crackle when you took them down. You had to take
everything down at night or it sure as hell wouldn't be there in the morning.
Somebody else would be sleeping on your frozen sheets or wearing your mother's brassiere.

Jimmy swerved to a stop in front of the housing project office. It was the
beginning of the month and we had to pay the rent. I didn't like going in there,
but I didn't want to fry to death in the car like I heard had happened to some
other kids when their father forgot about them. Plus I knew they had a fan in
there that I could stand in front of.

The lady who worked in the office perked right up when we walked in.
Jimmy flashed her a smile. His cigarette was dangling off his lower lip like it
might fall at any moment and cause a fire.

I made a beeline for the fan as Jimmy laid out some bills on the counter.

"Thirty-seven simoleons, baby. Don't spend it all in one place."

The lady giggled and turned all dopey-eyed. It made me want to smack her.

"Or maybe you want to take it and run away together."

"Oh, Jimmy, you're such a kidder."

"You think I'm kidding? Who's kidding? Who wouldn't want to run away with a beautiful doll like you?"

Jimmy looked like he might just plant one on her. I stepped in front of him. He elbowed me aside and leaned in closer to her.

"You're a real stand-up gal for not ratting me out to the main office."

She fidgeted a little. "I think nosy neighbors oughta mind their nosy business is what I think."

They were talking about the busybody who had sent an anonymous note to her last month complaining that Jimmy had bought himself a racehorse. The person didn't think racehorse-owning tycoons oughta be living in the projects, riding the gravy train, when honest poor people were on a waiting list to get in. The busybody said the horse probably cost a thousand simoleons, but Jimmy had only paid five hundred, so it showed what the busybody knew. A big fat nothing. Jimmy had a few hunches who the snitch might be but no solid leads. He just knew it hadda be a woman 'cause women were always flapping their big traps.

I was hoping to solve the mystery myself and then maybe get Jimmy to buy me and Virginia some bunk beds as a reward. Right now, there was barely enough room for us to walk around our two beds, never mind do the turkey trot or Watusi.

Jimmy said he'd buy the office woman something real swanky if the horse hit, which he said he knew it would. The damn thing was named Victory Bound, so you knew it was a winner. Until the big score, Jimmy said, he wanted to give the woman a token of his appreciation for not being a rat. He took out a gold lighter and laid it on the counter with the simoleons.

"Genuine gold-plated. I got it in France when I was in the merchant marine," he said. "Maybe you'll think of me every time you light up."

I'd seen that lighter before. There was a whole box of them in my bedroom closet.

The woman acted like nobody ever gave her anything. It almost made you feel bad for her. Almost.

She said no, she couldn't accept it.

He said she had to or his heart would break.

She said OK, it was gorgeous, just gorgeous.

Finally, we got the hell out of there.

It seemed even hotter when we stepped back outside. When you got cooled by a fan you always had to pay the price when you walked away 'cause it felt hotter than before. Everything—and everyone—had a price. That's what Jimmy said, anyway.

"That lady likes you," I blurted out.

"Ah, she's not my type," he explained. "Now, Ava Gardner, that's a real woman. Va-va-voom. She makes Marilyn Monroe look sick."

"Marilyn Monroe kicked the bucket," I reminded him.

"I know she's dead, dum-dum, but if she was alive. If both of them were standing here wanting to groove with me, there'd be no contest. Ava would win, hands down. Too bad Sinatra tapped her first."

We climbed back in the car and left the projects. We drove up the main drag, Elm Street, past the Blessed Sacrament school, where all the Catholics went, and Bakersville, where I went. I looked up at the darkened windows on the top floor, where my fourth-grade classroom would be. Fourth grade was supposed to be where the shit really hit the fan, where school got really hard and you weren't doing baby math anymore. Last year I had gotten all As, but how long could a person keep that up? I didn't even want to think about it.

We drove farther north, past the place where you got your TV fixed and the garage where you got your old clunker fixed and the Dunkin' Donuts where Jimmy knew the girl behind the counter and would get free maple crullers. We passed Central Avenue, where YaYa and Papou's beer joint was. We passed Zayre's, the cheapo store, where Shirley bought me jumpers that were too long and kneesocks that were too high so there was no chance of any leg showing and Jimmy blowing a gasket.

We finally made it to the nice part of town. I peered out the window at all the joints I planned to shop in when Jimmy's ship came in. The Bon-Ton Junior Miss Shop was where I intended to get most of my outfits. I figured that's where Susan shopped 'cause Virginia said that's where all the popular girls went. Candy-asses, she called them. The name candy-ass made you think maybe those girls ate a lot of candy and were lard-asses but they weren't. They all had cute asses like Annette Funicello. I asked Virginia if being a candy-ass meant they were sweet like candy, but she said, no, they were a bunch of stuck-ups. She didn't long to be a candy-ass like I did. She didn't want to wear shirts with Peter Pan collars and pleated plaid skirts and clodhopper saddle shoes. She wanted to wear dungarees and tight black sweaters and put black stuff around her eyes like the raccoon ladies in the Combat Zone. But unfortunately, she said, Jimmy made us dress like a couple of Greek yayas.

Jimmy barreled up the main drag so fast I couldn't get a good look at the candy-ass clothes. An ad came on the radio for Hank's Sports Center. Jimmy and I began to sing the Patti Page song that was the background music for the ad. I knew all the lyrics because Jimmy played the song whenever he got sloshed. It was about a merchant mariner who sailed around the world making women of many nationalities miserable. Patti told the joker to shape up or ship out. Jimmy said no broad would tell him what to do if she knew what was good for her, not even Miss Patti Page.

Cross over the bridge, cross over the bridge.
Change your reckless way of living, cross over the bridge . . .

Patti crooned in our ears.

And that's what we did. We crossed over the Amoskeag Bridge and pulled into Hank's place.

Susan Mans the
Ammo Counter

The store was jammed with men. Some looked like mucky-mucks and some looked like they didn't have a pot to piss in.

The smell of WD-40 hung in the air like a greasy fart.

Everywhere I looked I saw things I was afraid of tripping over. Fishing poles. Oars. Big, black rubber boots. One wrong step could send me flying into the blade of an outboard motor that would slice my head in two. Or a bowie knife could fall off a shelf and stab me in the gut. I watched guns being cocked and triggers being pulled and I wondered if some half-lit guy who traded in a gun had gone and left a bullet in the chamber. A bullet that would go straight through my kitty T-shirt and into my heart. And no one could save me. Not even kind Dr. Kildare on TV, or the darker, mean-looking Dr. Ben Casey, who Virginia thought was sexier.

Only Dr. Susan Piasecny could save me.

I saw her smiling at me.

She was standing behind the ammo counter. Jimmy was already there, kidding around with her. My legs went stiff. My tongue felt like it had been glued to the roof of my mouth. I couldn't even get a word out about wanting to be a lady doctor too or about how much I enjoyed the Good & Plenty she'd given me or about how I was now storing my Barbie accessories in the Good & Plenty box.

Apparently, she had spoken to me.

"Hey, dummkopf, get your ass over here and say hello to Susan," ordered Jimmy. "You were dying to come and now you're acting all tongue-tied like the Mummy."

I started to smile and then stopped myself. Some of my front teeth were coming in crooked. They were sticking out all funny, unlike Susan's, which were perfect. Jimmy said the crooked teeth made me look like Dracula. He had taken to wiggling his fingers in front of his mouth like they were rubbery fangs.

Trying to forget I had the Mummy's personality and Dracula's smile, I made my way over to Susan.

"Hi," I mumbled, looking down at the hole in my sneaker where my toe was poking through. My feet, Jimmy had said, were getting big as Frankenstein's.

"You've gotten so tall. Your hair looks so pretty," gushed Susan.

"What do you say?" asked Jimmy, starting to sound annoyed.

"Thank you," I replied, finally looking up. I stared into her warm brown eyes. They appeared to have dots of gold in them.

Jimmy playfully pinched Susan's cheek.

"You got cheekbones like Pocahontas. Must be that drop of Injun blood on your mother's side."

Susan swatted him away like he was a mosquito.

"Watch out. I just might scalp you," she said.

Jimmy laughed and backed off.

She moved away from him and came closer to me. She was wearing crisp cotton slacks, spotless sneakers, and a bandanna tied around her long, graceful neck. She seemed both warm and cool.

"I hear you're real smart. Mr. Personality here's been bragging. He says you got all As last year."

I felt warm and cool too. My cheeks were burning up. My tongue was still frozen.

"I told her to go break a window," Jimmy joked. "Get a B in behavior so the other kids don't think she's a brownnoser or a square."

Susan leaned closer to me. Like we were having our own private conversation. Like we were already best friends. "Don't listen to him. You just keep it up, study hard, and you'll be headed to Radcliffe before you know it."

I nodded. I didn't know where Rad Cliff was, but I thought it sounded wonderful—high up and far away. Possibly it was in KooKooLand.

"Radcliffe doesn't want a little greaseball like her. They want Yankee blue bloods," Jimmy butted in.

I wished he'd butt the hell out.

"She can go wherever she wants. Things are different. The world is changing."

"There you go again with that Martin Luther King utopian baloney. I keep tellin' you it's a divided world, Injun, and just 'cause you want it to be all hearts and flowers don't make it so."

"You'll see." Susan smiled, like she had some secret information.

"Those crackers down south are never gonna let little Elly Mae learn her ABCs with a nigger."

Susan's smile disappeared.

"Why would a smart guy like you use a dumb word like that?"

"C'mon, everybody said it in the merchant marine, even the niggers, and I oughta know 'cause I was drinking buddies with most of them."

"I don't see a merchant ship around here, do you, Jimmy? We got every other kind, so why don't you pick another ship to sail on?"

Jimmy cracked up. His mustache made a dashing smile on his upper lip.

"You're all right, kid. You're all right in my book any day of the week."

"Great. Put me down for Sunday. We can go to church together. You can give the priest a hot tip on the horses."

Jimmy laughed harder. She had him eating out of her hand like a racehorse with a cube of sugar.

I stared at the cross hanging around her neck. I begged God to let me be just like her. I vowed then and there to go to church. Even though Jimmy was dead set against churchgoing of any type and thought churchy people were squares. But Susan was a big Catholic and she didn't seem like a square, not even to Jimmy. So, by damn—no, by darn—I'd become a Catholic too. And then Susan and I could hang out at church together.

"Speaking of horses," I heard Jimmy say to Susan, "you still riding?"

"I just went riding with Mom," said Susan. "She's a great horsewoman. She's got a way with the most skittish horses."

Jimmy grunted, unwilling to concede Doris was good at anything besides aggravating Hank.

Just then a guy waddled up to the counter. He had a beer belly that made him look like a pregnant lady.

"Hey, Susan," he said with a snorty laugh, "gimme a pair of balls."

"Yeah, me too, Susan. What about my balls?" said his buddy, like it was the funniest goddamn thing in the world. Like he was goddamn Groucho Marx.

Balls were what hunters called a certain type of ammo when they wanted to be wise guys. When they wanted to make a girl get all red in the face. They seemed to like that one little word could get girls all bent out of shape.

I knew what balls were. Sort of. Besides being something fun and round you bounced against a wall, they had something to do with Down There. Something round Down There that guys thought was fun and funny. The shape is what threw me. I thought it was supposed to be long like a maple cruller.

The pregnant guy wasn't done having fun.

"You ever fired up any balls, Susan? You ever seen 'em shoot off?"

Jimmy stepped in. Right in the pregnant guy's face. The red-hot end of his cigarette butt was an inch from the guy's schnoz.

"Leave the kid alone. She's a good kid, a decent kid. Don't talk to her like that."

"I was just kidding around. I didn't mean anything by it."

"If I tell Hank what you said to her, he'll belt you so hard in the schnozzola you'll see more stars than Wile E. Coyote."

"I didn't mean anything by it," the guy repeated.

"Then maybe you want to open your stupid piehole and apologize."

"Sorry," the guy mumbled to Susan, staring down at the ammo.

"Maybe you wanna look at the person you're apologizing to so you at least give the impression you mean what you say."

The guy looked up at Susan. His stupid piehole was all twitchy.

"I'm sorry. Real sorry."

Susan gave him the ammo and he thanked her very much and slunk the hell out of there like a cat that had peed where it wasn't supposed to.

Jimmy had showed the guy who was boss. He had protected my best friend. He was the best goddamn father in the world.

"Any jerko bugs you, you tell your uncle Jimmy," he told Susan. "I'll straighten him the hell out."

"That's what I'm afraid of," she said.

A door banged open and a gruff voice boomed out.

"Look what the cat dragged in. A goddamn Greek."

It was Susan's father, Hank. The millionaire.

He didn't look so hot. He looked like he might've just gotten up or had tied one on the night before. I caught a glimpse of a makeshift bed in the smoky back room he had come out of. And a whole bunch of empty beer bottles. It made me think of a song I sang in the car to pass the time while Jimmy was in the bookie joint.

Ninety-nine bottles of beer on the wall
Ninety-nine bottles of beer.
Take one down, pass it around.
Ninety-eight bottles of beer on the wall.

You kept going until you had gone through all the bottles of beer or until your father came back.

I could smell the beer on Hank's breath when he got closer. He was puffing on a cigar as usual. Cigar smoke made my stomach do flip-flops worse than Jimmy's Lucky Strikes. I turned my head to the side and tried holding my breath. One Mississippi, two Mississippi, three Mississippi . . . I couldn't hold it long enough.

Hank handed Susan a wrench. He told her to go straighten up his place in the back, then finish putting that boat trailer together, then stock the shelves, then go buy him some more goddamn cigars, he was almost out. Susan took the wrench like she knew what to do with it.

Before she left she spoke to me again. "Don't forget about Rat Cliff."

"I won't. I won't forget." Rad or Rat Cliff, now I wasn't sure. I hoped it wasn't Rat Cliff.

Susan went into the back and closed the door. I could hear beer bottles being tossed into a garbage can.

Jimmy pulled Hank aside and started whispering to him.

I couldn't hear what they were saying, so I spied on them like Nancy Drew, trying to pick up clues.

Hank kept puffing away on his stinky cigar. Except for the cigar, he didn't look anything like I imagined a millionaire should look. He didn't wear a top hat or swill champagne like the swells in Fred Astaire movies. He wasn't even handsome like Jimmy. He was really old—forty-six, twelve years older than Jimmy—and a couple inches shorter. He had a bowlegged walk, but he had a swagger about him, and Jimmy said women were always throwing themselves at him.

He's like a bantam rooster, Jimmy explained. A cock of the walk.

Unlike Jimmy, Hank didn't like to throw the baloney. He always acted like he had someplace more important to be. If he thought a guy was full of shit, he'd turn his back on him and walk away. Like the guy didn't even rate a see-you-later-Charlie. If some rube took too long deciding between this rifle and that rifle, he'd order the greenhorn the hell off the premises. But if a guy knew which end of a gun was the business end, if, like Hank, he could track the biggest deer anyone had ever seen for three days until it gave up and said shoot me, he'd give him the goddamn gun for a test run. Or if a guy was like Jimmy and knew how to navigate a canoe through a hurricane to get to the biggest trout anyone had ever seen, then he was in the inner circle and got invited to Hank's hunting camp on the Allagash River, which was way the hell up near Canada in God's Country.

Big wheel or working stiff, judge or jailbird, they all wanted to go to God's Country with Hank.

"Everyone wants to be his buddy," Jimmy had once told me, "but nobody really knows him. Hell, I'm as close to him as anybody. We were both merchant seamen, we're goddamn brothers. But you can't cross a line with him. You can't get too chummy. I think that Polish mama of his has her claws into him pretty good. I did some landscaping for her. She's a tough customer, just like YaYa. I know the type. 'Go to church or else.' Nothing's ever good enough for them unless you're a goddamn choirboy. Well, that ain't me and it ain't Hank."

Hank was looking impatient. I edged a little closer to hear how Jimmy's matchmaking might be progressing.

"I've got something you can tap," I heard Jimmy say. "She's not bad looking."

"After my wife, who looks like a goddamn movie star, you want to set me up with something that's 'not bad looking'? Forget it, Greek."

"Look, she's not Ava Gardner, OK, but she's a nice-looking broad. Dark hair, like you go for. And a sweetheart, real quiet. Won't break your balls like Doris."

"Doris can be nice when she wants to be."

"You mean when she wants something. Like a new goddamn mink coat."

Hank didn't say anything, just puffed harder on his cigar. Jimmy watched him like a hawk.

"I heard she's back in town," Jimmy said. "Did you see her or what?"

"Yeah, I saw her last night. So what?"

"So what? Look at you. You look like you just took the slow boat up the devil's ass and back."

"Yeah, and you look like the devil's ass."

"Man, that broad just divorced you. Forget about her. How many times you gonna chase her tail across the country?"

"None of your goddamn business, Greek. That's how many times."

"Is she back to stay or what?"

"She wants to sell the house and move out to California."

"Sayonara. That's where she belongs. In KooKooLand."

"No, that's where you belong. You're the goddamn head case."

"Look, I'll have Shirley call this broad. We'll go out clubbing Saturday night. Just the four of us."

"All right. Fuck it. If it will shut you up."

Jimmy put his hand on Hank's shoulder.

"Forget Doris. Believe me, I know what I'm talkin' about. I had one just like her before Shirley. I may be a greaseball and you're a Polack, but we speak the same language."

Hank stubbed out his cigar and walked away. As he passed me, he said, "Your old man's a royal pain in the ass." Then he reached in his pocket and gave me a dollar. A whole frickin' dollar. I stood there, gawking at it.

Jimmy was already on his way out the door.

I ran to catch up with him, debating whether I would buy a Charleston Chew or Milk Duds or a Sugar Daddy.

I tripped over a fishing pole and went down into a sea of men's legs.

A meaty hand reached down and helped me up.

It was a cop. He was holding a hunting rifle. I froze. Froze at the sight of his shiny badge and his name. McSomething.

"Are you OK? Did you hurt yourself?" He actually looked concerned.

My knee was all scraped up. I knotted up every muscle in my body to keep from blubbering. I heard Jimmy's voice in my head. Always leave a cop on a stone wall. Meaning, don't tell them diddly-squat.

"I'm fine," I lied. "I didn't feel nothin'."

"Not a good place for little girls," he said.

"My daddy knows Hank," I barked at him, and ran off, doing my best not to hobble on my banged-up leg.

Outside, Jimmy was standing by the car, sucking on a Lucky.

"What the hell did you say to that fuzz?"

"Nothin', Daddy. I didn't say nothin'. I left him on a stone wall where he belongs."

"Good girl." Jimmy laughed. "I trained you good. Now hop to it. You're makin' me late."

I scrambled into the car. The seat was burning hot and my knee was stinging like a bastard and I still felt like blubbering. I cupped the wound so Jimmy wouldn't see my bloody scrape. I didn't want him to call me a dummkopf for falling. I just wanted to go home. I had some Chuckles jelly candies hidden in the Good & Plenty box with Barbie's shoes and pocketbooks. I wanted them bad.

But just my stupid Norris luck, Susan's younger brother, Terry, showed up.

Jimmy jumped out of the car and jogged over to Terry.

"And there he is, in the center of the ring, the one-and-only Manchester Mauler!"

Terry laughed and Jimmy grabbed him around the neck and mussed his wavy black hair. According to Jimmy, Terry was a dead ringer for John Garfield, the mauler in his favorite boxing movie, *Body and Soul*.

"So now you're a big high school graduate, you think you're a man? You think you can take me?"

"I could take you when I was ten, old man," Terry crowed.

They started throwing punches, messing around.

"Whoa, pretty boy," cooed Jimmy. "Lookin' good, lookin' good."

All of a sudden, I wanted to punch somebody, anybody.

I wanted to punch Terry. It didn't matter that he was nice as pie to me or was my future best friend Susan's younger brother or might one day be the boxing champion of the world. I hated his guts. Hated that he was keeping me from my Chuckles. Hated that Jimmy took him hunting and fishing and sat ringside with Hank at his boxing matches. Cripe, he was only in the Golden Gloves, but to hear Jimmy go on and on you'd think he was the Great Jack Dempsey.

The blood on my knee was starting to get sticky. I found a greasy gun-cleaning rag and tried to dab some of the blood off. The knee was now black and red and still throbbing and I was sure I was gonna get blood poisoning if I didn't get the hell home and swab it with alcohol the way Jimmy the Cut Man had taught me to do.

I heard Jimmy invite Terry to come up to Maine to watch our horse, Victory Bound.

"Come have your picture taken in the winner's circle," he said.

Goddamn it! I didn't want Terry horning in on my vacation. He wasn't part of our family and I didn't see where he got off being in the winner's circle. He already had a millionaire father and a movie-star-looking mother, even if they had just busted up. He already had a sister like Susan.

And he was a goddamn pretty boy. What more did he want?

Finally, Jimmy told Terry not to overtrain because with horses that was the kiss of death and people were the same as horses. Then Jimmy got back in the car. Terry gave me a little wave. I waved back at him.

Maybe he'll fall into a garbage truck or a snake pit, I thought. Maybe the Boston Strangler will get tired of strangling women and start strangling a few men.

You never knew. Something bad could always happen.

I still had hope.

Nick's Ringside Cafe

The Great Jack Dempsey was staring down at me. He had his arm around my grandfather, Papou Nick. Papou was wearing a fancy suit and a shiny tie and a white shirt with a collar all stiff and tight like it could choke him to death. Papou looked like a million bucks. Like a millionaire, even.

But that was a long time ago.

I studied the picture of Papou and the Great Jack Dempsey that hung above the cash register in Nick's Ringside Cafe. We had stopped there on the way back from Hank's. As I stared at the photo, I tried to figure out what had gone wrong. Why wasn't the Great Jack Dempsey in our lives now?

I glanced around the place. The truth was I didn't think a world champ would be caught dead in a joint like this. Everything was piss yellow from the haze of smoke that never went away. Even the picture of the Great Jack Dempsey was all yellow. There was sawdust on the floor that had beery spit in it, and three big dusty jars on the bar with gray things floating in them. Pickled eggs. Pickled pigs' feet. And kielbasa sausage, which was a Polack food for any Polacks who might be stopping by. I had seen a guy eat a kielbasa once, but nobody ever seemed to touch the pickled eggs or feet. I figured maybe they were just there for decoration like the picture of the Great Jack Dempsey. But then Jimmy had explained to me that you had to pretend to serve food in a beer joint or the city would shut you down. You had to have a grill in the back and a few hot dogs and some raw hamburger meat to throw on it when some pencil pusher from the city pulled a sneak visit. You had to offer the pencil pusher a grilled dog and a cold soda, which he would turn his nose up at before he got the hell out and let the paying customers get back to the business of drinking themselves half-blind.

The paying customers needed to drink themselves half-blind, Jimmy said, 'cause they all hated their Mickey Mouse, collect-a-paycheck-every-Thursday jobs. They were a bunch of poor alkie mill workers caught in a cage like Squirmy our hamster. The mill workers didn't own racehorses and had nothing to look forward to except a lousy week or two off in the summer and a frozen Butterball at Christmas.

No wonder they turn into rumheads, Jimmy said. I wasn't sure why he called them that since the only thing Papou and YaYa sold was ten-cent beers.

YaYa started to yell at Jimmy.

"Why do you do this? Why do you keep bringing her in here? You know we could get shut down again if a policeman sees her!"

"Relax, will ya?" Jimmy said to YaYa. "If a copper comes in, I'll hide her under the bar—she's skinny enough to fit anywhere. Skinny like her Olive Oyl mother. Besides, don't you want to see your own granddaughter? What kind of good-for-nothing grandmother are you?"

He was kidding around with her, yanking on the ties of her apron.

YaYa smacked him away and retied the bow on her perfectly starched apron. Then she smoothed down the front of her fancy blue dress. YaYa, like always, was dressed to the nines. Jimmy said she dolled up for the beer joint like she was going to the Carpenter Hotel, the place where all the Yankee ladies sipped their limey tea. She even wore diamond jewelry. Shirley told me the jewelry was as phony as a three-dollar bill, but I didn't see how anybody could tell the difference.

"Whose fault is it I don't see more of them?" YaYa snapped at Jimmy. "Why don't you let me bring her and Virginia to church this Sunday?"

I knew what he'd say about that. No f'in' way. No kid of his was going to have to suffer like he did when he was a boy with all that smelly incense and those priests in their big, goofy hats.

"These kids don't even speak Greek," he said. "It'll be mumbo jumbo to them."

"Whose fault is that?" she barked. "Who wouldn't let me send them to Greek school when I offered to pay for it?"

She shouted something at him in Greek for good measure. Jimmy answered her in English.

"I don't need your dough. Not one red cent. And she don't need Greek school. She's an American kid, for Chrissake. She don't want to be stuck in some dungeon after school learning a language she'll never use. She wants to be outside in the sunshine playing with the other American pip-squeaks."

He turned to me to back him up.

"Don't you, Dracula?"

He waited for my answer. YaYa waited too. Her eyes were black as licorice dots.

I didn't know the right answer. The answer that would make them both happy.

"I don't know," I mumbled.

"Of course she doesn't know," YaYa snapped. "Children do what their parents tell them to do—unless they're bad like you. I hope she doesn't take after you, that's all I can say."

"She does take after me. She does in spades." He pumped me again. "Don't you?"

"I don't know," I mumbled again.

I could see he wasn't happy with my answer.

"I guess so," I chirped.

I wanted out of there.

"Daddy, I'm hungry," I blurted out.

"How 'bout a pig's foot?" he suggested. He started to unscrew the top of the jar.

I stared panic-stricken at the floating feet.

Jimmy burst out laughing.

"Look at her. She thinks I'm serious."

He bopped me on the head.

"Take it easy. Nobody's gonna make you eat that. It's been here since the Stone Age."

He looked back over at YaYa, who was taking a dime from an alkie and putting it in the cash register.

"Make Dracula a hamburger," he ordered her. "Nice and bloody."

I didn't want it nice and bloody and said so, but Jimmy said that was the only way to eat meat. He said if I went to a swanky restaurant in Paris and ordered filet mignon cooked black as a nigger they'd call me a Yankee greenhorn and throw me the hell out of there.

YaYa went in the back and soon I could hear the sizzle of frying meat.

Jimmy covered the bar while she was gone. He poured frothy beer from the taps and collected more dimes from the alkies.

When he opened the cash register to drop the money in, I saw him slip some bills from the drawer and shove them in his pocket.

Playing the accordion, he called it. Skimming a little off the top.

I pretended I didn't see.

I had another secret and knew I had to keep it. Keep it on a stone wall.

Jimmy called me over and held out a nickel.

"Some music, maestro," he said.

I knew what he wanted me to play.

D-4. The buttons on the jukebox were hard for me to push with my pip-squeak fingers. The machine went and found the record I picked and dropped it on the spindle. Louis Armstrong's "When the Saints Go Marching In" started up.

I looked over at Jimmy. He nodded his approval. I knew in a few moments he'd be making trumpet sounds for the alkies and they'd be telling him he sounded pretty damn good.

YaYa put my hamburger on the counter with an Orange Crush and a slice of cool watermelon and I crawled up on a stool between two half-blind alkies. They made room for me.

I took the first bite of hamburger. No blood seeped out. I could see the outside was nice and black. I looked over at YaYa.

"How is it?" she asked with a wink.

"It's good," I said. "Mmm-mmm good."

YaYa went back to serving the alkies. She smiled and joked around with them. As I watched her yank on the tap, I thought about what Shirley had once told me. YaYa had been an alkie too when Jimmy was a kid. She drank like a fish in a barrel of booze until one day she took Jimmy out in Papou's car and drove right off the road. "Women drivers!" Jimmy woulda said if he'd been part of the conversation. Luckily nobody died and YaYa vowed to never touch a drop of the stuff ever again.

If you ask me, she meant to kill herself and your father, Shirley insisted. Papou drove her to drink. Drove her right off that road and into a ditch.

I gnawed off another hunk of hamburger. When I glanced back up, I saw YaYa's smile drop off her face. I didn't have to turn around to know why.

Papou Nick had just walked through the door.

Jimmy's Baptized and
I'm Saved

I wanted to run and hide under the bar.

Ever since I could remember, Papou scared the daylights out of me.

He's the toughest S-O-B going, Jimmy bragged, and nobody, not even Hank, would argue with him.

The person Papou most reminded me of was Edward G. Robinson in those gangster movies, except Papou was built like a boxer, not a shrimp like Robinson. You could easily picture him saying, "Go ahead, plug the guy," and not feeling bad about it for a second.

Once Papou had almost drowned Jimmy, and I was afraid he might try to do the same to me. Jimmy told Virginia and me the Almost-Drowned Story a lot to keep us in line.

The story went like this: Jimmy had been sickly as a baby and was crying all the time. When company came over Papou would hide him in a laundry basket in a tree 'cause Greek boys weren't supposed to bawl like babies. One day when Jimmy wouldn't stop bawling, Papou told YaYa to yank him outta the tree and stick him in the car. They drove to Salisbury Beach and Jimmy cried the whole way there. He cried from the car to the beach and he cried on the beach in the penicillin sunshine. Papou grabbed little Jimmy and ran toward the water. YaYa screamed and ran after them, but Papou told her to get the hell back to the blanket. He charged into the icy Atlantic ocean that would turn your feet into Popsicles in a lick. He held Jimmy under the water until he stopped his damn blubbering.

A Greek baptism, that's what Jimmy called it. He'd had the usual kind in the Greek Church, but this was the one Jimmy felt did him the most good. It toughened him up and after that he wasn't sickly at all. Well, except for that one time when he had a bellyache and Papou said he was faking and sent him to school and his appendix burst. But that could happen to anybody. That was just bad luck. Norris Luck.

Papou never had to give Jimmy a Greek baptism again, but he once gave one to Jimmy's cat. He threw the sickly cat into the canal and said it would sink or swim. It swam and found its way back home and lived a few more years. And that was proof that the almost-drowning cure really worked. It worked for animals as well as people.

Still that didn't mean I wanted it tried out on me the next time I got an earache. It was bad enough having Jimmy pour hot olive oil in my ear. I sure as hell didn't want him throwing me off the Amoskeag Bridge as well.

Not unless Susan ran out of Hank's and jumped in the Merrimack River to save me. Then I guessed it would be worth it.

"Hey you! Eat up! Kids are starving in Greece!"

Papou's voice made me jump. He was glaring down at me.

I jammed the rest of my hamburger in my mouth and tried not to choke on it. The last thing I wanted was Papou force-feeding me the way he had done with Virginia when she was little and wouldn't eat her scrambled eggs.

YaYa leaned down and kissed my meat-stuffed cheek that looked like Squirmy the hamster's. Then she hung up her apron and went home to fry some mackerel that Jimmy had brought for Papou's supper.

A new shift was coming in and the place was getting more crowded. Jimmy lit another Lucky Strike and Papou lit a cigar that was even bigger than Hank's. I took a bite of watermelon and spit the seeds onto the floor, trying to hit the ones that I'd already spit with the ones I was spitting. Then I tried to see how far I could stick my tongue down the neck of the Orange Crush bottle without getting it stuck.

Jimmy and Papou began talking about this horse and that horse and whether the horse Jimmy had bought oughta be hopped up or not.

Shirley said Jimmy and Papou were two of a kind.

Con artists. Operators. Flimflammers.

They were always cooking up scams. In one scam, Papou would call Tarzan the bookie from a phone booth to place a bet on a horse. Jimmy would be in the next booth getting the early results of the same race Papou was betting on from a guy he knew who worked at the track. Past posting, they called it. Cheating and stealing is more like it, Shirley said.

Nobody would've suspected Papou of pulling a fast one like that.

Everybody looks up to the old man, Jimmy would say. Even the Greek priests in their goofy hats.

The Greek priests in their goofy hats admired Papou 'cause even though he had become an American wheeler-dealer who rubbed shoulders with a heavy-weight champ, he still respected the ways of the old country. Even though he'd taught himself to read, write, and speak English—with no banana-peddler accent, Jimmy boasted—he still sent his sons to Greek school. And even though he'd changed his last name to something Yankees could pronounce, he'd kept every ounce of his Greek pride.

Most of all, though, Jimmy said the priests loved Papou because he greased their wheels. I couldn't picture Papou, who always dressed like a big shot, sprawled under a car greasing some priest's car, but then Jimmy had explained that wheel greasing was when you paid somebody to do stuff for you.

What did he pay the priests to do? I'd asked.

Get him into heaven, dum-dum.

Lucky for me, Papou had also done a little wheel greasing on my behalf. The year before, at the start of third grade, my new teacher, Miss Rogers, had stuck me in the back row and acted like she didn't know I was alive. At first, I'd tried some wheel greasing on my own. I spent some of my tooth fairy dough on the biggest, reddest apple I could find at the Temple Market. I blew on it and polished it with my sleeve until it was bright and shiny.

Miss Rogers took it from me like it was Snow White's poison apple.

I told myself maybe she wasn't a fruit lover. Or maybe she would've preferred a slice of cool watermelon instead.

But in my gut I knew it was because she had seen the name of the street I lived on. Ahern Street. One of the project streets.

"Those snooty teachers treat all the project kids like they're juvenile delinquents," Virginia had informed me as she was forging Jimmy's signature on an excuse note to cover the fact that she had played hooky.

"Not me," I argued. "I'm always the teacher's pet."

"That's 'cause you're a brownnoser and an egghead like Daddy says."

"And you're a crook and a cheater like Daddy."

"Hey, it's 'cause of me you're teacher's pet. Don't you forget it."

I couldn't argue with that. Virginia had taught me everything I knew. Before I was even in first grade, she had drilled me in reading, spelling, adding, subtracting. She'd also made me memorize the names of all the countries on the globe YaYa had given us so we'd know where the hell Greece was. Virginia didn't go in much for school herself, but she taught me stuff to amuse herself, just like she trained Squirmy to stand on his hind legs and eat feta cheese from her lips. Jimmy thought it was great that I had learned to read so early 'cause then I could slack off for the first few years. Plus, he was crazy about reading himself. He liked World War II stories and *The Call of the Wild* and Orwell's *1984* 'cause he said Big Brother was breathing down our frickin' necks.

But it was tough to show off your reading skills if no one ever called on you. And that's how it was in Miss Rogers' third-grade class, until one day I came home from school blubbering to Shirley about it and then Jimmy came home and asked what all the blubbering was about. When Shirley gave him the lowdown, he turned as red as that poisoned apple I had given Miss Rogers.

"I'll go pop that old biddy in the breadbasket!" he shouted, and started to head for the door.

"No, Daddy," I pleaded, "I'll get expelled."

"Have a drink first," Shirley suggested, trying to calm him down. "It's happy hour." She handed him the highball she already had waiting for him.

Jimmy took a slug of the highball and reconsidered his options. He mentioned something about popping the old biddy's kneecaps. He said he knew some dago gangsters in Revere who would do it for him, for nothing too, if they heard somebody had even looked at one of his kids sideways.

That sounded better to me. Unlike with Jimmy doing something himself, I didn't see how the dago gangsters could be traced to me. But then it occurred to me what if the dagos were squealers? What if they got caught and squealed and maybe I'd be seen as an accomplice and end up in the slammer along with them?

Right about then Papou called with a tip on a horse. Jimmy started ranting about the old biddy and the dago gangsters and Papou cut him off. Papou said forget the dagos, he knew what to do, he'd take care of it.

The next day an alkie from the beer joint, clean-shaven and dressed in one of Papou's fancy suits, delivered a whole case of Orange Crush to my classroom. Then he lugged in a case of grape soda and a box filled with Fig Newtons and Lorna Doones and some party hats left over from the big wingding Papou threw every year for all the alkies. Then he handed Miss Rogers a note and a red rose.

Miss Rogers got all giddy like the lady at the office when Jimmy gave her that Mickey Mouse lighter.

Miss Rogers asked me to read Papou's note out loud to the class. It said we should have a nice party on him and work hard and mind our wonderful teacher and he signed it Mr. Nick Norris, owner of Nick's Cafe. I noticed he had left out the Ringside part.

That very day Miss Rogers moved me to a seat in the front row and from then on it was smooth sailing. In June when I took home my final report card, there were nothing but As on it for the whole year.

Jimmy brought the report card to the beer joint and passed it around to the alkies and they had a round to celebrate.

He told them I was smart all right, but I should cut loose more. Live a little 'cause life was short and before I knew it I'd be grown up like them and life would be closing in around me. Life would be suffocating the life out of me.

It doesn't last, he lamented. The good old days are over before you know it and all you're left with is a bunch of bad new days.

I'll drink to that, one of the alkies had said. And they all downed another.

Jimmy and Papou were going on about the good old days right now. They had gotten off the subject of hosses and were starting in on boxers. The half-blind alkies were all ears even though most of them had heard the stories before. They sipped their beers and listened quietly like they were in church.

I drained my Orange Crush and leaned in closer so I wouldn't miss a word either.

Jimmy and Papou entertained us with stories about all the fighters Papou had managed. Fighters with funny names like the Cereal Kid, who was crazy about cornflakes. And the Fighting Bricklayer, who was built like a brick outhouse. And Kid Billodeaux, who had broken his hand logging and couldn't make a fist, so he would slap the other guy silly instead of punching him. And Red Conrad, who'd gotten some disease as a kid and had a gimpy leg and would limp around the ring.

We all laughed at the image of a boxer with a funny limp, as if we were seeing a Charlie Chaplin movie play out right before our eyes.

At long last Jimmy brought up Red's brother Norman. The Wilton Wraith. Papou's greatest fighter. One measly fight away from a title shot. A guy who would fight King Kong, he was that game. A guy who had almost gotten himself and Papou and Papou's little cut man Jimmy killed by some dago gangsters when he wouldn't take a dive like he was supposed to. Papou kept throwing the towel in the ring to get the ref to stop the fight, but crazy Norman kept kicking it out before the ref could see it. Finally Papou went over and threw the towel right on the ref's head and told him he was about as blind as Helen Frickin' Keller.

The half-blind alkies split a gut and I split a gut and then somebody asked what the hell happened to Norman, where the hell was he now.

Jimmy said Norman was still out in Wilton, but he had himself a new profession. He'd shoot a bunch of deer and sell them for a C-note to the New

Yorkers who drove up wanting to look like Great White Hunters but who couldn't hit the broad side of a barn.

How come Norman never got his title shot? asked another alkie who must've been so drunk the last time he heard the story that he forgot the answer.

Ah, he got clobbered by Sammy Slaughter, Papou said. Got clobbered by a nigger.

Powers Gonna Die

Finally, Jimmy said we had to get the hell out of there.

But that didn't mean I was going to get to go home.

Papou had given Jimmy a tip on a horse and it looked like a sure thing. So Jimmy drove on over to the bookie joint.

He parked outside and began to do some last-minute arithmetic on the *Racing Form*. I stared out the half-open window at the bookie joint. From the outside, it looked like a real rattrap. But I figured that must just be a cover. I imagined it was like those speakeasies in the TV show *The Roaring 20's*. Gangsters would do a secret knock on the door of some crappy building and a guard would peer out a window and see if you were a cool customer or a copper. If you were a cool customer, it was open sesame. Behind the crappy door, people would be playing roulette and rolling snake eyes and there would be rolls of cabbage as big as heads of cabbage and I figured some guy who was flush might give a cute little pip-squeak like me a fin for good luck.

Jimmy finished doing his math and opened the door.

"Can't I come in?" I begged, pinching the eagle on Jimmy's arm. "You take me in the beer joint and I'm not even twenty-one."

"The bookie joint's different, dum-dum. No broads allowed."

I never saw many ladies in the beer joint either. Now and then you'd spot a lady rumhead getting plastered.

But the bookie joint was a whole other story. Even Shirley couldn't go in there. Ever since Jimmy had taught her a few things about handicapping she was picking more winners than he was. But her superior handicapping skills didn't matter. She had to fork over her dough to Jimmy, tell him what to bet, and sit in the car and wait just like me.

Wait forever.

Jimmy bopped me on the head with the *Racing Form*.

"I'll be right back," he promised.

I nodded like I believed him.

He reached into the backseat and grabbed last week's newspaper that he kept there to wrap up dead fish.

"Here, read the funnies," he said, tossing it onto my lap.

"Oh boy," I said, trying to look grateful.

He slammed the door shut, jogged over to the bookie joint, and rapped on the door. Three knocks, two knocks, three knocks. I saw the sliver of a man's face.

Open sesame and Jimmy vanished.

I realized I had to pee.

I picked up the paper to distract myself and turned straight to the comics. I called them comics but Jimmy called them funnies. I figured *funnies* was an old-timey word from when Jimmy was a kid. Back then he'd had to stick the funnies in the bottom of his shoes when he got a hole in the sole, and then walk to school in the snow. I pictured those newspapers becoming all wet and maybe a picture of Blondie and Dagwood fighting getting on the bottom of his feet. Like the newsprint was now getting all over my hot, sweaty hands.

I finished the comics in a few minutes and then scanned the paper to see if there was any news about the Boston Strangler. There wasn't a mention. He was still out there and the dumb cops couldn't catch him 'cause they were too busy eating rum cakes that made their lard-asses lardier.

I read everything in the paper and was down to checking out the ads. The Wa Toy restaurant was having a special on their pu pu platter. Chink chow, Jimmy called it, and wouldn't touch it with a ten-foot pole. Supposedly they hid dogs and cats in the food like that maniac from *Blood Feast* hid eyeballs in his Egyptian stew.

I began to worry. What if some Chinese people came around the projects and tried to snatch our cat, Sylvester, for one of their pu pu platters? I told myself I better keep Sylvester on his leash from now on. And I better keep an eye out for slanty-eyed people. Then I closed the paper so I wouldn't have to think about dead dogs and cats anymore.

The intense heat in the car was making me sleepy. I imagined being baked alive like what nearly happened to the kids in my favorite fairy tale, "Hansel and Gretel." Those kids got dumped in the woods by their father and then a witch tried to roast them.

I hung my head out the window and tried to catch a breeze from an approaching truck. It thundered past, a few inches from my schnozzola. I fell back into the car, my heart pounding. I pictured my head being severed from my body and rolling down the street until it got squashed by a bus. Maybe that was a better way to go than roasting. At least it was quick.

I started singing about ninety-nine bottles of beer on the wall, but it made me too thirsty, so I stopped. I imagined crawling around in the desert with nothing to drink and dying that way.

I imagined exploding from pee.

Somehow, death was always popping into my head even though I didn't want it there. Death was like a toothache that just kept throbbing away.

Jimmy had first clued me in about death years before. We were up in Nova Scotia, visiting Grammy and Grampy. I was picking wildflowers. I called them powers 'cause I couldn't say *flowers* yet.

They're bootiful, I cooed to Jimmy.

Jimmy stared out to where the woods began, past where the wildflowers were. He looked sad about something. I tried to hand him a power.

They're beautiful, but they're all gonna die, he said. That's the lousy thing about life. Everything goes away. Everything dies. Even your mommy and me will die.

I dropped my powers and started screaming. I wailed so loud Shirley came running out of the house.

What happened? Shirley screeched.

Nothing, Jimmy said. She's crying over a big fat nothing.

I tried to tell her what was wrong.

Powers gonna die! Powers gonna die! I shrieked.

Hush, it's all right, she said, as she rocked me back and forth.

Powers gonna die. Powers gonna die.

What a crybaby, said Jimmy. Boo hoo hoo.

Shirley carried me away from him. Carried me up past the field where Grampy had built a baseball diamond for his seven kids. Up into the fields where the strawberries were. Rows and rows of strawberries that Grampy grew and sold for money.

She plucked a berry as big as my fist and handed it to me. I ate it and then ate another. The snot dripping down my chin mixed with the strawberry juice and made pink snot and I stopped crying.

She told me how she had loved berries when she was a little girl. How she would eat them when she was supposed to be picking them to sell.

I ate more berries and listened to Shirley's stories and couldn't get enough of either one.

Shirley had been born and raised right there on the farm. She picked strawberries all summer long and ate them with warm, sweet shortcake from Grammy's wood-burning stove and buttery cream from Grampy's cow.

Old Gutless is what they called the cow.

Hickville is what Jimmy called Tusket, Shirley's hometown.

Stump-jumpers, he called Shirley's family. Clodhoppers. Real greenhorns.

They didn't know the first thing about how to bet a trifecta. They didn't know where to get the strongest highballs in New York City. And they wouldn't be able to find their way around the Combat Zone with a map and a compass.

They played games with funny names. Pinochle. Parcheesi. Crokinole.

They bet matchsticks—if they bet at all—and surely not on Sunday.

They had no TV. The kitchen had a cold-water pump. And the bathroom was out in a shed that smelled like people had been doing their business in there for a million years. The curling strips of flypaper caught some of the flies buzzing around your keister but not all of them and the rest you had to shoo off with a newspaper from 1943.

In the winter it was too cold for flies or people out there and you did your business crouched over a pot with your legs trembling from trying not to move too much. Then you climbed into bed, where the brick Grampy had heated on the wood-burning stove to keep you warm was already stone cold.

The big deal of the day was going to the post office to wait for the mail. I went with my uncle Whitfield, but Jimmy wouldn't be caught dead in there listening to all the farmers talk about their chicken feed and their half-wit cousins. Instead, he spent the day hunting or fishing and getting half-lit. Then he'd sit around Grammy's kitchen at night and ask the stump-jumpers if they wanted to play crokinole for hard cash.

Not that he was serious or anything. He was just trying to get a rise out of them. He wouldn't be caught dead playing a game with a goofy name like crokinole.

Finally, everything came to a head one night when Jimmy called Uncle Whitfield's horse an old nag ready for the glue factory. Uncle Whitfield loved that horse and called Jimmy uncouth and Jimmy nearly decked Uncle Whitfield. Grampy took Shirley out to the barn and asked her if she had married an outlaw.

No, said Shirley, that's just how American men are.

Then maybe you want to come back home to Canada, he suggested.

But Shirley didn't want to go back home. Ever since she was a little girl she had dreamed of getting off that damn farm and seeing the United States of America. She had been picking red strawberries and churning white cream until she was blue in the face. Been doing it ever since she left school in the eighth grade to help out on the farm 'cause girls didn't go past the eighth grade up there. They just married boys in baggy pants with horse manure on their clodhoppers, had nine or ten kids like Grammy, and, according to Shirley, looked like old hags by twenty-seven.

By the time *she* was twenty-seven, Shirley didn't look like an old hag, but she wasn't married either. She'd been engaged once, but that didn't pan out. Most people in Tusket thought she'd end up an old maid. She was starting to think so herself. She got a job as a shopgirl in the nearest town and spent hours gazing at movie magazines and daydreaming about the States. She talked about the States so much that Grammy saved a little money every week from selling butter and eggs and bought Shirley a boat ticket to go visit her Aunt Cora in Massachusetts.

Jimmy was working on the boat and was looking for an old-fashioned girl like in the old country. He had just gotten divorced from the one who mouthed off like Susan's mother.

He spotted Shirley right away.

She had dark hair and was tall and had a shy way of going. She was dressed real nice but not too flashy, not too much makeup and not showing too much of her pretty long legs. She was talking to another passenger, a high yaller named Birdy who she'd just met and didn't even know was half-colored. Birdy was Jimmy's pal Be-bop's girlfriend, so Jimmy went right over and introduced himself. He told Shirley to come to the back of the ship that night, to the kitchen where he worked as a cook, and he'd make her a meal fit for a queen. He mentioned a filet mignon steak and Shirley thought that sounded real fancy. She mostly had deer meat on the farm, and she was sick to death of that.

So Jimmy made her the filet mignon and some duck with an orange sauce and some big, fat shrimp that tasted like the sea they were sailing on and something for dessert that he lit with a match.

He got her number.

He told her he'd take her for the thrill of her life. He'd take her to the backstretch 'cause he was known at the track and could get back there. He'd show her some beautiful horses. Didn't all girls like horses?

I like horses fine, said Shirley, who had seen more than enough of them on the farm and would rather go to a Red Sox game but didn't want to seem rude.

After that, we'll go dancing, he said, and Shirley perked right up. I'll show you the nightlife. I know all the jumpin' joints.

It was sounding better and better to Shirley.

But Shirley's Aunt Cora didn't like the looks of Jimmy one bit.

He looks like a sharpie, Aunt Cora said.

Shirley didn't care what old Aunt Cora said. She went on a date with the sharpie and even fell in love with those horses when they flew past her in the backstretch carrying their jockeys in their bright shiny shirts. She loved those horses even more when she saw Jimmy coming back from the betting windows with a stack of tenners and double sawbucks and when he gave her a tenner 'cause he bet a long shot for her that paid off big.

He took her to meet YaYa and Papou and told her they owned a restaurant. Nick's Cafe.

She asked Jimmy after they left if something was wrong with Papou 'cause he didn't smile or anything.

No, Jimmy said, he's just a tough hombre. That's how you gotta be in America. You just don't know any operators like him. You grew up in Hickville.

Tusket, Shirley corrected him.

There was something about Jimmy's tone of voice that didn't sit right, but she brushed it aside. American men are different, she told herself. They talked a language that she couldn't understand 'cause she was a strawberry farmer's daughter who didn't get past the eighth grade.

On the way back to Aunt Cora's, he pulled over and kissed her. It felt pretty good, but not as good as the kisses of the air force lieutenant she'd been engaged to. The one who had turned out to have a wife someplace else and who had broken her heart so bad she couldn't get out of bed for two weeks. The one she had taken this trip to forget.

Shirley pulled away from the kiss.

Jimmy smiled. That's OK, he said, I can see you're a good girl, not like most of the broads around the clubs.

Shirley had never heard the word *broad* before and didn't like the sound of it.

You're a real nice girl, Jimmy said. Not like my first wife.

Shirley nearly fell over. No one around Tusket ever got divorced. They were all religious folk and didn't believe in it. Shirley didn't believe in it either. Except for the lieutenant—she wished he'd divorce his wife and marry her.

Shirley decided maybe Aunt Cora was right after all. She had had fun, had even forgotten about the lieutenant for a while, but she had her doubts about the sharpie. She returned to Tusket and thought she'd never see him again.

But then while she was feeding the chickens she found herself thinking about that day at the races and about the filet mignon and about how he had told her she looked just like Ava Gardner.

A month later, Jimmy came to see her when his ship docked for an overnight. He brought Grammy a box of Fanny Farmer chocolates and Grampy some

Cuban cigars he got down in Havana. And he didn't use the word *broad* once.

One night, he snuck her some whiskey out on the porch and it was the best she had felt since the lieutenant went away.

But then he went and spoiled it by making a crack about Grampy's baggy pants.

Shirley still had her doubts.

And she might never have married Jimmy or moved to the States or had me at all if it hadn't been for what happened to her favorite brothers. Albert and Ernie. They were only twenty-two and twenty-three and they drowned one day when they went out fishing. It was July 6, 1952. Jimmy's ship had come in again and Shirley cried on his shoulder. He seemed to understand. He said life was a raw deal 'cause death was just waiting there to snatch any one of us at any damn moment. He said you might as well eat, drink, and bet the ponies as much as you could because before you knew it you wouldn't be able to pee straight.

Shirley up and married Jimmy six weeks later in Nova Scotia.

She'd known him four months and had seen him five times.

The Reverend S. F. Whitehouse performed the brief ceremony. Jimmy seemed anxious to get it over with and joked he'd give the reverend a fin if he made it snappy, but the reverend just looked confused 'cause he was a greenhorn and didn't know a fin was a five.

They drove back to the States in a car Jimmy had borrowed from a buddy of his. His own car was always breaking down and Jimmy didn't think it would make the trip. The friend's car wasn't much better. It broke down a few hours out of Tusket.

They stayed at the cheapest joint Jimmy could find.

They did the thing grown-ups do when they love each other, even though Shirley realized she didn't love him.

She didn't feel a thing that first time, although later on she said she got to like it, but only after a few highballs.

When they finally made it back to the States, they went right to YaYa and Papou's. YaYa handed over Jimmy's three-year-old daughter, Virginia. Papou handed over the want ads.

Greek women work, he told her. Not like these Yankee princesses.

Get a job, he ordered her.

And don't expect me to babysit, added YaYa. I've done my share already.

Jimmy dropped Shirley and Virginia at his crummy apartment and took off for the bookie joint. Shirley felt so alone she burst out crying.

Virginia began to cry too. Shirley tried to comfort her, but Virginia hauled off and kicked her, leaving a big, blue knot on Shirley's leg.

I want YaYa, wailed Virginia.

Well, YaYa doesn't want you, thought Shirley, but she didn't say it. Because despite being kicked, she was already feeling something for Virginia, who looked like a little blond doll.

We're two peas in a rotten pod, Shirley thought. All we have is each other.

There wasn't much food in the apartment, but Shirley was used to making a good meal out of nothing and made something for them both to eat before they fell asleep together.

Jimmy never came home that night.

Shirley got a job at the Chicopee mill, working the mothers' shift, from five to eleven.

After a few months, Jimmy said they might as well have a brat of their own.

A year and a half later I came along.

"I'm sorry," were the first words Shirley said when Jimmy walked into the hospital room. "I'm sorry it wasn't a boy."

Home Sweet Home

The car door slammed.

Jimmy was back from the bookie joint.

I jolted awake. The sun had sunk down and was now right in my eyes. My shorts were soaking wet. I panicked, thinking it was pee, then I realized it was only sweat. I still had to pee real bad.

Jimmy started up the car. He was as quiet as my Chatty Cathy doll after the string broke. Not a good sign. Usually he'd be talking a blue streak if he'd made some dough.

He yanked the wheel of the car and we screeched away from the curb, pulling out before the car already coming down the street could get in front of us.

"What's the matter," he said. "Cat got your tongue?"

He leaned closer to me.

"Or maybe Fuad Ramses's got your tongue?" He laughed and took a playful swipe at me with the Hairy Claw.

I exhaled. I was wrong.

He hadn't lost. Probably just broke even or mostly broke even, just picked up a fin or something.

"How'd you do?" I asked.

"Ah, I only made a fin," he groaned. "I coulda come outta there with a big score. A stupid jockey held my horse back when he shoulda let him run. He took him on the outside when he woulda run better on the rail."

The old Coulda Shoulda Woulda. That's what Shirley called it.

Every racetracker who sat at our kitchen table gobbling down Shirley's homemade bread and fried mackerel when he couldn't afford a square meal or who hitched a ride to Suffolk Downs with us in Jimmy's Pontiac when he couldn't afford a bus ticket had his own version of the Coulda Shoulda Woulda.

To me, they all sounded the same.

Finally we pulled up to the curb in front of our apartment.

I scrambled out of the car like a convict being sprung from the slammer and ran toward the house.

I glanced up at my bedroom window on the second floor and saw the faded paisley curtain move back into place. I knew that Virginia had been keeping one eye out for the Pontiac while she spun those 45s and now she was slamming the cover shut on the pink record player and flying down the stairs.

Jimmy raced me to the front door and got there first.

"Slowpoke," he chirped.

He pulled the screen door open. Virginia was standing in the kitchen, her face pink and sweaty from doing the twist around our bedroom. She was holding a dust mop as Exhibit A that she wasn't dancing around to colored people music.

"I was helping Mom," she said. "Cleaning up while she sleeps. And I rode the bike all the way to the cemetery."

"The sun gave you some color," Jimmy told her. "You don't look so pasty."

I ran upstairs and peed like a racehorse. Then I went into my bedroom and pulled out the Good & Plenty box from under my bed and stashed the wrinkled dollar Hank had given me inside it.

I took out a lemon Chuckle and shoved it in my mouth. The sticky jelly stuck in my teeth. One of my teeth ached a little, but I didn't care. I thought of Susan and tried to picture what she was doing at that very moment. She must've thrown out all the beer bottles and put together that boat trailer by now.

Maybe she was reading a doctor book or playing her clarinet or eating some Chuckles of her own. Maybe she was doing the exact same thing as me that very moment. I didn't know for sure if she liked Chuckles, but I couldn't imagine anybody not liking them.

I ate the cherry Chuckle next. Or maybe it was supposed to be raspberry. It mixed with the lemon one still in my mouth and made a lemon-cherry-or-raspberry taste. Then I shoved in the lime one, the licorice, and the orange.

Then I lost a tooth.

I felt it give way and get lost in the Chuckles. I fished it out. It was a bottom tooth and wouldn't show too much.

I went and got some toilet paper and wrapped the tooth up to give to Shirley when she woke up. I knew she'd make a big deal out of it and we'd stick it under my pillow for the tooth fairy. If Shirley had the money I'd get a quarter, and if not, a dime.

I chewed up the rest of the Chuckles without losing any more teeth, then took out my favorite board game, Candy Land.

I pretended Susan was there playing with me. I gave her first dibs on the playing pieces and then took one for myself. I rolled the dice for her and then I rolled the dice for me and then I rolled for her again.

We talked about whether we'd rather swap spit with Dr. Kildare or Dr. Ben Casey and about moving to KooKooLand to save people's lives and surf.

Maybe I cheated a little to win, but she was a good sport about losing.

Something Fishy

I wasn't hungry that night, but Shirley had fried up a mess of mackerel and I had to sit there and force some down.

"What's wrong with your appetite?" Jimmy asked, noticing my lack of enthusiasm for the fish. He thought if kids didn't pack it away like merchant mariners they'd waste away and die.

"She's eaten quite a bit," lied Shirley, who'd snuck some of my mackerel onto her plate.

"I don't want one morsel of mackerel going to waste in this house while little Greek kids are starving to death at this very moment," Jimmy said as he sucked the head of a fish and wolfed down the eyeballs.

Virginia avoided looking at him and managed to get down her mackerel by not chewing and guzzling Pepsi.

I did my best to copy her, trying not to breathe in the fishy smell. Supposedly I had been just wild about mackerel as a baby. Shirley said she would sing me a song as I stuffed fistfuls of it down my little gullet.

Little fishy in the brook
Papa catch him on a hook
Mama cook him in a pan
And baby eat him like a man.

I had no memory of being a mackerel-loving baby. Maybe Shirley had just made that up to get me to eat my mackerel now.

I felt a bone scrape the roof of my mouth and stuck a finger in there to try to fish it out of the fish.

"What're you doing?" Jimmy barked, even though he knew what I was doing. It was frickin' obvious.

"A bone," I mumbled, the word coming out all garbled since my finger was still in my mouth.

"She's got a bone," Virginia translated.

"Get your finger out of your mouth. Just swallow the bone, for Chrissake. A little bone won't kill you."

A little bone could so kill me. Tina had told me she knew some kid who heard about another kid who found a bone in a fish stick and got it stuck in her throat and died.

As I was sitting there with the bony lump of fish in my mouth not knowing what to do, some guys rapped on the screen door.

Two raps. One rap. Two raps. It was a different code than the bookie joint.

Jimmy jumped up from the table.

I spit the fish into my hand.

The two guys came in. I could tell they weren't from around the projects. They were dressed in madras pants that looked like they'd just come off the ironing board, and penny loafers with extra-shiny pennies in them. They seemed surprised to see me and Virginia and Shirley and got all fidgety.

"We're here for the pancakes," the shorter guy mumbled.

"They're right upstairs," said Jimmy. "Come on up to my office."

The penny loafers hurried up the stairs.

I couldn't believe I had gotten stuck eating mackerel when there were pancakes on the premises.

"I want pancakes too," I whined.

Shirley got all fidgety like the guys.

"I didn't make pancakes. That's just a figure of speech."

I wasn't buying it.

"What kinda pancakes are they?"

Shirley started clearing away the dishes. She didn't answer me.

"What kind are they?" I repeated. "Blueberry?"

I heard the sound of our Super 8 projector whir to life in the bedroom upstairs.

"He's showing our home movies?" I wailed.

I could never get enough of our home movies, even though I had to sit through a lotta shots of dead deer to get to ten seconds of me falling down on the ice as I was practicing to join the Ice Capades.

"He's not showing our home movies," Shirley said. I could tell by her voice that she was ticked off at Jimmy.

"What's he showing, then?" I asked.

She didn't say anything for a long time. I was getting ready to ask her again when she answered.

"They're grown-up movies. Not nice movies. Not movies for sweet little girls."

I finally got it. They were movies about Down There.

"Like in the Combat Zone," I stated, no longer asking questions.

"Yes," said Shirley, dumping her own mackerel in the garbage, hiding it inside the egg carton from that morning's breakfast.

I suddenly remembered the mackerel that was still in my hand. A circle of fishy wetness had seeped between my fingers and onto my pedal pushers.

I jumped up and washed my hand, washed the mackerel mush right down the drain.

Shirley started doing the dishes, moving extra fast 'cause she had to leave for work soon. I decided to head back up to my room so I would be closer to the action and maybe could hear what Jimmy and the guys were saying about the pancakes.

I started to make my way toward the stairs.

"Where are you going?" Shirley asked. "Stay down here."

"I'm going to play Candy Land," I lied.

"All right. But keep your door closed," she told me. "And why don't you play some records? But not too loud. We don't want to disturb Daddy when he's working."

I headed for the stairs again.

She called after me.

"I'll make you pancakes for breakfast."

Holy Mackerel

The next day we had to go fishing for more mackerel. We were a mackerel-less household and that would not do. Not when the mackerel were running good, if you knew where to find them, and Jimmy surely did.

"Rise and shine," he said, throwing open the bedroom door at six that morning. "You lucky kiddos are going fishing."

Seeing Sylvester, our black and white cat, curled up in Virginia's arms, he had a brainstorm.

"And, hell, Sylvester's going too!"

Jimmy pulled the cat's tail. "You want to go, don't you, Sylvester, baby?" He had named the cat after his cartoon hero who was always scheming to gobble up Tweety Bird.

Sylvester shot out of bed and flew down the stairs. I could picture him scratching on the door to go out, pretending he had to pee, but really planning to slink off and hide somewhere.

"He's gonna be in pussycat heaven with all those fish," said Jimmy. "C'mon, make like Sylvester and get your lazy asses out of bed."

As an incentive, he informed us a special breakfast was waiting for us.

"I made milk toast," he announced, and went back downstairs.

So much for those pancakes I had been counting on.

Virginia pulled her pillow over her face. I felt like barfing all over Barbie. Milk toast was worse than mackerel. By themselves milk and toast were not terrible, especially if you poured a mound of sugar and cinnamon on the toast and added half a can of Hershey's syrup to the milk. But put the toast and milk in a bowl and let it soak and it would make you gag worse than Sylvester with a hair ball.

That morning I managed to choke down half the milk toast. The garbage got the other half when Jimmy went upstairs to get something from his bedroom.

Outside, Sylvester was pacing on the front stoop. Jimmy had tied a length of rope to his rhinestone collar and secured it to the metal pole of the clothes-line so Sylvester couldn't run off.

When Jimmy came back downstairs, he was carrying a couple of the other kind of pancakes. He put them in a brown bag and stuck them in his tackle box. He wrote a note for Shirley to read when she got home from making sunglasses.

Took the brats fishing. I'll wake you up early to fry the mackerel. Love, Jimmy.

He raced me to the car. I lost.

Virginia grabbed the backseat of the Pontiac and I got stuck with the front. Sylvester wedged himself under my seat and began to meow like he was going to get a distemper shot.

We were off. I prayed to God that the mackerel knew we were coming and were heading for the deep water.

Jimmy's Claw lunged over and pinched my scrawny arm. I yelped.

"I've got a big surprise," he crooned. "Guess where we're going first?"

I tried to ignore my stinging arm.

"Benson's Wild Animal Farm?" I blurted out hopefully.

"Hell no," Jimmy said. "Who wants to see Bambi in captivity looking miserable when you can see him happy and running free in the woods?"

Free until you blow his brains out or shoot his mother, I thought.

"Guess again," Jimmy said.

He looked in the rearview mirror at Virginia.

"You too, teen-rager, what do you think?"

Virginia shrugged and picked at her cuticles.

"Are we going to Dunkin' Donuts for coffee?" she mumbled. Coffee and Pepsi were her favorite food products, chased down with a cancer stick when Jimmy wasn't around.

"No, dummkopf." Jimmy laughed, lighting a cancer stick of his own. "You girls aren't too swift, you know that?"

A sly grin spread across his face and the smoke poured out of it.

"How we gonna go fishing without the canoe?" he hinted.

It was only then that I realized Jimmy's canoe was not strapped to the roof of the car. Usually it was tied up there year-round 'cause fishing season led to deer hunting season which led to duck hunting season which led back to fishing season. It didn't matter if we were going to the drive-in or to some cousin's fancy Greek wedding. The canoe was up there.

The only time it wasn't was if we were headed to the Combat Zone. Jimmy was always afraid some lowlife there would swipe it.

"We're going to the Combat Zone!" I sang out, picturing a fun day of cannoli and maybe a Charlie Chaplin movie.

"Wrong again, dum-dum. Not when the mackerel are running like a nigger from the KKK. No, we're going fishing all right, but not in the canoe. We're going in . . ."

He made a sound like a drumroll.

". . . our brand-new motorboat."

"You bought another boat?" Virginia exclaimed, looking PO'd. I suspected she was mad he'd blown a wad on a boat when he still gave her only a twenty-five-cent allowance.

"A canoe and a motorboat do not serve the same purpose," he lectured her. "With a canoe you can get into narrow places all quiet like an Injun, but with a motorboat you can go way far out into the deep ocean. We can get even more mackerel."

I wanted to hurl myself from the moving car.

I suddenly thought about the Project Snitch. If she found out we now owned a motorboat as well as a racehorse I felt certain we'd be thrown out.

But Jimmy said he knew how to take care of snitches. Then he did his trumpet imitation the rest of the way to Hank's.

The motorboat was lying in Hank's parking lot. It was about twelve feet long and pretty beat up. Jimmy had already painted on the name he had given it. I craned my neck to read the words, since the boat was upside down.

"*Aristotle Onassis*," Jimmy announced. "She's called the *Aristotle Onassis*."

Hank came out of the store.

"You goddamn Greeks are always late," he barked.

"How the hell would you know?" Jimmy shot back. "You goddamn Polacks can't tell time."

Hank scowled at him but proceeded to help Jimmy load the *Aristotle Onassis* onto the roof of our car.

"The motor's a little tricky," I heard Hank say. "You gotta pull the string just so or you could end up flooding it."

"So you sold me a Thanksgiving special, a frickin' turkey, is that what you're sayin'?"

"I don't sell any goddamn turkeys, you cheap Greek. This is a good little motor. I coulda sold it for double, but you jewed me down."

"If we get stuck out on the water, I'm gonna frickin' kill you. I'm gonna wrap that string around your frickin' Adam's apple."

"Try it and I'll wrap my meat hooks around your throat."

"The only thing those meat hooks know how to hold is a greasy kielbasa."

"Christ, I oughta have my head examined for doing business with a greaseball."

"You oughta have your kookoo coconut examined anyway, you crazy Polack."

They went on and on like that. If you didn't know better, you'd think they hated each other's guts. But apparently they didn't. In fact, Jimmy said he was closer to Hank than to his own brothers, one of whom was a wimp music teacher who didn't know a rifle from a baton and the other who had moved out to KooKooLand and was black as a nigger from baking in the sun.

Susan came out of the store. She walked right up to me.

I held my breath. I stood up straighter.

"Well, hello again," she said.

She was wearing a funny little smile.

"Your father's a real shipping magnate now."

I thought it must be a figure of speech. I thought she must mean he was drawn to the sea like a magnet.

"Yes," I agreed. "He loves the sea."

Susan motioned to Jimmy and Hank.

"They're a real pair," she said. Then she added, "You hang in there. Don't let them drive you too nuts out there on the water, OK?"

It was then I realized that Hank was coming with us. A millionaire was coming fishing with us in our crappy little boat, the *Aristotle Onassis*.

"Are you coming too?" I asked. My voice sounded all high-pitched and squeaky like somebody was strangling my Adam's apple with his meat hooks.

"Being trapped at sea with the two of them might drive *me* nuts," she whispered to me, laughing.

Jimmy finished tying the boat on the roof and Hank dropped the Johnson outboard motor into the trunk.

Jimmy took the pancakes out of his tackle box and slipped them to Hank.

"Maybe these'll put a smile on your sad-sack kisser," he said.

Hank snatched the pancakes and shoved them in his pocket.

"Announce it to the whole goddamn world, why don't you," he hissed.

"Relax," crooned Jimmy. "What're you, a yellowbelly? Afraid the fuzz are gonna come get you?"

Susan looked upset when she saw the pancakes. She turned and started to go back inside. Hank grabbed her arm and said some things. Susan got all frozen-looking. I heard him say something that began with "And tell your goddamn mother . . ."

Whatever it was he wanted her to say, Susan didn't want to do it, I could see that.

I strained to hear more.

Jimmy told me to get my damn keister in the car.

I climbed in the back next to Virginia, who had her hand under the seat and was petting Sylvester.

"What kind of nosy little buttinsky are you?" Jimmy snarled at me. "You don't stand there listening to people's family business."

I looked down, feeling my face get all hot.

I was a nosy little buttinsky and now Susan probably hated my guts.

Hank got into the front seat.

I glanced out the window, hoping to wave good-bye to Susan, but she had already gone inside.

"She's stubborn, just like her goddamn mother," Hank said to Jimmy. "Doris screwed her up, that's for sure."

Jimmy just said, "Screw Doris. We're going fishing."

He gunned the engine and headed for the coast.

We got there in record time.

"Forty minutes and change," said Jimmy, checking his phony Bulova as we pulled into a patch of mud near the bait shack.

Sylvester had been quiet the whole way, but sensing he was about to head out to sea, he began to meow.

Hank nearly choked on his beer.

"Is there a goddamn cat in here?"

"Yeah, that's Sylvester," Jimmy said. "I've taken him out in the canoe before. He loves it."

"Maybe you can take a cat in a canoe," Hank shot back, "but you can't take him in a motorboat. The sound of the motor's gonna spook him. He could jump ship."

"So? He knows how to swim," Jimmy said proudly. "I taught him when he was a kitten."

"You taught the cat to swim?"

"Yeah, I threw him in the kids' wading pool. Sink or swim. They learn real fast."

Hank drained his beer and tossed the bottle on the floor. It rolled under the seat toward Sylvester and he meowed louder.

"He yowls 'cause he's not cut like a sissy cat," explained Jimmy.

"For Chrissake, why can't you get yourself a goddamn dog like every other guy?" demanded Hank. "A cat's no good for hunting. It can't pick up a scent or retrieve a duck."

"I don't need Lassie to help me find a goddamn duck when it drops. I can find it myself unlike the ding-dong judges and crooked cops hanging around your joint who call themselves hunters but can't find their own ding-dong to take a piss."

Hank split a gut.

"Anyway," Jimmy added, "cats are smarter than dogs. Dogs would wag their asses and follow you into the devil's rumpus room. Cats are sharp enough to be suspicious of people."

Cats were also easier to hide, since the projects didn't allow pets. But Jimmy didn't say that. He just asked Hank a simple question.

"C'mon, if it came down to it, who would you rather be? Top Cat, who's a wheeler-dealer, or goddamn Huckleberry Hound, who goes around sniffing petunias?"

"I don't wanna be either one," snapped Hank. "They're goddamn cartoon characters."

"Cats have spunk. Dogs are droolers. That's all I'm saying."

Hank was fed up. His bulbous nose was becoming all pink and veiny.

"I'm not going in any goddamn boat with a yowling tomcat, you crazy greaseball."

Jimmy suddenly started laughing his head off.

"Cool your keister. I was never really gonna take him. I just wanted to get a rise out of you. I wanted to get that Huckleberry Hounddog look off your kisser."

Hank's expression darkened.

"I'm never going hunting or fishing with you again," he barked.

"You say that every goddamn time," said Jimmy.

"Well, this time I goddamn mean it."

"Well, then it's my goddamn lucky day."

"Just get the goddamn bait."

And that's how it went. We finally got the goddamn boat in the goddamn water and Hank showed Jimmy how to pull the goddamn string so as not to flood the goddamn motor and we went out for some goddamn mackerel.

Sylvester watched us shove off. Virginia had made him a bed out of Jimmy's smelly old shirt.

"Poor Sylvester," she whispered to me.

I thought it was his goddamn lucky day. This was one time I would've rather parked my keister in the car. I didn't want to be trapped in that floating rust bucket with a goddamn greaseball and a goddamn Polack and no place to pee.

But all that changed once we got out onto the open sea. The cool salt air smacked me in the kisser and it felt good. The brine shot up my nose and into my brain and flushed out all the worried thoughts that were stuck in there like crusty boogers. Blue was all around me and I felt happy. Dolphins jumped out of the water to greet us. I saw bobbing seagulls, and laughed when Hank shouted in my ear that they were Polish eagles. Jimmy said they were dumb and dirty like Polacks and tried to run them over. He was going too fast, but I didn't care 'cause there were no poky old ladies or pissed-off truckies to crash into.

Virginia grabbed my elbow if I leaned out too far and tried not to get her Keds soaked from the water sloshing around in the bottom of the boat.

Jimmy dropped anchor in just the right spot in that whole big ocean. We caught fish after fish—except Virginia, who never wanted to kill a fly and said she'd rather watch. I forgot they were mackerel, and just had so much goddamn fun. I reeled them in as fast as Jimmy and Hank could bait my hook. Heard them flopping around in the wet burlap bag at my feet and pulled up another one.

I didn't even mind when Jimmy and Hank cracked open the whiskey and warm beer and started telling their old stories about being in the merchant marine. Stories about sailing under the same captain, E. J. Christianson, who was a good skipper and never talked down to his men. I learned about what Jimmy called "the Religion of the Sea," and pretended that I, too, could one day join the merchant marine, join the brotherhood of men, even though I was just a goddamn girl.

We fished until the burlap bag couldn't hold any more.

Then we filled the bottom of the boat.

And even Hank didn't look so sad anymore.

I was sorry when Jimmy pulled anchor and we headed back to shore.

Sylvester was glad to see us. He got a mackerel head for staying in the car all afternoon without spraying.

Virginia and I snuck off and peed behind the bait shack, keeping a lookout for one another.

When we came back, Jimmy and Hank were having a contest to see who could gut the most fish fastest. Jimmy won, but Hank said Jimmy cheated 'cause he took the best knife.

On the way home, Hank bought each of us a mug of A&W root beer, even though Jimmy said that Virginia and I could share. Hank told him to quit being a cheap Greek where his kids were concerned and I thought that sounded like good advice. I imagined Hank was my father and Susan was my sister and we never had to share a root beer unless we wanted to, with two straws, for fun.

Finally, we dropped Hank back off at his store. I was hoping to see Susan again and brag about how many fish I caught, but she was long gone.

When we got back to the projects, we went door-to-door passing out the mackerel. All the mothers were tickled pink to get them. They had something besides Rice-A-Roni to put on their tables that night, something to feed their nine or eleven or thirteen kids.

If one of the mothers was the Project Snitch, I thought maybe we had even won her over and she wouldn't squeal on us anymore.

The Grass Is Not Greener

Hank asked Jimmy to check on his goddamn lawn. The thing was, it wasn't really his lawn anymore. Doris had gotten the house in the divorce and was planning to sell it and move to KooKooLand. But Hank was still all worked up about that lawn. Jimmy had put it in for him a couple of years before and now Manchester was stuck in the worst drought in fifty years and the lawn had some brown spots. Hank had seen them when he drove by.

"Let the goddamn lawn rot," Jimmy had told him. "And Doris along with it."

But Hank wanted the lawn green as a rube so the house would look better and sell for more dough.

"More dough for her to spend at that Jew clip joint Neiman Marcus," said Jimmy.

Hank told him to quit being a goddamn pain in the ass and go over there and check on those spots.

So that was how, a few days after the fishing expedition, Jimmy and I ended up at Hank's old house.

Jimmy walked around the lawn throwing down new seed and watering those brown spots with a hose.

I saw Susan watching him through the window. I stuck my head out of the car so she'd see I was there and maybe come on out.

It worked like a charm. She walked right up to the car and asked if I wanted to come in where it was nice and cool.

"You poor kid. What does he do, drag you all over the city?" she asked.

"Just about," I said. "Everywhere except the bookie joint."

Susan just shook her head and opened the door for me.

She told Jimmy she was taking me inside and he told me not to break anything or he'd golf me one.

I followed Susan inside, staring up at the back of her head and wishing I was as tall as her.

The house was dark. Most of the shades were down. Susan poured me a glass of Pepsi. The glass was made of real glass, not plastic like our free tumblers. I gripped it tight with both hands so I wouldn't drop it and break it and get golfed.

My eyes darted around, looking for bullet holes. I'd once heard Jimmy tell Shirley that Hank had shot his gun at Doris in the house. Jimmy insisted Hank had only done it to scare Doris, to get her to straighten up and fly right. He didn't want her to keep driving her Cadillac out to KooKooLand, spending money at every Jew joint along the way every time they had a little fight. After all, little fights were something husbands and wives had all the time, especially when one thought the other was cheating or when somebody was spending too much dough or when the husband's hamburger was burnt black as a nigger and not all nice and bloody.

I didn't see any bullet holes around. I figured maybe they had hung a picture over them or covered them with a fuzzy throw rug.

I took a sip of soda and found myself once again staring at Susan's gold cross.

"I like your necklace," I blurted out.

People ate up compliments. I had learned that from Jimmy. When he wanted something from you, you were a beautiful doll or a stand-up guy. I wanted to be Susan's friend and I was willing to use any means—including Jimmy's—to achieve my goal.

"Do you go to church?" Susan asked me.

"Oh yes," I lied.

It wasn't a total lie. It was a white lie as opposed to a full-out whopper. The truth was when we were in Nova Scotia the previous summer Shirley had dumped me at Sunday school, which was like church only you got to color pictures of the Three Wise Men.

"Then you know Christ died for our sins?" Susan continued.

Right away I was getting into deep water. My knowledge of churchy stuff beyond the Three Wise Men visiting baby Jesus and bringing him toys was strictly limited.

But suddenly a word my friend Tina had mentioned floated into my head.

"You mean our venal sins?" I asked, certain this would impress Susan.

She laughed.

"Venial sins," she corrected me. She spelled it—V-E-N-I-A-L—like it was a spelling bee. "He died for all of our sins, mortal and venial."

"Yes," I said, trying to figure out a way to change the subject but not coming up with anything.

"My friend Tina is a Catholic," I announced. "There are lots of Catholics in the projects."

Susan's face got all sad-looking.

"There are a lot of people in need in this world," she said. "That's why I want to be a doctor. To help those children." Then she started talking about other bad things in the world, like people fighting each other with A-bombs and prejudice against black people, which confused me 'cause I thought they were colored.

"Life's a raw deal, I guess," I said. "'Cause people are starving and we all die—even our parents."

"Death isn't a bad thing," she said. "There's something better after we die if we don't sin. There's heaven."

Heaven. I pictured it like a planet in another galaxy but without the blood-sucking aliens. I sure hoped it existed, but Jimmy said there were no guarantees. It wasn't a sure thing like a six-to-five shot.

I heard Jimmy's voice boom out from the other side of the screen door.

"That goddamn lawn looks like hell," he said.

It sounded like he wanted to blame somebody but didn't know who.

"It's my fault," offered Susan. "I'll take better care of it from now on."

"A lawn's a living thing," lectured Jimmy. "If you don't take care of it, you're killing a living thing."

"You're right. I'm sorry," said Susan. After a moment she added, "I remember when you put that lawn in."

"C'mon, Dracula, let's go," he called out. "Hop to it."

I jumped up. I hopped to it.

I was almost to the door when Doris appeared from a back room.

I stopped in my tracks.

She looked so different.

Different from the ladies I saw around the projects and different from my teachers and different from my mother even though I once heard Jimmy tell Shirley they looked like sisters when he was trying to butter her up.

Maybe it was because Doris had been hanging out in KooKooLand that she seemed so different. Hank said she looked like a movie star and I had to agree with him. Her shiny dark hair was done up like she'd just come from the beauty parlor and her nails were painted the color of the reddest red in the Crayola 64 box.

I suddenly felt bad for my mother. She had never even been to a beauty parlor. She just gave herself a Toni home permanent every couple of months, and her nails were usually split from doing piecework and dotted with bits of Scotch tape to keep them from splitting even more. Besides, Jimmy wouldn't let her paint them anyway.

"Hello, Jimmy," said Doris, blowing the smoke from her cigarette out between her red lips that matched her red nails.

"Yeah, hi," said Jimmy, barely looking at her. "C'mon, Dracula, get a move on," he snapped at me again.

I realized I was still holding my Pepsi and gulped down the rest of it because there were starving, Pepsi-less kids in this world and I didn't want Susan to think I didn't care about them.

I handed the empty glass to Susan, but she barely noticed.

"You feeling better, Ma?" she asked Doris, a worried look on her face.

"Yeah, sure," said Doris, not sounding like she meant it.

Doris walked closer to the screen door. "So how's Shirley?" she asked Jimmy.

"She's OK," grunted Jimmy. He was not making the least attempt to shoot the baloney with her.

"You letting her get behind the wheel yet?"

Jimmy didn't like the question one bit, and Doris looked like she knew he wouldn't like it.

I hurried over to Jimmy so we could leave before he got all riled up and maybe smacked my best friend's mother in the kisser.

"I don't need my wife driving so she can take off on me," Jimmy snapped. "Take off to KooKooLand."

"KooKooLand?" Doris laughed. "If you ask me, this whole city is KooKooLand."

"Good. Then you can just drive your ass right outta here," he said. "And as for Shirley, she don't want to drive anyway. She's a good woman. She knows who's boss in our family."

Doris moved a little into the light and I noticed that there were dark circles under her eyes like Shirley had from never getting enough sleep.

"Well, thanks for checking on the lawn, boss," she said before she turned her back on Jimmy and disappeared.

Bad Cop, Good Cop

On the way home, Jimmy wouldn't shut up about Doris. She had done the worst thing anyone could do. She had called the fuzz on poor Hank more times than he could count instead of toeing the line like Shirley. She had made Hank's life a living hell and now Jimmy just wished she'd hurry up and sell that house with the bad lawn and take the dough and get out of Dodge and never show her face again.

And about that kisser of hers? Did I see how much face paint she was wearing?

I admitted she was wearing lipstick and maybe some rouge.

She looked like a damn Injun, he said. Or like she belonged in the Combat Zone.

I suddenly felt bad for Susan. She had a mother who wore too much face paint and a father who had shot up their house. Maybe being a millionaire's daughter wasn't all it was cracked up to be.

I wondered where Susan would live when Doris sold the house with the bullet holes and the bad lawn and moved away. Susan very well might move out to KooKooLand too and I would never see her again.

I looked out the window and tried not to think of anything 'cause everything I could think of made me feel like blubbering.

I was making a friend and losing her at the same time. It just wasn't fair. It was a goddamn raw deal.

The more Jimmy said mean things about Doris, the faster he drove, until we heard a cop car's siren wailing behind us.

"Oh, Jesus. A fuzzmobile," Jimmy said.

There were some pancakes on the dashboard. Jimmy grabbed them and stuffed them under the seat next to his butcher knife.

He swerved over to the curb and watched in the rearview mirror as the cop made his way toward us.

"We're living in a police state," he muttered. "Big Brother, here we come."

The cop asked for Jimmy's license and registration and Jimmy handed them over with a *go ahead and arrest me, lard-ass* expression.

The cop saw Jimmy's name on the license and broke into a grin.

"Well, well, Jimmy Norris. The one and only. You've got quite a reputation."

"Yeah? Says who?" Jimmy shot back.

"All the guys at Hank's. I hear you're the best duck hunter in New England."

Jimmy leaned back and took a slow drag off his cigarette.

"I do OK," he said, acting like he didn't want to toot his own horn, but you knew he thought so too.

"I hear you do better than that," insisted the cop.

I could tell he didn't want to give Jimmy a ticket anymore. He wanted a few duck-hunting tips.

"So, you think it's going to be a good season?" the cop asked.

"There's always a lotta ducks if you know where to look. It's the damn quotas that are a pain in my ass." Jimmy smiled, almost like he was letting the guy in on a little secret. The little secret being that Jimmy broke the law by shooting too many ducks almost every time he went into the marshes, but the dummkopf wardens could never seem to catch him doing it.

"So, where you headed?" the cop asked, making a stab at doing his job.

"I'm just coming back from Hank's house," Jimmy said, knowing that would make the right impression.

He cocked his head in my direction.

"I was just trying to get home in time to watch *The Three Stooges* with my kid here. She's crazy about the Stooges. Aren't you, kiddo?"

I thought the Stooges were pretty lame, but I played my part and nodded like I was the biggest Stooges fan in Manchester, possibly all of New England.

"My kids love the Stooges too," the cop said.

I wondered if his kids lied about being Stooges fans too.

"Well, you better get going then," he finally said. "I don't want to disappoint a little girl."

Jimmy fired up the engine.

"But take it easy, OK?" the cop told Jimmy. "You don't want to get in an accident and miss opening day."

Jimmy agreed he sure didn't want to miss it, and off we went.

When we were back on our way, Jimmy said the guy was OK, that once in a while you found a flatfoot that was OK, not too often but once in a great while.

"But I bet he can't hit the side of a barn," he laughed. "Put us both out in the woods and he'd have nothing on me. He couldn't touch me."

Don't Touch the Merchandise

We didn't make it home in time for the Stooges because we had to drop those pancakes off to some guy who lived in the North End, some mucky-muck Jimmy knew from Hank's who called himself a hunter. The mucky-muck's lawn was big and bright green, as if the worst drought in fifty years had bypassed his house completely. Jimmy said the mucky-muck had a bunch of deer and elk heads on the walls in his mansion, but that he'd bought them for a couple of C-notes from a guy like Papou's ex-fighter Norman. I asked Jimmy why he didn't shoot a few deer for some of these big shots himself and make some easy dough. I was still angling for those bunk beds. But Jimmy said he didn't believe in that kind of killing. Just like he didn't believe in jacking deer, which was when you turned a big light on in the woods and the deer froze and you could blow them away like nothing. There was a Law of the Woods, Jimmy said, just like there was a Religion of the Sea. And knocking down a beautiful buck just so some freeloader could stick the buck's head on his wall was not in the rule book.

After the mucky-muck's we went to the lowlife section around Lake Avenue and met up with Sad-Sack Barney, who was standing on a street corner waiting for us. Barney was a Greek guy a little taller than me who was one of Jimmy's business partners. I was surprised Jimmy had a Greek business partner since he said Greeks would steal the eyes right out of your head and sell them as diamonds. But Barney was different. Barney was like family.

"Hi, Uncle Barney," I said, as I scrunched over next to Jimmy to let Barney into the front seat, and also because he smelled.

"Hello, sweetheart," he said. "How's my little girl?"

He gave me a wink. He was cockeyed and you never knew which eye to look in.

"Never mind the hearts and flowers. What've you got for me?" snapped Jimmy, who said Barney would talk your ear off and then keep blabbing into the hole in your head.

Barney reached into one of his shopping bags. He always had three or four bags with him at any one time and you never knew what would be coming out of them. Cartons of cancer sticks in brands nobody smoked. Gillette razor blades. Last year's model of genuine ladies' Timex watches. Sometimes the items were large, like chain saws or watermelons, and you had to follow him to a shed where he had stashed them.

Uncle Barney pulled a windup monkey out of his shopping bag.

"Look at how cute this damn thing is," he said, as he wound it up and set it on the dashboard. The monkey clapped its cymbals once and tumbled into my lap. Its motor continued to make a grinding sound.

"What am I gonna do with a bunch of goddamn windup monkeys?" snarled Jimmy.

"There are a lot of kids in the projects," Barney said. "Many of them have allowances."

"You know you get goofier by the day," Jimmy told him. "What else you got?"

I started to hand the monkey back to Barney.

"Keep it, sweetheart. Consider it a birthday present from your uncle Barney."

My birthday was in February, but I thanked him anyway.

"C'mon, hurry it up, Barney. I haven't got all day. Some of us have to work for a living."

"OK, you're gonna flip over this," Barney assured Jimmy. He pulled a Roman candle out of the bag. "Some guy in Revere got them off a boat from China."

Jimmy had gotten fireworks from Barney before, but that shipment had all been duds and he'd had to give some people their money back even though he never sold anything with a money-back guarantee.

"I'll put you on a slow boat to China if these are like the last ones," warned Jimmy.

"These are real Fourth of July quality," Barney assured him.

So Jimmy gave Sad-Sack Barney some of the big-shot's money and took a shopping bag of Roman candles home to the projects.

The fireworks were hot sellers with the greaser punks in the neighborhood. I watched them come and go all afternoon as I jumped rope in front of the house, singing:

Mickey Mouse
Had a house
Couldn't pay his rent
So he got kicked out.

By early evening most of the punks had left. Jimmy warned them to be careful and not blow their stupid hands off or he'd get fingered. The punks laughed and said they knew what the hell they were doing.

After the last punk left, Jimmy told Virginia and me to go get our friends and bring them around the back of the building. He said he'd saved the best fireworks for us. So we rounded up everybody—Tina and her brother and his wiseass friends; and the Greek girls, Aphrodite and Stephanie; and the Loomis family, who never got to go anywhere; and the Riggs kids, whose old man was in the Valley Street jail sleeping off a bender. Word spread and other kids showed up, and some of their parents, carrying a six-pack under one arm and a baby under the other. Jimmy said the babies could stay as long as they didn't squeal, but one peep outta them and they'd be booted out like a football. Somebody had a transistor radio tuned into the Red Sox game and Jimmy said he'd be booted out too if he didn't turn those bums off.

Shirley was upstairs getting ready for her double date with Hank and the other Shirley, but Jimmy told her to get her keister outside. Her hair was still half up in pin curls, so she tied a kerchief around her head.

Jimmy had all the fireworks set up and ready to go. Whenever some nosy kids got too close, he'd tell 'em, "Don't touch the merchandise." He lit the fuses with the glowing end of his Lucky Strike and, one after the other, they shot up into the starry night.

They were the loudest and brightest fireworks any of us had ever seen.

And only a couple were duds.

After the last one, Jimmy said, "That's it. The show's over. Beat it." He went in the house to get ready for the double date and Shirley went back to undoing her pin curls.

But none of the neighbors wanted to go home. They stood around behind the building under the cloud of white smoke that had settled there, breathing in the burnt odor that lingered.

Tina began to worry that just watching illegal fireworks might be a sin, even if you hadn't bought them yourself or even touched them. She told me she was probably going to have to confess the whole thing to Father McSomebody.

I said if she squealed on my father and the cops stuck him in the Valley Street jail with Mr. Riggs I would never speak to her again if I lived to be a million billion trillion years old.

Telling a priest was like telling God, she assured me. Even if the Boston Strangler came and confessed, the priest would have to keep his trap shut. The pope made the rules and Rule Number One was no squealing.

"The pope oughta make an exception for the Boston Strangler," I said.

"The pope knows what he's doing," Tina insisted, starting to get hot under the collar. "If you're going to bad-mouth the pope, I won't be your friend anymore."

"I didn't say anything against the pope," I argued, knowing Susan wouldn't like that. "The pope's OK in my book. Anyway, I don't think the Boston Strangler is the churchy type, so he probably won't be confessing any sins."

"The Boston Strangler couldn't be a Catholic," stated Tina. "President Kennedy is a Catholic."

Tina was always bringing up the fact that President Kennedy was a Catholic whether it made sense to or not.

I figured now was as good a time as any to drop my big surprise on her.

"I'm thinking of becoming a Catholic."

Tina looked confused.

"I thought you were a heathen. That's what my mother said."

"I am not," I said, not knowing what a heathen was. But it didn't sound good.

"If you're a Catholic, you have to go to church."

"I know that. I'm not some ding-dong," I replied. "I have another friend who's Catholic who I might go to church with."

Tina looked jealous, which was just the reaction I was going for.

"I was your friend first. You oughta go with me."

I acted like I was thinking it over. Who was my favorite Catholic? Her or Susan? Finally, I slipped my arm through hers.

"OK," I said. "It's a deal. I'll go with you."

We locked pinkie fingers.

Then we talked some more about President Kennedy. And about Mrs. Kennedy, who I said looked like a movie star, even though she was as big as a house from being in the family way.

And that got us to talking about sex. We'd picked up a few things about sex from our older sisters—a guy put his thing from Down There in your pee-pee and then peed in you. It seemed like something no girl would ever want to do. It gave us the creeps to picture the president and Mrs. Kennedy doing it.

"They're good Catholics. They only do it to have children," Tina said. "I'm sure they don't like it."

"They do it for the country," I added. "So there'll be a First Family."

Shirley opened the back door and told me to come inside. She was wearing a blue satiny dress with gold flowers on it. It was fitted but not too tight.

Around the knee but not too short. Colorful but not too loud. She was wearing a little face paint, but not too much. And her hair was done up but not too high.

Tina gawked at her and told her she looked prettier than Annette Funicello. I felt bad for Tina. Her mother didn't have a husband and was big like Tina and never went out clubbing or double dating. She only went to church as far as I could tell.

Shirley smiled and said thank you and told Tina to run along home before her mother had a conniption fit. Then she went back inside.

I promised Tina I'd ask my mother to keep an eye out for another millionaire for her mother and then maybe they could all double-date.

Tina said her mother didn't like men 'cause they only liked one thing. She spelled it out. S-E-X.

Some of them also like hunting and fishing, I said, and went inside.

Double Date

In the living room, Hank was slow dancing with Shirley.

Not the miserable, husbandless Shirley. My mother Shirley.

They were waiting for the miserable Shirley to show up so they could head off to the Pericles Club. They were already half-lit.

Jimmy had put on some music and was crooning along with it.

You belong to my heart
Now and forever . . .

I ran into the kitchen and got myself one of the free tumblers. Jimmy poured me some Canada Dry ginger ale so I could pretend I was having a highball and join in the fun.

I watched Hank give Shirley a twirl. She was stiff as a dead duck. I knew she didn't want to look like she was having too good a time or dance too close to Hank, or Jimmy might give her a hard time about it later.

I heard Hank tell Shirley her dark hair was beautiful.

That perked Shirley right up. It had taken her half an hour to twirl all those pin curls after coming home from Foster Grant and at least her effort was paying off.

"She's not bad-looking for a Nova Scotia farm girl," joked Jimmy as he cut in. He began to croon in Shirley's ear. I watched her loosen up and try to follow his fancy footwork.

Hank sat next to me. He hadn't bothered to get too dressed up, but he acted like he didn't have to bother.

I sat very still beside him and tried not to stare at the line of dried blood under his chin where he had cut himself shaving or at his much-broken nose or at his hands like meat hooks.

He downed one beer and Shirley quickly replaced it with another. He took out a cigar and Jimmy lit it with one of his phony-baloney gold lighters that he had to click a half-dozen times before it would light.

Hank's cigar smoke found its way right into my kisser. I wanted to get the hell out of there, but I didn't want to blow my chance for getting more dough out of Hank. I figured if he was really looped I might get a deuce. Or if he was really, really looped he might mistake a fin for a buck and I'd have my candy covered for the foreseeable future.

While I was racking my brain for a compliment to butter him up, he spoke to me.

"Who do you think looks sharper, me or your old man?"

I wanted to tell him he did, but I didn't want to get on Jimmy's bad side.

"You both look sharp," I offered. "Super-duper sharp."

"Ah, I've got that two-bit Greek beat a mile," he boasted.

"Screw you, you ugly Polack," Jimmy called out. "You got the dough, but I got the looks."

"Not with that Greek hook of yours. You could use it to catch a barracuda," Hank shot back. He was talking about Jimmy's nose, which had gained him the nickname Captain Hook when he was a kid.

"Look who's talking. Your schnoz looks like you went twenty rounds with Dempsey."

"Where the hell is that Shirley, anyway?" Hank suddenly snarled. "If she's not here in five minutes, I'm takin' off."

"Cool your keister. Have another beer."

Hank drained his beer and started searching around for the bottle opener to pop open another.

I spotted the opener next to Jimmy's La-Z-Boy, snatched it up, and handed it to Hank.

Surely my efforts deserved a little reward, I thought. But Hank just took it, didn't even look at me.

I tried another angle. "We watered your lawn," I blurted out, including myself in the lawn maintenance, even though I hadn't lifted a pinkie finger to help.

The subject of his house did not put Hank in a generous mood.

He glared at me. "That's my goddamn house. My goddamn lawn."

I knew right away I had blown it. I wouldn't be adding any dough to the Good & Plenty box that night.

I took off and nobody noticed.

I went up to my bedroom. Virginia was sprawled on her bed reading *True Confessions* magazine. Her hair was slicked with Dippity-do and had been wound around a couple of empty frozen OJ cans.

"Aren't they ever gonna leave?" she wailed. "If I have to hear any more of that old-fogy music, I'm going to kill myself."

"The other Shirley isn't here yet," I informed her.

"Maybe the other Shirley is going to stand Hank up." Virginia smirked. "Who would want to go out with him anyway? He's about a million years old."

"He's loaded," I said. "Whoever marries him will lead the life of Riley."

"I'll never marry for money," declared Virginia. "Only for love. Mad, passionate love."

"I never want to get married," I announced.

I was going to be a lady doctor like Susan, a stewardess, and a writer of detective stories. I didn't see why I needed a husband to do any of those things.

"You don't want to be an old maid," Virginia insisted. "There's nothing worse."

"I wouldn't be an old maid," I argued. "I wouldn't."

"That's what an old maid is. A girl who doesn't get married and turns into a prune. Do you want to turn into an old prune?"

"No, but I don't want some guy p-p-peeing in me," I stammered.

"It's not like that," Virginia said. "It's not pee that comes out. And it's supposed to be wonderful, except for the first time, which hurts like hell."

I was convinced.

"I'll never do it."

Virginia started to tease me.

"What if Little Joe wanted to marry you?"

I had it bad for the youngest of the Cartwright brothers on *Bonanza* and Virginia never let me forget it.

As I was standing there trying to figure out what I'd do if Little Joe proposed, the music downstairs stopped with a loud scratch as the needle was dragged across the record.

I heard the voice of the miserable Shirley.

I opened the door and leaned over the banister so I could hear how she was getting along with Hank so far.

Somebody's footsteps approached the bottom of the stairs and I ducked back.

"We're going now!" my mother shouted. "You girls get to bed by eleven."

"We will!" we shouted back.

I heard the front door slam. I raced to the bedroom window and peeked around the curtain.

The miserable Shirley had dolled herself up and was making goo-goo eyes at Hank. Hank had his arm around her waist and was guiding her to his Cadillac. He opened the door and she slid onto the leather seat. He got behind the wheel and pulled out fast to keep up with Jimmy's Pontiac, which was already halfway down the block.

I wondered if Hank and the miserable Shirley would end up getting married. If they did, I figured Susan would be pretty miserable herself. Tina had told me the pope put the kibosh on Catholics getting a divorce and then marrying somebody they liked better.

"Thank God they're gone," said Virginia. "I thought *I'd* turn into an old maid before they cut out."

She yanked the OJ cans out of her hair, put on too much face paint, and made me swear on our mother's life that I'd never tell anyone she'd gone out, not even if I was tortured to death.

I swore with my fingers crossed behind my back.

She took off into the steamy darkness and I locked the door behind her. I figured the Boston Strangler wouldn't be able to get in unless he had a crowbar. Or unless he found that key Jimmy lost out by the garbage cans a few weeks back when he was half-lit.

I poured myself another shot of ginger ale, which by then was flat and piss-warm. I checked for loose change under the seat cushion where Hank had been sitting. I found a peppermint Life Saver, rubbed the fuzz off of it, and ate it.

Then I danced around the living room, pretending I was on a double date with Susan and the Bonanza brothers—Hoss and Little Joe.

We were half-lit and rockin' the Ponderosa.

Home Movies

After I got tired of dancing around by myself like a dummkopf, I settled down to watch a movie. The movie on TV that night was *Invaders from Mars*. In the movie, some space aliens landed a flying saucer in this kid's backyard and turned his parents into killer zombies. The parents looked the same, but they were mean instead of nice and they tried to turn the kid into a killer zombie too.

At the end the army blew up the aliens and the parents became nice again, but I didn't see how the kid could trust them. Once a Martian messed with your parents' brains, who knew what was going on in there.

When the movie was over, I went to the window and peered into the backyard. I didn't see any flying saucers out there, but the saucer in the movie had burrowed into the ground so you couldn't see it. If you stepped in the wrong spot you got sucked down into it. There could be a saucer out there and I wouldn't even know it.

I grabbed Jimmy's loaded gun from under the La-Z-Boy for protection and ran upstairs and turned on all the lights. I checked under my bed and then checked in Jimmy and Shirley's bedroom closet to make sure no aliens were hiding behind the ammo, rifles, and other firearms.

I saw the Super 8 projector. I saw the box of pancakes.

I forgot all about the aliens and picked up one of the pancakes. There was a rubber band keeping the film from unraveling. I slipped it off.

I unraveled the film and held it up to the light. The pictures were too small. I ran and found the magnifying glass I had gotten in a box of Cracker Jacks.

I put the magnifying glass up to the film. I saw a lady wearing an apron and high heels. She didn't have a top on. I unraveled the film some more. A man showed up. I unraveled some more. The lady bent over the kitchen table. I unraveled. The man took down his pants. I unraveled. He touched his Down There. I unraveled. He put his Down There between the lady's legs. I unraveled. Nothing else happened. The man just kept his Down There in the lady until the pictures turned into blackness. I stopped unraveling. The film was piled up on my sneakers. My own Down There felt all tingly. I put my hand inside my pedal pushers and began to rub. It felt strange. It felt good. I couldn't imagine why I had never done it before.

Then I remembered YaYa had told me never to touch my Shame. That's what the old Greek ladies called a girl's Down There.

I didn't care. I rubbed my Shame anyway. I rubbed until my hand got all tired and my eyes got all sleepy.

Then I heard the front door open. I tried to shove the film under the bed, but it kept getting caught around my feet.

I heard the sound of footsteps coming up the stairs. I wished the ground would swallow me up.

Virginia appeared at the bedroom door.

She screamed like she had just seen a zombie.

"What are you doing?" she cried. "You shouldn't be looking at those."

"I wanted to see our home movies," I lied. "I was just looking for our home movies."

"He'll kill us if he finds out," she said.

She grabbed a pencil off the dresser and stuck it through the hole in the reel and began to roll the film back up, twirling it like a pinwheel.

It seemed like she had done this before.

It took forever to roll the movie back up. I could imagine the pictures going in reverse. The man taking out his Down There. The lady standing up. The man disappearing. Until the lady was just standing there without a man again.

Virginia put the rubber band back on the film and we went to bed.

After Virginia fell asleep, I rubbed my Barbie against Virginia's stuffed dog Poochie, who she didn't play with anymore. Then I rubbed my stuffed lamb Lambykins against my mute Chatty Cathy.

I heard Jimmy and Shirley come home, and when Shirley checked on me, I pretended I was asleep.

As soon as she left, I crept out of bed, put one of the free tumblers against the crack in the door, and squashed my ear against it.

I wanted to find out how the double date had gone.

I listened for a long time while Shirley made Jimmy a fried bologna sandwich and Jimmy complained about the cheap Greek who owned the club and watered down the drinks so it served him right that Jimmy had smuggled in his own bottle of booze.

Finally, I heard Shirley say, "I hope Shirley got home OK. Hank got a little grabby with her at the car."

"Grabby, my ass," Jimmy said. "That broad was all over him like a case of poison ivy."

"She was a little forward," Shirley quickly agreed.

"A *little?*"

"You're right. She was too forward."

"I'll tell you one thing. Hank's probably making it with her right now."

"She wouldn't do that. She's Catholic."

"Those Catholic broads are always on the make. When I was in Italy and France in the merchant marine they were all over me for a pair of stockings. And in the whorehouses, they all had a cross hanging from the bedpost."

There was a big empty space in the conversation. Every time Jimmy brought up whorehouses in Europe, Shirley would clam right up.

"Oh, come on, baby. That was before I met you. You know I don't tomcat around anymore."

There was another big empty space. Then Shirley answered back in a sharp voice that only came out when she'd been drinking highballs.

"How do I know what you do? I work all night and the rest of the time I'm sleeping dead to the world and you're off doing who knows what with who knows who."

"Look, don't start. I told you once I'm not making any other broads. I don't wanna have to tell you again."

"You danced so close to Shirley it looked like you wanted to go home with her yourself."

"You're crazy. I was just trying to give the miserable broad a little thrill."

"Hank didn't like it. He looked like he was going to punch you."

"You don't know what you're talking about. Me and Hank, we kid around like that with each other. Like when we're out in the marshes together and we see who can bag the most ducks. We try and get each other's goat. You don't know anything about it. So don't try and talk about what you don't know. You're a farm girl and you don't know the score."

Shirley was quiet again. I heard her blue satin shoes start heading up the stairs and Jimmy's heavy black shoes follow.

My arm was getting tired. I moved the tumbler to the other ear.

They were now in their bedroom. Jimmy's voice had changed.

"Come on, baby. You got that Shirley beat by twenty lengths. You made every broad in the joint look like a hundred-to-one shot. You left them at the starting gate, for Chrissake."

I heard some kissing. I heard the zipper on the blue and gold dress being pulled down.

"Come on, baby," Jimmy said again. "Don't I show you a good time? Most wives gotta beg their husbands to take them out. But those pencil pushers are so tired from punching a clock all they can do is conk out in front of Lawrence Welk on a Saturday night. You get to go out clubbing and to the track. You're gonna get your picture taken in the goddamn winner's circle in a few weeks. Jesus, you had your own private fireworks show tonight, how about that? You never had any of that up on the farm. No Nova Scotia farm boy would show you the world the way I have."

I could hear another zipper being pulled down. And the bedsprings on their half-paid-for bed creaking.

I pressed my ear harder against the tumbler and listened to the S-E-X sounds. I knew it was wrong to listen but I did it anyway.

I knew they weren't doing it to make a baby. I'd once heard Jimmy tell Hank they each had two brats and that should be enough for any man. More than that could crimp a guy's style.

When the S-E-X sounds died down and the creaking stopped, I got back into bed. I lay there putting the pictures from the pancake I'd seen with the sounds I'd just heard. Making my own movie. My own dirty movie.

If there was a God and if I died in my sleep, I knew I would go straight to hell.

Susan would be playing her clarinet in heaven and I would be sucked into an underground world like in *Invaders from Mars* except instead of aliens, the devil would be there stabbing my keister with his red-hot pitchfork.

I vowed to change my evil ways.

I vowed that the next day I would save myself.

Absolution

Lucky for me, Jimmy dragged Shirley off to Maine early the next morning to see about Victory Bound. Uncle Bobby, the horse's trainer, had called from Scarborough Downs and said Victory Bound wasn't eating his oats. The horse appeared to be on a hunger strike. Uncle Bobby thought Jimmy oughta come by the barns and talk to the animal, since Jimmy knew how to look right in a horse's eyes and tell what the hell was bugging him.

While Virginia was still dead to the world, I put on the outfit YaYa had bought me for Greek Easter but which I hadn't gotten to wear. YaYa had bought the outfit in case Jimmy would let her take me to Easter Mass, but Jimmy had said no frickin' way and had taken me to see Alfred Hitchcock's *The Birds* instead.

When I stepped into the Blessed Sacrament church that morning, I was afraid God would strike me dead. Either that or the priest would look into my eyes the way Jimmy looked into Victory Bound's eyes and see I was a sinner and toss me out.

But I wasn't struck dead, and nobody rushed up to kick me out. Instead, a man in a dark suit smiled at me and handed me a program like what you got when you entered the racetrack.

I followed Tina and her mother up the aisle, holding on to the doily Tina had bobby-pinned to my hair. I didn't want the doily falling off because Tina had told me God didn't like it if you didn't have a doily or a kerchief or a big, frilly Easter bonnet on your head. I didn't know why, but I figured I'd be finding out soon.

We sat on a bench up front. It was hard as a rock. I wondered why they didn't put some throw pillows on it or something.

"Boy, this bench is hard on your keister," I said.

Tina's mother gave my hand a little swat.

"We don't say bad words like that in church. We don't say bad words at all unless we're little heathens. You don't want to be a little heathen, do you?"

"No, ma'am," I said. "I want to be a good Catholic."

"That's good. The Lord has spoken to you."

"Yes, he has," I chirped, realizing as soon as the words were out of my mouth that I had just lied. I hadn't been in church five minutes and I had already committed a sin.

"It's not called a bench, stupid," Tina corrected me. "It's a pew. And it's supposed to be hard so you don't fall asleep or anything. Everybody knows that."

I could see Tina was really enjoying lording it over on me, since I was usually the big know-it-all.

"You better just follow me," she said. "Like in Simon says, do what I do. Except when I go up to the altar to eat the body of Christ and drink his blood. You have to stay put for that."

"That's fine by me," I choked. It sounded like *Blood Feast* up there at the altar.

"It's just a cracker and some grape juice," Tina snickered. "I bet I had you going. I bet I had you quaking in your Mary Janes."

I was dying to tell her I knew all about the cracker and grape juice, but I kept my mouth shut so I wouldn't tell another lie.

The priest finally showed up wearing a dress. He started spewing a bunch of mumbo jumbo.

"Is the whole thing in Greek?" I asked Tina.

"It's Latin, stupid," she hissed. "The Greeks got their own church. You'd know that if your father wasn't a heathen."

"He's not a heathen, stupid. He's an agnostic."

Her jaw went all slack. She didn't know what the hell I was talking about. I gave her a smug look.

An agnostic, Jimmy had taught me, was a person who looked up in the sky and saw a big, fat question mark. A person who didn't know whether God was up there and wouldn't know until he saw God with his own two sober eyes. Until God showed up with beams of light shooting out of his keister and sat down and had a drink man-to-man and explained every screwed-up thing in the world. Like why some people got all the breaks and other people got the shaft. Why starving kids with giant bellies croaked while porky pipsqueaks slurped down sundaes. Why the workingman shoveled manure while the bosses were digging for caviar with a silver spoon. "If God exists, somebody oughta shoot the bastard." That's how Jimmy had summed the whole thing up.

Tina jabbed me with her elbow.

People were now sliding off the rock-hard benches and kneeling on rock-hard stools.

I flinched as the scrape I'd gotten at Hank's pressed into the stool. I watched Tina close her eyes and begin to pray. I closed my eyes too. I was dying to unburden myself, to wipe the slate clean like an Etch A Sketch with a dirty picture I had once seen Virginia shake away when I came into the room.

Praying didn't feel strange. I took right to it.

Dear God, please don't let anyone find out what I did last night and forgive Poochie and Lambykins and Barbie and Chatty Cathy. I made them do it. I made them have S-E-X. Please, God, don't make me fry in hell. Let me go to heaven, if there is such a place and I hope there is, because I want to be where Susan is. I want to do everything just like her and go where she's going. And forgive my daddy for having those movies in the first place. He's just trying to make a buck and no one will give him a break. He'd tell you that himself if he was here, but he couldn't be here because he's got a starving horse and, well . . . he's not really sure if you exist, he sees a big question mark in the sky where other people just see clouds with maybe a clown's face in them. But he talks about you all the time, he talks about you even more than Tina talks about you, and Tina can talk your ear off, I'm sure you know that. Anyway, God, if you'd just give Daddy a big score he wouldn't have to sell those movies anymore and I wouldn't look at them or even think about them.

The lady in the apron bending over the table flashed into my head and I tried to get her the hell out of there.

Stop it. Stop it. Stop it, I shouted to myself. God is going to fry your keister.

There, I did it. I said *keister* again.

God, I didn't mean it. I didn't mean to say *keister* and I didn't mean to think about the lady.

I saw the lady again.

Get lost, get lost, lady, I told the lady in the apron.

The harder I tried to get her to go away, the more she kept bending over that table. Like a movie you watched over and over because you liked it so much. Only this movie I didn't like. I didn't. *I didn't.*

But the truth wouldn't go away.

I *did* like it.

I felt Tina's elbow jab me again.

People were leaving the hard stools for the hard pews. I clambered back onto the pew, wondering if God had made Tina elbow me so I would stop thinking my bad thoughts.

I tried harder to pay attention to the priest. He was now speaking my language. He talked about Christ dying on the cross and pointed to a cross with a bloody man nailed to it.

Blood Feast popped into my brain again. I saw the bloody woman hanging by her arms, and pushed her away.

It wasn't easy getting bad stuff out of your head. I could see that now. That must be why it was so hard to be a good Catholic and only a few people like Susan ever qualified.

The priest kept going on and on about the cross. He said God the father loved his son so much he had to make him suffer. He did this so people would understand sorrow.

"What did he say about Zorro?" Tina whispered.

"Sorrow, not Zorro, numbskull," I shot back, happy that I understood something a priest said and that she didn't.

Then it was time to go eat the body of Christ and drink his blood.

I sat there watching the people go up to the altar. Only a few heathens like me didn't go.

When Tina came back she stuck her tongue out so I could see the melting cracker. Her mother told her to shut her mouth.

After that, men began passing around big silver plates. I expected the plates to have doughnuts on them. Tina had told me they passed out doughnuts after church to reward people for showing up. But these plates didn't have any refreshments on them. People were putting money on them. I started to panic. Hank's buck was stashed in my sock. Tina and I had planned to go to the Temple Market after church to buy candy.

I wondered if God really wanted me to put my dough on the plate.

I didn't want to. I wanted Chuckles.

My heart pounded as the plate got closer. I slipped my hand in my sock and grabbed Hank's buck in my fist, not knowing what I would do when the plate got to me.

Finally, the dinner plate was at our row.

The lady in the apron flashed through my head, how I had touched my Shame flashed through my head, what I had made my poor stuffed animals do flashed through my head, and I thrust my fist out, ready to pay for my sins.

But before I could drop Hank's buck on the plate, Tina's mother reached across me and put an envelope on the plate.

"Don't worry. That's for all of us, dear," she whispered to me in a kind voice. And she passed the plate down the row.

God had spared me. He had seen that I was sorry and had forgiven me and was rewarding me with Chuckles.

Hallelujah. Hallelujah. I sang it loud.

Candy Land

After church I ate a cruller and a maple-frosted and then we went off to buy candy. Tina's mother gave Tina a list of what she wanted at the store and told us not to dillydally.

We pushed open the door to the Temple Market. Horrible Heddy, the woman who worked the cash register, looked up from her movie magazine and frowned.

"Hi, Heddy," I said, trying to butter her up. "We've just been to church."

"Pick out what you want and twenty-three skidoo," snapped Horrible Heddy. "I got no time for shenanigans. I got paying customers in here."

The store was empty except for us.

Tina grabbed a shopping cart with wobbly wheels and started rolling it through the cramped aisles, scanning items on her mother's list. We filled the cart with Devil Dogs, Ring Dings, Marshmallow Fluff, Skippy peanut butter, Bosco, Mrs. Paul's fish sticks, Cheetos, Cheez Whiz, Wonder Bread, and Swanson TV dinners in both the fried chicken and Salisbury steak varieties.

Horrible Heddy kept her peepers glued to the big round mirrors mounted on the ceiling, watching us like we were a couple of convicts just outta Sing Sing.

Finally, Tina and I headed for the candy display.

The Chuckles were all gone.

I shoved my hand way in the back and came up empty. Now I didn't know what to do. I picked up a Baby Ruth and put it back and picked up a PayDay and put it back and picked up the Baby Ruth again.

Horrible Heddy came up behind us and made sure no Baby Ruths had ended up with the PayDays.

"Something don't look right," she said. Then she figured it out. "The Chuckles are missing."

"You're all out," I replied.

"That's a likely story," she barked. "Empty your pockets."

"I didn't swipe anything," I insisted. "I didn't."

"She didn't," Tina backed me up. "Me neither."

I started to feel all clammy. What if a Tootsie Roll had fallen in my pocket when I wasn't looking? What if Horrible Heddy found an old gumball in there that I had forgotten about?

"Empty your pockets, both of yous, or I'm callin' the cops," she snapped.

She bent down so her face was right next to ours. Her breath smelled like she had just smoked a carton of Kool menthols while sucking on a Vick's cherry cough drop.

Tina quickly dug into her pockets. She pulled out the crumpled shopping list, the money her mother had given her, and the necklace she called rosary beads.

"See, I don't got nuttin'," said Tina.

Horrible Heddy turned away from Tina and zeroed in on me.

"Now you," she said. "What're ya waitin' for, Christmas?"

"No. I won't," I blurted out.

Tina looked like she was about to keel over.

"I didn't swipe anything," I repeated.

"We'll see about that, Little Miss Liar," Horrible Heddy shot back. She grabbed the phone and made like she was about to dial the fuzz.

I felt my lower lip quivering and bit it to get it to stop. I didn't want to bawl. I wanted to strangle her with my meat hooks. I wanted to whack her with a Swanson Salisbury steak.

But instead I turned my pockets inside out.

There was nothing in there. Not a frickin' thing. Not even Hank's buck. I had stashed it back in my sock in case I got my pocket picked at church like had happened to Shirley once at the racetrack.

Horrible Heddy patted me down. I stood there with my linty pockets hanging out vowing to return to the Temple Market one day when I was a world-famous writer/stewardess/lady doctor. I would show Horrible Heddy I wasn't a project kid anymore. She'd be so surprised she'd have a heart attack right then and there and I'd have to save her life even though I hated her guts. Then she'd get down on her knees and thank me and beg me to take anything I wanted in the store—anything. To take the whole damn store.

And I'd tell her to take her crappy store and shove it up her keister.

She finally took her mitts off me.

"Hurry up and get what you're gonna get," she said, looking unhappy that she hadn't found anything.

I grabbed the Baby Ruth *and* the 5th Avenue and a few Tootsie Rolls and a couple of *Archie* comic books. I'd show her I had dough. I wasn't just some project kid without a pot to piss in.

"You got enough to pay for all that?" she asked, hanging over me.

She didn't think I could add two and two. But *she* was the one. Always adding things in her head and gypping you.

"I have enough," I fired back. "I have a whole dollar from my father's friend Hank Piasecny who owns Hank's Sports Center in the North End. I'm best friends with his daughter, Susan."

I could see Tina's face drop when I said somebody else was my best friend. I felt like a traitor, but I had to straighten Heddy the hell out.

"Don't lie," she said. "Don't be a little liar. You probably stole that money."

"I did not," I insisted. "Hank Piasecny the millionaire gave it to me." I choked back the sobs welling up in my throat again.

Tina backed me up. "It's true," she said. "I seen his Cadillac parked right outside her house."

"She doesn't live in a house, she lives in the projects," said Horrible Heddy.

I started lying my head off and couldn't stop.

Hank Piasecny gave me money all the time. Hank Piasecny took me to Benson's Wild Animal Farm. Hank Piasecny bought me bunk beds for my birthday. Hank Piasecny was taking me to Disneyland. Oh yeah, and Hank Piasecny and his whole family were coming up to Maine with us to have their pictures taken in the winner's circle when our racehorse won.

"Well, that's a real whopper," Heddy snorted. "People in the projects owning racehorses."

"You wait. I'll bring you my picture in the winner's circle. You'll see. You wait."

"I won't hold my breath," she said.

"My Swansons are melting. My mother's gonna kill me," Tina said. She began pushing the cart with the wobbly wheel toward the checkout counter. Horrible Heddy followed, giving her a little shove.

I wanted to put my candy back and tell Horrible Heddy I was never shopping in her Mickey Mouse establishment again. I wanted to tell her I was taking my frickin' business somewhere else. But there was no somewhere else. No other store I could walk to or even ride my bike to. The closest was out near the cemetery and Jimmy didn't let me go that far.

I suddenly remembered those dago gangsters in Revere. The ones Jimmy had said would pop off my teacher's kneecaps. I realized if I went home and told Jimmy all about Horrible Heddy, all about her making me empty my pockets and calling me a little liar, and trying to gyp me by adding in her head, he would do something. Something really bad. He would take all my hurt and make it his 'cause we were family and nobody hurt one of us without hurting all of us. That was the Greek Code, something the dagos apparently believed in too.

The dagos would probably torch the joint 'cause that's what they did to get even. Plenty of times Jimmy had pointed out blackened buildings in Revere where somebody had tried to gyp a dago and had been taught a goddamn lesson.

I pictured the Temple Market bursting into flames. I pictured Heddy's lacquered hair lit up like a Roman candle. I pictured all the Baby Ruths melting and the *Richie Rich* comic books burning.

But then, where would I buy my candy?

Revenge was sweet, I heard Jimmy say once.

But candy was sweeter. So I kept my big mouth shut.

I laid my purchases out on the counter and Horrible Heddy added them up in her head.

"One dollar, missy," she said.

I reached into my sock and took out the dollar that I had folded and folded and folded into a small square. Horrible Heddy cursed and unfolded and unfolded and unfolded the dollar.

It wouldn't lay flat in her cash register drawer.

It was my only sweet revenge.

Jimmy's Lucky Horse

Sure enough, Jimmy got Victory Bound eating his oats again. The horse had just gotten depressed, Jimmy explained when he returned from Maine.

Until a few weeks ago, Jimmy had been visiting Victory Bound almost every day. The horse had been living on a pretty farm not far from Manchester. The lady who owned the farm had been fattening up Victory Bound and exercising him so he could go out and win races and we could get our picture taken in the winner's circle. Now that Victory Bound had been moved to the track in Maine, the only people he saw were ding-dong grooms and Uncle Bobby the Trainer, who the horse had not warmed up to yet.

So Jimmy had talked to Victory Bound and told him not to worry. Told him we'd be up there in a week. Then Jimmy tied the old shirt he wore when he gutted fish onto the door of Victory Bound's stall. Apparently the horse, due to his superior sense of smell, could make out Jimmy's odor underneath the rotting fish smell. He began nuzzling that shirt right away. Then he ate all his oats, with an extra helping of molasses, while Jimmy rubbed the white markings above his eyes just the way he liked it, and whispered all gentle in his velvety ear.

He told Victory Bound he was the most beautiful creature on the face of the earth. He told him he could run like Seabiscuit and nobody could beat him. He told him he loved him more than anything in this godforsaken world.

I listened to Jimmy's story and began to feel all down in the dumps myself.

I wished I wasn't a crummy little pip-squeak.

I wished I was a big, beautiful horse.

I wished I was Victory Bound.

Goin' to a Beach Party

A week later, I packed up Lambykins, Poochie, Barbie, and Chatty Cathy. Virginia packed up the record player and her OJ-can hair rollers. We dropped Squirmy off at YaYa and Papou's house because Jimmy said we could only bring one goddamn pet, and Sylvester was going because he could gobble up any fish guts left over from Jimmy's planned fishing expeditions on the Maine coast.

I could tell YaYa wasn't too happy about hamster-sitting. She told us to stick Squirmy in the basement. I kissed his furry belly good-bye and left him in her cobwebby dungeon, promising I would feed him a hunk of feta cheese when we returned.

As we were leaving, Jimmy invited YaYa to come up to Maine and get her picture taken in the winner's circle. YaYa spit on him to ward off the evil eye and told him she couldn't get away from the beer joint. Jimmy insisted she could get somebody to cover for her for a night, but YaYa said he was a dreamer and a fool and that the horse would probably fall and break its leg.

Let's get the hell out of here, Jimmy said to Shirley.

And we were off on our vacation. Off to win a race.

We were all wearing our Foster Grant sunglasses—quality-control rejects with a few missing rhinestones or off-color speckles in the plastic or misshapen earpieces so they sat on your head funny and you were always adjusting them.

The car was crammed with horse feed, binoculars, liniment, Jimmy's lucky hat, fishing poles, tackle boxes, waders, and the boat motor. Virginia was holding Sylvester and I was balancing a box of groceries on my lap. We were lugging our own groceries because the stores in Maine charged tax on everything and Jimmy would be damned if he was gonna pay it. New Hampshire had no taxes and the state motto as much as told you so: Live Free or Die. Maine's license plate said Vacationland, but Jimmy said they oughta change it to ClipJointLand.

We drove and drove forever. After a while the box of groceries made my legs feel numb. I tried to shift the weight from one thigh to the other. Virginia took pity on me and shifted half the weight on her leg. Sylvester didn't like being crowded off her lap, but we all had to suffer a little.

Finally, we made the turn onto the main drag of Old Orchard Beach and I forgot all about my suffering. I remembered the priest at Blessed Sacrament describing how people would feel once they reached the promised land and now I knew what he was talking about. I breathed in the smell of saltwater taffy, clam grease, and coconutty Coppertone and my spirits soared. I ogled the souvenir shops as we drove past and wanted everything, absolutely everything—the giant towels that said BEACH BUM, the Styrofoam surfboards, the candy-striped umbrellas, the itsy-bitsy teenie-weenie yellow polka-dot bikinis on hangers swinging in the breeze.

Bam! Jimmy slammed on the brakes.

Hordes of people were strolling around with their beach gear, crossing the street where they felt like it, forcing the line of cars to stop and let them cross. Jimmy said the ding-dongs were in the goddamn road where he had the goddamn right-of-way. I wished he'd just wait, just look at the people and see how much fun they were having. Instead, he blew his horn, swerved around the ding-dong drivers, and plowed through the ding-dong crowd. The tourists were shocked out of their beachy trance and scattered like ants when you poured Kool-Aid on their anthill.

"Maybe I'll hit a few and do the world a big favor," Jimmy cracked. "A few less goddamn tourists."

"Aren't we tourists?" I asked hesitantly.

"No, we're not goddamn tourists. We're goddamn racetrackers. In a few days these dubs are gonna be paying money to watch us have our picture taken in the winner's circle."

As Jimmy swerved to get off the main drag, Sylvester leapt from Virginia's lap and tried to dive out the open window. Lucky for us, his leash got caught on the lever that moved the seat forward. Halfway out the window, he strained at his collar, his eyes bugging out with disbelief that his escape had been foiled.

"Don't let that putty tat get away or I'll moider you!" Jimmy shouted at Virginia, in a voice like Sylvester the cartoon cat.

Virginia wound the leash around her hands and held on for dear life.

Sylvester's meows of misery filled the car the rest of the way to our apartment.

Deflated

We unpacked our crap on the double. Jimmy supervised the operation, barking orders like we were a bunch of wet-behind-the-ears merchant mariners who needed to shape up or ship out. I arranged Poochie, Lambykins, Barbie, and Chatty Cathy on my cot in the living room. I placed them far apart so they wouldn't engage in any hanky-panky. Then I opened the crammed suitcase that Virginia and I had borrowed from YaYa. It smelled like her basement and made me think of Squirmy. It didn't seem right he was stuck in a dungeon while I was going to be sprawled in the sun working on my Coppertone tan. I prayed to God to forgive our family for abandoning Squirmy and reminded God it was not my doing.

I pulled out my new one-piece bathing suit and shimmied into it, wishing it was a polka-dot bikini. Then I unpacked the beach ball that Shirley had given me for Christmas a few years back. At the time I'd thought Santa had given me the beach ball, but Jimmy had set me straight.

There is no Santa Claus, dumdum, he'd said.

There is so a Santa. I just had my picture taken with him, I'd shot back.

That joker with the phony beard? He's an alkie geezer who gets soused at Papou's beer joint the other fifty weeks of the year. Didn't you recognize him?

I know you're kidding, I'd insisted. I know there's a Santa.

There is not, kiddo. All that ho-ho-ho is just a lot of ha-ha-ha this country crams down people's throats so they'll shell out for more toys.

What about the reindeer? I'd pleaded, holding out hope that at least they were real. What about Comet and Cupid and Donner and Blitzen? What about Rudolph?

Only ducks, geese, and Tweety Birds can fly, Jimmy had said, pretending to aim at one and blow it away. You oughta be smart enough to figure that out. You're supposed to be the egghead around here, with the straight As.

I started blubbering.

You killed Santa. You killed Santa.

Shirley rushed into the room and tried to comfort me. She asked Jimmy if it had really been necessary to tell me so soon. I was still a baby. He said I was no squalling brat even though I was acting like one, and the longer I went on believing in Santa, the worse it would be for me when I found out. He said he had done me a big goddamn favor and she should quit making a federal case out of it. She was the killjoy 'cause she was the one picking a fight. And if she wanted a fight for Christmas he'd sure as hell give her one with a silver bow.

Then he turned on me.

You're always starting something. Always turning your mother against me.

His eyes were like two mad hornets.

I stood there, stung.

Shirley plastered on a smile thick as calamine lotion. Everything's fine, she cooed. Nobody was turned against anybody. Everybody loves everybody in this house.

Then she offered to cook Jimmy a steak, nice and bloody.

To make up for the fact that there was no Santa, Shirley got me more presents than Santa ever had—including the beach ball I had just unpacked.

I filled my cheeks with air and began to blow up the ball. I couldn't believe what a dummkopf I was to be thinking about Christmas in the middle of summer when there was a great big beach only a hop, skip, and a jump away.

I got the ball nice and full and bouncy, and capped it off. Right away, I could hear the hissing of air. I couldn't imagine how the ball had sprung a leak. I was always so careful with my toys. I never lost a LEGO or mangled Monopoly money. I wouldn't even play marbles with my marbles 'cause I didn't want them getting dirty.

It's not like I could blame the damage on anyone else. Ever since Tina had pulled the string too hard on Chatty Cathy, I had a firm policy: Nobody plays with my goddamn toys. You never knew how something would come back— with a chocolate smudge on your favorite Barbie outfit or a spring that wasn't quite as springy or a page torn out of a good book, ruining a whole damn story. I'd been given secondhand toys when I was younger, but now that Shirley was doing piecework and buying me new toys, I sure as hell didn't want them looking like hand-me-downs.

I let the air back out of the beach ball and vowed to get Shirley to buy me a new one at one of those souvenir shops. Maybe I'd get one for Susan, too. I was already trying to decide what to bring her.

I skipped out into the kitchen in my new bathing suit. Shirley was putting away groceries and Jimmy was studying the *Racing Form*. Virginia was trying to coax Sylvester out of a cupboard.

Jimmy looked up and smirked. "Where do you think you're going, Esther Williams?"

"To the beach," I answered.

Wasn't it frickin' obvious? Wasn't it why the hell we were here?

"We're not going to the beach, dummkopf. I got work to do. We're heading to the track."

My happiness deflated.

Jimmy said he needed to check on Victory Bound's appetite and get some tips on that night's racecard from Uncle Bobby.

Virginia and I begged him to let us go to the beach instead. We reminded him that the sun was out and we hadn't gotten our daily dose.

"You'll get plenty of sun playing around the barns," he insisted. "And we can take a dip when we get back."

Shirley tried to make us feel better. "We'll be here for two whole weeks," she reminded us. "Two whole weeks of fun in the sun."

I put my shorts back on. Jimmy put on his lucky hat.

And we piled back in the car and left the beach behind.

Shit

Victory Bound was happy to see us.

He kept nudging me with his nose and pulling at my pockets for sugar cubes.

The horse was raring to go, Uncle Bobby told Jimmy. He was eating Bobby out of house and home and was kicking his stall like a wild stallion. He had even chewed Jimmy's fish-gutting shirt to shreds.

Jimmy thought the horse had bulked up real good, like a boxer before a big fight, and his coat had a nice goddamn shine to it. Jimmy looked into Victory Bound's eyes and said, "This baby's a winner. I'd stake my goddamn family on it."

I spit on Victory Bound to ward off the evil eye the way YaYa had taught me to do.

"OK, let's talk turkey. Let's retire to the drawing room," Jimmy cracked to Uncle Bobby, making a sweeping motion toward the shitty tack room where Uncle Bobby slept, right next to Victory Bound's stall.

They went in and plopped down on a creaky cot and began discussing the evening's wagering. Jimmy wanted to know which horse was lame, which jockey had been eating too many T-bones, which trainer was juicing his horse, and which trainer was pulling his horse 'cause some two-bit dago gangster from Providence told him he better or else.

I fed Victory Bound my last sugar cube. Well, it wasn't really my last—that one I was keeping for myself—but it was my next to last.

With no more sugar left, Victory Bound got sick of me and I got sick of him. He started to kick his stall and I began to kick at the dirt.

I wished my mother would save me. I wished she'd take me to the track kitchen for some gummy lemon pie or rubbery chocolate pudding. But Shirley had her hands full. She'd been cornered by Uncle Bobby's girlfriend, Aunt Hazel, a plump woman with hair like tangerine cotton candy. Hazel wasn't married to Bobby, so I didn't see where she got off calling herself my aunt, but since Bobby wasn't really my uncle, I let it pass.

"Take a load off," Aunt Hazel said, offering Shirley a filthy lawn chair with a few dangling straps.

"Oh, I've been sitting all day," Shirley stammered. "You go ahead."

Aunt Hazel sank down on the chair and I held my breath to see if it would hold. Her ass nearly touched the ground, but the straps didn't snap. Right away, Hazel began telling Shirley her troubles in her high, squawky voice that sounded like a crow that had just found some roadkill. Her troubles were always the same. She was madly in love with Bobby, but he was a cheating lowlife who wouldn't make her an honest woman.

Jimmy just said Hazel was a fat pig with a big mouth. He thought a catch like Bobby could do better and told him so every chance he got.

I got away from Aunt Hazel's squawking and went looking for Virginia. I found her behind the barn. She had made friends with a litter of wild kittens and was petting them as they fought to lick her with their rough little tongues.

"Look at these poor little things," Virginia moaned. "I wish I could smuggle one home. It could live in our bedroom."

I bent down to inspect the kittens and the runtiest one dug its claws into my earlobe.

"Goddamn sonofabitch!" I cried out, already failing in my efforts to be a good Catholic.

"Quit swearing," Virginia hissed. "Daddy will moider you."

The truth was, Jimmy was the one who had taught me to swear in the first place. One Christmas Eve when he was half-lit he had coached me to sing Christmas carols with swearwords.

Deck the halls with boughs of bullshit.
Fa la la la la . . . na fas skata.

Na fas skata, he had said, laughing, was Greek for "eat shit."

He insisted we were gonna sing the song together for YaYa on Christmas. But, when I started to belt it out the next day, it was a whole different tune.

"Girls don't curse," he snapped, "unless they're no-good whores. Any daughter of mine talks like a no-good whore, I'll cut out her tongue. I'll murder her."

He didn't say *moider.* He wasn't kidding around.

While he was chewing me out, one thing kept going through my head.

Na fas skata! Na fas skata! Na fas skata!

And that's what I felt like saying now—to Jimmy, to Victory Bound, to Aunt Hazel, to that mean little kitten.

But I knew better and kept my trap shut.

I dabbed at my ear to see how bad it was bleeding. There was only a smear of blood, so at least I wasn't bleeding to death. I did, however, begin to consider the possibility of cat scratch fever.

"You shouldn't have put your face so close, dummkopf," Virginia said.

"You'll smuggle one of them home over my dead body," I replied, and got the hell away from those goddamn kittens.

I stomped down to the other end of the barn, navigating an obstacle course of horseshit. This racetrack, I decided, was even crummier than the other ones Jimmy hung around. Everything was encased in mud and dried shit. The entire time I'd been here, I'd been flapping my arms to keep away the horseflies. They were big as Jimmy's thumb and gave a nasty bite.

Finally, I spotted a flyswatter hanging on a nail and decided to play a game. A killing game. How many of those sonofabitches could I murder, not moider? How many could I smack the living life out of?

And, oh boy, that's when I started to have fun. I zigzagged around the place killing horseflies like it was an Olympic event and I was going for the gold. I kept score as the body count mounted. Twenty . . . thirty . . . thirty-five. I was going for a new world record. I even whacked one on my leg before it could get me. It hurt, but I didn't give a shit.

"Die, die, you sonofabitch," I said to the horsefly.

Finally, I heard Jimmy call out to me.

"Hey, pip-squeak, let's go for a dunk. That is, unless you want to bunk down here for the night with Victory Bound."

I threw down the flyswatter and ran to Jimmy, leaping over the piles of horseshit.

I was so glad to be getting out of there I jumped up and kissed him.

Down by the Sea

I rode Jimmy all the way to shore.

The water was so cold I couldn't feel my hands wrapped around his sun-tanned neck or my feet hooked around his muscled thighs. We rode through seaweed that got all tangled around our legs. It felt like a killer octopus, but I didn't care. Well, I almost didn't.

"I'm a man-of-war and you're my first mate!" Jimmy shouted as his wiry body sliced through the choppy sea with me on board.

We shot past other kids on their flimsy Styrofoam boards and swerved around their fathers with their potbellies and flabby, lobster-red arms.

I sailed on Jimmy until goose bumps covered my entire body and my teeth were chattering like Squirmy's.

"Race you to the blanket!" Jimmy finally called out, dumping me off his back. He charged out of the water and I staggered after him.

He drew a line in the sand with his big toe and I stood behind it.

"Ready, set, fire!"

I tore away from the starting line.

He gave me my usual head start. I dug my frozen feet into the sand and pumped my frozen arms. I heard Jimmy's breath gaining on me and pushed harder. My lungs felt like two ice-water balloons about to burst.

Our horse blanket was just a few strides away. I was beating him this time, I was. I glanced back with a triumphant smile and he went flying by me.

"Sayonara, dum-dum."

He threw himself down on the blanket and I threw myself down a few miserable seconds later. I lay there gasping and spitting out seawater and snot.

Shirley wrapped a towel around me.

"Can't you let her win once?" I heard her whisper to Jimmy.

He snorted with laughter.

"You don't know diddly-squat about raising brats, do you? I'm building her competitive spirit. You need that in this world so nobody pulls anything over on you. If I didn't have it, all the other hunters would be outgunning me. If Jack

Dempsey didn't have it, he wouldn't be world champ. If Victory Bound didn't have it, he wouldn't be tearing up his stall and headed for the winner's circle. You catch my drift?"

"Yes," said Shirley. "I catch your drift."

"I'll race you again right now," I blurted out.

Lucky for me, Jimmy didn't take me up on it or I really might've burst a lung.

"Nah, kiddo, I gotta do some handicapping."

He bopped me on the head.

"But you almost had me that time."

I began to shiver and Shirley rubbed me with the towel.

After a while she warned Jimmy it was getting late.

"We got plenty of time," he insisted. "Plenty of goddamn time. This is the best time of day. Look how beautiful it is with the sun going down and the sky like a painting by Winslow Homer and all the ding-dong tourists gone off to stuff their faces with fried clams. We got our own private beach here like millionaires."

He gestured from one end of the empty beach to the other. Then he turned his attention back to the *Racing Form*. Shirley, Virginia, and I wrapped our damp towels tighter around ourselves and turned our backs to the stinging wind.

Virginia buried her nose in *1984*—a book that Jimmy had insisted she read to get a better understanding of the police state that would soon be facing us.

I drew a picture of Susan in the sand. She had shells for eyes and seaweed hair and a big, half-moon smile like the moon rising in the cloudy sky above us.

Jimmy sat with his arm draped around Shirley. They studied the *Racing Form* and discussed which horses were a sure thing for the daily double and how they were going to box the trifecta.

Shirley strained to catch the Red Sox score on a distant radio and Jimmy told her to quit daydreaming.

Finally, Jimmy checked the waterproof Bulova that he had gotten from Uncle Barney. Beads of moisture were clouding up its face, so he had to squint to read the time.

"Jesus Christ, why didn't you tell me it was so late?" he barked at Shirley.

"I *did* say something."

"No you didn't."

"I thought I did. . . ."

"You weren't thinking, dummkopf. You weren't thinking at all."

He shook out the blanket and got sand all over us.

We raced back to the apartment.

Jimmy took a shower while Shirley threw together mackerel sandwiches for them to eat on the way and highballs to wash them down.

Shirley sprayed herself all over with Off 'cause someone at work had told her Maine mosquitoes would eat you alive. She offered to spray Jimmy too when he got out of the shower, but he said he wasn't worried about any puny skeeters.

"They really go for me," Shirley said. "My blood must be sweeter than yours."

"They go after females 'cause they smell weakness. You never hear a hunter bellyaching about mosquitoes. If we did, we'd be laughed outta the woods."

He went to get his binoculars and Shirley slipped Virginia and me each a fin—our entire vacation money. We were allowed to cross the street to buy Pepsis and Ring Dings at the dumpy East Grand Market, but that was it.

On the way out, Jimmy told us to finish up all the mackerel 'cause it was starting to stink. Then he warned us not to open the door to anybody 'cause it could be the Boston Strangler. I locked the door behind them. Jimmy scratched on the door like a madman, and they were off to make a killing.

Lobsters for the Poor

As soon as they were gone, Virginia teased her hair, put on short shorts, and drew some raccoon circles around her eyes with Shirley's eyebrow pencil.

"We're only going across the street," I said. "Not to Hollywood."

"They won't be back for hours," drawled Virginia. "I'm going to the main drag and I can't leave you alone, so you're coming with me."

My throat tightened up like the Strangler had his mitts wrapped around it.

"What if they find out?" I squeaked.

"They're not going to find out—not unless some little snitch snitches."

"I'm not a little snitch. I'm not some goddamn snitch."

"Watch your mouth. And put on long pants so the mosquitoes don't eat you alive."

"Look who's talking," I said, eyeing Virginia's shorts, which barely covered her keister.

"I'm fourteen. I can do what I want when Hitler's not around," Virginia replied as she bit the price tag off a padded bra. I couldn't imagine where she got the money to buy the new bra and the short shorts. I hoped she wasn't sneaking money out of Shirley's purse since that would make it harder for me to hide my own occasional stealing.

Then I remembered my stealing days were over. I was a good Catholic now. Supposedly.

I put on my plaid pedal pushers and stuck the money Shirley had given me deep in my sneaker.

Virginia and I held our breath and sprayed each other with Off.

I turned on the outside light to see if the Boston Strangler was hiding out there. Mosquitoes immediately began to swarm around the light. Otherwise, the coast was clear.

We were about to head out the door when Virginia froze.

"Oh, crap. We forgot about the mackerel."

"I'm gonna puke if I have to eat any more smelly mackerel," I wailed.

"Maybe Sylvester will eat it," Virginia said.

We brought the mackerel over to the cupboard where Sylvester was still hiding, but he only scrunched farther back into the cupboard.

"Poor baby. I know just how you feel," Virginia purred.

She wrapped up the mackerel in some aluminum foil and dropped it in her purse.

"The Polish eagles will eat it," she said. "They eat garbage."

"Good thinking, Einstein," I replied.

We headed for the main drag, smelling a little fishy.

I glanced behind me several times to see if the Boston Strangler was following us. Virginia told me to quit yapping about the Strangler. I was ruining all of her F-U-N. Besides, she said, whoever the nutcase was, she didn't think he'd be leaving the Boston area and hanging out in Vacationland. Wackos didn't take vacations. They were too busy chopping up their nagging mothers and collecting stuffed birds like Norman Bates in *Psycho*.

Suddenly it occurred to me that Jimmy collected stuffed birds like Norman Bates. There was a glassy-eyed mallard on the TV and a pair of black ducks above the couch.

And Jimmy fought with YaYa all the time. Once he even shoved her down when she told him he wouldn't amount to a hill of beans.

A terrifying thought raced through my mind: What if my father was the Boston Strangler?

I weighed the evidence.

He liked to prowl around Boston. He sometimes stayed out all night when Shirley was working. He loved watching women get their tongues yanked out. And what about those bloodstains in the trunk of his car? How could I be sure they were from moose meat and not from some pretty, long-haired secretary who was asking for it by living alone with no man to protect her?

Even Tina had once said her mother thought Jimmy was a maniac and wouldn't let Tina go anywhere in the car with us. Maybe he really was a maniac. How could I know for sure?

Another thought popped into my head and fought off the other thoughts. Maniacs didn't have children! Norman Bates didn't! The Sadist didn't! Fuad Ramses didn't!

I told myself I was safe. Maniacs weren't fathers and fathers weren't maniacs. I chanted that four times 'cause four was my lucky number. I crossed my fingers and crossed my eyes to make it stick.

I kept my fingers crossed until we hit the main drag.

And then I forgot all about maniacs. Forgot about Jimmy.

The place was lit up like a frickin' Christmas tree. Rides were blinking and twirling and plunging and people were screaming in fear but nobody was bleeding or dying.

Virginia took some of my money and bought me a string of tickets as long as my scrawny arm. Then she told me to scram and meet her later at an arcade she had already scoped out.

"Have F-U-N, kiddo, and don't talk to any goddamn maniacs," she said as she hurried off.

I went on the scariest rides first.

I went on the Mighty Mouse roller coaster, the Jack-and-Jill slide, and the Noah's Ark fun house. I went on the world's biggest Ferris wheel and the world's fastest merry-go-round. I rode the bumper cars and rammed as many dummkopfs as I could.

I played pinball and skee-ball and had my fortune told by a lady who said I'd be rich beyond my wildest dreams, which I took to mean Victory Bound would win for sure.

I played ringtoss, hoping to win a giant giraffe, but settled for a lobster key chain instead.

I ate pizza, french fries, saltwater taffy, cotton candy, a candy apple, and a cashew bar.

After stuffing myself to the gills, I went out onto the pier that stretched for miles. I listened to the water sloshing under my feet and looked over the side. I stared at the ancient moss-covered pilings and wondered how long they'd been there and if they might collapse while I was standing there.

I soaked it all in. I ate it all up. I spent all my dough in one night.

Then I hung around the ticket booth with a long face until some rube tourists asked what was wrong. I told them I'd lost my tickets and they took pity on me and bought me a few.

I rode the Mighty Mouse three more times and the bumper cars twice and then I walked over to the arcade and found Virginia. She was standing with some punks watching a greasy-haired punk play pinball. She didn't look thrilled to see me.

Tommy, the pinball player, started teasing us, calling us jailbait.

I told Virginia we should vamoose and she said to quit being a killjoy. We watched Tommy play pinball some more. Watched him until he flipped his flippers too hard and punched the machine and made it freeze and say TILT.

"Look what you made me do," he snapped at us. "You were breathing down my neck."

"Sorry," said Virginia, and lent him money to play again, although I didn't think he'd ever pay her back.

Finally it was late, really late. We ran all the way back to the apartment, concocting alibis in case Jimmy and Shirley had beaten us home. The one we settled on was we had smelled something burning and ran out of the house to save our lives.

But the alibi wasn't necessary 'cause they weren't home. We jumped into bed without even brushing our teeth and I lay there with Poochie, Lambykins, Barbie, and Chatty Cathy and thanked God for saving my keister once again. Virginia and I talked about what a blast we'd had and how we couldn't wait to do it again and we finally fell asleep.

How long I was asleep, I don't know. I woke up to the crash of pots and pans.

It was still dark outside, but the light in the kitchen was on and Shirley appeared to be cooking up a storm. I heard Jimmy's voice and a young wiseguy's voice.

Jimmy said, "You shouldn't have done it," but he was laughing and I could tell he didn't mean it.

The young guy answered Jimmy. "Hey, man, if you don't want any, all the more for me."

I heard a weird scratching sound that I couldn't quite place, like somebody trying to get out of a coffin. Or, rather, like a bunch of people trying to get out of a bunch of coffins.

I got up and staggered into the kitchen.

All the stove burners were fired up and covered with pots of boiling water. Shirley was dropping a big, black lobster with waving claws into one of the pots. Three bushel baskets of the lobster's relatives were on the floor. The lobsters were scratching against the sides of the baskets and against each other, vainly trying to escape a similar fate.

"Hey, who's this?" the young guy said. He had a goofy, friendly smile and dirty blond hair that hung in his blue bloodshot eyes.

"That's Dracula," joked Jimmy. He put his hand in front of his mouth and wiggled his fingers.

"Quit it," the guy said. "She's a cute little kid. You call her that again and I'm takin' back my lobsters."

"All right, all right," said Jimmy, backing off. "She knows I'm just kidding around. Don't you, kiddo?"

"Yeah, sure," I said, smiling, careful not to show my choppers.

Shirley kept drowning more lobsters. A chorus of screeches rose up from the boiling water.

"Who's gonna eat all those lobsters?" I asked.

"We are," said Jimmy. "We're gonna eat lobster like there's no frickin' tomorrow."

"Do you like lobster?" the young guy asked me.

"Don't know. Never had one," I mumbled.

"Well, step right up, sit right down."

He pulled out a chair for me like we were in some swanky joint.

"Lobsters are what rich people eat," explained Shirley.

I was stuffed to the gills from all the crap I had eaten, but I didn't care. I absolutely positively wanted to eat like a rich person.

The young guy sat down next to me, still grinning like a goofball. He began drumming on the table to music only he could hear. He smelled like horseshit and seaweed.

"Are you a fisherman?" I asked.

"Only when there's no moon in the sky," he laughed.

Jimmy split a gut and I laughed too, covering my mouth, though I didn't know what was so goddamn funny.

It turned out the guy's name was Bruce. He was a groom down at the track who messed around with a few other things on the side. One of those things was lobsters. When the moon was dark, Bruce would go out in his crappy boat and pull up other people's traps. He'd swipe a few lobsters from each trap and nobody'd be the wiser. Sometimes he sold the lobsters for a few bucks and sometimes, if he liked you, he'd give 'em away.

I knew right away Bruce was going to be a part of our lives, at least for a while. I was used to Jimmy adopting punks like him. Guys named Ron or Ronnie or Bob or Bobbie. Guys like Susan's brother, Terry, who knew how to throw a goddamn punch. Jimmy always insisted it was a great deal for me having the punks around since I didn't have a big brother. But the punks never gave me the time of day. As far as I was concerned they were just big-fisted boys. Big-mouthed boys I wanted to moider 'cause Jimmy mouthed off about them so much.

But at least this one, this Bruce, had stood up for me.

When the first batch of bright red lobsters was yanked from the pot, he scooted his chair closer to mine and tied a dish towel around my neck like a bib. He showed me how to twist the claws off the beady-eyed creature that was staring me in the face. Then he held up the claws so I could drink the briny juice from them. He crushed the claws with his big, strong fists and dug the meat out all in one piece shaped like a mitten.

He fed me my first taste of lobster.

I decided he could be my big brother forever.

I forgot how full I'd been and filled myself with lobster.

We all did.

"This is the life," said Jimmy. "The life of Riley."

"Imagine eating like this every day," sighed Shirley as she cooked batch after batch of lobsters, piling them up on the table, on the counters, on sheets of yesterday's *Racing Form* spread out on the floor.

Sylvester finally crept out of his cupboard. Jimmy threw him a lobster carcass to pick over and he grabbed it with his big, fat, double paws and tore into it.

Virginia came out to see what all the commotion was about. Jimmy told her to join the party. Virgina watched Shirley plop another live one into the water and I could tell she didn't like staring into its beady eyes as it was boiled alive.

"I'm not hungry," she said.

"Try it or I'll golf you one," said Jimmy. "They're a present from Bruce. Somebody brings you a present, you don't turn your nose up at it."

"That's OK," said Bruce. "She can try it tomorrow. I think there'll be a knuckle or two left over." He was trying to be funny, trying to lighten things up.

"She's going to try it right now. She's gonna be polite."

Virginia forced down a bite of lobster.

"Mmm, it's yummy," she said. "Can I go back to bed now?"

"Go ahead, killjoy," snapped Jimmy. "More for us."

"Now, Jim . . . ," said Shirley, her face sweaty from all the steam coming out of those pots.

"Now, what? I try to do something nice for her, for all of you, and she acts like the Queen of Sheba."

"I'm just tired from havin' so much fun," yawned Virginia as she slipped away.

"Lobster isn't good enough for some people," he called after her.

"How am I ever going to fit them all in the fridge? It's impossible," Shirley said, trying to distract Jimmy from Virginia's snubbing of the lobster. Shirley knew Jimmy would rise to the fridge-packing challenge just as he always did whenever she panicked after he brought home twenty-five ducks or fifty mackerel or one hundred pounds of deer meat.

"Relax, will you," he told her. "None of these sweet babies are going to waste. I'll fit 'em all in there."

And that's what he did. After Bruce took off, Jimmy packed dozens of lobsters into every crevice of the fridge.

I went back to bed with a lobster bellyache. I lay there and suddenly got a whiff of something going bad. I realized Virginia had forgotten to leave the mackerel for the Polish eagles and it was stinking up her pocketbook.

If I didn't get rid of it there would be holy hell to pay in the morning.

I waited until I heard Jimmy begin to snore. Then I grabbed the mackerel, crept down the back stairs, and stuffed it in the neighbors' trash can.

Early the next morning we were woken by a loud pounding on the door.

"Open up! Police!" a deep voice barked.

This is it, I thought. We're all going to the slammer. I grabbed Lambykins and held on tight.

I could hear Jimmy trying to hide stuff in the bedroom.

The knock came again.

I peeked out into the hall and saw Bruce's face in the window of the front door.

"Open up, Jimmy. It's just me," Bruce said.

The rustling in the bedroom stopped. Jimmy stormed out in his boxers and I thought for sure Bruce was gonna get golfed.

"I oughta kill you, you crazy son of a bitch," he hissed.

"Can't you take a joke?" Bruce asked. He had the same goofy smile, but he was all fidgety and his eyes were glassy and even more bloodshot.

"No, I can't take a goddamn joke. You're as high as a kite, aren't you?"

"I'm not feeling any pain," Bruce said. "You want a taste?"

"I told you I don't do that crap. What the hell do you want? You're gonna wake my goddamn kids."

"I think they're already awake." Bruce had spotted me looking around the corner. He waved. "Hey there, little lobster-eater."

I waved back.

"Vamoose. Get the hell back to bed," Jimmy barked.

I vamoosed. But the apartment was so small I didn't even need a glass against the wall to hear every word they were saying.

"Spit it out, hophead. What are you doing here?"

"Some fishermen reported the locks on their traps had been sprung. The cops are nosing around the barns."

"I thought you knew how to pick the locks so no one would know they'd been skimmed."

"I guess I fucked up a little, busted a couple."

"How the hell'd they trace it to the track?"

"Beats me. They just think racetrackers are a bunch of lowlifes."

"Yeah, and it's numbskulls like you that give them that impression. C'mon, Bruce, who knows about the goddamn lobsters besides us?"

"I dunno. I owed this guy fifty bucks and paid him off in lobsters. Maybe he shot his big mouth off."

"I oughta shoot your big mouth off. I oughta go in the bedroom, get my goddamn .38 special, and shoot your big mouth off."

"They're never gonna trace it to us, Jimmy. I'm one hundred percent sure, OK? One hundred percent sure. But just to be one thousand percent sure, I think we oughta put the lobsters on the next train outta town."

There were train tracks right behind the house. Cargo trains rumbled by every few hours and shook the house like an earthquake.

"Are you nuts?" said Jimmy. "I'm not throwing away any goddamn lobsters on any goddamn train. I'm not wasting lobsters when people are starving in this world."

"A lotta winos still ride those trains," said Bruce. "They'll have a poor man's picnic, I promise you that."

Bruce also promised Jimmy he'd get us more lobsters when things quieted down. But, for now, he said it was better to be one thousand percent safe than one million percent sorry.

I heard them pack up the lobsters and drag them down the stairs.

After a while, a train came by and blew its horn and took the lobsters far, far away.

Paralyzed for Life

A few days later, we were back at the beach. Jimmy and Shirley were lying on the blanket, drinking highballs and handicapping, and Virginia was frying herself to a crisp 'cause Tommy the greaser had said tan lines were S-E-X-Y.

I went out bodysurfing on my own, without Jimmy. I was pretending I was on a surfin' safari in KooKooLand with Susan and the Beach Boys.

All of a sudden a big wave hammered me from behind and sucked me under.

It slammed me hard against the sandy bottom. I gulped in mouthfuls of salty sand and felt myself tumbling around. I tried to get to the surface, but just ended up tangled in seaweed that seemed to tie me to the ocean floor.

I'm going to die, I thought. I'm never gonna make it to KooKooLand.

And then I had a revelation.

It's OK. I've been to church. I'm going to heaven.

I relaxed.

And the ocean spit me out onto the shore.

I stood up, heaving water out of my lungs, my eyes burning, my neck bent at a strange angle. I hobbled back to our blanket.

Shirley went to wrap a towel around me.

I screamed bloody murder when she touched me.

Jimmy threw down the *Racing Form*. I had done it now. I had disturbed the genius at work.

"What the hell's the matter with you?"

"Her neck's all weird," I heard Virginia say.

"Oh, my God, she's got a broken neck!" Shirley wailed. I could hear the terror in her voice and I started to shake.

"Straighten up, Quasimodo," Jimmy ordered me. "You're scaring your mother."

I tried to straighten up. I screamed again.

"I can't," I heard my strangely calm voice say.

I tried not to move an inch. If I didn't move, it didn't hurt so bad.

Jimmy felt around my neck bones like he did with a deer whose head he was about to chop off. I yelped some more and other people began to gather around.

A woman with a French Canadian accent shrieked at Jimmy to call an ambulance, call a policeman, call *somebody* for God's sake. She said a neck injury could paralyze me for life.

Jimmy barked at the woman to quit scaring his kid. He told her to shut her big Frog trap or he'd shove his fist in it.

The Frog beat it.

Jimmy asked if anyone knew a doctor. A lobster-red man said he did, and Shirley followed him to his house to call since we didn't have a phone.

The other people, seeing the situation was under control, wandered back to their blankets.

Jimmy took a swig of his highball, puffed on a Lucky Strike, and stared at me through the smoke.

"Nice going, Quasimodo," he said. "It was a beautiful day and you had to go and spoil our fun."

"I didn't mean to," I told him. "I didn't mean to spoil everybody's fun."

"She didn't spoil my fun," Virginia piped up, looking miserable.

"Don't stick up for her, Florence Nightingale," he said, and turned back to me.

"Just wait. The next thing you know, that Frog buttinsky's gonna flag down a copper and the copper'll show up at our place and maybe he'll see something that's none of his goddamn beeswax. Then he'll drag your old man off to the slammer and it'll be all your goddamn fault."

I felt my face get hot. I couldn't believe he was worried about getting pinched when I might be paralyzed for life.

I hope God locks you up in sing sing for life and throws away the frickin' key!

The second I had the thought, shame washed over me.

What kind of a dirty rat of a daughter was I?

How would I feel if Jimmy really got fingered and it was all my stupid fault? All because I had squealed to God and God had granted my wish 'cause now I was a churchy person that he actually paid attention to.

I asked God to forget what I'd just said. Forget about sending Jimmy away for life. I begged him to just fix my Quasimodo neck instead.

Finally, Shirley returned, clutching a piece of paper with a doctor's address. She and Virginia gathered up all our stuff. Jimmy grabbed the *Racing Form*.

On the way to the car Virginia nervously asked Jimmy if I could really be paralyzed for life.

"Don't be a dummkopf," he said. "She's walking, ain't she?"

Virginia glanced at my hobbling gait and seemed to have her doubts.

"If Papou was here, he'd just chuck her back in the ocean. Or if Dr. C was around, he'd straighten her out, bingo bango."

Lucky for me, Papou was many miles away. And Dr. C, our Greek family doctor, wasn't officially practicing medicine at the moment. Not since his license had been suspended for performing a secret operation on a teenage girl while half-lit. An operation that didn't go so well.

Jimmy was half-lit himself as he drove us to the doctor. He ran a couple of red lights and got us there in no time flat.

After a few minutes in the waiting room a nurse came to get me.

"Dr. Skillings will see you now," she chirped.

"Wooo," said Jimmy in his Boris Karloff voice. "Dr. *Killings* is coming for you, little girl."

"There's nothing to be afraid of," the nurse assured me, glaring at Jimmy.

Shirley clasped my hand and led me into the back room.

Dr. Skillings looked delighted to see a little girl with a pretzel neck.

"This is going to be a piece of cake," he said. "A big piece of chocolate cake. How does that sound?"

"Good," I croaked.

He laid me down on his examining table and crossed my arms over my chest.

"Hug yourself tight, honey," he said.

"Don't hurt me," I begged.

He smiled and threw the whole weight of his chest down on me.

I heard a crack like thunder. I saw stars like Wile E. Coyote when the Road Runner dropped an anvil on him.

"I'm paralyzed for life," I wailed.

"No, you're good as new," the doctor said brightly.

He uncrossed my arms and helped me back up.

He was right. I was a little sore, but I was standing up straight.

Shirley kissed me like I was back from the dead.

Dr. Skillings walked us out to the waiting room.

Virginia ran up and hugged me so hard she nearly smothered me.

Jimmy said, "Looks like you're gonna live after all." Then he asked the doctor, "So what was it, Doc, her C-5, right?"

"Yes," Dr. Skillings said, looking stunned. "Are you in the medical field?"

"Nah, I just read a lot," Jimmy said. "Anatomy, physiology. Mostly for hosses. But people are a lot like hosses. They both got seven cervical vertebrae."

"That's right." Dr. Skillings nodded, impressed.

"The biggest difference between hosses and people is obviously in the brain—people are dumber."

Dr. Skillings burst out laughing.

He turned to me with a big, toothy smile.

"Your daddy seems pretty smart," he said. "And I'm sure you're the apple of his eye. So you be careful the next time you go in the ocean, OK? I don't want to see you back here again, little lady."

I agreed. I didn't want to see his kisser again either.

But, as it turned out, we all ended up right back there the very next day.

An ugly rash had broken out all over Virginia. She had been baking too long in the sun, trying to make tan lines for Tommy and trying to bleach her dirty blond hair till it was no longer dirty, just blond.

"She's got sun poisoning," Dr. Skillings announced.

"Sun poisoning, my ass," Jimmy croaked. "The sun's the best medicine there is."

"Not for this little lady. She's allergic to it. She's got to stay out of it for at least the next two weeks."

Jimmy was flabbergasted.

"Some vacation." Virginia pouted.

And that's how Jimmy became, in his words, the first goddamn Greek father of the first goddamn Greek kid in history ever to be allergic to the sun.

Black and Gold

The big day had finally arrived.

Shirley did her hair in pin curls and Virginia put hers up in OJ cans and I left mine straight and shiny like Victory Bound's mane. Jimmy slicked his back with extra Wildroot and put on his lucky shirt.

Virginia rubbed Sylvester's double paws for luck and I spit on everybody and Shirley spotted two crows, which had always been a sign of good luck ever since she was a girl.

We entered the racetrack through the special back gate. Jimmy flashed his Owner's Pass clipped to his visor even though the guard knew him by now since there were no other cars with a boat named the *Aristotle Onassis* tied to the roof going in and out all the time.

We bumped along the dirt road leading to the barns and Jimmy didn't even complain like he usually did about how that goddamn road was massacring his goddamn shocks.

When we got to the barns Victory Bound was prancing around in his stall like he already knew the race was in the bag. Uncle Bobby had on a clean shirt and Aunt Hazel wasn't complaining about him as much and I barely noticed the horseshit.

Jimmy and Uncle Bobby strapped the saddle on Victory Bound as I patted his mane and rubbed the special white spot above his eyes.

I looked in his eyes and begged him to win. I promised him a gazillion sugar cubes if he did.

The jockey came striding out of the tack room. He was just a little taller than the Munchkins in *The Wizard of Oz*. He was buttoning up the brand-new racing silks that Shirley said had cost an arm and a leg. The silks were black and gold with a big *N* on the back. *N* for Norris. *N* for the whole goddamn Norris family.

That Munchkin was riding for us.

Jimmy and Uncle Bobby huddled with the jockey for a while, telling him when to take the horse on the inside and when to hold him back and when to just let the sonofabitch go go go. The jockey nodded like they'd told him this a million times before, which they surely had.

Jimmy boosted him up on the horse.

And all of a sudden he didn't look like a Munchkin anymore. He looked like a giant.

And Victory Bound looked like a stallion. His coat was sleek and his muscles were bulging. He held his head up like a champion.

I felt tears rush to my eyes. It was all so beautiful. The horse was beautiful and the jockey on him was beautiful and everything around us was beautiful.

I saw tears in Jimmy's eyes too. He turned and brushed them away.

"If he doesn't win, those poor kids are gonna be heartbroken," Aunt Hazel said to Shirley.

"Shut up. Don't be a jinx," said Uncle Bobby.

I spit on Victory Bound to make up for Aunt Hazel's big mouth.

Then we headed to the grandstand. It was packed with down-on-their-luck racetrackers and two-bit gamblers and ding-dong tourists.

"Fifteen minutes till post time. Place your wagers early," the announcer called out over the sound system.

Uncle Barney was there with a few shopping bags, trying to move some merchandise to the ding-dong tourists. And Bruce was there with his glassy eyes. And Charlie, the gas station owner who'd given us the free tumblers. And some of the guys who bought pancakes. And Jimmy's other friends from the bookie joint and the Greek coffeehouse and even a few alkies from Nick's Ringside Cafe.

Everybody except YaYa and Papou. YaYa had turned down Jimmy's invitation, but Papou woulda been there except he and Jimmy had had a fight. Jimmy had asked to borrow some dough for our vacation, but Papou had told him to get a goddamn job instead. Papou told him he shouldn't be taking a goddamn vacation if he couldn't pay for it.

"Screw you," Jimmy had said. "You don't want your grandkids to have a vacation? I'll find the money. I'll go to a goddamn loan shark."

And that's what he had done.

And here we were.

"It's too bad your folks couldn't come," one of the alkies said to Jimmy.

"Yeah, too bad," said Jimmy. "Too goddamn bad."

"I bet Nick put down a big bet with Tarzan, though," said one of the guys from the coffeehouse.

"Yeah, he bet against me," cracked Jimmy, and walked away to place his own bet, dragging me with him.

I shot Virginia a reassuring grin as we left. She looked like a nervous wreck with her scaly red rash.

When we got inside the clubhouse, Jimmy pulled me into a corner.

"I'm betting it all on the goddamn nose," he announced. "No betting to place or show this time, no covering myself for the short money. I'm betting to win."

He made me stand in front of him like a shield.

"Hold that," he said, handing me his just-lit Lucky. He wanted two hands to count out all his dough.

By the look of it, he was planning to wager most of the loan shark's money.

"Don't go anywhere or I'll golf you one," he barked, and took off without the Lucky.

He got in line at a betting window. There was a shorter line next to his, so I knew that must be his lucky window. When he got to the front, I watched him throw the baloney with the guy selling tickets.

I couldn't see how much he put down. I couldn't see the color of his tickets. He slipped them right in his wallet. All except for one. That one he gave to me.

"Bring me some good luck, kiddo," he said. "Bring us all some good god-damn luck."

I clutched the two-dollar ticket as tight as I could. I didn't want to lose it. I didn't want to blow the whole shebang.

Some racetrackers moseyed up to us. They'd been tailing us but acted liked running into us was just a happy accident. They were hoping to get a line on how Jimmy was betting. They didn't know whether he was pulling the horse or juicing it or what. Uncle Bobby was known for pulling and juicing, and it turned out he had just had his license suspended for pulling and juicing. Even if Victory Bound won, Uncle Bobby would have to keep his ass out of the winner's circle and let the ringer pretending to be Jimmy's trainer take his place.

Jimmy told the guys everything was on the up-and-up, but, as for win-ning, he just wasn't sure. The horse hadn't finished all his oats last night. The racetrackers looked concerned about the oats. Jimmy acted concerned too. He didn't want those racetrackers spreading the word that the horse was a sure thing and then killing his odds, cutting into his big payday. I did my part and looked concerned too, even though I knew that Victory Bound had gobbled down all his oats and practically eaten the bucket they were in.

Jimmy was on the move again. I dodged trash cans and weaved around people to keep up with him. I was still holding his cigarette butt, which was barely an inch by now and nearly burning my fingers. He snatched it back and sucked down the last few puffs without frying his lips.

We stopped again so Jimmy could shoot the baloney with some more racetrackers. I rubbed my two-dollar ticket and repeated to myself: Victory Bound's a winner. Victory Bound's a winner. Victory Bound's a winner. Victory Bound's a winner.

Four times.

I looked over and saw Shirley standing at a window to place her bets. She was hiding behind a crowd of ding-dong tourists, trying to keep Jimmy from spotting her.

Shirley was always trying to hide her betting from Jimmy. Because she mostly won and he mostly lost, Jimmy always wanted her to make him whole. He'd ask her to show him how much she'd made, then proceed to peel off most of it, leaving her a few bucks to buy groceries. To protect her earnings, Shirley had taken to pretending she was going to the ladies' room and hiding most of her winnings in her underwear. Jimmy complained that women were always going to the damn bathroom 'cause their bladders were too damn small, but Shirley blamed it on all the watery racetrack coffee she was drinking between highballs.

Jimmy snapped his fingers at me and we were off again.

He ducked into the men's room and I waited for him. It seemed like he was gone a long time. I walked in a circle, feeling more and more nervous about the race. I wanted to pee too, but I didn't want Jimmy to bark at me for having a small bladder, so I held it.

Finally, he came out. He looked a little green around the gills and I wondered if maybe he had thrown up. He told me to shake a leg and we beat it back to the grandstand.

When we got there, I couldn't believe my eyes. Shirley was sitting with Hank and the miserable Shirley. The miserable Shirley didn't look miserable at all.

Jimmy lit up like the tote board when he saw Hank.

"Jesus," he said. "My old man wouldn't make the goddamn trip, but here you are."

"Yeah, here I am, greaseball," Hank said. Hank didn't give a goddamn about the horses, so it was a big deal he had shown up.

"We flew up here in no time in the Caddy," said the other Shirley, hanging on to Hank. "That car rides like a dream." She said it like the car was hers. Like it was her goddamn dream.

Jimmy and Hank gave the other Shirley a look like she oughta shut her trap, but she didn't seem to notice.

I wanted to tell the previously miserable Shirley she was going to be miserable again if she didn't watch it.

Hank took out a cigar and the other Shirley hurried to light it for him.

"So this nag of yours, is it gonna win or what?" Hank asked Jimmy.

Jimmy pulled Hank aside and started whispering to him. I knew he was giving it to him straight up. I heard him say the horse looked good. He had eaten all his goddamn oats. Hank could bet the goddamn store on it.

Hank took off for the windows.

I got a sinking feeling. If Hank lost the store, Susan might have to quit school. She might never get to be a doctor who saved the lives of poor little colored children.

I clutched my ticket and prayed to God to let things go our way just this once. I promised never to do anything bad with a stuffed animal again.

A big truck rolled by, spraying clouds of mosquito repellent.

Virginia came back from the ladies' room smelling like smoke and carrying a Pepsi with two straws.

I realized I had to pee really bad.

"The horses are entering the track," said the announcer with no excitement in his voice whatsoever.

I strained to see the black and the gold. I finally saw it. Victory Bound was the last horse to enter the track.

As the horses cantered in front of the grandstand, Jimmy peered at Victory Bound's ankles and knees and at how he held his head.

Hank came back and sat on the seat in front of me. I could see the stack of tickets bulging in his pants pocket.

"Did you buy a ticket for me?" cooed the other Shirley.

"No, I didn't," said Hank. "But here." He pulled out a ticket and handed it to her—a two-dollar ticket like mine. I could see a lot of other two-dollar tickets in his pocket. He could've gotten a few expensive tickets instead of a big bunch of deuces, but I figured he got more tickets to make a bigger bulge. Jimmy told me that was what a lot of guys did to look like big shots.

"I don't like to bet. I just like to watch," the other Shirley said to Jimmy, who was trying to look through his binoculars.

Jimmy got the hell away from her and stood by the railing.

The other Shirley opened one of the beers she was carrying in her big purse and handed it to Hank.

"Can I get you anything else? How about a nice kielbasa?"

"Just watch the goddamn race," Hank said.

"The horses are approaching the starting gate," droned the announcer.

I was so excited I could barely breathe. I squeezed my legs together so I wouldn't pee on myself.

Don't blink, I ordered myself. If you keep your eyes on the black and gold from this moment on, Victory Bound will win.

Hank stood up in front of me, blocking my view. Then the other Shirley stood up, 'cause she would've followed Hank if he did a swan dive off the grandstand.

No, I silently cried, still not blinking, but unable to see a thing. Please don't do this. Please don't make me make him lose.

I struggled to see around their big asses.

I gave up and stood up on the bench and then Virginia stood up, and then the people behind us had to stand up and the people behind them. Everybody had to stand 'cause of Hank, the big shot.

"The horses have entered the starting gate," the announcer said.

I could see the black and gold and I still hadn't blinked, so maybe everything would be OK. Maybe I hadn't jinxed it.

"And they're off."

I heard the clang of the gate opening and the hooves pounding the dirt and I lost sight of the black and gold.

The horses were all bunched together and the announcer had suddenly come alive and was talking so fast you couldn't hear a goddamn thing he was saying.

I didn't blink. I kept my eyes on that knot of horses, straining to see the black and gold.

The people behind me were screaming for another stupid horse—"Go Nutmeg Gal!"—and Virginia and I tried to drown out their stupid voices.

"Go Victory Bound! Go Victory Bound! Go Victory Bound!"

We couldn't stop yelling it.

The horses came unbunched and I finally caught a glimpse of the black and gold in the backstretch. He was in the back of the pack.

My body went limp. Tears flooded my eyes. And I couldn't help it.

I blinked.

And then I knew for sure it was over.

I closed my eyes, 'cause it didn't matter anymore. I felt more tears and tried to squish my eyelids against my eyeballs to make them stop, but it didn't help.

I hated the people in the row behind me who were screaming louder and louder, urging their horse on when I had just gone mute.

We lost, and it's all my fault, I thought.

I wanted to take a swan dive off of the grandstand. I wanted to kill those goddamn people behind me.

And suddenly Virginia was grabbing my arm and pulling so hard I nearly fell off the bench.

I opened my eyes and the black and gold was miles in front—miles and miles—coming down the home stretch and Jimmy and Shirley were screaming and Hank and the other Shirley were screaming and all our friends were screaming and I was screaming—*govictoryboundgovictoryboundgovictorybound*—and the people behind me had gone mute.

He went over the finish line all by himself and I finally heard the announcer's voice, and even he sounded excited.

"And it's Victory Bound by six furlongs! Victory Bound is the winner!"

Everybody was jumping around and Shirley grabbed my hand and Virginia's hand and she looked so stunned, like she couldn't believe it, none of us could, and we were racing toward the winner's circle after Jimmy, all of us: Hank and the other Shirley and Uncle Bobby and Aunt Hazel and Uncle Barney and gas-station Charlie and hopped-up Bruce and the guys from the bookie joint and the Greeks from the coffeehouse and the alkies from the beer joint.

Victory Bound came prancing up to the winner's circle and Jimmy wanted everybody in the picture, but the guy said there were too many of us and Jimmy started to argue with him, but Hank told him to just get in the goddamn winner's circle with his family.

So it was just us, the Norris family—minus Sylvester and Squirmy—and the ringer who was pretending to be the trainer.

"Ain't this the life?" Jimmy cried out.

Yes, we all agreed. This was the life.

And then the flash went off.

And we were all blinded for a few moments.

Good Luck, Bad Luck

"My lucky number is six now," I announced to Virginia in the car on the way back to Old Orchard Beach that night. "Because Victory Bound's number was six and he won by six furlongs and today is August sixth."

"Six-six-six is the mark of the devil," intoned Virginia. She had just read a book about witchcraft and was convinced she had been burned at the stake in a previous life.

"Don't jinx my lucky number, Satan-lover," I snapped at her.

In the front seat, Jimmy and Shirley were having a few highballs to celebrate Victory Bound's winning.

"Poor Shirley," I heard Shirley say. "She's really got it bad for Hank."

"She's a numbskull," spat Jimmy. "I never shoulda introduced her to him in the first place."

He was PO'd 'cause he'd asked Hank to stay over and go fishing with him the next day. But right after the race Hank told him the other Shirley was smothering him to death and they left. The other Shirley smiled and waved toodle-oo like she didn't know Hank was about to give her the heave-ho and she was gonna be Miserable Shirley again.

"If she'd just been smart enough to back off, she woulda been on goddamn easy street eating bonbons," continued Jimmy. "A guy like Hank, you can't crowd him. He's like a boxer—you corner him, he's gonna come out fighting."

"Maybe I should tell her that."

"Keep your snout out," said Jimmy. "Hank don't need another woman nosing around in his business. Besides, it wouldn't do any good. The real problem is he's still carrying a torch for that goddamn Doris."

"I never thought Doris would go through with the divorce," sighed Shirley. "Her being Catholic and all. People back in Canada said you make your bed, you lie in it."

"Hank oughta thank his lucky stars she finally went through with it, 'cause he never woulda pulled the trigger. He's a loyal SOB. And she woulda just kept blubberin' to the cops every time they had a little spat."

"At least she waited until Susan and Terry were out of high school. At least those kids didn't have to grow up in a broken home."

"Give her a prize for that," said Jimmy. "Give her the goddamn Cracker Jack prize."

Hearing about Susan and her broken home made me more determined than ever to buy her a nice present. Not some piece of crap like a lobster key chain. Something special she could take back to college that would remind her I was her best friend in the whole goddamn world.

I slipped a finger into my sneaker to make sure my winnings were still safe in there. I could feel them—four simoleons. Jimmy had kept the two he had staked me for the ticket, 'cause he said that was like a loan. Then he took a cut of the winnings, 'cause that was like interest on the loan. If he were a loan shark that's how it would work, is how he explained it.

I felt like telling him he was an Indian giver, but I didn't want to hear about what an ungrateful little weasel I was. It was true I wouldn't have had any dough at all without him, so maybe he had a point. Maybe he deserved a cut. Maybe I *was* an ungrateful little weasel. Nobody had given Jimmy diddly-squat when he was my age. He had worked in Yanco's butcher shop every day after school and all day Saturday, and Papou always took his cut. So maybe all fathers took a cut. Maybe that's just how things worked.

That night when we got home, we all hid our money. Shirley's went into her underwear drawer and Jimmy's went under the mattress and mine went into the Good & Plenty box. Virginia didn't have any to hide 'cause she'd blown all of hers on cancer sticks and Pepsi. Jimmy had gotten everybody started on hiding their money. He didn't think money belonged in a goddamn bank. He didn't want some busybody banker knowing when he was making a killing and squealing to Uncle Sam. He didn't want his money all locked up after three in the afternoon when he might need to lay down a big bet or buy some hot merchandise or hightail it up to Canada if the fuzz came looking for him. Just to be safe, he made Shirley stay a Canadian citizen so we could get across the border easy—bingo bango.

I could imagine other situations in which we might need to use Jimmy's escape plan—an alien invasion, for instance. Or an A-bomb attack by Communists.

Awful things happened. They happened all the time. They happened out of the blue.

It didn't matter who you were. Or even if you were a big shot. Anybody could get sucker punched.

The day after Victory Bound won, I was lying on the beach, still basking in the glow of victory, when I heard two women sobbing. They were saying that Jackie Kennedy's baby had been born too soon and was probably gonna die.

It's a son, too, one of the women blurted out, which seemed to make it worse.

People all over New England are praying, the other woman said.

The pope's praying too, said the first woman. All good Catholics are.

I joined in. I closed my eyes and prayed with the pope and all the good Catholics of New England.

I prayed with Susan 'cause I knew, wherever she was, she was praying too.

But two days later, the Kennedy baby died anyway. Maybe somebody, one person, hadn't prayed hard enough. Maybe it was me.

But I knew what Tina would say. What Susan would say. God wanted that little baby. God had a scheme and it wasn't our business to know God's family business. We just had to pray now for the Kennedys not to suffer too much, even though the prayers we'd prayed before hadn't worked. Every time you prayed and your prayers didn't come true, you just had to keep on praying. Tina said that's what you did if you were a good Catholic.

So I lay down on the beach again and closed my eyes and prayed for the Kennedys to be less miserable.

But I couldn't concentrate. Jimmy's voice kept butting into my prayers.

He was going on and on to Shirley about Papou and YaYa. He had called to tell them about Victory Bound's victory and all YaYa had wanted to know was when we were coming back 'cause she was sick and tired of having a filthy rodent in her basement. Then, when Jimmy asked Papou if he wanted a photo of us in the winner's circle to put up in the beer joint next to the picture of the Great Jack Dempsey, Papou had told him not to waste his goddamn money.

Shirley said she was sure Papou was happy about the horse winning, that he just had a funny way of showing it. It was the Greek way, which was not to show happiness at all, 'cause then the evil eye would come looking for you and misery would rain down on you. Shirley had first learned about the evil eye when YaYa spit on me after I was born so I wouldn't die.

Since the Kennedys weren't Greek I figured nobody had spit on their baby. Maybe if some Greek had done that, everything would be different. Maybe that was why I had lived and Jimmy had lived, even though, according to YaYa, we had both been born too soon and both been sickly, just like the Kennedy baby.

"Who wants a nice cold root beer?" Shirley sang out.

I figured I could do more praying later and opened my eyes.

Virginia was walking up to the blanket carrying my sand bucket. Jimmy had sent her to the Normandie Inn to steal some ice from their cooler. Virginia handed the bucket of ice to Shirley, and Shirley plopped ice cubes into high-balls for her and Jimmy and into root beers for Virginia and me.

"What have you been doing, dum-dum?" Jimmy asked me, gnawing on a hunk of ice.

I tensed up. I knew Jimmy wouldn't be keen on the idea of me praying. He might turn it into a joke. Or he might start talking about all the starving babies in the world and ask why I wasn't praying for them, too. He might make me defend what was so special about the Kennedy baby in relation to those other babies and I knew I wouldn't be able to do it to his satisfaction.

"Nothing," I said. "I haven't been doing anything."

"In other words, you're wasting your vacation. The vacation your mother and I worked so hard to take you on."

"No," I said. I didn't see how that followed. "I'm having fun. I'm getting a nice tan. See." I held out my browning arm as evidence.

"Tanning is for idiots," he said. "KooKooLand idiots. The time you waste lying there like a corpse you could be reading a book or the newspaper to make yourself less of a dum-dum."

I obediently reached for the newspaper. A picture of President Kennedy looking sad was on the front page.

"They're making a federal case outta one dead kid," Jimmy complained. "Kids die every day. It's a big, bad world."

I nodded like I agreed with him.

"C'mon," he said suddenly. "Let's go for a dip."

I thought he must be joking.

There was a freak invasion of jellyfish going on at the moment and every-body was staying out of the water. Some of the jellyfish were pink and some were white and one kind was harmless and the other stung you and I couldn't remember which was which.

Jimmy insisted all the jellyfish were harmless. He said he knew all about jellyfish from being a merchant mariner and a fisherman and from swimming amongst jellyfish lots of times. Even if one kind did sting a little, it wasn't poi-sonous and you would barely feel the sting.

"What are you, a chicken?" asked Jimmy. "A little baby chicken?" He started to make his clucking sounds.

Pluck pluck pluck.

"I don't think she should go in the water," Shirley piped up.

"Oh, look, it's the mother hen trying to protect her baby chick," said Jimmy.

"I don't want her to get stung. Even if it's not poisonous."

"What about me?" asked Jimmy, draining his highball. "You don't care if I get stung? You only care about her? You don't care what happens to me?"

"No, of course not. Of course I care about you." I could see Shirley was trying not to get boxed into a corner. "You said the stinging wouldn't bother you. But you're a big, strong man and she's a little girl. Besides, nobody else is in the water."

"These goofball tourists are all chickens."

"Jimmy . . . please. I don't want her to go."

"Why do you have to take up for her all the time? Ever since she's been born you've been doing that and I don't like it. I don't like it one bit. You're always taking her side."

"I'm not taking anyone's side," said Shirley. "I just—"

"I don't see you taking my side. I don't see you ever taking my side. And you should be taking my side. You should be taking my side all the time. I'm your husband. I'm the head of this family and you treat me like I'm Joe Palooka."

I knew he was going down a road that wouldn't end until Shirley cried and he told her they had been having a great time and she had messed it all up.

Unless I saved the day.

"I want to go in the water with Daddy," I blurted out. "I'm not afraid of those stupid jellyfish."

Jimmy looked over at me with his angry face, and for a breathless moment I thought he was going to start in on me.

But he broke into a grin.

"All right then. Now you're talking. That's my kid. That's what I like to hear."

I jumped up. I prayed to God to protect me from the killer jellyfish. At least if I get stung, I prayed, please don't let it hurt too much 'cause I'll have to pretend it's nothing, really nothing, or she'll be right and he'll be wrong and then I'll get blamed for ruining the whole goddamn day.

"I'll race you to the shore," he said.

As I got into my starting position, he turned back to Shirley for one more parting jab.

"Your daughter's got more goddamn guts than you do."

Shirley looked at me helplessly. Her eyes said I'm sorry. I put on a big smile so she wouldn't feel so bad.

I raced him to the shore. Raced him faster than I ever had, dreading the destination.

I'm gonna beat you, you bastard, I thought. I'm gonna beat you if it kills me.

He let me get close. He let me get my hopes up and then he pulled away like Victory Bound.

He charged into the ocean ahead of me, splashing water back into my face.

"You'll never beat me. You'll never beat your old man," he crowed, and dove head first into the water thick with pink and white jellyfish.

I edged into the water, trying to avoid the jellyfish, but it was impossible. They sloshed against me, blobs of pink and white potential pain.

There was nothing left to do except ask God to protect me, even though I knew he was probably busy right now with the Kennedys.

Jimmy waved me out into the deep water and I went toward him, pushing my way through the sea of fear.

I closed my eyes and pretended I had a force field all around me. Like the robot in *The Day the Earth Stood Still*, nothing could touch me.

I went in over my head and somehow I didn't get stung.

"See?" Jimmy laughed. "I was right. Remember, your old man is always right."

"You're right," I repeated, and this time it was true.

I lay back and floated in a sea of beautiful jellyfish and never wanted to go back to shore again.

What's in the Box?

It was our last night at the beach and I had to make up my mind once and for all. I needed to find the perfect present for Susan. I felt like our whole friendship was riding on my decision.

There were several items in the running. There was a framed Jesus that had OLD ORCHARD BEACH, MAINE stamped across the sea he was walking on. There was a bongo drum, which was what *I* wanted, but which I thought Susan might like too since she already played the clarinet and might want to learn a new instrument. There was a jewelry box shaped like a pirate's chest that smelled like cedar when you opened it. I figured Susan could store her gold cross in there. That is, if she ever took the cross off, which was something I didn't know about one way or the other.

The truth was I was beginning to realize there were lots of things I didn't know about Susan. Like what her favorite color was and whether she liked chocolate better than vanilla or Top Cat more than Huckleberry Hound. I began to see Susan as a mystery and realized how few clues I had. I felt Nancy Drew wouldn't be in such a predicament. She'd know what to buy her best friend. She'd have solved that goddamn mystery by now.

To make matters worse, as I dragged myself up and down the main drag, Virginia was breathing down my neck. I'd begged her to come shopping with me, but she was dying to get back to the arcade. She wanted to spend her last night with Tommy. She'd gotten crazier and crazier about him over the two weeks we'd been there. She said he reminded her of James Dean, but all I could see was a freeloader who bummed money from her to buy pizza and then wouldn't even give her a bite.

As we went from souvenir shop to souvenir shop, Virginia kept pushing me to make up my mind. I hadn't told her I was buying something for Susan, so she thought I was just dicking around trying to pick out something for myself.

"How about that bongo drum?" she suggested. "You haven't stopped talking about that since we got here. Or those giant sunglasses? You thought those were a riot when you first saw them."

"I thought they were *cute*. I didn't think they were a riot. I thought the giant pencil was a riot. I thought I could write a whole lotta mystery books with that."

"So get it then."

"I really want a lot of things. That doesn't mean I'm gonna buy 'em."

"What about candy? You love candy. What about that chocolate lobster?"

"I don't want to think about lobster ever again."

Virginia frowned. I figured like me she was thinking about those lobsters on the train.

"Daddy's crazy," she suddenly said. "You know that, don't you?"

"He's not crazy," I said. "He just gets mad when he loses at the track."

"Yeah, stark raving mad. I can't wait till I'm eighteen. It'll be sayonara, Hitler."

"Fat chance. He won't let you go. You oughta know that, dummkopf."

"It's the law, dummkopf."

"Ha! The law doesn't scare him."

"Then I'll just take off one night. Just disappear. And he won't know where to find me."

"If Hank could find Doris all the way in KooKooLand, he'll find you, that's for sure, 'cause he's a better hunter than Hank."

"Then I'll go far away. Across the ocean. To France or England or anywhere." She corrected herself. "Anywhere but Greece."

"Anywhere but Greece," I echoed.

And then I saw it. The perfect present.

A snow globe. A giant snow globe with a beach scene inside. With palm trees and beach umbrellas and two girls—two teen-ragers—in bikinis and Foster Grants lying in the sun.

I shook it up. Snow swirled around the girls like they were in a blizzard on the beach. It didn't make any sense why it would be snowing at the beach, but it looked so pretty I didn't care.

I held my breath and turned it over to see the price. I had enough. I had enough and would still have enough left over to buy the giant pencil for myself and a few pieces of saltwater taffy for Tina.

"This is it," I told Virginia. "This is what I want."

"Whoopee-do," said Virginia. "Let's beat it."

I carried the snow globe around the rest of the night like it was an A-bomb. Don't drop it, I told myself. Whatever you do, don't drop it, dummkopf.

Virginia disappeared down to the beach with Tommy for a while. After they came back, Virginia went to the bathroom, and I heard Tommy's friend ask him if he'd got any. Ask if he'd opened her box.

"Nah," said Tommy, sulking. "She's just a cool way to get my finger wet."

I didn't know what it meant, but I felt my face get all red.

"You're a lousy goddamn pinball player," I snapped at him, and stormed off.

The next day, we packed up the car. I said good-bye to our apartment and good-bye to the beach and good-bye to a flock of seagulls. I waved good-bye to the last train conductor on the last train that was going by, hoping he had gotten a few of those poached lobsters for himself.

I realized I was gonna miss it all so much. I was trying not to start blubbering when I noticed Jimmy take his handicapping pen out of his shirt pocket and scribble something above the front door.

I love this place, he wrote. And he signed his name, *J. Norris*.

"Someday," he told me, "you'll remember this summer and you'll realize it was the best one of your whole goddamn life."

"Someday," he repeated. "We'll all be dead and no one will even know we were here."

I ran out of the apartment, trying to block out what he'd said. But I knew I never would.

On the way home, nobody said a word. Jimmy and Shirley smoked and drank, Virginia petted Sylvester, and I played with the snow globe, pretending I was living in a beachy bubble with Susan.

Since we'd eaten up all the groceries, at least I didn't have to carry a box on my lap.

Or that's what I thought anyway, until we pulled over at a truck stop somewhere near Rochester, New Hampshire. Jimmy got out of the car and climbed into a tractor-trailer with some guys I had seen at the house. Chubby Somebody and Louis Somebody Else.

Shirley, Virginia, and I waited in the car. We heard laughter coming from the truck.

Shirley started up a game she'd taught us years before to keep us entertained while we were parked outside of bookie joints, truck stops, or junkyards.

I'm thinking of something red, Shirley would say. Then you'd have to guess what it was. The bull's-eye on her pack of Lucky Strikes. A Baby Ruth wrapper in the gutter. A bloodstain in the snow. We played for matchsticks like the clodhoppers in Nova Scotia. Sometimes we played until we ran out of things to guess.

Finally, Jimmy emerged from the tractor-trailer carrying a big box. I managed to snatch the snow globe from between my legs a second before he slammed the box down on my lap.

"Here's a present for you," he joked. I could smell fresh booze on his breath.

"Ain't that merchandise a little heavy for the kid?" asked Chubby Somebody.

"Nah," replied Jimmy. "Dracula's OK."

"Don't worry, kid," snorted Louis Somebody Else. "The way your old man drives, you'll be home before your legs need to be amputated."

"Shut up, numbskull," said Jimmy, before he sped off.

I balanced the snow globe on top of the box of merchandise. I didn't know what was in the box and, for once, I didn't care.

I just wanted it the hell off me.

The Transformation
of Squirmy and the Bunk Beds

Our first day back we went to pick up Squirmy. YaYa couldn't wait to get rid of him. Virginia wiggled her finger in Squirmy's cage, but Squirmy didn't nuzzle her like he usually did. He bit her. Virginia screamed and yanked her bleeding finger out of the cage.

YaYa went flippy. She yelled at Jimmy that hamsters were vicious rodents and shouldn't be kept as pets and said it would be all his fault if Virginia got rabies and died.

Then she spit on Virginia.

Virginia looked like she was gonna faint. We'd both been terrified of rabies ever since Jimmy'd told us about a hunter who'd gotten chomped by a raccoon and then had to get a bunch of needles stuck in his breadbasket.

Jimmy yelled at YaYa that it was all *her* fault, that she'd taken lousy care of Squirmy, that she never liked animals, never let him have a dog 'cause they made too much of a mess and that there was something wrong, really wrong, with anybody who didn't like furry little animals.

Then he grabbed Squirmy's cage and we beat it.

In the car, Virginia kept squeezing her knuckle, trying to get out any rabies poison. I scrunched away from her, not wanting to catch anything. I asked her if she felt weird, like the Wolfman before a full moon. She told me to shut my trap and then Jimmy told us both to shut our traps, told us we were a couple of dummkopfs for thinking we could get rabies from a hamster.

When we got home, Jimmy deposited Squirmy's cage in our bedroom and Squirmy began running around in circles like he had really gone off the deep end.

"Don't stick your schnozzolas in there," Jimmy warned us before leaving to settle up with the loan shark. He said the bloodsucking loan shark was charging an arm and a leg and would chop off an arm or a leg if he didn't hurry up and pay up.

I asked if I could go with him to see the bloodsucker. I asked if we could stop at Hank's on the way back.

"Some of us gotta work for a living," he replied. "You're a lucky kid. You're still on vacation. I gotta go mow some rich lard-asses' lawns. I gotta climb back on the hamster wheel to put Twinkies in your breadbasket and support a dippy rodent."

I did my best to look sorry for being a lucky kid with a dippy rodent.

As soon as he drove away, Shirley kissed us and went off to bed 'cause she had to go back to making sunglasses that night.

Virginia and I watched Squirmy run around in circles.

"Squirmy, calm down. It's me," Virginia cooed. "Remember I fed you feta cheese from my mouth?"

Squirmy looked like he wanted to tear her lips off.

"Maybe he ate some radioactive bugs in the basement and now he's like Dr. Jekyll and Mr. Hyde," I offered. "Or maybe he smacked his head against the cage and got amnesia."

"He loved us and now he hates us," moaned Virginia.

"No, he's just mad. He's mad and he'll get over it. Like Daddy."

To take Virginia's mind off of the whole Squirmy situation, I suggested we play Life.

Life was my second-favorite board game after Candy Land. It had a wheel you could spin and dough you could win and you got to drive a car even if you were a girl. You drove through the ups and downs of life, collecting a husband and adding pink or blue kids to your car. You either ended up a Millionaire or went to the Poor Farm.

Virginia hated Life. Besides which, she was too old for toys. That's what she'd informed me, anyway, when she turned fourteen. I knew she still secretly played with her tiger puppet, but rather than use that to convince her I simply said that someday . . . someday . . . we would be old and shriveled up and maybe crippled and she would be sorry she hadn't played one last game of Life with me, her only sister.

"Quit it," she said. "You sound just like Miserable Daddy." She yanked a *True Confessions* magazine out from under her mattress, then tossed it aside. "OK, one lousy game."

"Yabba dabba doo!" I cried.

Now all I had to do was win. Had to. It was a matter of Life and death.

In the past, I didn't hesitate to cheat. I'd sneak my playing piece onto a different square or steal money from the bank or add another kid to my car. But now that I was aiming to be a good Catholic, cheating was outta the question.

So I played it straight. And Virginia clobbered me. Her family got big and rich and mine stayed puny and poor.

"Your face is so long, it's dragging on the board," Virginia said.

"This is a stupid game," I choked. "I like Candy Land better."

When Virginia finally realized I wasn't going to cheat, she took pity on me and cheated herself. She snuck her car backwards and miscounted and ended up on bad squares. My mood lifted. I acted like she'd just had a sudden turn of bad luck. Norris Luck. Hell, that happened all the time. You thought you were a winner and then you got robbed. As long as I wasn't the one cheating, I figured I was OK with God. If Virginia wanted to go to hell, that was her business.

We heard Jimmy's car pulling up to the curb—the worst sound in the world.

"Hitler's back," said Virginia.

"Oh no," I moaned, the joy of my near victory evaporating.

I peeked out the window to see Jimmy and Uncle Barney unloading some TVs from the Pontiac. They lugged the first one inside and up the stairs and into our bedroom.

"Hey, little girls," Uncle Barney grunted as he entered, struggling with the TV.

He gave a cockeyed glance around the room, looking for a spot to drop his heavy load.

"Move that game," grunted Jimmy. "Make it snappy."

We grabbed Life and threw it into its box.

They dropped the hot TV in its place with a thud.

"How're my good little Greek girls?" asked Uncle Barney. "Bet you can't wait to get back in that winner's circle."

"Cut the crap and help me move this bureau," said Jimmy. They shoved the bureau back against the closet, creating space for another couple of TVs.

Jimmy turned to us. "You kids have too many toys. There's no room for anything else in here."

"Ah, leave 'em alone, Jimmy. We got enough room. We'll pile 'em on top of each other."

"Oh yeah? You want to scratch the finish? You think customers wanna buy a scratched-up set? I'm talkin' regular people, Joe Frickin' Blow, not a bum like you."

"We can stuff rags between 'em," suggested Barney.

"And while we're at it, you can stuff two in my ears so I don't have to listen to your bright ideas anymore."

"Your old man's a comedian," said Uncle Barney. "A regular Jack Benny."

"Jack Benny's a moron," countered Jimmy as he studied the room, figuring out where the other TVs would go. Finally, he looked over at me.

"OK, Dracula," he said. "You win. Tomorrow you get your goddamn bunk beds."

"Ohboyohboyohboyohboy!" I squealed.

I felt like kissing those hot TVs.

Lying in bed that night, I tried to picture what the new bunk beds would look like and how much fun it would be to climb the little ladder from one to the other. I lobbied Virginia to let me have the top bunk, but she said she didn't care, I could take my pick.

The next day I planned to go bunk bed shopping with Jimmy, but he had already left the house by the time I got up. I kept listening for the sound of some truckie in his big rig—some guy who owed Jimmy a favor—driving up to deliver our bunk beds so Jimmy wouldn't have to pay the store to do it.

But no truckie appeared. I waited in my bedroom for hours, staring out the window. Finally, Jimmy's car drove up. Bruce, the hopped-up groom and part-time lobster poacher, stumbled out of the passenger seat. He had a drill, which he dropped on the ground.

I figured the bunk beds would be following along any minute.

But still, no truck appeared. Jimmy and Bruce tromped up the stairs and came into my bedroom. When Bruce saw me, his yellowish eyes seemed to brighten.

"Hey, it's the lobster lover and future bunk bed owner."

"Are you putting together the bunk beds?" I asked, getting right to the point.

"Yeah, he is," said Jimmy. "So gangway."

Bruce plugged his drill in and began to drill a hole in the bedpost of Virginia's bed and I knew right then and there I wasn't getting any bunk beds. I was getting our twin beds stacked on top of each other, engineered by a guy who could barely see straight.

Right away I saw the complications.

"How am I gonna get onto the top without a little ladder?"

"You'll hoist yourself up, for crying out loud," said Jimmy. "We did it all the time in the merchant marine. It'll build up those jigaboo arms of yours."

I watched Bruce drill the holes. They didn't look very straight.

Squirmy chattered and rammed his head against the bars. I figured he didn't like the sound of the drill.

"Take Psycho outta here," Jimmy ordered me.

I gingerly grabbed the handle on Squirmy's cage and brought him downstairs. I set him on the kitchen table.

Squirmy wouldn't stop chattering. Virginia got some feta cheese and dropped it through the top of the cage, hoping to jog his memory of happier times. He got up on his hind legs and tried to bite her finger again.

And that's when I noticed the little white marking on his belly.

"Squirmy never had a white spot like that!" I cried out, like Nancy Drew cracking a case.

"Oh, my God! It's not Squirmy!" Virginia screamed.

The jig was up.

Jimmy heard us shrieking and stomped down the stairs. We told him our discovery.

He glared at the fake Squirmy and then came clean about what had happened.

Squirmy had run away. He had escaped his cage right after we left for Maine. YaYa couldn't find him until a few days passed and she smelled something rotten coming from behind the washing machine.

Virginia started to bawl when she heard about the rotten smell. I started bawling too. And Shirley came running downstairs in her nightgown.

"See what you did, Olive Oyl?" Jimmy snarled.

It turned out it had been Shirley's idea to pull a bait and switch. She had raced down to Woolworth's the morning after we got back and bought another hamster. She thought if they pretended nothing was wrong we wouldn't notice.

"I meant well," she moaned. "I guess I did the wrong thing."

"You sure as hell did!" yelled Jimmy. "The Grim Reaper ain't no Santy Claus. He's real. And they might as well get used to it."

"It's OK," Virginia croaked, forcing a smile.

"We'll get used to the new Squirmy," I piped up. "I'm sure he'll stop trying to bite us."

"He's just scared," Virginia managed to say. "It's only natural."

"He's awfully cute," insisted Shirley. "He's just a little nervous."

"He must be a goddamn she," snapped Jimmy. "I told you to get a male, but you screwed up as usual."

"They thought it was a boy. It's hard to tell."

"No it isn't. It's loco, so it's a goddamn female."

Squirmy chattered at Jimmy.

"I'm gonna drown that little—"

"No, Daddy, don't!" I wailed. "I love him—her—already!"

"All right, all right, quit your moaning and groaning. Just get it out of my goddamn sight before I wring its furry neck," he said. "And go try out those new bunk beds. You wanted 'em and now you got 'em. No other kids in the projects are lucky enough to have bunk beds, right?"

"Right," answered Virginia.

"Right," I chimed in.

We took the imposter Squirmy's cage back up to our bedroom. Our twin beds were now stacked on top of each other. Bruce was sniffing the tube of glue that he had used to put them together.

He quickly screwed the cap back on the glue and flashed his goofy smile.

"Don't squeal on me to your old man, OK?" He turned to Virginia. "And I won't tell him about those magazines hidden under your mattress. Deal?"

He stuck out his pinkie.

We nodded and hooked pinkies with him.

"Cool," he said. "You two are cool c-c-customers."

We stood there in silence for a moment. I watched Bruce's head bob around like a jack-in-the-box. I could hear Jimmy and Shirley downstairs, still arguing about whether Squirmy was a boy or girl.

Bruce cocked his thumb in the general direction of the bunk beds.

"They *should* more or less hold together. Just don't jump on 'em too hard."

"Oh," I said, starting to get worried.

"I mean you can jump on them, just not too h-h-harm."

"Not too *hard*," I corrected him.

"Right-o, kiddo," he mumbled, attempting to light the filter end of his cancer stick. I pointed out the problem and he snorted with laughter.

"Don't tell your old man," he said again.

"We won't," I assured him again.

"Lemme demonstrate how to get up there," he said.

"No, that's OK," I replied, picturing him cracking open his coconut.

But Bruce insisted. After slipping a half-dozen times he managed to climb onto the footboard of the bottom bed and shimmy his body onto the top. The beds swayed and creaked but didn't fall apart.

"See? Great, huh?"

"Great," I said, wishing I'd never brought up bunk beds in the first place.

Bruce finally left and Virginia and I lay on the beds and tried to come up with a name for the new hamster. Nothing seemed right, so we ended up calling her Squirmy Two.

She was just like Squirmy, only different. Like the bunk beds were like bunk beds, only different.

Bleeding Hearts

Another shipment of TVs came in the next day. The guys who'd knocked off the TV store had hit the very same store again. They'd gone back for what wouldn't fit in their truck the first night. Nobody in their right mind would hit the same store two nights in a row, but Uncle Barney said these guys weren't in their right minds. They were a couple of wackos from Revere.

Jimmy had his hands full trying to sell all those TVs. He had to move them fast 'cause he was afraid the Snitch might get wind of the TV showroom in our bedroom and send somebody from the office to check it out. I kept hounding Jimmy to take me to see Susan, but it was a week before we headed over to Hank's. By that time, I had grown attached to the snow globe and didn't want to give it up. But I reminded myself if God could sacrifice Jesus, his only kid, I could surely give up my snow globe.

We stopped by the house that wasn't Hank's anymore to check on the lawn, but nobody was home. Jimmy watered some brown spots, complaining all the while that ever since Hank had been given the heave-ho the place had gone to hell.

We left Hank's house that wasn't his and made only one stop, at the bookie joint, before we ended up at Hank's store. The place was a madhouse. Guys were getting ready for hunting season and everybody wanted Hank to fix their guns.

Hank was in a lousy mood. He said he was up to his goddamn ears in broken guns. Jimmy said he knew how Hank felt. He was up to his goddamn eyeballs with his own baloney.

I scanned the crowd of men but didn't see Susan.

"How's it going with that Shirley?" Jimmy asked Hank.

"Don't ever mention that broad again," snapped Hank. "I'm done with her, but she won't take the hint. She found out I was at a boat show and just showed up. Do me a goddamn favor, Greek, and don't fix me up with any more nutty broads."

"Hey, she was just something to tap, just a quick piece of action."

"I can get my own action," snarled Hank. "With no strings attached."

"All right, all right," said Jimmy. "Take it easy. I didn't know she was loco. I'm sorry, OK? Shirley shoulda known—it's her fault. So, where's the kid anyway? Where's Susan?"

"She's gone up to that girls' college. She's outta my goddamn hair."

My heart sank. I wondered if God was punishing me for wanting to keep the snow globe.

"When will she be back?" I blurted out.

"Who the hell knows? Thanksgiving, Christmas," barked Hank.

"Shut up. Don't bug Hank," ordered Jimmy.

He threw his arm around Hank.

"Cheer up, Polack," Jimmy said. "It's almost hunting season."

A beefy guy standing nearby grumbled, "They oughta make it hunting season on coons. And I don't mean raccoons."

A few guys laughed. Hank and Jimmy joined in.

"I don't know about you," the beefy guy said, "but I'm sick to death of listening to that Martin Luther King. I have a dream he shuts the hell up."

"I have a dream he gets his black ass thrown in jail for firing up those niggers," laughed the beefy guy's buddy.

"I have a dream somebody plugs his black ass with buckshot," cracked Hank, getting into the spirit of things.

My stomach started to hurt. I didn't like what they were saying.

I wasn't sure why all the hunters seemed to have it in for this Martin Luther King. I'd just seen him on TV a few nights before and he seemed OK. It was August 28, Jimmy's birthday. I'd made Jimmy a birthday card that showed me hitting myself on the noggin with a hammer. Above the picture I'd written *I'm nuts about you*. The card was propped up on top of the new TV set we'd gotten from Uncle Barney. The news was on and Martin Luther King was giving a speech. It seemed like a million people were cheering him on. From what I could tell, he was saying he had a dream people wouldn't go at each other's throats all the time. He had a dream they would live in peace and little white kids could play ring-around-the-rosy with little black kids.

Jimmy said he had a dream all right, a goddamn pipe dream, and made me change the channel. He was in a bad mood. He said now that he was thirty-five, the best years of his frickin' life were over.

And here we were, a few days later, and he was still in a bad mood. All the hunters at Hank's seemed to be in a bad mood. They kept getting more and more fired up about the Martin Luther King "situation."

"Somebody oughta drop an A-bomb on him and all those bleeding hearts," shouted the beefy guy.

"Don't count on Kennedy to do it. He's another bleeding heart," shouted another guy, even louder.

"My daughter's a goddamn bleeding heart," said Hank. "And so is her goddamn mother."

"Then it's a good thing you're not married to her anymore," the beefy guy said.

"Shut your frickin' mouth," barked Hank, and walked away. He went into the back room and slammed the door, leaving all the men standing there with their broken guns.

"I have a dream that frickin' Doris never shows her painted face around here again," spat Jimmy before he grabbed his guns and headed back to the car.

On the way home, I asked Jimmy what a bleeding heart was.

He swerved around a slow car and I had to wait for his answer.

"A bleeding heart is a do-gooder," he finally said. "A person who wants the whole damn world to get along even though since time began people in different tribes have been clobbering one another."

"Why?" I asked. "Why are people always clobbering one another?"

"Because we're animals," he said. "Wild animals. Animals fight each other. That's nature. You put a tiger in a pen with Bambi, the tiger's gonna have Bambi for breakfast. The tiger and Bambi ain't gonna have a goddamn Sunday picnic. If you're stronger, you dominate. The bleeding hearts want a perfect world where everybody gets along. If I'm a tiger, they want to pass laws telling me I have to picnic with Bambi. They want to make the strong animal weak so the weak animal doesn't get a goddamn inferiority complex. They want me to share my jungle with Bambi. Well, it ain't gonna happen. Bambi better move outta my jungle and into the woods where he belongs so he has a shot to live out his life, far away from me."

"What about boys and girls?" I asked. "Boys are stronger than girls, so wouldn't it be better if boys went to one school and girls to another so girls wouldn't get clobbered by boys?"

I was thinking about a particular boy in my class, a kid everyone called Billy from the Projects. He had bombarded me with snowballs all last winter. Sometimes he threw ice balls and they hurt like hell. Shirley had told me that Billy from the Projects hurt me because he liked me and didn't know how else to show it. That seemed idiotic, but Shirley said that I would understand it when I got older. In the meantime, I was angling to be sent to an all girls' school, especially now that I'd heard Susan was going to one.

But Jimmy wasn't taking the bait.

"Don't be a numbskull," he said. "Separating boys and girls isn't natural. That's what the crazy Catholics do. You wanna be a crazy Catholic? You wanna be taught by a bunch of penguins?"

"No," I said, knowing that was the right answer even though it was a lie.

"But, you're right about one thing," he continued. "The female animal is weaker than the male animal. They're the weaker sex. And not just 'cause they're smaller. They're mentally weaker too. Unstable. Like that Shirley that's driving Hank nuts or that Doris he was married to. Doris will probably go off her rocker out in KooKooLand once it sinks in how tough she's gonna have it without Hank around. Women go nutty without a man to keep their head screwed on straight."

"They do?"

"Sure. Remember *Whatever Happened to Baby Jane?* and *Sunset Boulevard?* Those women went loco without a man."

"What about men? Do they go loco without women?"

"Are you kidding? They got no aggravation. They got it made."

I bit my lip to keep from crying like a girl.

"I hate being a girl," I blurted out. "I wish I was a boy."

"I wish you were too, kiddo," he said, bopping me on the head. "But what're we gonna do? Them's the breaks."

When we got back home Jimmy got right on the phone to try to move those last few TVs and I ran up to my room. I took out the snow globe and shook it over and over, watching the snow fall all around the two girls on the beach. It made me feel better. It made me feel like being a girl wasn't so terrible. I told myself girls could have their own fun without mean boys throwing snowballs at them. I decided I'd give the snow globe to Susan for Christmas and that that would be even better, 'cause she would love it more than any of her other presents. I would have the best Christmas ever, even without our stolen Christmas ornaments. I told myself someday . . . someday . . . those girls on the beach would be Susan and me, out there in KooKooLand. A place where it never snowed, so nobody threw any frickin' snowballs.

Rats

The night before school started, Jimmy decided to take Virginia and me to the dump to shoot some rats. He wanted to get in a little target practice before hunting season began. And he thought we oughta blow off some steam before we got stuck behind our desks all day like a couple of pencil pushers.

On the way to the dump, we stopped to pick up Boozer Eddie. Boozer did landscaping jobs with Jimmy and he was crazy about rat shooting.

Jimmy pulled up in front of Boozer's house and waved his .22 out the window. Boozer came out with a half-gnawed pork chop in one hand and his .22 in the other. Boozer's wife, May, ran after him.

"Finish your dinner. Let that crazy Greek wait!" May shouted.

"Shut up or I'll belt you one!" Boozer yelled at her as he jumped into the front seat.

"Hey, May, we'll bring you back a nice fat rat you can fry up for breakfast," Jimmy called out, emphasizing the word *fat* since May was big as a house.

"I'll feed it to you, Norris. Right up your ass!" May screeched.

"Your wife's got a mouth as big as her keister," Jimmy said to Boozer.

"Don't I know it," laughed Boozer. "Let's get the hell outta here."

Jimmy peeled rubber.

As Boozer finished his pork chop, he told us what he'd been up to.

"I shot eight squirrels today with a slingshot," he crowed, his milky-blue eyes all bright and glossy. "Right outside my house. You oughta seen 'em drop outta those trees."

He made a corkscrew motion with his pork chop and whistled loudly to create a sound effect for the falling squirrels.

"I skinned one alive. Boy, did it squeal."

I felt my stomach clench. Virginia scrunched her eyes closed.

We'd come to the conclusion that Boozer was a nutcase some time ago, when May had called Jimmy all worked up because Boozer had strung their cat up by its front paws. Apparently Boozer had been trying to train the cat to walk on its hind legs. but the cat was not getting the hang of it. So Boozer tied ropes around the cat's front paws and hoisted it up. The cat had flipped out and hurt itself and May said there was blood all over the place.

"He killed the goddamn cat?" bellowed Jimmy, sounding like he might string up Boozer.

May said no, the cat was alive, but his paws were all skinned up.

Jimmy rolled his eyes like he thought May was getting hysterical.

"All right, all right. I'll come over. I'll fix him up good as new," Jimmy the Cut Man assured her.

He hung up and proceeded to gather together alcohol, a needle and thread, and some Gold Bond Medicated Powder.

Shirley, Virginia, and I stood there, horrified.

"Boozer's sick," choked Shirley.

"He's mean," I wailed.

"He's a cat torturer," moaned Virginia.

"Boozer's OK," Jimmy snapped. "He got a little carried away with training the cat, that's all. He loves that cat same as I love Sylvester. So shut your traps."

We shut our traps. We were stuck with Boozer.

Once we got to the dump, Jimmy mixed up some highballs and we waited for the sun to go down. The stink of the place made me feel like barfing, so I breathed through my mouth. To kill time before the rats came out, Jimmy set up some cans for us to practice on. I had gotten to be a pretty good shot. I blasted away some Snow's Clam Chowder, Campbell's Cream of Mushroom, and Green Giant Niblets corn. Pretty soon my ears were ringing like a pinball machine. I was afraid I might go deaf, but earplugs were out of the question since Jimmy said they were for sissies.

When it started to get dark the rats began to slink out of their hiding places. Jimmy raked the piles of garbage with a flashlight and Boozer blasted away. Then Boozer held the flashlight and Jimmy blasted away. I kept score so they'd know who had killed the most rats and who could lord it over the other one. Sometimes it was hard to decide whether to count a rat as dead if it was still stumbling around, but usually I gave the shooter the benefit of the doubt.

Finally, Jimmy passed his gun to me. My hands started to shake. It wasn't that I felt bad about shooting rats. I didn't. Rats weren't cute like squirrels. They didn't frolic through the treetops or nibble peanuts you left for them on the windowsill. They didn't have a TV cartoon made about them like Rocky the Flying Squirrel did. Rats were what YaYa would call filthy rodents. They slunk around at night like criminals. The only reason my hands were shaking was 'cause I wanted to prove I was the best goddamn rat-killer around.

But I was so anxious I couldn't shoot straight. To be good at killing you had to be relaxed. Loosey-goosey. Jimmy had taught me that. Then you had to picture the thing you wanted dead as stone-cold dead already. But I just couldn't do that. Those rats were as alive as I was.

I didn't manage to blow away one rat that night.

"Gimme my gun back, Helen Keller," Jimmy barked. "You're wasting my ammo."

I handed over the .22.

Jimmy turned to Virginia, who was hanging off to the side, trying to be inconspicuous.

"What about you, Four-Eyes?" he asked. That was his latest nickname for her now that she was wearing glasses—or, at least, wearing them when he was around.

"I don't wanna waste any more of your ammo," she replied. "You always say I'm a lousy shot."

"You are. You're both lousy shots. You got none of my genes, that's for sure."

I heard Virginia mutter, "I hope not," under her breath.

I gave her a look and quickly went back to scorekeeping.

Jimmy beat Boozer like he always did. Boozer said I was probably fixing the score 'cause I was Jimmy's daughter.

"I'm no scammer. He won fair and square," I insisted.

Boozer said next time he'd keep score himself.

Jimmy plopped the fattest rat into a burlap bag.

"Give this to May. You'll really get a rise outta her."

"Oh boy," said Boozer, forgetting all about losing. "I know just where to put it."

"Where?" asked Jimmy.

"Under her pillow," Boozer laughed. He began to sing one of Shirley's favorite songs.

Sweet dreams of you
Every night I go through . . .

"I'd give anything to see the look on her kisser," said Jimmy as he threw the rat into the backseat next to where I was sitting. I scrunched closer to Virginia.

The ride back to Boozer's seemed to take forever even though Jimmy was hauling ass. He slugged on his highball and talked about other times he was so loaded he couldn't remember driving home.

"Even half-cocked, I got the instincts of a homing pigeon," he insisted.

"What do you think would happen if you got a homing pigeon drunk?" asked Boozer. "Would it still be able to find its way home?"

"A homing pigeon wouldn't drink booze, numbskull."

"You could prop open its beak and pour some down its throat," suggested Boozer.

"Why waste good booze on a frickin' pigeon?" asked Jimmy.

Finally, we got to Boozer's.

Boozer stumbled out of the car.

"Hand me the bag," he said to me.

I froze.

"What're you, deaf?" asked Jimmy.

Actually, I was only half-deaf due to the ringing in my ears.

"Or maybe you're a fraidy cat," taunted Jimmy. "A fraidy cat of a little rat. Fraidy cat. Fraidy cat."

"I am not," I snapped. I grabbed the bag and quickly shoved it at Boozer.

Boozer took his good-looking time before taking the rat from me. He had a crooked little smile on his face. I could see he was enjoying making me squirm. Jimmy's gun was right next to me and I felt like shooting his crooked lips right off his face. Unlike with the dump rats, I didn't think I'd miss.

Finally, Boozer took the rat and brought it into the house.

When we got home I wanted to take a bath, but Jimmy said it was too god-damn late. So I lay in my top bunk listening to Squirmy Two's angry chattering and still smelling the stink of the dump in my hair. I prayed to God to make the smell disappear by morning. I didn't want my new fourth-grade teacher getting a whiff of me and sticking me in the back row with the morons.

Virginia was in the same boat. Tomorrow was her first day of high school and I knew she wanted to make a good impression even though she acted like she didn't give a flying you-know-what. Her voice wafted up from the bottom bunk.

"I stink," she moaned.

"No you don't," I said, trying to make her feel better. "It's just me."

Fall Back

"And what did you do over your summer vacation?"

Miss Morrissey was smiling at me and I was smiling back, trying to ignore Billy from the Projects who was picking his schnoz with his new pencil and rubbing his boogers on my desk.

"I went to Old Orchard Beach," I replied sweetly, knowing better than to include *Blood Feast*, rat shooting, or the Combat Zone in my answer. "My dad raced me on the beach and taught me how to ride the waves."

"He sounds like a very nice father. What does he do for a living?"

"He does landscaping at the North End," I chirped. "I help him sometimes. I took care of Hank Piasecny's lawn. He owns a gun shop. He's loaded."

Miss Morrissey frowned and I knew I'd gotten a bit carried away.

"Well, I'm glad you got some fresh air. Being outdoors is very important, children. President Kennedy wants us all to be active, healthy Americans."

I nodded and smiled without showing any of my Dracula teeth.

I already knew Miss Morrissey was big on healthy stuff. Virginia had had her for a teacher when she was in fourth grade and had given me the lowdown.

"Please stand, children," she ordered us that first morning. Then she started reeling off a list of breakfast foods. "Juice or fruit? Eggs or cereal? Ham, bacon, or sausage? Toast or English muffin? Milk or cottage cheese?"

You were supposed to have had one from each food group. If you had, you could sit your ass down. If not, you had to remain standing and tell Miss Morrissey where you had screwed up. By the third day of school, everybody had got the hang of it and just sat their ass down even if they'd had a Devil Dog for breakfast. All except for Billy from the Projects.

"I had coffee and a jelly doughnut," he told Miss Morrissey every day, even though it sent her into a conniption fit.

"Just sit down, for cripes' sake," I whispered to him on day three.

"Mind your beeswax," he shot back, "or I'll beat you up."

"You try any baloney this year," I hissed, "and my father'll beat *you* up."

Billy from the Projects suddenly looked like he was quaking in his Buster

Browns. Everybody in the projects knew Jimmy had punched a punk that summer and threatened him with his .22. The punk had been carving his initials into the tree in front of our house—one of the only elm trees left in Elmwood Gardens—and Jimmy had to teach him a lesson 'cause the boy had no goddamn respect for the great outdoors.

Billy from the Projects sat his ass down from then on and pretended he'd had a healthy breakfast.

But it wasn't just breakfast Miss Morrissey got on our case about. We were supposed to be in bed by eight thirty and sleep with the window open. And on Mondays she asked if we'd changed our underpants.

Before the first week was out I'd decided Miss Morrissey was pretty dippy.

But I didn't care 'cause at least she liked me. Papou didn't even have to grease her wheels with a case of Orange Crush. Once she heard from my third-grade teacher that I wasn't a dummkopf, she wouldn't leave me alone. She kept me after school to hang her holiday decorations and to listen to her stories about the glorious cruise she took to Cuba before the evil Commies took it over.

And fourth grade didn't turn out to be so hard after all. I could usually do my homework in under ten minutes. I'd time myself with Jimmy's stopwatch and kept a running list of my times.

One night Shirley watched me breeze through my homework. She said she wished she coulda followed the principal's advice at the end of the previous year and skipped me a grade. But Jimmy had told the buttinsky principal that when a horse is going good that's no time to bump him up in class. I might get all shook up and lose my appetite like Victory Bound when he was moved to another track. Hell no, Jimmy had said. He wanted to keep me back with my class.

"No Caspar Milquetoast pencil-pushing do-gooder is going to tell me how to run my own family," Jimmy had said to Shirley when they returned from the meeting with the principal. "Who's the boss around here anyway—me or him?"

"You are. You're the boss," Shirley had replied stiffly.

"Really? Gee, you don't sound too convincing."

"You're the boss!" Shirley had repeated, trying to sound more enthusiastic.

"Wow—what a performance. Give Ava Gardner here an Academy Award."

"Jimmy, please, don't start—"

"Start what? I'm not starting anything. I'm just trying to get the facts straight. I'm trying to see where I stand in this family. 'Cause you seem to think another man knows better about raising my kid than I do."

"You know best, Jimmy. You always know best."

"That's right. Just like the TV show—*Father Knows Best*. And don't you forget it."

Then he turned to me.

"See what you did? You're always causing trouble around here. If it wasn't for you, things would be smooth sailing."

"I'm sorry," I mumbled, not sure what I was apologizing for.

"Now you've made me late," Jimmy barked, and took off for the track.

"Thank God for the horses," Shirley groaned as she poured herself a highball. I stuffed my mouth with Chuckles and we snuck on a Red Sox game. Watching forbidden baseball with Shirley had turned me into a fan too.

But, unfortunately, Jimmy's luck with the horses turned that fall. Victory Bound ran one more good race and then came up lame. Everybody told Jimmy the horse should be sent to the glue factory, but Jimmy said Victory Bound had so much goddamn heart he might come back. Shirley told me that the horse was eating us out of house and home. She had to work longer hours to try to pay for him. Most of the time she wasn't even home before I left for school.

Jimmy worked longer hours too, at the bookie joint. He started making bigger bets, looking to make a killing so he could buy another racehorse. He pictured a whole stable of Victory Bounds running under the Norris banner. Then if one was going bad, the others could help make up for it. He explained it all to me and it made sense.

In order to make a big killing, Jimmy needed to come up with more dough to bet. Uncle Barney had a bunch of air conditioners and Jimmy thought he could move them, no problem. Virginia and I helped Jimmy carry the heavy boxes up to our bedroom as he barked orders at us to "keep her steady" and "steer to the left" as if each air conditioner were a World War II battleship. He stacked the boxes up to the ceiling.

But it turned out Jimmy couldn't move any of those air conditioners. Instead, after a few weeks he decided to take one to a pawnshop. He lured me to go along by saying he'd be stopping at Hank's old house on the way back. Hank had asked Jimmy to trim a few trees there before the frost set in. Jimmy said Susan might be home visiting from college for the weekend. He told me Susan had been made head of her school newspaper and had a poem that was going to be published in a book. I couldn't wait to congratulate her. I decided it was the perfect time to give her the snow globe instead of waiting till Christmas.

On the way to the pawnshop Jimmy seemed down in the dumps. He said he was glad I had come along 'cause he wanted some company. He felt Shirley was abandoning him 'cause she worked so goddamn much. He said Virginia was a dopey teen-rager with her head in the clouds and he was afraid she was turning boy crazy on him. He said I was the only female in the family he could rely on and it was a damn shame I hadn't been a boy.

The whole conversation made me down in the dumps too. I was glad when we arrived at our destination, and leapt out of the car so fast Jimmy didn't even have to tell me to "Hop to it, Dracula."

The pawnshop was crammed to the gills with junk. The owner seemed to know Jimmy pretty well.

"You crazy Greek," he laughed. "Who the hell's gonna buy an air conditioner in October?"

"Smart people. People who don't wanna get soaked buying one in June, that's who," replied Jimmy. "Just take a look at it, you cheap Frog." He had lugged the sample specimen into the shop and was prying open the box. "It's brand spanking new, unlike most of the crap you got in this fleabag joint."

"I'm tellin' ya, they won't sell till summer and I got no place to store 'em."

"All right, dummkopf," Jimmy said with a shrug, closing the box back up. "I got other customers who want these babies. I was doin' you a favor, givin' you the first shot."

"What I could really use right now is more of those fancy old Christmas ornaments. You got any more of those?" asked the pawnshop owner.

I froze.

Jimmy saw my face and offered a quick explanation.

"I found some ornaments at the North End. Some mucky-muck was throwin' 'em out."

"Why would a mucky-muck be throwing out fancy Christmas ornaments?" I blurted out.

"How the hell should I know? Rich people got more stuff than they know what to do with, while the rest of us are scraping by."

"How come you didn't keep those North End ornaments for us since ours got stolen?" I fired back, trying to catch him in a big fat lie.

"Because I found 'em *before* ours got swiped and we didn't need any more frickin' Christmas ornaments. Now let's go," he snapped, lifting the air conditioner off the counter.

"Sorry," said the pawnshop owner.

"Yeah, thanks for nothing," replied Jimmy.

On the way to Hank's old house Jimmy tried to butter me up.

"I bet I know what you'd like. A nice, thick, coffee milk shake."

"Oh boy," I mumbled.

We headed over to Cremeland, which was a hop, skip, and a jump from the Valley Street jail. As we drove past the jail I wondered if the lard-ass cops were ever gonna nab Jimmy or if, like he always boasted, he was just too goddamn smart for them.

At Cremeland, Jimmy sent me up to the window to buy a coffee milk shake. As usual, we had to share and he drank most of it. But this time I didn't care 'cause I had a stomachache. I felt like puking into the milk shake and passing it back to him.

When we got to Hank's old house it was dark and empty. Susan was nowhere around. I wondered whether she was ever supposed to be there. I wondered whether Jimmy had concocted the whole thing about her being there just to get me to go along.

As I watched him trim the trees, swaying on his rickety old ladder, I imagined him falling and breaking his frickin' neck and me being free at last, free at last.

When we got home, I helped him lug the air conditioner back up to my bedroom. He shoved it on top of the other air conditioners and then took off for the track. I climbed up on my wobbly bunk bed and lay down. I balanced the snow globe on my forehead and scrunched my eyes closed as tight as I could. I was hoping Susan could feel me thinking about her, or that I could read her mind like the swami I had once seen at a county fair. I was hoping to see what the future had in store for us.

But nothing came to me. Everything was quiet.

That's when I realized something was wrong. There was no sound coming from Squirmy Two's cage. No creaking of her hamster wheel. No angry chattering. No scratching of her nasty little claws.

I looked down and saw Squirmy Two lying in her cage. Her tongue was hanging out and any dummkopf could tell she was dead. Immediately I wondered if it was my fault. Had I killed Squirmy Two? Had I neglected to feed her 'cause I was afraid to go near her cage? Had she died of loneliness 'cause I never played with her? Had she died 'cause I wished Jimmy dead?

She was mean and I didn't like her, but even so, I started to cry.

Sufferin' Succotash

Hunting season was upon us. But even that didn't seem to cheer Jimmy up. Hank had invited Jimmy up to his hunting camp near Canada to get away from it all and I was hoping he'd go. It was like a vacation for me when he did. I could watch all my favorite TV shows, the ones Jimmy had banned. Shows like *The Adventures of Ozzie & Harriet*, in which the father wore a necktie, or, as Jimmy called it, a noose. But Jimmy had a million reasons that year why he didn't feel like going to Hank's camp. It was too goddamn far. The other hunters who were going were a bunch of ding-dongs. And Jimmy always got stuck cooking for the ding-dongs and butchering their deer since he was the best goddamn cook and the best goddamn butcher in the bunch.

So Jimmy stayed put.

Then he regretted that he'd stayed put and felt even worse.

He became convinced he was dying. At first, he thought he had spinal meningitis and had me and Virginia tap on his spine to see if it hurt. When that didn't pan out, he thought he probably had the Big C. So he dragged me with him to see Dr. C, who had finally gotten his license back. Dr. C told him he was sick all right, sick in the head, and gave him some tranquilizers—black-and-green capsules called Librium—that Jimmy washed down with his highballs. But they didn't seem to make a lick of difference.

He tried watching some of his favorite TV shows, *The Three Stooges* and Sylvester and Tweety cartoons, hoping to cheer himself up. He made me watch with him 'cause he said only wackos laugh alone. Normally, every time Sylvester said "sufferin' succotash," we would both crack up. But not this time. Instead, Jimmy just sat there pointing his .22 at Tweety and pretending to blow him away.

When cartoons didn't work, Jimmy decided eating some of his favorite foods might make him feel better.

"Maybe if I had some brains . . . ," he said to Shirley.

So Shirley fried up a whole mess o' crispy brains. YaYa had taught Shirley how to make all of Jimmy's favorite foods. Glands. Intestines. Spleens. Stuff normal Americans chucked out and, as far as I could tell, only Greeks and movie cannibals like Fuad Ramses ate. Jimmy kidded YaYa that Shirley's brains made hers look sick, but YaYa didn't think that was funny. She said Jimmy's fresh mouth made *her* sick and that his two brothers beat him by a mile.

But it didn't really matter whose brains Jimmy ate. He said the tranquilizers had screwed up his goddamn taste buds and everything just tasted like spit.

All this time Jimmy was miserable I was dying to sneak back to church. I wanted to say a few Hail Marys to make Jimmy feel better in order to make up for wishing him dead. But I didn't think I could risk it. In his miserable state, if he caught me going to church, there was no telling what he might do. So instead I coughed up fifty cents for a collection Tina said the church was taking to give Thanksgiving turkeys to poor people. It hurt to give away so much dough, but Tina said God would like me better, so I did it.

With less money to spend on candy, I was really looking forward to Halloween. Jimmy said I didn't need a costume that year, I could go as Dracula, and waved his fang fingers in front of his mouth.

"He doesn't mean to be mean," insisted Shirley. And she went out and bought me the prettiest princess costume she could find to make up for it.

I couldn't wait to show off that costume at the school Halloween party, but when the day came, Jimmy kept me home to go duck hunting with him. He said I wasn't gonna be learning anything that day and we'd be back in plenty of time for me to go trick-or-treating. He said trick-or-treating should be enough Halloween festivities for any person for one day.

Shirley hugged me extra tight before I left. I knew she was worried about me going with him. But she said she couldn't make a fuss about it 'cause he was sick in the head right now and might go off the deep end if anybody got on his case.

"We have to act like nothing's wrong and do what he says and make sure he knows he's the man of the house. That's what Dr. C says. OK, honey?" asked Shirley.

"But what if he wants me to race him across the highway or swim in the freezing ocean or eat a dead duck's eyeball?"

"He's not *that* crazy," she assured me, but I could tell from her fake smile she wasn't that sure.

"Don't worry," I said, reassuring her instead. "I'll be OK."

I raced Jimmy to the car and lost by a mile and we headed off to kill some ducks.

We got to the coast in record time and hunkered down in the canoe at

Norris Point. That's what the wardens had dubbed that particular jut of land. They called it that 'cause Jimmy owned the goddamn place. He shot as many ducks as he pleased, screw their kill quotas, and they could never catch him.

I'm like the Road Runner, Jimmy said. I always get away.

Meep meep, dummkopfs.

The wind was howling in my ears. My eyes and nose were dripping frozen tears and snot. I wiped them both on my sleeve when Jimmy wasn't looking. While we were waiting for some ducks to swoop in, Jimmy had a few highballs and asked me if I thought my mother was cheating on him like no-good Doris had cheated on poor Hank.

"If you ever see a guy in the house, you have to report it to me. You're like my deputy. Get it? I'm deputizing you," he said.

I nodded, not wanting the job.

Then I thought, I hope she is cheating. I hope she leaves you for a North End doctor who isn't sick in the head and who takes me to church. Better yet, I hope she moves to KooKooLand with Doris, Susan, and me and marries Ozzie Nelson after he divorces Harriet.

"You can't trust any woman," Jimmy continued. "They're all as flighty as these ducks."

He began luring the ducks to him with his duck call.

Quack quack quack.

"All women are capable of cheating."

Quack quack quack.

"It's in their genes."

Quack quack quack.

"Even YaYa cheated on Papou when I was a kid."

Quack quack quack.

"Poor Papou never knew. All these years I've kept it on a stone wall."

I wasn't sure if what he was saying was true or if he was just wacko. YaYa seemed as scared of Papou as I was. I couldn't picture her cheating on him.

Fortunately the ducks began to fly in, drawn by Jimmy's quacking.

"Come to Daddy, Daffy Ducks," he whispered as he picked up his rifle.

Before the day was over, he had shot a mess of ducks. I tracked them down wearing Jimmy's waders, which were ten sizes too big for me. All except for one. I searched and searched for the last one but couldn't find it. Jimmy said the poor duck was out there suffering because I was a dummkopf, and sent me out to look some more.

But that goddamn duck had disappeared and I cursed it and wished I could do the same.

Finally, Jimmy called me back and grabbed the waders from me. He sloshed around for a long time, but he couldn't find the duck either. He came back, disgusted.

"It's all your fault that poor thing is in agony," he spat. "I shoulda shot you instead."

Guts

When we got home, Jimmy and I plucked the ducks over a garbage can on the front stoop. Then Jimmy gutted the ducks in the kitchen sink and I burned off their pinfeathers on the stove. The smell of burning duck flesh filled the apartment. It was getting late and I was getting worried I'd miss Halloween altogether. Trick-or-treaters were already banging on our door. Virginia passed out some penny candy that Shirley had bought from Uncle Barney, and Jimmy gave the kids a real scare by waving some real guts at them.

Finally, all the ducks were dressed and Jimmy let me go get dressed. I leapt up the stairs two at a time, afraid all the good candy would be gone by the time I got out there. I yanked on my princess costume, ripping one of the sleeves in the process and calling myself a dummkopf. Normally I would've woken up Shirley and gotten her to safety-pin the sleeve, but there was no time to waste.

I ran into the bathroom and tried to wash the dried blood off my hands. But the blood was caked under my bitten nails and didn't want to come off.

Then it occurred to me. With my ripped sleeve and bloody hands I could be a different kind of princess. A killer princess. That was my costume. That's who I told myself I was.

Virginia handed me an old pillowcase and took one herself even though she said she was too old to trick-or-treat.

And off we went into the night. We ventured out of the projects into the neighborhoods with real houses. Houses with cozy front porches lit by smiling jack-o'-lanterns. Houses where the good loot was.

Fortunately, there was still lots of candy out there. And cinnamony cider and homemade doughnuts and creamy hot chocolate, all handed out by ladies in frilly aprons and men in woolly sweaters who looked like they belonged on *Leave It to Beaver*. I trick-or-treated like a maniac, racing from door to door to door screaming *Trick or treat, smell my feet, give me something good to eat* as fast as I could, so I could get on to the next house, and the next. My ratty old pillowcase got so full, it started to rip.

"Oh no," I moaned. "Some old bat musta slipped a couple of goddamn apples in there." I rooted around for the offending healthy snacks, found them, and tossed them into the bushes.

But the damage had been done. My pillowcase had sprung a leak.

"Why don't you put your candy in with mine?" suggested Virginia.

"No way, stealer," I shot back.

"Well then, we better get home before you lose it all," said Virginia. "Besides, Hitler's gonna kill us if we stay out much later."

So we turned and headed back to the projects. I had to cradle the pillowcase in my arms all the way home. Like Hansel and Gretel, I left a trail behind me.

But there was still plenty in the pillowcase when I got home. I emptied my loot onto my bed and organized it into candy groups. I stuffed my face with Sugar Daddies, Sugar Babies, Baby Ruths, 3 Musketeers, candy corn, candy cigarettes, Turkish Taffy, Charleston Chews, Good & Plenty, Good & Fruity, and Chuckles. I ate so much candy my stomach felt like one big Sugar Baby. Suddenly I realized all those Chuckles, Good & Fruity, Good & Plenty, Charleston Chews, Turkish Taffys, candy cigarettes, candy corn, 3 Musketeers, Baby Ruths, Sugar Babies, and Sugar Daddies were on their way back out.

Dizzy with nausea, I scrambled down from the top bunk. The swaying bed made me feel even worse. I crept down the stairs and stumbled out the back door into the night.

Dropping to my knees on the dewy grass littered with candy wrappers, I puked out my whole frickin' Halloween haul.

And nothing tasted sweet coming back out.

No Thanks

T he next day I peeled the ghosts and goblins off of Miss Morrissey's class-room windows. My second-favorite holiday was over, but at least we were in the home stretch heading toward my favorite holiday, Christmas.

First, though, we had to get through Jimmy's least favorite holiday. Veter-ans Day was his least favorite 'cause he said merchant mariners had been given a raw deal. The government didn't consider them veterans even though more of them died in World War II than any other group of servicemen. Jimmy said the day made him feel like plugging every government pencil pusher in Wash-ington and strangling them with an American flag. But usually he just went hunting instead.

After peeling the battleships and soldiers off of Miss Morrissey's windows, I stuck up the Pilgrims and Injuns. As far as I was concerned, Thanksgiving really only had pie going for it. Otherwise there was just turkey that, according to Jimmy, was dry as an old turd. No self-respecting Greek would eat it, he said, but since YaYa and Papou were trying to be like Yankees, we had to go over to their house and pretend.

Every year, while Jimmy and Papou handicapped the horses, Shirley and YaYa cooked till they were red in the face. Then YaYa would set the table and wouldn't let anyone help. Normally her fancy gold dishes resided in a locked cabinet and you spent the rest of the year admiring them behind a glass door. But on Thanksgiving and Greek Easter the dishes came out and YaYa was a nervous wreck. Jimmy would snatch a plate off the table and toss it in the air like a Frisbee just to drive her nuts.

That year I was really dreading Thanksgiving. Ever since Halloween I'd had an awful ache in my guts and never felt like eating. For days I plotted how I could make an entire Thanksgiving dinner disappear from my plate without Jimmy or Papou seeing that I wasn't eating and force-feeding me.

I was worried sick and feeling sicker by the day when a maniac killed the president.

Miss Morrissey broke down crying when she told us. And then most of the kids in the class broke down crying. And I knew somewhere Susan was crying and Tina and her mother and the pope and all the Catholics in New England. I wanted to be like them, to be crying right along with Susan. But I just sat there, confused. I didn't know the president. I didn't think about him constantly the way Tina did. He didn't even seem as real to me as Howdy Doody. I had bawled my head off when Howdy went off the air a few years before. I had even bawled my head off for mean old Squirmy Two. But somehow I couldn't squeeze out even one lousy tear for the president.

Cry, dummkopf, cry, I ordered myself.

I put my head down on my desk and pretended to bawl so Miss Morrissey wouldn't think I was a heartless heathen.

Through my phony sobs, I heard her say we were getting dismissed from school.

I coulda jumped for joy. My stomach was killing me and now I had an excuse to go home and crawl into bed.

Or that's what I thought, but I should've known better.

"I don't want any blubbering or bellyaching about any president going on in this house," Jimmy barked at Shirley and Tina's mother, who were sitting at the kitchen table doing just that when I got home.

"Men die every day, real men on merchant ships. Kennedy's just one man, no better than any other, and worse 'cause he was a bleeding heart."

He looked right at Tina's mother and smirked.

"Now he's a bleeding, bleeding heart."

"God should strike you dead!" shouted Tina's mother. She jumped up and ran out our front door.

"God didn't protect the president," he called after her. "You remember that the next time you're in church listening to a bunch of Catholic mumbo jumbo."

As I watched Tina's mother run across the street, I knew she wouldn't ever be bringing me to church again and I was probably going straight to hell.

After she left and for most of the weekend, Jimmy took a powder. There was nothing on TV except people talking about the president. No Sylvester cartoons. No Three Stooges.

"Frick the president. And frick that idiot box," said Jimmy.

He grabbed his rifle and the Racing Form and slammed the door on his way out.

"He's the only person in the whole world who isn't miserable about the president," sobbed Virginia.

"Maybe he's right," I said. "The president is just one person and people die all the time. What about those women the Boston Strangler killed? Don't you feel bad about them too?"

"You're just like him!" Virginia shouted at me. Then she grabbed her coat and took a powder too.

Shirley went up to her bedroom and I could hear her blubbering. I made her a highball and brought it up. She hugged me tight until I squirmed away. She told me she was exhausted and had better get a few hours of sleep before work. She didn't wanna nod off and get her hand mangled in one of the machines like had happened to somebody else on her shift.

"Maybe they'll cancel work 'cause of the president," I suggested, hoping she'd stay home and I could finally work up the courage to tell her about my stomachache.

Shirley looked panicked.

"God, I hope not. We need the money," she said.

She took a big slug of the highball.

"Life goes on, I guess."

"Why didn't God protect the president?" I suddenly asked. "Does that mean there's no God?"

Shirley guzzled down the rest of the highball.

"Maybe God was asleep, honey. Just like Mommy needs her sleep."

I took the hint and twenty-three skidooed. I went back downstairs and turned on the idiot box. I sprawled in front of it, holding my aching belly. Unlike Jimmy, I couldn't get enough of watching people be miserable about the president. Watching other people's pain seemed to take my mind off my own.

Most of all, I wanted to know everything about the maniac who pulled the trigger. Was he big and hairy? Small and weaselly?

Did he have any pip-squeaks like me?

When they finally showed the guy, it turned out he was small and weaselly and looked like a million guys I'd seen hanging around Hank's. I wondered if he was a hunter too. I wondered if he'd murdered the president for being a bleeding heart or just for the fun of it.

The next day another maniac shot the first maniac.

"Everybody's going kookoo!" shrieked Virginia, and it sure seemed that way.

When Jimmy came home from hunting, I told him a second maniac had plugged the first.

"Yabba dabba doo," he said. "Maybe now they'll put your cartoons back on the air."

But that didn't happen, not right away. First we had to get through the Kennedy funeral. Jimmy sure as hell wasn't gonna stick around for that. So off he went hunting again.

I sat glued to the idiot box. I searched the crowd for any glimpse of Caroline Kennedy. I tried to imagine how she must feel, having a father who was dead. I wondered if she'd ever wished him dead like I'd wished Jimmy dead. Probably not, since she was a good Catholic and I was a heathen. And, besides, her father had gotten her a pony named Macaroni and a puppy and I only had a lame racehorse that I couldn't even ride and a cat that tried to run away from home every chance he got.

After the funeral, the cartoons came back on, but I didn't feel much like laughing and neither did Jimmy.

"Nothing's funny anymore," he said.

A few days later we got dressed up and headed over to YaYa and Papou's for Thanksgiving. Well, only Shirley, Virginia, and I got dressed up. Jimmy was still wearing his hunting clothes and wouldn't change even though Shirley had starched and ironed a white shirt for him.

"I'm not wearing that cardboard straitjacket. No broad tells me what to wear. Not you, not my old lady, not Ava Gardner," he said, and Shirley quickly put away the shirt.

"You look fine," she chirped.

"Yeah, well, you don't," he said. "Change that goddamn dress. I can see your knees when you sit down. You wanna embarrass me in front of my old man?"

We waited while Shirley tried on dress after dress, demonstrating how much of her knees showed when she sat down. Finally she found something droopy and black that passed the test and we were off.

I had hidden the snow globe in my purse, hoping for the chance to finally give it to Susan. Jimmy had mentioned she was home from college and spending Thanksgiving with Hank, Doris, and Terry at Hank's old house.

"Maybe Hank and Doris will get back together," said Shirley when she heard about the Piasecny holiday plans.

"I hope not," said Jimmy. "I sure as hell hope not."

I asked Jimmy if we could stop by Hank's old house after we ate our dried-out turkey.

"We'll see how the stupid day goes," he said.

When we got to YaYa and Papou's, Jimmy drank a bunch of highballs. Like me, he didn't seem to feel much like eating. He pronounced the turkey a frickin' turkey, the sweet potatoes too sweet, and the stuffing too goddamn salty.

"Don't start," warned YaYa. "We're trying to have a nice day even though the president's dead and you're dressed like a bum."

"Nice? What's so nice about it?" Jimmy sneered, draining his highball and then shoving the glass at Shirley to make him another. "Thanksgiving . . . my ass. Thanks for nothing! What does anybody have to be thankful for? Being kicked around and then kicking the bucket?"

"Quit whining," growled Papou. "I pity your poor wife, having to listen to that."

"Go ahead, take her side. Everybody else does."

"Shut up!" bellowed Papou.

"I can say what I want. It's a free country—ha ha ha—haven't you heard?"

"Shut your mouth or I'll kick your ass!" yelled Papou.

"Try it and I'll deck you!" Jimmy yelled back, making a fist.

"You're crazy in the head! You ought to be locked up!" screamed YaYa.

"Get out of my goddamn house," boomed Papou, grabbing the carving knife slicked with turkey fat and coming at Jimmy.

Shirley choked down a scream. Virginia started to cry.

"You don't scare me! I'm not a frickin' kid anymore!" shouted Jimmy.

"Don't hurt my daddy!" I yelled at Papou.

Jimmy whipped around. I saw a flash of fist and ducked. He threw his arm around me.

"My goddamn kid sticks up for me better than you ever did," he snarled at YaYa.

"I should've killed you before you were born!" screeched YaYa.

"I wish you had," spat Jimmy.

And we got the hell outta there.

For once, I didn't have to clean my plate.

"What about going to Hank's?" I asked when we got in the car, hoping I might get repaid for standing up for Jimmy.

"Susan doesn't want to see your ugly face," he barked. And nobody said another word all the way back home.

Comfort Food

Over the next few days, Jimmy got more riled up. Any little thing could set him off.

One night when he was half-lit, he decided my bangs and Virginia's bangs were too goddamn long. He sharpened a pair of scissors on the steel rod he used on his boning knives and came at us.

"Look at me. I'm Raymond. I'm a little fairy," he said in a high-pitched voice, doing an imitation of YaYa's best friend's son, a beautician who often did YaYa's hair.

I scrunched my eyes closed, afraid he'd jab out my eyeball. He ended up hacking our bangs so short that Virginia and I thought we looked like a couple of retards. We had to scotch-tape our bangs at night to try to stretch them out.

After that, a neighbor's dog got Jimmy all worked up. Since dogs were banned in the projects, the neighbor kept the animal cooped up in his apartment. The dog was barking at night and keeping Jimmy up, and Jimmy threatened to plug the dippy mutt and its owner. Boozer Eddie said he had a better idea and came over to discuss the situation.

"Stuff some lye in a hunk of deer meat," he said. "And then feed it to the son of a bitch when the owner is gone. I did it once and it works real good. The mutt keels over foaming at the mouth like the son of a bitch ate a bar of soap. That's what the owner thinks, boo hoo, and no one knows a goddamn thing."

"The mutt's locked up all day. How you gonna get the meat to him?" asked Jimmy.

"Toss it through the mail slot," replied Boozer. "Special delivery for Big Mouth."

They both cracked up, like they were talking about a cartoon dog getting a stick of dynamite through the mail slot.

I didn't think it was funny at all. Not that I liked that yapping mutt myself. I didn't even like to walk past his apartment—I was afraid he might get loose and chew my face off. But still I didn't want to see Big Mouth poisoned. If they were gonna kill him, I didn't want the poor mutt to suffer.

Anyway, I thought they were just kidding around.

But a few days later, the barking stopped. I told myself the Snitch had probably reported the dippy dog to the office. I told myself the owner had probably brought him to a nice farm in the country like where lame ole Victory Bound was now. I told myself that wherever he was, Big Mouth was better off 'cause at least he wasn't cooped up anymore.

Once the barking stopped I prayed with all my might that Jimmy would cheer up. But God must've been napping again, 'cause things only got worse. Things got so bad Jimmy didn't even wanna go hunting.

Hank called one morning while we were having breakfast and told Jimmy to go out and shoot a few things and he'd feel better. Jimmy said the only thing he could shoot that would make him feel better was himself or Shirley. Then he hung up and shoved some breakfast dishes on the floor.

Sylvester took off like a bat outta hell.

Jimmy went to get his rifle.

Shirley yelped at Virginia and me to go upstairs to our bedroom. We were too scared to leave her down there alone and only went as far as the living room.

What had set Jimmy off was that Shirley had been late getting home from work. She said she was working overtime, but Jimmy was convinced she'd been cheating on him. Shirley told him to call Foster Grant and check the time she punched out and he told her he'd punch *her* out. But then he went ahead and called. Sure enough, the woman said Shirley had worked an hour later. But Jimmy wasn't satisfied. He said maybe Shirley had gotten the woman to lie for her. He said women were like that. He said they stuck together like two pieces of dirty flypaper.

Jimmy returned to the kitchen with his rifle. Virginia and I snuck closer and crouched in the hallway. I slipped Jimmy's rat-shooting pistol out of the closet and hid it behind my back.

I couldn't hit a rat at thirty feet, but I figured I could hit him at ten if my hand would stop shaking.

Please God, don't let me miss. Please God, don't be asleep. Please God, do something.

I edged forward and peeked into the kitchen.

Jimmy was pacing around, crunching the broken dishes under his rubber hunting boots and tracking egg yolk across the floor. The rifle dangled at his side. Shirley was huddled next to the stove.

Jimmy started ranting about *The Honeymooners*.

"You know what Ralph Kramden says. 'To the moon, Alice.'" Well, forget the moon. You're going past the moon. You're going to goddamn Pluto. You're going into the great goddamn beyond."

"Jimmy, I was working late. I promise—"

"You promise? You promise, what? Not to be a whore? How's that possible? That's not possible. 'Cause you are a whore. So how can you promise to be something you're not?"

"I'm not— I didn't—"

"Don't contradict me. Don't you ever contradict me. I'm the man in this house. Do you see another man in this frickin' house? I'm the only man in this house. I'm the only man 'cause you couldn't even give me a frickin' son. You couldn't even do that right. You're useless, you know that? Nobody would even miss you if I blew your frickin' brains out."

Right about then Hank walked through the door.

"Jesus Christ," he said when he saw Jimmy, Shirley, and the broken eggs.

"I told you I'm not going hunting," Jimmy announced.

"Gimme the goddamn rifle," Hank growled.

Jimmy shook his head, pointed the gun at Shirley.

"They're all alike. Shirley, Doris, the whole bunch of them," Jimmy said.

Hank snatched the rifle from him.

"Sit the hell down, Norris!" Hank barked like a drill sergeant.

Jimmy sat the hell down.

"Call the goddamn doctor," Hank ordered Shirley. "Can't you see he's in a bad way?"

Shirley rushed for the phone. She slid on some egg yolk and went down on one knee, then got up and made the call.

She got Dr. C on the phone and explained the situation and he said he'd be right over.

While they were waiting for Dr. C to show up, Jimmy gave Hank some advice.

"Do me a favor. Don't get another goddamn ball and chain, OK?"

"I don't want another goddamn wife," Hank replied coldly. "Now shut up."

"They just break your heart," Jimmy continued. Then he flashed a goofy grin. "Oh, I forgot. You're a mean old Polack. You got no goddamn heart."

"That's right, Greek. I got no goddamn heart."

"Goddamn Doris ground it up in a goddamn meat grinder along with your goddamn balls," said Jimmy as he rooted around in his shirt pocket for a Librium.

"Lay off those goddamn pills with the goddamn booze," Hank said.

"They don't do a goddamn thing," said Jimmy as he popped another itty-bitty black-and-green capsule.

Just then, he spotted Virginia and me peeking around the corner.

"Get in the other room or I'll belt you!" he yelled.

We scurried out of sight. Virginia sat on the couch and rocked back and forth. I stayed close in case Jimmy got a notion to snatch his rifle back from Hank and I had to rush in and shoot him.

Dr. C finally arrived, carrying his black bag.

By now, Jimmy was so worked up he was panting like Victory Bound after he won that race. Dr. C took one look at Jimmy and pulled a needle out of his bag.

"What the hell is that?" asked Jimmy.

"Medicine. Don't move," said Dr. C as he jabbed Jimmy in the arm.

"I gotta go," choked Hank, once he laid eyes on that needle. He shoved Jimmy's rifle back in the closet and took off.

Jimmy's panting started to slow down. Dr. C turned to Shirley.

"What happened?" he asked Shirley. "Did you have a fight? I told you to go easy on him."

"I did. I did go easy on him," replied Shirley, her voice sounding all tight. "I just worked a little later to pay for the horse. I thought it would make him happy."

"Happy, my ass," snorted Jimmy. Then he turned to Dr. C. "That's what I really need. A happiness pill. You got that in your little black bag?"

Dr. C grabbed Jimmy's shoulders.

"Dimitrios!" he bellowed, calling Jimmy by his Greek name. "Straighten the hell out! You're a tough, proud Greek, not some weak Yankee!"

Then he talked to Jimmy in Greek until Jimmy's head started to droop like a dead daisy.

Dr. C turned back to Shirley.

"Take him upstairs, lay him down, and then make him something nice to eat."

"Lamb and orzo," said Jimmy, slurring his words. "Not too much tomato."

"I'll make that farina cake you love, too," said Shirley, trying to sound cheerful.

Dr. C helped Jimmy up and he and Shirley each put an arm around him.

"My wife's the best goddamn Greek cook around, you know that?" Jimmy mumbled to Dr. C.

Dr. C nodded. "Maybe if I'm lucky she'll make me a farina cake too."

"Two farina cakes, coming up," chirped Shirley.

As they headed upstairs, I heard Jimmy say one more thing to Dr. C before he passed out.

"Mark my word, Doc. One day she could slip some poison into that cake. You know, like Medea. If you find me dead one day, you'll know what happened."

Worried Sick

God woke up and answered my prayers and Jimmy seemed better.
"I just had to blow off a little steam," he assured Shirley a few days later as he gave her a double-decker box of chocolate-covered cherries, her favorite sweet.

Shirley took the box like it was radioactive.

Jimmy hooked his arm around her neck, kissed her tenderly, and then took off for the bookie joint.

Shirley opened the box. There was a note inside written on a page from the *Daily Racing Form.*

You're the best thing in my whole crummy life. Love, Jimmy.

"Poor Daddy," said Shirley, melting like those cherries on a hot day. "He tries so hard."

"I don't care. I hate him," I said.

"That's a terrible thing to say about your own father."

"He's mean."

"He's sick. He can't help it."

"I wish he was dead."

"Don't say that! Think how you'd feel if something bad happened to him."

I thought about it. I pictured him outta the picture. And all I could feel was sad that it wasn't true.

Shirley thought I was feeling sorry about what I said.

"It's OK, honey. Daddy loves you. And he loves Mommy. You know that."

"He almost shot you."

"He was just making believe. Trying to scare me. Like in a scary movie."

"He wishes I was dead. He wishes I was a boy."

"He's just joking when he says that. Don't pay any attention. Just let it roll off you, like water off a duck's back."

"I hate ducks."

"You hate everything today, I guess. But I know there's one thing you still love."

She held out the box of chocolate-covered cherries, giving me first dibs. That's what she always did. Fed everyone else first. Took the smallest piece of pie, the one burnt biscuit, the gristliest piece of lamb.

Normally I would've gobbled down four or five of those cherries and then snuck a few more later, spreading out the remaining ones so the box wouldn't look so empty. But my stomachache had gotten so bad I couldn't even look at them.

When I shook off the box of cherries, Shirley knew something was up and I finally blurted it out.

"I hurt bad," I said, terrified my appendix was gonna burst like Jimmy's had when he was a pip-squeak like me.

"Where, baby? Where do you hurt?"

"My stomach. It's been hurting for a long time."

Shirley pressed lightly on my belly and I cried out. The look on her face got me even more scared.

She got right on the phone and called the doctor. Not Dr. C. My doctor. His name was Dr. Joy but Jimmy called him Dr. Killjoy. When Shirley got him on the phone he said to come over to the hospital, where he was looking in on his patients.

"I don't wanna go to the hospital," I wailed.

"It's the same as his office. He's just not in his office right now, so we're gonna see him at the hospital."

"I don't feel so bad," I lied.

But Shirley wasn't buying it. She called a cab and brought me to the hospital.

They laid me on a table in the emergency room. Dr. Joy pressed on my stomach with his big mitts and I screamed bloody murder and started blubbering.

"Is it her appendix?" asked Shirley, looking as white as the sheet I was lying on.

"I don't know," said Dr. Joy, which wasn't very comforting.

"I don't want it to b-b-burst like my d-d-daddy's," I cried, picturing a balloon filled with blood exploding in my breadbasket. I was blubbering so hard it was tough to get the words out.

Dr. Joy stroked my forehead.

"That's not going to happen. You're in a hospital."

He pressed on my stomach again and I yelped some more.

"Did you swallow anything you shouldn't have? Something in a bottle? Or a toy? A marble?"

"I didn't do n-n-nothin.'"

"She said she's had the pain for a while," Shirley told him.

"I'm afraid we're going to have to keep her."

"You t-t-tricked me!" I screamed at my mother.

"I didn't think you'd have to stay, honey," she said.

"I w-w-wanna go home," I wailed, but nobody listened.

They brought me up to a room and I wailed the whole way. They stuck me in a bed and I kept on wailing.

A nurse pinned me down and another nurse took some blood and I screamed like Fuad Ramses was draining me dry.

Shirley held my hand and I clutched hers like a life raft.

Finally, she stood up to leave and I went totally bonkers.

"I have to go, baby. Daddy'll be worried sick if he comes home and no one's there."

"Don't tell him I'm s-s-sick! He'll k-k-kill me!" I cried.

"What a silly thing to say. Daddy loves you."

Shirley flashed the nurse a stiff smile.

"She's just scared," she said.

"You run along. We'll take care of her," cooed the nurse.

Shirley leaned in and kissed me.

"Go quickly," the nurse whispered. "It hurts them less that way. Like pulling a Band-Aid off a boo-boo."

Shirley nodded and twenty-three skidooed, blowing me a final kiss.

As soon as she was gone the nurse turned to me.

"No more crying, young lady," she snapped. "Big girls don't cry."

"Oooo, I love that song," said the pretty teen-rager in the bed next to mine. She didn't look sick at all. In fact, she started singing.

Big girls do-on't cry-ay-ay.

"F-f-f-rankie Valli's a f-f-f-fairy," I said through my blubbering, repeating information I'd gotten from Jimmy.

"We don't talk about bad things like that!" scolded the nurse.

Then she twenty-three skidooed too.

I didn't know how fairies could be bad. They brought you dough when your teeth fell out. Besides, they were just make-believe.

I kept on blubbering.

"I want my m-m-m-ommy."

"Whatsa matter wit ya?" asked the Frankie Valli fan. "Are ya dyin' or sumpthin?"

"L-l-l-leave me alone, n-n-numbskull," I replied.

"Jus' my luck. Gettin' stuck with a kid," she snorted, and then picked up a movie magazine and left me the hell alone.

After a while, a man came and wheeled me away for X-rays. He told me to make believe I was on a ride at Disneyland.

"I n-never been to D-d-disneyland," I told him, all the while thinking that now that I was dying I would never get there or anywhere else in KooKooLand.

After the X-rays, the man brought me back to my room. I was so tired from all the crying I finally konked out.

When I woke up, Dr. Joy was pressing on my guts again.

"Well, hello, Sleeping Beauty," he said.

"Am I gonna kick the bucket?" I asked straight out.

"No, you're going to be fine." He smiled, and for a moment I believed him.

Then I saw Jimmy standing at the foot of the bed.

"When you gonna quit frickin' around and slice her open?" he barked.

Dr. Joy didn't look happy about Jimmy being there. "Where's Shirley?" he inquired, sidestepping the whole question of slicing me open.

"She has to work tonight. I told her to stay home to get some sleep."

That was a big lie. I knew he just wanted to keep her away from me. Keep her from *pluck pluck plucking* over me like a mother hen.

"We're not operating on her. It's not her appendix," said Dr. Joy. "I have to do a few more tests."

"Oh, Christ," said Jimmy. "Leave it to Dracula to get something nobody knows what the hell it is. She's always causing trouble."

Dr. Joy gave him a stern look.

Jimmy faked a laugh.

"Relax, Doc. She knows I'm just kidding around. I'm just tryin' to take her mind off that pain in her gut. Just tryin' to make her feel better. Right, kiddo?"

My gut was feeling worse, but I forced a grin.

"Right, Daddy."

Dr. Joy patted me on the shoulder.

"She's a great little kid."

"Oh, she's a regular Shirley Temple," Jimmy replied.

Dr. Joy gave him another sharp look.

"Let's step out into the hall," he said to Jimmy.

Jimmy looked surprised. He sauntered out after Dr. Joy, lighting a cancer stick.

"I'm dyin' for a ciggie myself," announced the numbskull in the next bed before she disappeared into the bathroom.

I ignored her, my eyes fixed on the doorway, hoping Jimmy would take a powder and Dr. Joy would return with a toy like he did when I went to his office.

But it was Jimmy who came back in, looking ticked off. He walked up and hissed in my ear, "Just when I was feeling better you had to go and ruin it, didn't you? Well, I know what you're pulling."

"I—I'm not p-pulling anything," I said, trying with all my might not to start crying again.

"Go ahead. Cry, little crybaby. They'll blame me for that too. Like they're blaming me for your bellyache. You always wanna get me in trouble, don't you? And I know why. You want me outta the picture. You want your goddamn mother all to yourself. Well, get this through your conniving little squash. One of us will end up gone, but it won't be me."

Then he pinched my arm so hard I yelped.

"Oooh, poor little pip-squeak. Guess you still got that bellyache," he said loudly.

"That all she got? A bellyache? I thought she was dyin'," said the teen-rager as she came out of the smoky bathroom. She sashayed back to bed in her bobby socks and hospital gown.

Jimmy noticed how cute she was and turned into Mr. Charming.

"You don't look so sick yourself. What're you in for? Being too pretty?"

The teen-rager giggled.

"I'm gettin' my wisdom teeth out."

"Baloney. I bet you're just playin' hooky. You got better things to do than go to school."

"That's for sure."

Jimmy spotted the movie magazine she was reading. Sandra Dee was on the cover.

"Anybody ever tell you you look just like Sandra Dee?"

"I do not."

"Do too. Spittin' image. 'Cept you're prettier."

She giggled again. I was right. She was a total numbskull.

"I'm dying for another ciggie," she told Jimmy. "But I'm all out."

He removed a Lucky Strike from behind his ear and slipped it and a book of matches under her sheet.

"Don't set yourself on fire under there," he said.

"I won't," she promised.

"And don't tell Nurse Ratched where you got it, OK? Don't get me in trouble like my pain-in-the-ass kid here."

"My lips are sealed," she said, pressing her lips together in a pout that made her look like a trout.

A nurse came into the room and Jimmy stepped away from the teen-rager's bed. The nurse told Jimmy visiting hours were done.

He kissed me gently on the forehead and whispered one more thing in my ear.

"Wait till you get home, troublemaker."

Then he took off, giving the nurse a little wink.

She came over and took my temperature.

"You're a lucky girl to have such a nice daddy, aren't you?"

Fortunately I didn't have to answer 'cause I had a thermometer stuck in my trap.

After the nurse left the room, the numbskull put in her two cents.

"Your dad is sooo cool."

"You don't look like Sandra Dee one bit," I snapped, and turned my back on her.

I lay there and tried to figure out what to do. If I didn't die in the hospital I'd have to go back home, where I felt Jimmy would murder me for sure. My only hope was to run away. I closed my eyes and began to dream up my escape—from Jimmy, from the hospital, from my whole stupid life.

This was my plan. I'd wait for the numbskull to fall asleep and then vamoose out the window. I'd hitch a ride with a truckie to Susan's college up north. She'd be thrilled to see me and let me hide out in her dorm room. She'd cure my stomachache with medicine she cooked up in chemistry class. After I was better, we'd have picnics on her bed with my stuffed animals. We'd snatch the stuffed animals from my old bedroom one day when Jimmy was out hunting and Shirley was asleep. Eventually Susan would bring me to her teacher, who'd skip me a bunch of grades and put me in Susan's class. We'd sit next to each other and pass notes back and forth and still get straight As. We'd go to medical school in KooKooLand and find a cure for the Big C. I'd marry Dr. Kildare and she'd marry Dr. Ben Casey and we'd live next door to each other and go surfing in polka-dot bikinis every single day for the rest of our lives.

To make it all happen, I only needed one thing. Dough. I decided to steal some from Shirley's purse the next day when she came to visit and then make my getaway that night.

But my plan never got off the ground. The next morning Dr. Joy came in and told me I was going home.

"I still got that pain," I groaned, hoping to make him change his mind.

"I'm going to give you something to make your tummy all better. What do you say about that?"

"Yabba dabba doo," I muttered.

It turned out he had found worms crawling around in my guts. I pictured big, slimy earthworms slithering up my gullet and out of my mouth, nose, and ears like a corpse in an Edgar Allan Poe movie. But he said these were itsy-bitsy worms you could barely see. He asked if I'd been on a farm lately or touched any dead animals.

"Just the ducks my daddy shoots," I told him. "I find them for him after they fall out of the sky."

"Well, maybe he can get himself a nice little doggy to do that from now on. I bet you'd like a puppy."

"Yeah, sure," I said, humoring him, resigned to the fact that I was going home and was as good as dead.

"I'll call your mommy to come get you. I know you can't wait to go home and play with your dolls. And here's a new friend for them."

He pulled out a Troll doll and gave it to me. I pretended to like it, but those ugly dolls gave me the creeps. After he was gone, I stuffed it under my pillow and suffocated it.

A short while later, Shirley showed up carrying a lollipop as big as my head. She was taking me home in a taxi 'cause Jimmy was out hunting again with Hank. I prayed Jimmy'd get trampled by a moose or eaten by a bear or, better yet, accidentally plugged by Hank. I figured if Hank killed Jimmy he'd feel so bad he might adopt me and then Susan and I could really be sisters. I'd be a millionaire's daughter and move out of the projects.

On the way back home Shirley had the taxi stop at a drugstore. She picked up a big bottle of medicine that the whole family was supposed to take. When we got home, she gave me a tablespoon of the stuff. It was the color of old blood and tasted like vomit.

Shirley, Virginia, and I washed it down with Dr Pepper.

Jimmy refused to take it at all. He said there was nothing wrong with his guts that a couple of good stiff highballs couldn't fix.

But, I guess the medicine must've worked anyway 'cause my stomachache went away.

And luckily Jimmy didn't make good on his threat to kill me. Instead, he just iced me out.

"Stay outta my sight," he snarled the first day I was back, and after that he didn't say another word to me.

Then he proceeded to butter Virginia up by telling her how pretty she was and how she was his favorite daughter and how he had been crazy in love with her mother, Jacqueline, more than my mother Shirley.

"Don't worry," Virginia said when we were lying in bed one night. "He won't stay mad at you forever."

"I don't care," I snapped.

"C'mon, don't rock the boat, dummkopf. He's in a good mood and Christmas is coming."

"He hates Christmas. He'd kill Santa if Santa was alive."

"He's not so bad when he's winning at the track. He gave me five bucks and told me I could play hooky."

"He's just trying to get you on his side."

"Well, you have Mom and I have him."

"Mom loves you too. Just as much as me."

Virginia didn't look convinced. And, truthfully, I wasn't sure Shirley did love her as much.

I felt bad for Virginia, that she couldn't even remember her own mother. She didn't even have one lousy picture of her. Jimmy had torn up every last one after Jacqueline took off. Before she left, Jimmy'd told her if she hauled her ass out of there she wouldn't be taking his goddamn kid with her. Shirley said Jacqueline tried to get Virginia back, but Jimmy told the judge she was a lousy mother for abandoning her baby girl. He said she drank like a fish when she shoulda been on her knees washing out diapers. He even got one of his buddies to say she cheated on Jimmy with him. The judge decided Virginia would be better off with YaYa until Jimmy could find another wife. Which, of course, he did in no time flat. And Virginia never saw her mother again. Jacqueline tried to see her a few times, but YaYa turned her away and threatened to call the cops if she showed up again.

"Mom loves you more and always will," Virginia insisted. "That's what Daddy says."

"He's a big fat liar," I shot back.

"Maybe you're just jealous 'cause he likes me better. Maybe you just don't like how things are around here now 'cause you're spoiled rotten."

I couldn't believe my ears. While I'd been in the hospital Jimmy had turned my own sister—scratch that, my half sister—against me.

I felt more determined than ever to run away and be with Susan, the sister I was meant to have.

I turned my face to the wall and said one last thing to Virginia.

"You'll miss me when I'm gone."

Sayonara, Baby

"We heard you were a goner," said Billy from the Projects when I returned to school.

"I was just playing hooky, numbskull. I got better things to do than hang around this stupid joint."

"We heard you were in the hospital throwing up green pus."

"I was just faking. I got to watch cartoons all day with my best friend, Susan. Her old man's a millionaire."

Billy from the Projects threw an eraser at me. It hit me on the noggin.

"I'll kill you dead!" he yelled.

"My father's gonna kill *you* dead when I tell him what you did!" I yelled back.

"If he touches one hair on my chinny chin chin, my mother'll call the office. And the cops'll come and they'll throw him in the Valley Street jail where he belongs. He's nothing but a lousy crook who's riding the gravy train."

"Oh yeah? And your mother's a big fat snitch," I shot back, figuring I now knew who the snitch was. "And you know what happens to snitches." I hung my tongue out of the side of my mouth like a corpse. "They get plugged by dagos from Revere."

Billy from the Projects turned as white as the chalk on that eraser.

"Nobody in my family's a snitch."

"My old man's got friends at the office. He knows who the snitches are."

Billy from the Projects looked like he was about to pee his pants.

"We won't say nothing. We won't say nothing. We won't say nothing."

He kept repeating the words like my broken Chatty Cathy.

"Good," I said. "You and your old lady better clam up from now on."

When I got home from school, Jimmy was standing in the kitchen ripping open a piece of mail addressed to Shirley. It was a Christmas card from Grammy in Nova Scotia and there was a present for Shirley—a double sawbuck—inside. Jimmy slipped the cash into his wallet and stuffed the empty card back in the envelope.

"Don't you snitch on me," he warned. "I'm gonna use this dough to buy your mother a Christmas present. You want her to have a nice Christmas, don't you? You don't want her to be left out in the cold while you and your sister are tearing into your presents like greedy little pigs?"

I shook my head. The picture of my mother with no presents to open on Christmas morning was too much to bear.

"What do you think we oughta get her?" he asked.

"Can we get her a new washing machine?" I said. The one she had with the wringer was always leaking and flooding the kitchen.

"A washing machine? She doesn't need that, dummkopf. She already has one. It just needs a screw tightened or something."

I nodded like I agreed with him even though I knew he'd never ever tighten that screw.

"Hey, I know just what to get her," said Jimmy. "Barney just got a shipment of Chanel No. 5. Broads go wild for perfume."

I felt certain Uncle Barney's Chanel No. 5 would not be at the top of Shirley's Christmas list. Jimmy had gotten her some perfume from Barney once before and she said it smelled like toilet water from a toilet.

"Well, I've got homework to do," I said, starting to edge out of the room.

He blocked my way.

"Only a brownnoser does homework as soon as she gets home. The other pip-squeaks in your class must think you're a real ass-kisser."

"No they don't."

"Sure they do. And you're not even sharp enough to see it. You know it's not enough to be smart in life. You gotta be clever too. You gotta know how to work your points."

"I know."

"Nobody's gonna like you if you're a brownnoser."

"Susan likes me. She doesn't think I'm a brownnoser. She told me to study hard."

"Susan doesn't know you like I do. If I told her what you're really like, she wouldn't like you at all. She'd find another poor little pip-squeak from the projects to fawn all over."

I started to panic.

But before I could defend myself, he began to laugh and bopped me on the head.

"Take it easy, brownnoser. I'm just riding you. C'mon, let's go get you a stupid Christmas tree."

Somehow, without doing anything, I was back on his good side.

We took off in the Pontiac and headed over to a plant nursery where Jimmy sometimes bought landscaping supplies. He knew a guy who worked there and the guy had agreed to trade a Christmas tree for a few pancakes. The only thing was, the guy's boss couldn't know about it. So we had to wait around back until the guy finally ran out and tossed a tree over the fence to us. Jimmy tossed a couple of pancakes back over to him and they were square.

When we got home and put the tree in its stand, even Jimmy, who didn't give a goddamn about Christmas trees, had to admit it was a scrawny-looking thing and that the guy had stiffed him.

"That no-good weasel thinks he pulled a fast one on me, but I've got news for him. Nobody pulls a fast one on this Greek. I knew he was a chiseler all along. The pancakes I gave him stank. They weren't the good stuff. So who came out ahead, kiddo? Who's the Top Cat?"

"You are," I admitted, impressed that he had stiffed the guy before knowing he was gonna get stiffed himself.

"Anyway, that runty little tree gave up its miserable life for you, so you better ho ho ho enjoy it," Jimmy said before he got changed into some sharp clothes, splashed on enough Old Spice to choke a horse, and took off.

I woke up Shirley early that Friday night so we could trim the scrawny tree before she left for work. Shirley, Virginia, and I piled a bunch of lights on the tree and a ton of tinsel and some crappy ornaments Shirley had bought at Woolworth's to replace the antique ones Jimmy had pawned. I kept picturing our beautiful ornaments on some other kid's tree and it made me wanna plug somebody—the kid, Jimmy, Santa. But plugging anybody was out of the question. So instead I took one of the candy canes I was supposed to be hanging on the tree and made believe it was a .22. The straight part was the barrel, the hooked part the trigger. I blew away those Woolworth ornaments, the stuffed mallard above the TV, and the highball in Shirley's shaky hand.

Around ten thirty, Shirley left for work and I went upstairs to bed sucking on my candy cane gun.

Oh no. Oh no. Oh no.

I awoke to Shirley wailing and leapt out of bed like I'd been zapped by a string of Christmas lights with a bum plug. It was the next morning. Shirley was home from work and I figured Jimmy was already wound up about something. I stumbled over to the bedroom door and cracked it open. Jimmy's transistor radio on his bedside table was blaring. Jimmy often turned the radio on as he was getting dressed to go hunting, not caring how goddamn loud it was or who he might be waking up.

I could hear Shirley sobbing and Jimmy telling her to shut up.

Then I caught some words that the guy on the radio was saying.

Henry Piasecny. Fatal stabbing. Two people. Family home.

I felt myself go stiff and limp at the same time.

I strained to make out more words. One victim was a woman.

Please don't let it be Susan, I prayed. Please don't let it be Susan.

Then I heard Jimmy's voice.

"That goddamn bitch had it coming."

That's how I learned it was Doris. Doris and some guy clueless enough to mess around with the woman Hank Piasecny was still carrying a torch for.

I edged out into the hall, trying to hear more details, but the announcer had moved on to the weather. A cold snap was on the way.

Jimmy came storming out of his bedroom and spotted me.

"Get back in your goddamn room!" he shouted.

Shirley flew out of the bedroom after him. The faint smear of rouge on her cheeks was streaky with tears.

"Everything's fine," she croaked.

They raced down the stairs and I could hear Jimmy slamming around.

"Goddamn Doris. Why didn't she stay in goddamn KooKooLand? Why did she have to show her painted Injun face around here again?"

"I can't believe it. I can't believe it," Shirley kept saying.

A short while later, Jimmy left the house carrying his rifle. He hadn't planned on going hunting, but he told Shirley he really needed to shoot something to take his mind off poor Hank's predicament or he'd go off his rocker himself.

I watched from my bedroom window as he scraped ice off the windshield, his steamy breath pouring out with every angry scrape.

After he drove away, I crept downstairs and found Shirley smoking a cancer stick and drinking a highball and staring into space. She snapped out of it when she saw me and put on a smile.

"Who wants *blueberry* pancakes?"

I was taken aback. Usually she only made blueberry pancakes for special occasions like my birthday.

"OK," I said, figuring this qualified as a special occasion.

While Shirley got out the fixings for pancakes, I pumped her for more information.

"Do you think Susan knows? Does she know her mommy's dead?"

"I suppose she does by now."

"Where's Hank? Did the coppers get him?

"He was arrested, honey. But don't you pay any attention to this. These are big-people problems."

"I wanna see Susan," I blurted out. "I bought her a snow globe at the beach and I wanna give it to her for Christmas."

"I don't think she'll be having much of a Christmas this year."

"I hate Hank! I don't care if he is a millionaire!"

"I never liked him," admitted Shirley. "I never liked the way he looked at me. I hope they lock him up and throw away the key." Then she quickly added, "Don't tell your father I said that."

"Maybe Susan's back from college. Maybe she wants to come over."

"She can't come over. She needs to be with her family."

"It's not fair! I wanna see her."

"I'm sure Daddy will take you to see her when things have settled down."

She mixed up another highball and I turned on the kitchen radio to listen for more news about Hank and the murders. Shirley lowered the volume so it wouldn't wake Virginia, who smoked and read magazines till all hours and hated getting up in the morning. I stuffed myself with blueberry pancakes and then studied the reflection of my blue tongue in the toaster and wondered if that's what it would look like when I was dead. After breakfast, I continued to hover by the radio, while Shirley drank and defrosted the refrigerator. I watched as she placed pots of boiling water in the iced-up freezer and then chipped away at the melting ice with a large butcher knife. I tried to imagine what it would feel like if that knife sliced through my body like what had happened to Doris.

Over the next few days, I couldn't stop thinking about the murders and about poor Susan. I pumped Jimmy for information and poured over the front-page *Union Leader* stories written by a newsman who was an old racetrack buddy of Jimmy's. I pieced together the details as best as I could but it wasn't easy. There were all sorts of rumors flying around. Everywhere you went people were talking about the murders and everyone had an opinion. Some thought Hank Piasecny should get his goddamn keister fried and some thought he should get a goddamn medal. Like I said, everyone had an opinion. But some things nobody could know for sure 'cause the only people who would know the truth were either dead or possibly off their rocker.

So, here's what happened, sort of.

A Night Out

That Friday night as Shirley and I were trimming our scrawny tree, Susan's mom, Doris, was getting all dolled up to go out on the town. She was forty-two, three years older than Shirley, but lots of people said she still looked like a million bucks. It was December 13, 1963—Friday the thirteenth, one of the few days Jimmy steered clear of the bookie joint and a day I always considered myself lucky to get through without anybody dying on me.

Doris wrapped herself up in a fur coat Hank had bought her when they were still married and headed on over to a local cocktail lounge, the Venice Room. She began drinking a few stiff ones with a half dozen of her friends. Some of the friends were married and some weren't, and the ones that weren't were most likely on the make. Shortly after midnight, a big-shot architect named John Betley came into the bar for a nightcap. At fifty, John had four years on Hank, but that wasn't all he had on him. He was better looking and college-smart and more hoity-toity than Hank. Jimmy said he was a real lady-killer and normally that was a compliment, but not in this case.

"He thought he was better than us working stiffs," Jimmy said, "but Hank showed him who was boss."

I dug up as much as I could about John Betley. I learned he was the only boy in a Catholic family of five kids. He'd gone to a fancy architecture school all the way over in London, England. During World War II, he'd been an officer, fighting the dirty rotten Nazis all over Europe and getting all sorts of medals. He'd never had a ball and chain and still lived with his parents and Jimmy said that made him a mama's boy.

On that Friday night, he'd eaten a lobster dinner at home with his parents, which made me think they must be loaded. After dinner, he took off in his sleek white convertible. I don't think he was looking for trouble like Jimmy and Hank often were. I figured he was probably just looking for fun.

He arrived at the nearby Venice Room for a nightcap, and spotted Doris and her friends. He joined them. Maybe he was lonely and wanted some company. Maybe Doris had her eye on him and drew him over like the floozy Jimmy said she was. Either way, he didn't plan to stay long. The place was closing at one and he told everyone he was going back home to bed. But the others weren't ready to call it a night. Doris invited them all back to her house. The house with the bad lawn that was now frozen solid. The house she got in the divorce and was gonna sell soon 'cause now she would be residing in KooKooLand, where the lawns were always soft and green. John said he didn't want to go to Doris's place, but his drinking buddies wouldn't take no for an answer. He finally agreed to go for a quick one.

Nobody noticed that the back door of Doris's house had been forced open. They were probably having too much fun. John didn't just have one drink and twenty-three skidoo. He stuck around. Finally, everyone else took off. Doris and John were left alone in the living room.

But, they weren't really alone. Hank was hiding in the house, listening to them. Some people, like my friend Tina, said they were having S-E-X. Some people said they weren't. Jimmy said bullshit, of course they were, 'cause what else would a whore and a ladies' man be doing alone together at five in the goddamn morning. That was when Hank came out of his hiding place and, as he told Jimmy some time later, ordered John to get the hell out of his goddamn house. John, he said, told him *he* should get out, that the house didn't belong to him anymore and that he should buzz off and leave Doris alone.

Hank didn't say what Doris's reaction was to his showing up. No doubt, if she was half-lit, Hank's appearance would've sobered her right up. After all, she knew better than anybody what Hank was capable of. It was one year to the day since she'd gone and squealed to the coppers. Gone and gotten an order from a judge to keep him the hell away. A piece of goddamn paper that Hank had said frick you to many times by showing up at the house anyway since the coppers always went easy on him. Ever since then, Doris had told people, had even told Susan, that it was only a matter of time before Hank did her in. She told Susan that Goodwin Funeral Home should handle all the arrangements. She didn't want her daughter to be at a loss when D-day came and Hank blew her brains out.

Except he didn't use a gun, which Jimmy said would've been too goddamn easy. Like shooting fish in a barrel or jacking a baby deer. Hank gave them a fighting chance, said Jimmy. He used an ordinary kitchen knife. Well, two ordinary kitchen knives. Knives that used to be his knives from a kitchen that used to be his kitchen.

Maybe John Betley wasn't looking for trouble that night, but trouble found him anyway. I wondered, if he hadn't stood up to Hank, whether he might still be alive. But any guy who had defended his country against an army of bullies sure as hell wasn't gonna walk away from just one. One who was shorter than him and who probably seemed like somebody he could take. But unfortunately for John, Hank was good and mad. And, from what I could tell, when somebody was good and mad it made them big and strong.

Jimmy thought Hank had every reason to be good and mad.

"In the old country, if a wife cheated on her husband and ruined his good name, she disappeared," he said to me the night after the murders. "She fell off a goddamn cliff or something, and nobody asked any goddamn questions. That's the way it's been for thousands of years. A man's wife embarrasses him, she pays the price. Sayonara, baby."

"But Doris wasn't Hank's wife anymore," I pointed out.

"Don't be an idiot," Jimmy replied. "Hank's a goddamn Catholic. Even if he never went to church. To Catholics, divorce is a goddamn sin. Once you marry somebody, even if she's a whore like Doris, you're stuck with her. That stupid church and Hank's old lady drummed that into his squash ever since he was a pip-squeak. So if you ask me, it's their goddamn fault he carved up Doris and her big-shot boyfriend. Maybe they oughta lock up his mother and the goddamn pope."

I nodded because I didn't want Jimmy to think I disagreed with him. But I didn't really see how Hank's mother and the goddamn pope could be blamed for what Hank did. They weren't anywhere near the house with the bad lawn.

Hank was the one who killed two people.

Here's how he did it.

He stabbed John thirteen times, in the lungs, liver, all over his breadbasket. He stabbed him through the palm of his hand, probably as John tried to defend himself and Doris. He stabbed Doris eleven times. The blow that killed her went right into her heart. He left the knife sticking out of her chest. Maybe he couldn't get it out, or maybe he just wanted to leave it in there like some warrior planting his flag on the battlefield. The newspaper said Hank and Doris's marriage had been like a twenty-three-year war. It had looked like Doris had won the battle, but Hank pulled a sneak attack and had come out on top.

John bled to death on the floor between the living room and the dining room. Doris was attacked in the kitchen and laundry room. The cops figured John was killed first and then Doris.

I tried to imagine how long Doris had to watch the bloodbath, how long it had taken Hank to stab John thirteen times. When no one was around, I ran an experiment to find out. I opened Jimmy's special drawer in the kitchen. The drawer had nothing but knives in it. Knives of every shape and size for cutting up anything from a buck to a flounder. Some of the knives were rusty and some were shiny. Some still had dried blood on them. I picked a good-sized one and pretended I was Hank. I sliced into thin air and timed myself with Jimmy's stopwatch. Allowing for the time I figured it would take to yank the knife out of human flesh, I was amazed to see that Hank could've done it in under fifteen seconds. Even so, that still would've left Doris enough time to escape. Maybe that's what she was trying to do when she went toward the kitchen, since the back door was in that direction. Or maybe she was going for a knife of her own to fight Hank off.

There was no real way of knowing the details. Hank was the only one left who'd been there and his recollection wasn't so hot. Or so he said. Some time later he told Jimmy the whole goddamn thing was like a dream. He said he woke up at one point and he was on the floor. Doris was standing over him telling him everything was OK and that they should get married again. Then he realized he was standing over her body, and she was the one lying dead on the floor.

So he twenty-three skidooed.

He got into his truck and drove off into the early-morning darkness, leaving the house ablaze with lights. He headed out onto the turnpike and drove toward his sports shop. Near the Amoskeag Bridge, not far from the store, he crashed his truck into a guardrail. Maybe he was trying to kill himself, or maybe he was just driving like a maniac and lost control. He abandoned the truck there and walked the rest of the way.

A short while later, a state trooper was flagged down by a passing driver who reported seeing an accident on the other side of the turnpike. When the trooper got to the scene, all he found was a smashed-up truck. No people, no bodies, nothing. Fortunately, the truck had the name of Hank's store written on the side, so the trooper sped on over there.

The trooper pulled up in front of the sports center at about seven a.m. The lights in the store were off, but it was light enough out that he could see inside. He spotted Hank stumbling around the back of the store. Guns and ammo had been knocked or shoved all over the place. Hank appeared to be bleeding from a head wound and trying to sop up the blood with a paper towel. The trooper tried the door, but it was locked. He banged on the door. Hank looked over and gestured for him to buzz off. The trooper realized this wasn't gonna be a routine traffic accident. He got on his radio and called for backup.

Shortly after, a Manchester cop arrived in his cruiser. The two coppers approached the store and peered through the window. They saw Hank weaving and falling down. They rapped on the window. Hank snatched a rifle and struggled to load it.

The trooper knocked on the window one more time.

Hank shouted at them to get the hell out of there. To show them he meant business he kept trying to load the rifle, and this time it looked like he might succeed.

"We better get out of here. He's a crack shot," the Manchester cop warned the trooper.

They took off toward the corner of the building. A shot rang out from inside the store. Moments later, they heard a loud thud. Then silence.

The cop quickly radioed for more backup and an ambulance.

The two coppers crept back toward the entrance and peered through the window again. They could see Hank lying on the floor. It didn't look like he'd shot himself. It just looked like he'd passed out.

The coppers didn't bust down the door. They waited until more coppers arrived. When the new guys got there, they decided someone oughta drive over to Doris's to see if she had a key to the store.

And when that someone got to the house on that freezing December morning he found Doris and John, all hacked up.

Meanwhile, back at the sports center, the other coppers discovered that a guy who worked at a nearby gas station had a set of keys to the store. The coppers unlocked the door and found Hank wasn't all that bad off. He came to and was taken to the hospital to get his bloody noggin stitched up.

A makeshift courtroom was set up in Hank's hospital room. Hank knew most of the guys there—the judge, the clerk, the chief of police. Shortly after noon, Hank was charged with killing his former wife, Doris Piasecny, and a man she had taken a shine to, John Betley. As fate would have it, Hank's longtime lawyer, a guy who had gotten him out of scrapes before, was the cousin of the man he had just murdered. Hank expected the guy to represent him anyway, but the cousin wanted no part of it. So Hank was left that morning without a lawyer. Or, as Jimmy described it, without a goddamn shyster. The judge entered innocent pleas for Hank, giving him time to find himself a new lawyer.

Hank didn't seem worried about losing his lawyer, or about anything else for that matter. When he was handed copies of the murder charges, he flipped them onto the foot of the bed without even glancing at them. As the clerk began to read the charges, he cut the guy off and asked if it was really necessary to read through all that stuff about the murders.

The chief of police put his hand comfortingly on Hank's shoulder and let him know there was no way around it. So the murder complaints were read and Hank sat there fidgeting and gritting his teeth like he couldn't wait to get it over with.

A newspaper photographer wanted to snap some photos, but the chief wouldn't allow it. At least he spared Hank that embarrassment.

When it was all over, Hank asked for a cigar and somebody lit one up for him. I figured men smoked cigars in that hospital all the time when someone was born. I don't know if anybody had ever smoked one after someone died, but I guess there was nobody or nothing stopping Hank from doing it.

A Real Live Dead Woman

The next morning, Hank was transferred from the hospital to the Valley Street jail and I trudged off with Tina to the Temple Market. Tina pumped me for information about the murders and I told her what I'd heard Jimmy and Shirley discussing over breakfast.

"Some people say Hank cut off the guy's Down There and put it in Susan's mother's mouth."

I demonstrated how Jimmy, as a joke, had pretended to stuff his Jones breakfast sausage down Shirley's gullet.

"*Eeewww!*" shrieked Tina. "*Now I'm gonna have to say a million Hail Marys.*"

"Don't be such a baby," I said. "It's no worse than what I saw that killer in *Blood Feast* do."

"You think you're so tough! Just wait till Hank breaks outta jail and shows up at your house. He'll chop up your whole family. Sylvester even."

"He's not getting out, numbskull. They're gonna lock him up and throw away the key, probably. And, anyway, if he does bust outta jail and come around, I'll just plug him with Jimmy's .22."

"I know one thing. He's going straight to hell. He'll be down there with Lee Harvey Oswald and the Boston Strangler and Judas and all the other bad men."

"My father says what Hank did is all the pope's fault 'cause the pope won't let people get divorced even if they hate each other's guts."

Tina's face got all red like a big blister.

"Your father's goin' straight to hell for saying that! And for all the bad things he said about President Kennedy. I bet President Kennedy's up in heaven right now helping God make a list of who's good and who's bad and your dad's on the bad list."

The way Tina described it heaven sounded just like the North Pole, which made sense since hell was hot, so heaven hadda be cold. God sounded like Santa Claus and President Kennedy was like an elf.

Picturing heaven as eternal Christmas, I could suddenly see it a whole lot clearer. And I knew it was where I, who cherished Christmas above all other days, belonged.

It made sense that Jimmy, who hated Christmas more than Ebenezer Scrooge, would be going to hell. It was kind of comforting to think that if the dummkopf cops didn't nab him, an all-knowing God would. The only thing was, I didn't wanna be stuck down there with him.

"Do you think there's any chance I'm goin' to hell too? Or is it just men down there?"

Tina looked very serious.

"Girls can definitely go to hell. Unless you become a good Catholic you're gonna be frying down there with Hank."

"How do you know that?"

"The priest and the nuns and my mother said so."

"How do *they* know?"

"They just do. They're grown-ups."

"My father says it's all a crapshoot and nobody knows what happens when we die."

"He's a big liar who's going to hell. How can you believe anything he says?"

As much as I liked to consider myself smarter than Tina, I had to admit she had a point.

"I'm not going to hell," I blurted out. "Starting today I'm gonna be the best Catholic in the whole world."

"Ha. You won't be better than me. I got a big head start."

"I'll catch up. I'll beat you. You'll see."

"Yeah, how you gonna do that when your father won't even let you go to church?"

"God *knows* he won't let me go. 'Cause God knows everything, right?"

"Yeah," Tina admitted grudgingly. "Maybe God'll give you a dispensation until you grow up. But then you'll have to go to church a hundred times more to make up for it. Until then, you better pray a lot. You better pray like a maniac."

"I am a maniac!"

I grabbed an icicle and pretended to stab Tina. Stabbed her all over just like Hank had done to Doris and that guy unlucky enough to cross his path.

When we got to the Temple Market, Horrible Heddy had her snout buried in the *Union Leader*, devouring every detail of the murders. I was afraid she'd remember what I'd told her about being bosom buddies with Hank, but she didn't seem to have a clue about my association with the madman she was reading about. Not until Tina opened her big trap.

"Her father's best friends with that maniac," she reminded Heddy.

Heddy looked up from the paper, annoyed.

"Yeah, tell me another one. . . ."

"Her father says Hank cut off the guy's you-know-what and fed it to the lady like a sausage," Tina blurted out.

Heddy nearly fell over.

"Holy Christ!"

"It's a sin to take the Lord's name in vain," Tina sniffed.

"The papers don't say nothing about nobody cutting off anybody's you-know-what."

I figured now that the cat was out of the bag, I might as well try to impress Heddy with my inside knowledge.

"That's 'cause the coppers are covering up for Hank. My dad says half of 'em been deer hunting with Hank and the other half wish they'd been."

"Yeah, well, that ain't gonna save him."

"My dad says he'll beat the rap."

"Dream on. They're gonna lock him up or string him up, one or the other." She shook her head. "It just figures you project kids would know a lunatic."

"I never met him," Tina protested. "And I never want to. He might stab me in the eye." She demonstrated with a Tootsie Roll what Hank might do to her.

I suddenly felt bad for Hank, felt the need to defend him, if for no other reason than that he was Susan's father.

"He didn't mean to do it. He was probably just trying to scare Doris. Anyway, she drove him to it."

Heddy got as cold as that icicle I'd tried to stab Tina with.

"I heard enough outta you. Buy what you're gonna buy and beat it. And don't show your puss around here again."

Tina started to tremble. "Me too?"

"You're all right. But not your little friend. Anyone who defends a murderer isn't welcome in this establishment."

On the way back to the projects Tina volunteered to buy me my candy until I was eighteen and could get to another store.

"She can't keep me outta there," I insisted. "If she tries to keep me out, her store'll get hit with Jewish lightning."

"The Jews don't make lightning," Tina said. "God does."

"Jewish lightning isn't real lightning, dummkopf. It's when people burn stuff down on purpose, like the Jews do all the time, even more than the dagos, so they can collect the insurance money."

"I never met a Jew," said Tina. "I guess I never want to 'cause they killed Jesus."

"They all live in the North End where the rich people are," I said. "My father cuts their lawns. They give good tips at Christmas even though they don't believe in it."

"If your father gets one of those Jews from the North End to burn down the Temple Market, you'll all go to hell with Hank."

"He won't get a Jew to do it. He'll get a dago 'cause they torch stuff to teach people a lesson, not for money. And anyway, I won't go to hell 'cause I won't be the one doing the torching."

"But God will know it's your fault, dummkopf."

"But it won't be my fault. 'Cause here's the thing. God says we gotta honor our mother and father, right?"

"Yeah, that's true," admitted Tina, starting to look uneasy.

"So if my father sends me to the store for a pack of Luckys, I gotta go, right? 'Cause I gotta honor my father. So, I go to the Temple Market and Heddy won't let me in. When I come home with nothin' I gotta tell my father the truth—I got thrown out 'cause I was stickin' up for Hank. Well, you know what happens next? My old man calls up some dagos and *kaboom*. I didn't do anything wrong. I honored my father *and* I told the truth. So I'm in the clear, right?"

"If you put it that way, I guess you're in the clear," said Tina. Then she started to look miserable. "But I don't want the Temple Market to burn down. Then my mother won't have anywhere to buy food and my whole family will starve to death."

I could see Tina had a point. Her mother didn't own a car, so she was stuck doing all her shopping at Heddy's puny joint. Tina's mother had tagged along with us to the A&P a few times, but that hadn't worked out so well. Jimmy had swerved around every corner extra fast just to scare her and she squeezed my arm so hard I got a bruise. And now that Jimmy had bad-mouthed the corpse of President Kennedy, I knew nothing would get her back in our car. Not even starvation.

"Then I guess if my old man sends me for Luckys, *you'll* have to go in and buy 'em," I conceded.

"Maybe after a while Heddy'll forget she kicked you out. Just don't ever bring up Hank in there again."

"I'm not the one who bought him up. You did."

"I did not."

"You did too."

"Did not."

"Did too."

"Did not."

"Did too."

We kept at it like that all the way home. But I was right and I knew it and I was glad to see even a good Catholic like Tina lied once in a while.

That night Jimmy got some good news. Hank had hired a big-shot lawyer to replace the one who was the cousin of the guy he killed.

"He's got Stanley Brown in his corner. He's going for a knockout," Jimmy crowed to Shirley, pretending to sock her in the jaw. Stanley Brown was the law partner of some mucky-muck Jimmy did landscaping for. The mucky-muck was OK in Jimmy's book 'cause he liked to shoot the baloney and once told Jimmy he was such a good talker he oughta have been a lawyer himself.

"Hank's gonna beat the rap," Jimmy insisted. "You wait and see."

The next day, Monday, was the beginning of the last week of school before Christmas vacation. The temperature was below zero. It was only a short walk from the projects to school, but I thought I was gonna have to get my nose amputated by the time I got there.

Billy from the Projects was waiting for me when I arrived.

"My mom told me your old man's friend sliced up a bunch of people with a sword." He pretended he was Zorro, making the sign of the Z.

"Maniacs don't use swords, dummkopf. They use butcher knives. Big, bloody butcher knives."

"I never knew anyone who knew a maniac before," he said. "You're lucky. You got a racehorse and a new TV and you know people who kill people."

"Wanna touch me?" I bragged. "Maybe some of it will rub off on you."

Billy from the Projects reached out and grabbed my freezing hand. I felt a jolt of static electricity and yanked my hand away.

"Don't get your cooties on me!" I yelled.

Billy from the Projects looked hurt. I felt bad, but I didn't say I was sorry.

After that, word got around about me knowing a murderer. Miss Morrissey pulled me aside and told me to quit going on about Hank. Apparently, I was scaring some of the crybaby girls. I said I couldn't help it. I was all broken up about my friend's mother dying. I put on a big, sad hound dog face. Miss Morrissey bought it and asked if I needed to go home. I said I hated to miss any school but that that was probably a good idea.

When I got home Shirley wasn't asleep like she normally was. The school had called and told her I was on my way. She met me at the door with a smile plastered on her dog-tired face. She sat me down next to the radiator. Then she heated up her hands on the radiator and pressed them to my frozen cheeks. After a while, she got me thawed out. Then she made me cocoa with extra marshmallows.

As I slurped down the sticky sweetness, I felt an intense rush of love for my mother.

"If Daddy ever tries to stab you, I'll shoot him in the head," I said.

Shirley recoiled as if I had stabbed her myself.

"Daddy will never hurt Mommy like Hank hurt Doris."

"How do you know?"

"'Cause Daddy loves Mommy."

"But Hank loved Doris. Daddy said he was still carrying a torch for the broad."

Shirley frowned, tried a different angle.

"Mommy and Daddy aren't divorced like Hank and Doris. If Doris hadn't gotten a divorce, none of this would've happened."

"If you divorce Daddy we could move to Disneyland."

Shirley stared out the frosted-up window.

"If I divorce your father, I won't end up in Disneyland. I'll end up six feet under like Doris."

"He wouldn't follow us to KooKooLand. He thinks the place is for dummkopfs."

"That doesn't matter. He'd track us down and there'd be hell to pay."

She blinked back a few tears.

"When you were a baby, I thought about leaving. I thought about going back to Canada. I even saved up some money. But I knew I wouldn't get far. I knew he'd find me."

"We could hide in Grampy's barn," I said, without much conviction, knowing she was right.

A tear plopped onto the kitchen table and Shirley quickly wiped it off with her bathrobe sleeve.

"I was afraid he'd take you away from me like he took Virginia from her mother."

"I'd shoot him if he tried that. I'd shoot him right between the eyes."

"Nice girls don't talk like that."

"I don't care. I won't let him take me."

She plastered on a smile again.

"He's not taking you anywhere. I shouldn't have said that. Mommy's just tired. Mommy's not leaving Daddy. Mommy loves Daddy."

"Why? Why do you love him?"

She took her time answering. I wasn't sure if she couldn't think of a good answer or if there were too many answers floating around in her head.

"'Cause no one else loves him. Not even YaYa and Papou. I'm the only one. Daddy needs me."

She looked at me apologetically.

"And I need him."

"Why?"

"I don't know. I don't want to be alone in my old age."

"You'll have me. I'll take care of you."

"You'll have a husband of your own."

"I don't want a husband. I hate boys."

"Someday you'll want one. All girls do."

"Not me."

"They're not all like your father. Some of them are like my brothers who drowned. They were good to everybody."

She poured herself a drink.

"But the good always die young, I guess."

"Does that mean I should be bad like Daddy?"

"No, you're Mommy's good little girl."

"But if I'm good like your brothers am I gonna die?"

"No. Nothing bad is going to happen to you."

"How do you know? How do you know nothing bad's gonna happen to me?"

"I won't let it."

"Was Doris bad? Did she deserve to die like Daddy says?"

"No. Maybe she was no angel. But she didn't deserve to go to heaven yet."

In a little while, Jimmy came home from duck hunting. I couldn't believe he could sit out in a duck blind all day and not freeze to death, but apparently whiskey kept you warmer than cocoa or a radiator.

While he stood at the stove, burning the pinfeathers off the bloody ducks, Shirley told him that Doris's funeral and church Mass were being held the next day.

"Do you think we should go, at least to the funeral?" she asked him. "For Susan and Terry's sake."

"Are you nuts?" he said. "Then it's gonna look like we're taking Doris's side."

"Well, what if just me and the kids go? We'll sit in the back. No one will even know we're there."

Jimmy considered that scenario, taking a swig of his highball to help him think better.

I had all sorts of mixed-up feelings about attending Doris's funeral. On the one hand I was terrified at the prospect of seeing a real live dead woman. This wouldn't be a movie dead woman, covered in Karo syrup, but an honest-to-God dead lady, staring me right in the face. I might scream or start bawling or faint and fall into the coffin and get her cooties all over me. On the other hand, I felt going there could make me Susan's friend for life. I pictured myself sitting beside her, holding her hand while she cried on my shoulder. I pictured myself bringing her over to our apartment for hot cocoa with extra marshmallows and finally giving her that snow globe.

But Jimmy put the kibosh on the whole thing.

"I feel bad for those kids, I really do. I love 'em like my own," he said. "But they're better off without that whore of a mother. And Hank's buddies gotta stick together. We gotta show everybody in this city what we thought of Doris. A big nothing. A big fat zero."

So no one from the Norris family went to the funeral or to the church Mass. We stayed the hell home to show we were on Hank's side.

But as it turned out, Hank ended up going himself.

That Monday he appeared in court dressed in a nice suit, a white shirt, and a tie. I'd never seen Hank decked out in a suit before, but Jimmy said Stanley Brown had to make him look like an upstanding citizen, like John Q. Public. Hank stood before the judge and pleaded innocent to killing his ex-wife, Doris, and a guy he barely knew. Well, actually, Hank didn't say a word. Stanley Brown did all the talking. One of the county attorneys wasn't too thrilled about that. He pushed to have Hank speak for himself. To have him stand up there and look everyone in the eye and say he was innocent, even though everyone in the goddamn city knew he wasn't. But the judge said that wouldn't be necessary. Hank could keep his mouth shut, which he did until the hearing was over and he was carted back to jail.

Later that day, Stanley Brown made his next move. He asked the court for permission for Hank to attend Doris's Mass.

"That's a smart strategy," Jimmy explained. "Brown wants to make it look like Hank's sorry. Like he didn't mean it. Boo hoo hoo."

The judge granted the request even though, as Jimmy pointed out, an accused murderer going to his victim's church service was not something you saw every day.

Bright and early the next morning, Hank walked into Our Lady of Perpetual Help church escorted by the county sheriff and the chief of police, who had seemed sympathetic to him at the hospital.

In keeping with Doris's instructions to Susan, the Goodwin Funeral Home handled all the arrangements.

Hank and the cops sat in the back of the church—supposedly so Hank wouldn't seem so conspicuous. Frankly, I didn't see how that was possible. I figured most of the people there must be gawking at Hank the whole time or trying their damnedest not to. Some of them were probably pretty riled up at having the dead woman's murderer in their midst. Any way you cut it, a lotta them would've ended up thinking about Hank, not Doris, which kinda made sense since Jimmy said Hank always had to be the goddamn center of attention.

As for how Hank felt attending the service of his ex-wife, the police chief told a reporter that from up close where he was sitting, Hank had seemed very remorseful and had even cried.

Just like Jimmy had said. *Boo hoo hoo.*

When it was all over, Hank was whisked back to the Valley Street jail.

But he didn't have to stay cooped up there very long. The next day, the day of John Betley's funeral and church Mass, Stanley Brown filed a petition to have Hank moved to the state hospital in Concord—or, as Jimmy called it, the cracker factory. The judge immediately granted the request.

"Yabba dabba doo! Brown got him sprung from the slammer in four days," Jimmy said, having a highball to celebrate. He raised his glass to Hank. "We'll be throwing one down together soon, my brother."

Jimmy insisted I have a little sip to join in the celebration, since Shirley was at work and he was too goddamn happy to drink alone. I slugged it down fast, but it still stung like hell. He put on some Louis Armstrong records and made his trumpet sounds. He told me to have another sip. And then another.

Finally, he told me to get my pip-squeak ass to bed. He thought it was a riot that I was stumbling around like a pint-sized alkie as I made my way up the stairs. Somehow, I managed to climb up onto the top bunk. I lay in bed with the room swaying and told Virginia I'd never, ever drink again, even if Jimmy tried to pour booze down my gullet the way Boozer Eddie had threatened to do with that pigeon.

"Booze makes you wanna barf at first, just like ciggies," Virginia said, blowing perfect smoke rings from the cancer stick she was puffing on. "But then you get used to it and you feel like you're on top of the world."

I didn't want to be on top of the world. I didn't even want to be on the top bunk. I wanted to be on solid ground.

"Will you switch beds with me, just for tonight?" I asked her. "I'm too dizzy up here."

"All right, kiddo. But you owe me one."

She helped me down from the top bunk and tucked me into the bottom one. I closed my eyes to stop the spinning and finally I fell asleep.

I woke up all groggy. I tried to drag myself out of bed but my legs felt heavy, like two fallen tree trunks. Jimmy laughed and said I was just having my first hangover. He said not to worry, that after a while I'd be able to hold my liquor 'cause all the Norrises were good at that.

Then he told me I could stay home from school, which was pretty cool. Just like getting sprung from jail.

Fruitcake

My hangover didn't hang on. By ten a.m. I made myself some breakfast—a baseball-sized blob of vanilla ice cream drowned in a mud puddle of chocolate syrup. I checked out the newspaper for more stuff about the murders. There were no new developments. I read an article on the front page titled "Negro Full of Hate." It said colored people were mad as hell 'cause they stirred up their hatred toward white people over their whole lives. They lived lives of hate.

I didn't know whether that was true or not. I didn't know any colored people to ask. But if it was true I could sort of understand it. Sometimes I felt like I was living a life of hate too. I hated so many things it wasn't funny. I sat down and made a list of everything.

Mackerel, rats, and prunes were on the list.

Insects of all shapes and sizes. Spiders, june bugs, even ants. I once stomped an anthill to smithereens just for the hell of it until a boy came and stomped all over my feet and shouted, "See how they feel!" His old lady made him apologize, but what he said got me to thinking and I hadn't done it since.

There were a lot of people I hated too. I made another list.

Billy from the Projects. Some other dummkopfs in my class. My stupid teacher. Heddy. Boozer Eddie. Hank. I put Jimmy on the list, erased him. Put him back on.

I made another list. A list of the people I loved. That was shorter. Shirley. Virginia. Susan. I added Sylvester to make the list longer even though he was a cat.

The next day I went back to school. I looked around at my classmates and thought about who belonged on what list.

While I was figuring all that out, Hank's lawyer was figuring out some stuff too.

He went over to check out the crime scene.

In the five days since the murders, the cops had been guarding Hank's old house like it was Fort Knox. By the time Stanley Brown headed over there, the place had been pretty well gone over. The main evidence Brown could see were the signs that someone had broken in and two big bloodstains where Doris and John had taken their last gurgling breaths.

Brown left the house and came back the next day with a photographer to take pictures of the evidence. But, when they got there, presto chango!—the bloodstains had disappeared. Someone had scrubbed them away. You couldn't even tell where the bodies might have been.

Except for the fact that two people were dead, it was almost like the murders had never happened. Like it was just a bad dream that only two people were never gonna wake up from.

Because of this turn of events, Brown asked the court to toss out all the charges against Hank. He said he'd been robbed of the chance to examine evidence and was hamstrung as far as defending Hank. Any blood that he could have sent to a lab to prove that someone other than Hank had carved up Doris and John was now gone. Hank, he argued, couldn't possibly get a fair trial and should be set free. Free as a Polish eagle.

Brown didn't get into who might have made those stains disappear. All he said was the house was still being watched by the cops when he returned.

The court put off making a decision until after the holidays, which left Hank cooped up in the mental hospital.

In the meantime, a whole mess of headshrinkers began examining him. Headshrinkers who worked for the cracker factory. Headshrinkers who worked for the state. And a big-deal headshrinker who Stanley Brown brought in, Dr. Harry Kozol of Harvard University, who was an expert on violent nutcases.

"Is Hank crazy?" I asked Jimmy on Christmas Eve. "Crazy like Norman Bates in *Psycho*?"

"Hank's no crazier than I am," Jimmy replied. "But if Brown asks me to testify to that effect, I'll swear he's nuttier than a fruitcake."

"Speaking of fruitcake, who wants a piece?" asked Shirley trying to inject some Christmas cheer into the conversation.

"Count me out," said Jimmy, pretending to gag. "I'd rather eat Victory Bound's saddle."

"I'd rather eat Charlie Chaplin's shoe," I added, figuring that would make Jimmy crack up, which it did.

"I'm stuffed," said Virginia, who was sulking 'cause Jimmy wouldn't let her hang out with her no-account friends.

"Well, somebody's gotta eat it," sighed Shirley. "I guess it'll have to be me."

She sawed off a tiny sliver of fruitcake and washed it down with a big slug of the boozy eggnog she had just made.

Watching her chew, I could almost taste that soggy, pruney cake. Fruitcake was the only dessert I wouldn't touch with a ten-foot pole. Every December, Grammy would send one wrapped in tinfoil and tied with string. The fruitcake weighed a ton and Jimmy said if you clocked a person with it their skull would crack open and their brains would squirt out and make a tasty frosting.

"You better get to bed, girls. Santa only comes when you're sleeping," Shirley trilled, acting like Jimmy hadn't already killed off Santa.

"OK," we said, pretending we'd gotten amnesia and still believed in him.

Shirley put out some Lorna Doones on a plate for the make-believe Santa.

"Why don't you leave the old geezer some fruitcake?" Jimmy laughed. "Once it lands in his gut, he'll never get off the ground again and that'll be the end of goddamn Christmas."

"Daddy's just kidding," said Shirley. "Sleep tight. Don't let the bedbugs bite."

Virginia and I trudged off to bed. Since it was Christmas Eve, I tried to get away without brushing my teeth, but Virginia scared me into doing it by saying if I didn't I'd end up with false choppers like YaYa's that I'd have to plop into a tumbler at night.

Virginia rolled her hair around two OJ cans and then lit up a half-smoked butt that she had hidden under her bed. She sucked as many drags as she could off the butt, then stubbed it out in the small puddle that collected beneath the hissing radiator. She sprayed some Alberto VO5 hair spray around to cover the smell, and before long she had conked out.

I was way too excited to sleep. I was picturing Shirley wrapping presents all night. Every year, she went crazy at Christmas. Any toy advertised on the idiot box that I hadda have went on her list. She put toys on layaway and paid a dime or a quarter a week on them. When the toys were finally paid for, she'd lug them home on the bus, carrying them with throbbing arms from the bus stop. She'd find clever places to hide them, in the far recesses of closets and behind the leaky washing machine. I could've found them if I wanted, but only a dummkopf spoils her own surprise.

That year the toy I wanted most was the Deluxe Dream Kitchen, a doll-sized assortment of kitchen appliances. The Dream Kitchen had a dishwasher, something I'd seen in the North End houses Shirley cleaned. I had a dream of one day buying Shirley her very own dishwasher. I wanted to give her a kitchen as dreamy as the one I hoped she was placing under our scrawny tree at that very moment.

I had a dream, yes, I had a dream.

But I had a whole lotta worry too that Christmas Eve. I worried that maybe I wouldn't be getting the Dream Kitchen at all. Maybe Shirley hadn't been able to come up with enough dough to buy presents 'cause Victory Bound had eaten it all up. Maybe Jimmy would put the kibosh on giving us any toys that year 'cause we were too goddamn old. Worst of all, maybe God was gonna punish me 'cause I was thinking about toys like a greedy little pig while Susan was probably lying in a bed somewhere bawling her eyes out.

I wondered if Doris had already done her Christmas shopping before she'd been murdered. Were there still presents waiting to be wrapped in the house that had been scrubbed clean of blood? Did the police take the presents as evidence? Was Susan gonna get any presents at all? If only she knew I had that snow globe for her. If only I knew where she was, I'd creep out of the house and hitchhike there and bring it to her.

But all I knew was that she wasn't at college anymore. After the Colby Junior College dean had broken the terrible news to her, Susan had left school and returned to Manchester. Jimmy said she was staying with some family members 'cause the murder house was off-limits. Even if it wasn't, I was pretty sure she wouldn't ever want to stay there again.

I prayed that somewhere somebody was putting presents under a tree for Susan since her mother was now lying under the ground and wasn't able to do it. I made another pact with God then and there. If you give Susan some presents, I told him, you can take my Dream Kitchen and give it to another kid.

But maybe God was asleep again or maybe he didn't like me telling him what to do or maybe he just didn't take me up on my offer. Maybe he was rewarding me for my generosity, like at church when I didn't have to put any dough in the collection plate. All I know is I got my Dream Kitchen.

But knowing Susan might be present-less that Christmas morning took away some of my fun.

"What's the matter, honey?" Shirley asked. "Isn't that what you wanted? Did I get the wrong thing?"

"No, no. This is just what I wanted."

"Then act like it, for Chrissake," growled Jimmy. "Your mother paid good money for that. Some kids got no goddamn presents this morning."

"I know," I choked. "I know."

I jumped up and hugged my mother as tight as I could. I didn't ever want to let her go.

"I love it, Mommy. I love it love it love it."

Shirley's face was bright with relief.

"I just want you to be happy."

"I am. I'm the happiest girl in the world."

"Yeah, what about me? Don't you want me to be happy?" Jimmy asked Shirley.

Shirley's face tensed and she popped up like a jack-in-the-box.

"Of course we want Daddy to be happy. Let's get Daddy his presents."

She piled a mountain of packages on Jimmy's lap.

"I don't want all this," he groused. "I tell you every year, just gimme some dough. That's all I want for goddamn Christmas."

She quickly pulled a card from her bathrobe pocket and handed it to him.

"I didn't forget," she said. "But I wanted you to have some packages to open too. You needed a few things."

"I don't need anything. All I need is this," he said, tearing into the envelope like a greedy little pig. I caught a glimpse of the front of the card. It said *Merry Christmas to My Wonderful Husband.* Jimmy opened the card and counted out the money, not letting us see how much was in there. Shirley watched him nervously, hoping he'd be happy with how much she'd managed to squirrel away during the year.

"Is that all?" he said when he'd finished counting.

Shirley's shoulders sank.

Then he broke into a huge grin.

"That's my baby," he said. "My Nova Scotia baby."

He took her into his arms, dipped her back, and gave her a big, long kiss on the mouth.

After a few seconds, I looked away and so did Virginia.

Jimmy stuffed the money in his wallet. Then he put the card in an old seaman's chest where he kept all the cards and notes we had given him and my report cards with the straight As.

"OK," he barked like a merchant mariner. "Let's open the rest of those goddamn presents. Hop to it, pip-squeaks. On the double."

Virginia and I tore into our gifts. I would rather have opened mine slowly to make Christmas last longer, but that was out of the question. Jimmy wanted us to hurry the hell up, get on with it, move our keisters.

That year I got almost everything I wanted. A pogo stick, outfits for Barbie so she wouldn't go naked and do bad things, a Ken doll so she could do bad things anyway, and Barbie's sports car, which Jimmy said she'd better let Ken drive or she'd end up in Barbie's Graveyard.

While we were opening presents, the phone rang. It was Uncle Barney. He had obtained some new merchandise on Christmas Eve when the stores closed early and were a piece of cake to knock off.

"It's *Christmas*," Shirley said, frowning. "Can't it wait?"

"Hey, some of us gotta work on Christmas," said Jimmy, and took off to meet Barney. Before he left, he told us to hold off on opening the rest of the gifts. He needed to make sure they passed his inspection.

But once he was gone, Shirley brought out our Secret Presents. She always kept a few things under wraps that she knew Jimmy wouldn't approve of. That year Virginia's Secret Present was the palest of pink lipsticks and mine was a pair of black patent leather Mary Janes—something I'd been hounding her for for months. Shirley warned me to wear the shoes only when Jimmy wasn't around. He had banned patent leather shoes 'cause they were something loose women like Doris wore. Something they wore so men could see up their dresses and get a glimpse of their Shame and be driven crazy.

I hid the shoes under our bunk beds and a few hours later Jimmy came back. He tossed a couple of ugly snowsuits at Virginia and me—the dregs of some store's Christmas inventory.

"Merry Christmas from Barney. Let's finish this thing off."

We raced through the opening of the last few presents. The only things Shirley got were some Jergens hand lotion from Virginia and a card I had made. Jimmy didn't even get her a bottle of Uncle Barney's shitty toilet water. He said he wouldn't be turned into a present-buying patsy by the capitalist Christmas machine.

Shirley said she didn't need anything. *We* were all she needed. And Christmas, she insisted, was really just for kids.

I didn't believe her, but I told myself I did so the whole day wouldn't be ruined.

After that, we piled into the Pontiac and headed for YaYa and Papou's. I dreaded Christmas at their house even more than Thanksgiving. YaYa always got us crummy presents—scratchy, too-big nightgowns and sad-looking dolls from Greece with strange hairdos. Papou would growl about how much dough YaYa had blown and Jimmy would start in telling the Rifle Story, even though YaYa told him to shut up.

The Rifle Story went like this: Jimmy had wanted a rifle for Christmas when he was eight, but YaYa thought he was too young. Jimmy begged and pleaded and wore YaYa down and finally she took him to Sears. But seeing Jimmy with a rifle in his hands, she got cold feet. She dragged him, kicking and screaming, out of the store, and Jimmy didn't get a rifle until he was my age, nine. Jimmy said he'd be an even better shot if he'd had that extra year to practice. But YaYa had lied to him and broke his heart and that's why he couldn't stomach Christmas—or her—very much at all.

"Grow up and get over it," YaYa finally snapped at him.

"Greeks never forget their oppressors. *Never,*" Jimmy said. "Maybe you want me to forget about what the Turks did to the Greeks too? Maybe I should go kiss a Turk on the keister?"

"How dare you speak those words in this house? Get out, get the hell out!" barked Papou.

And so we left.

There was still Christmas dinner to get through.

We returned home and Shirley got cracking getting the big meal on the table. Jimmy had shot a Canadian goose and Shirley had slow-cooked it the previous night while she was up wrapping presents. Usually there were still shotgun pellets in the geese Jimmy shot and I was afraid I'd crack a cavity-rotted tooth on one.

But Shirley made sure there were no pellets in the slices of goose she fanned across my plate. The goose was crisp and juicy and the potatoes Shirley cooked in the goose fat were better than any french fries you could eat and her spanakopita was bursting with feta cheese.

For dessert we had Shirley's pumpkin custard slathered with whipped cream. And her baklava, golden brown and oozing honey and better than YaYa's. And plates and plates of Greek cookies Shirley had been baking for weeks when she shoulda been sleeping.

Shirley put out the fruitcake too, but I don't think anybody touched it.

After dinner, Shirley called Grammy in Canada to tell her how much we all loved the fruitcake. Virginia and I had to get on the phone and lie and tell her it was delicious. Jimmy grabbed the phone from me and told Grammy he'd used the fruitcake to saddle up Victory Bound. Just kidding.

When Shirley was about to hang up, Grammy asked if she'd gotten her Christmas card, and Shirley said, oh yes, she almost forgot, it was a beautiful card, not knowing to thank her for the money that had been inside.

Muscle Beach

Virginia always said the days after Christmas would make you want to blow your brains out. It didn't even matter if Shirley had given her everything she'd wanted for Christmas or if Jimmy was blissfully gone, holed up at the bookie joint blowing his Christmas dough. It didn't even matter that there was no goddamn school for a week. Christmas was over and there was nothing, really nothing to look forward to. Just short, gray days leading to long, black nights. Endless frickin' winter.

New Year's came, but nobody felt like tooting the horns Shirley had bought. "One year closer to annihilation," Jimmy said, draining his highball.

I kept hounding him about seeing Susan but nothing came of it.

One night when he was making me arm wrestle him at the kitchen table, he announced that Susan had left town.

"She's been shipped off to Doris's sister in KooKooLand," he said, as my trembling arm hit the table.

Doris had been planning to say sayonara, baby, to New Hampshire right after Christmas and fly back to California. But now Susan was heading out there instead. Jimmy said she didn't feel up to going back to college. She couldn't concentrate on human anatomy with her old lady a corpse and her father having his head examined.

All I could think was, she's never coming back. She's gonna forget all about me. Forget all about this stupid place.

And at first, it seemed like I was right.

Jimmy found out Susan was settling in pretty good. At least that's what Terry said when Jimmy brought him some of Shirley's spanakopita so he wouldn't waste away.

Like Doris, Susan had always dreamed of moving to California. She was outdoorsy and a bleeding heart, so Jimmy figured she'd fit right in. But it didn't turn out that way. California was a nightmare for Susan. Everywhere she looked she saw her mother starting over her life at forty-two, tanned as honey from all that sunshine and full of excitement.

207

It didn't help matters that Susan found a cheesy crime magazine at Aunt Irene's that had a story about the murders: *Man Goes for a Walk and Gets Ventilated!* The story was mostly about John Betley, about how going out for a belt of booze with a floozy had caused the poor sap to get stabbed to death. It got Susan all riled up.

All in all, KooKooLand didn't make Susan feel any less crazy.

Before long, she returned to New Hampshire.

I finally got Jimmy to take me over to Hank's store to see her. Hank's family had been running the place for him while he was locked up in the loony bin.

I left the snow globe at home. Christmas was over and I thought Jimmy would call me a dummkopf if I brought a present.

On the drive over I tried to rehearse what to talk about with Susan. Her dead mother. My Christmas presents. Hank. Nothing seemed right. When we pulled up, I still hadn't figured it out.

The shop felt strange without Hank. People weren't hanging around and throwing the baloney.

I didn't notice Susan right away. She looked different. Older. More like her mother. She didn't seem to be working. She was just standing there, looking lost.

Before I could get a word out, Jimmy began blabbing away to her.

"You look like a paleface, Injun. Didn't you get any sun out there in KooKooLand? That's all that goddamn place is good for."

"Aunt Irene took me to Muscle Beach," she said flatly. "But it wasn't very sunny."

"I know Muscle Beach," boasted Jimmy. "I was there when I was in the merchant marine, docked in San Pedro. It's just a bunch of fairies who think they're he-men. I could swab the deck with 'em without leavin' a streak."

Susan looked away from Jimmy. I tried to catch her eye, but I seemed to be invisible to her.

"I'm going into the hospital," she mumbled. "In Massachusetts. McLean Hospital."

I froze. Maybe she was dying.

"McLean? That's the best goddamn joint around," Jimmy assured her. "They'll get your head screwed on straight. Hell, after everything that's happened, I wouldn't mind goin' there myself."

"Well, the more, the merrier," she said.

I relaxed a bit. She was just going to a loony bin.

Jimmy lowered his voice and leaned closer to her.

"Your old man didn't know what he was doing. You know that, don't you?"

"I know," said Susan. "I know."

"Good," said Jimmy. "That's good. Kids gotta respect their father no matter what. He needs you right now. Your old man needs you. You gotta be strong for him, OK? You're a tough kid. You'll bounce back. You'll be back at college before you know it, making him proud. I'm counting on you. I'm counting on you to become a doctor and find a cure for the Big C before it grabs me by the throat."

Susan managed a weak smile.

Jimmy hugged her and we left.

The only thing I ended up saying was good-bye.

I'd wanted to tell her how sorry I was that her mother was dead. I'd wanted to say it but couldn't open my frickin' mouth. I was afraid Jimmy would yell at me for taking Doris's side.

On the way home, I asked Jimmy if we could drive down and see Susan at the loony bin. He said Susan didn't need a little pip-squeak bugging her when she was trying to get her head on straight. He said I was a dummkopf for even asking. He said he understood Susan better than I ever would 'cause he knew what it felt like to be going off your rocker and I was just a happy-go-lucky kid without a care in the world.

He pulled over just outside the projects and told me he was in a hurry and to hoof it the rest of the way home. I jumped out and he sped off.

I went home and sat in my room and chewed some Chuckles on the side of my mouth where my teeth ached the least. As I sat there, I came up with a new plan.

I'd ditch school one day and hitchhike to the loony bin. I'd find Susan in her hospital bed on the verge of dying. She'd be so glad to see me she'd perk right up. I'd feed her some Chuckles and make her laugh. I'd give her the snow globe with the two sunbathing teen-ragers and she'd say it was the best present she ever got in her whole entire life. She'd ask if we could be pen pals and I'd shout yes yes yes. She'd promise to write every day and to draw hearts and flowers all over the envelopes and to send secret messages only we could understand.

At the end of the visit, I'd steal a needle from the nurse. We'd prick each other's finger and press our fingertips together. I'd feel my blood flow into her and hers into me.

It wouldn't hurt at all.

Then I'd hitchhike home.

I'd get back before school let out and walk in the door like nothing happened.

I'd talk Virginia into forging a note for me. *Please excuse my daughter for being absent, she had a lousy toothache.* At least that part wasn't a lie.

But the more I thought about my plan the more I pictured a million things going wrong. I pictured a hot-rodder trying to pass a truckie as I was hitchhiking and running me over. I pictured freezing to death by the side of the road and being eaten by a bear. I pictured the Boston Strangler coming along and saying, Get in, little girl.

And, just like that, I knew the whole thing was a pipe dream. I was too much of a Chicken Little—*pluck pluck pluck*—to go anywhere. It was Susan who was going somewhere. Going right outta my life.

Not long after that, the snow globe sprang a leak. I picked it up one day and a drop of water plopped onto the floor. I looked closer and saw there was a tiny crack in the plastic. Before long, those teen-ragers would be high and dry. I couldn't believe it. I'd been so careful with the snow globe, watching over it like Jimmy with Victory Bound or like Shirley with Jimmy's favorite supper in the oven. I'd been careful, and still something had happened. Something I couldn't explain.

I wanted to blame somebody. Cockeyed Barney. Hopped-up Bruce. My stupid sister. Sylvester the goddamn cat. Somebody must've been in my bedroom and knocked it over and didn't tell me. I felt like murdering whoever it was. Stabbing them to death like you-know-who. But there was no one around to blame.

I was left with nothing. Nothing but being mad. Good and mad.

I stormed downstairs. I went and got a hammer from our junk drawer. The hammer had a wobbly handle but it worked good enough. I put the snow globe on the floor of my bedroom and didn't even hesitate. I brought the hammer down on it as hard as I could. It splintered like a bar of Turkish Taffy when you smacked it against a counter. A puddle of water was left on the floor looking like Sylvester had peed there.

For the first time I could see how destroying something, really smashing the living daylights out of it, could make you feel better.

I felt powerful. I felt like Popeye when he ate a can of spinach.

Like I could swab the deck with those musclemen just like Jimmy.

Good and Mad

Feeling good didn't last.

Feeling mad didn't go away.

I was mad when I had to go back to school after the holidays.

Mad when I turned ten and realized I'd never be a single digit again and my life was as good as over.

Mad when the birthday present I was given—a ladies' Timex from Uncle Barney—stopped ticking the very next day.

Mad when the Beatles were on Ed Sullivan and Jimmy made me change the channel 'cause they were a bunch of fairies.

Mad when I went to the dentist and had seventeen cavities in my Dracula teeth.

And mad—really mad—when Shirley told me they'd sold Victory Bound. Sold him to someone with lots of dough who could take better care of him. She promised we'd get another horse, but I yelled I didn't want another goddamn horse. I ran up to my bedroom and slammed the door and bawled. And every time I looked at that picture of us in the winner's circle hanging on the wall, I wanted to smash it.

I decided Jimmy had been right all along. Life wasn't fair. It just wasn't fair. Look at Susan. She'd been on top of the world and now she was just trying to keep her head above water. She'd been skiing down mountains and publishing poems and on her way to being a doctor for poor kids and now she was stuck in a nuthouse.

Things didn't seem to be going Hank's way either. The judge refused to toss out the case against him even though somebody had destroyed evidence by mopping up those bloodstains. Jimmy said the judge was as blind as goddamn Helen Keller if he couldn't see that Hank was being railroaded. He talked about getting a dago from Revere to gouge the judge's eyes out so that everyone would know what a blind bastard he was.

But that didn't end up being necessary because, one by one, all those head-shrinkers said Hank was mad. Not just angry mad like me, but crazy mad like

Norman Bates. The headshrinkers told the grand jury—twenty-one men and one woman—that Hank was as nutty as a fruitcake on the night of the murders and was still nuts. They said Hank had no memory of ventilating two people, but they were worried he might ventilate himself if he suddenly remembered. For Hank's own safety, he should be locked up in the nuthouse for life. Or at least until he wasn't nutty anymore.

The grand jury didn't indict Hank for murder.

"He beat the rap!" crowed Jimmy when he heard the news. "*Meep meep,* dummkopfs!"

The jury only made a ruling in the death of John Betley. They didn't even consider Doris's death. I asked Jimmy why that was and he said she wasn't worth anybody's time, she was a goddamn whore.

Hank was committed to New Hampshire Hospital on February 26, 1964, a little more than two months after the murders. He was forty-six years old.

Once again, the city was divided. Some people thought Hank had gotten away with murder. Others thought being married to Doris had been punishment enough.

Personally, I hoped he rotted in there.

I hoped Hank Piasecny was out of all of our lives forever.

I hoped we could adopt Susan.

But none of those things happened.

Still, it was a year before we saw Hank again. Jimmy, of course, wanted to visit him right away. But for the first year only family members were allowed to see him.

"They oughta make an exception for merchant mariners," Jimmy complained. "But those pencil pushers don't know crap about the Brotherhood of Men."

Through the grapevine Jimmy heard that Hank was holding up great and still tough as nails.

The house with the bad lawn and the disappearing bloodstains was sold and the money went to Susan and Terry. Jimmy said Terry could use the dough since he'd gone and screwed up and gotten married and had pip-squeaks instead of playing the field like Jimmy always told him to do.

Susan got out of the fancy nuthouse near Boston. She returned to New Hampshire and began working at a medical lab. She visited Hank all the time. She forgave him for murdering her mother because she'd been raised a good Catholic and she believed in forgiveness.

In 1965, about a year after Hank was committed to the hospital, he was moved to an area where he could mingle with the other patients. He quickly became top dog in the place. Before long, he had the other patients waiting on him hand and foot.

He kept in good shape playing pitch-and-putt golf. Sometimes Susan played with him, but she was always careful to let him do better than her.

Finally, anybody could visit Hank. At first, the hospital had a hard time handling all the people who wanted to see him. They ended up forcing people to make appointments.

One Sunday, Jimmy loaded us all into the Pontiac and drove to the nuthouse.

On the outside, the place didn't seem scary at all. It looked like what I imagined a college would look like: stately old brick buildings on a big lawn with leafy trees and picnic tables. It seemed peaceful and a whole lot nicer than the projects.

I noticed the name of the street the place was on. Pleasant Street.

"Hank was on easy street, now he's on Pleasant Street, poor bastard," said Jimmy as we headed inside.

At the front desk, Jimmy tried to joke around with the woman who was checking us in.

"You've heard of the Mad Monk, Rasputin? Well, we're here to see the Mad Polack Piasecny," he said, laughing.

The old bat glared at him.

"We don't use words like that around here."

"Oh yeah? Which word? *Mad?* Or *Polack?*" He said the words louder to get a rise out of her.

The woman didn't answer. She just sent someone to find Hank.

While we waited, I checked out the other nutcases, wondering how many of them had killed people. Some of them looked pretty kookoo. I was sure Hank would look kookoo too after killing two people. I pictured his eyeballs spinning like pinwheels and his mouth drooling like a Saint Bernard's. But when he showed up he looked the same. Maybe a little happier.

Maybe he was just happy to see us.

"Give your Uncle Hank a kiss," Jimmy ordered Virginia and me.

It ticked me off that Hank, who had never before been called my uncle, was now related to me after ventilating two people, but I forced myself to peck his sandpapery cheek.

Virginia kissed the air near his kisser.

"You look good. You don't look wacko to me," Jimmy kidded him.

"I'm not as wacko as you, greaseball," said Hank.

"Same old Hank!" Jimmy laughed, sounding relieved.

"I gotta talk to you," Hank said to Jimmy. "In private."

They moved off to the side and Hank began to whisper to Jimmy. I wondered if he was giving Jimmy the lowdown on what happened that night, whether he actually cut off the guy's Down There and put it in Doris's mouth. That's what I was hoping to find out.

After a few minutes, Jimmy came back over to us.

"I gotta go run an errand for Hank. You girls keep him company," he said.

Shirley looked panicked.

"I don't know what to say to him," she said.

"He's still Hank. He's the same son of a bitch."

"I'm afraid to be alone with him."

"Don't be an idiot. There's dozens of people around. He's not gonna slice and dice you and the pip-squeaks."

"Can I come with you?" I begged.

"Nah, Dracula. Stay with your old lady."

"I don't know what to say to him," Shirley repeated.

"Just butter him up. Tell him he looks like a million bucks. You know how to do it."

"I'll try," squeaked Shirley.

"Don't try," snapped Jimmy. "Do it." Then he left and drove off the premises.

"Let's get the hell out of here," Hank said to us.

We went outside and sat on a bench with him. I tucked myself behind Shirley so she could shield me if Hank went berserk. Virginia pretended to be fascinated by a nearby stump.

Before Shirley could start buttering Hank up, he started buttering her up.

"You're a sight for sore eyes," he told her.

"Oh, I look like a fright," protested Shirley. "But you, you look like a million bucks," she said with the same frozen smile she wore so often around Jimmy. "You don't look sick or anything, Hank."

"I'm not sick, so why would I look sick?" he asked with a slightly threatening tone that made me scrunch closer to Shirley.

"Of course you're not sick," she said quickly, looking flustered.

"I'll tell you one thing, the crap they serve for food around here could make anybody sick. I sure could use some of your deer stew. Bring me some the next time."

"Of course. I shoulda brought some today. I didn't think. I'm so stupid."

Hank suddenly reached out and stroked Shirley's hair.

"You got hair like Doris."

Shirley nearly choked.

"I shoulda done it up better. I was working all night."

"Jimmy shouldn't let you work that night shift. A woman shouldn't be out at night. You could run into a nutcase like me."

Shirley stiffened up even more. "Oh, Hank, you're not a nutcase."

"I'm just kidding, Shirl. Lighten up, OK?"

Shirley forced out a little laugh.

"I'm slow on the draw, Hank. Jimmy tells me that all the time."

Hank pulled out a cigar.

"Gimme a light," he commanded her.

Shirley rummaged through her purse and came up with a book of matches. As she lit Hank's cigar I could see she was trying to keep her hand from trembling.

One of the other patients, a jittery-looking guy, rushed up to Hank and Shirley with two cups of coffee. Shirley took the coffee politely, but she looked like she was scared the nutcase might have spit in it or something.

"Can I get you anything else, Hank?" the guy asked. "Anything else you need?"

"Nah, beat it," Hank said, and gave the guy a tip.

Soon after, Jimmy returned from his errand.

"I got the milk shakes," he said loudly to Hank.

Yabba dabba doo. At least I was gonna get something outta being forced to spend the afternoon with a maniac.

"Where is it?" asked Hank.

Jimmy nodded in the direction of the parking lot.

Hank stood up.

"Let's take a little stroll," he said.

We all followed Hank. None of the nurses or attendants gave us a second look. Nobody seemed to care that Hank was slipping away. When we got to the car, Jimmy jumped behind the wheel. He told Shirley to slide next to him to make room for Hank, and make it snappy. Virginia and I scrambled into the backseat.

"Where's the milk shakes?" I blurted out.

"Shut up," said Jimmy. "Don't make me have to tell you again."

"I guess you were convincing," Hank laughed. "Nobody can bullshit like a Greek."

Suddenly it hit me—we were kidnapping Hank.

I pictured us screeching out the front gate and Jimmy having a shoot-out with some coppers and me taking a bullet right in the breadbasket.

But Jimmy didn't even turn on the car. He just pulled a bottle of whiskey and a bottle of vodka out of a paper bag and told me to hand him a couple of those free tumblers that were on the backseat.

Then he passed Shirley an unopened bottle of ginger ale and told her to do the honors, because she made the best goddamn highballs in the world, always the right amount of whiskey and not too much ginger ale to water them down.

Hank was having vodka, straight up.

"Where's the bottle opener?" asked Shirley, doing her best to orchestrate mixing drinks while sandwiched between Jimmy and Hank.

"Check the glove compartment," Jimmy told Hank.

Hank opened it and found the bottle opener. He handed it to Shirley.

Then something else in the glove compartment caught his eye. He reached in and pulled out a large knife I had never seen before.

"That's a real beauty," said Hank, holding it out and admiring it as I held my breath, afraid he was gonna stab my mother and then me and maybe Virginia too if she wasn't fast enough to get away.

"A guy came into my old man's beer joint last week and was selling it," said Jimmy. "It's the real McCoy. A Nazi knife."

Hank turned the knife over and I saw there was a swastika on the handle.

Hank ran his hand along the blade of the knife.

My stomach knotted up so bad I had to bite my lip to keep from going in my pants.

I knew Jimmy would yell at me if I asked to go to the bathroom, so I held it in. Held in all the shit that seemed to want to come out.

"I wish I had a dozen more of those," said Jimmy. "I could sell 'em and make a killing."

"I'd buy one," said Hank, still admiring it.

Finally he put the knife back in the glove compartment.

Jimmy made a toast to his seafaring brother and they started talking about the merchant marine.

But I couldn't stop thinking about that knife.

I knew what a swastika was. Several months back, Jimmy had shown me a book about Nazis. He told me he admired them 'cause they were military geniuses.

If they were so smart, how come they lost, I had asked, feeling pretty smart myself.

Hitler made one wrong move, he said. He never shoulda invaded Russia. He made one wrong move and all of history was changed.

But you wouldn't have wanted him to win, would you? He was a bad man, wasn't he?

Don't believe everything you hear, kiddo. Some people would call your old man bad too. But those people are a bunch of milquetoasts. They do what they're told and are led around like a donkey with a ring in its goddamn nose. Other people like your old man and Hitler are leaders and outlaws and they're respected and feared and they don't win no popularity contests.

But didn't Hitler kill a lot of people?

He didn't kill as many as they said. That Holocaust is overrated.

What's a hollow cost?

Hitler killed a few Jews. Boo hoo hoo. He also killed a bunch of Lithuanians, Russians, and Poles. Hell, a lot of goddamn Greeks died too, but they're tough and don't go around bellyaching about it all the time like the Jews. The Jews, they're weak people. Look at them. Most of them wear glasses. They wouldn't even see the enemy until it was too late. You need good eyesight to be able to defend yourself. Like me. I got better than 20/20 and that's why I'm a goddamn crack shot and nobody's ever gonna mess with me.

Virginia wears glasses, I said. Does that mean she's weaker? I didn't let on that my own eyesight wasn't so hot lately and that I often found myself squinting at the blackboard in school.

Yeah, Virginia's weaker than you even though she's older. She don't have your moxie.

He took a hit off a cancer stick and then said, the Jews are smart though, I'll give 'em that. If anybody's gonna come up with a cure for the Big C, it'll be a goddamn Jew.

Maybe Hitler killed the Jew who was gonna come up with a cure for the Big C, I said.

Jesus, leave it to you to come up with that. I hope you're not turning into a bleeding heart.

I'm not, I said, I'm not. But really, I wasn't sure.

"So, what about Doris?" I heard Jimmy ask Hank, and that snapped me right out of thinking about Nazis.

Jimmy was peering around Shirley to get a better look at Hank.

"How're ya doin' with all that? You got your head on straight?"

Hank took a slug of booze and turned toward Jimmy. With his face in profile, I could only see half a smile.

"All my troubles are six feet under," he said, sounding pretty carefree.

Jimmy grinned.

Pretty soon Hank slipped the bottle of vodka in his pocket and said he hadda get going. A whole lotta other people were coming to see him.

Jimmy offered to bring him a bottle anytime, but Hank said he had it covered. The attendants would get him whatever he wanted.

Hank gave Shirley a good-bye kiss. She smiled with gritted teeth.

As we drove away from the hospital, Jimmy was high as a kite.

"He's crazy, my ass," he said. "Crazy like a fox."

Then he sang the theme song to *Zorro*.

Zorro, the fox so cunning and free . . .

Usually, I sang along with him. But that day I just didn't feel like it.

Paint It Black

After that, hunting season rolled around and something wasn't right with Jimmy's rifle. He really needed Hank to take a look at it. He just didn't trust anybody else not to screw it up. So, Jimmy drove the rifle up to the nuthouse with me riding shotgun. When we arrived, Jimmy went to get Hank and I moved from the front seat to the back to make room for him. I wasn't so nervous about seeing him this time.

Hank didn't too look happy to see us or to be messing around with Jimmy's gun. He told Jimmy the gun was shot and said Jimmy was too much of a cheap Greek to buy a new one. Jimmy told him he was a stupid Polack, the gun was a sweetheart, and he better not mess it up. They had a few drinks and Hank fixed the gun up almost as good as new. Word got around that Hank was back in business, and other hunters brought their guns up to the nuthouse.

Hank kept seeing the headshrinkers and they thought he was almost as good as new too.

Jimmy, on the other hand, was not doing so hot.

He began seeing a headshrinker of his own. He didn't let on to Hank or his hunting buddies or even to Dr. C, his Greek doctor. It was a big secret and we had to keep it on a stone wall.

A Yankee doctor had been the one to tell Jimmy to see the headshrinker. Jimmy had gotten friendly with the guy while trimming his arborvitaes. Before long, Jimmy was showing up at the doctor's office all the time, certain he was dying of the Big C. The doctor thought a headshrinker might be able to convince Jimmy of what he kept telling him—that he was as strong as an ox except in the noggin department.

At first Jimmy said he wouldn't be caught dead going to a headshrinker.

I'm not crazy, he insisted. I'm sick.

The Yankee doctor said he didn't think Jimmy was crazy or sick. He just thought Jimmy was reading too damn many medical books from the library. He said Jimmy knew more about the Big C than most doctors and that it was a shame he wasn't cutting out tumors instead of clipping hedges.

Finally Jimmy agreed to give it a shot. He started going to a headshrinker in Massachusetts so nobody would find out about it. Sometimes he took me along to keep him company during the long ride.

On the way home after one of his appointments I asked him what went on with the headshrinker. He said he talked about what a raw deal life was. And about how YaYa had made him less of a man by not giving him a rifle when he was eight. And about how Papou had made him a goddamn hypochondriac by letting his appendix burst, which nearly killed him.

Your goddamn parents screw you up, he said. They screw you up good. But you still gotta respect them. Remember that the next time you feel like sticking a shank in my breadbasket.

I said I would. I'd respect my parents. I knew that's what the Greeks believed and the Catholics too. It's what Susan had to do. She had to respect Hank even though he had stabbed her mother in the breadbasket. She had to keep going to visit him and act like nothing had happened.

Jimmy kept going to the headshrinker, week after week, and it seemed that, like Hank, he was getting better too. Christmas season of 1965 rolled around and he didn't complain about it nearly as much. He even bought Shirley a present. A ladies' Timex from Uncle Barney that I hoped wouldn't stop ticking and end up in the bottom of a drawer like mine had the previous year.

Unfortunately, Jimmy's good mood didn't rub off on Virginia. She got even more down in the dumps after Christmas than usual. She started cleaning our room constantly and washed her hands all the time. She walked around with soapsuds on her hands, rubbing them until the skin cracked and bled.

Jimmy said she took after YaYa, who was so clean she washed every can of goddamn corn that came in the house. He said YaYa had screwed Virginia up when she took care of her when she was little just the way she had screwed him up.

He told Virginia to quit washing her mitts or he'd chop 'em off and feed 'em to Fuad Ramses.

So Virginia stopped hand washing and started shoplifting.

And it turned out she had a real knack for it. She filled our bedroom closet with stolen loot. Rolling Stones records. British rock magazines. Black stockings. Black boots. Black miniskirts. More black stockings.

One day Virginia came home from school looking big as a house. Under her baggy, black, Greek-lady coat she was wearing several layers of S-E-X-Y black clothes with the tags chewed off.

"He's never gonna let you wear any of that stuff," I choked.

"I change on my way to school, dummkopf," she said. "Hitler doesn't have a clue what I'm wearing. And if you don't wanna be the laughingstock of sixth grade, you'll do the same thing."

She was older and knew the score so I did what she said. I changed in doorways, behind bushes, between cars. Virginia let me borrow anything that she didn't have first dibs on.

We were the two grooviest-looking birds in the projects.

Then it all came crashing down. Like a numbskull, Virginia wrote a note to her best friend, Carol, explaining why she was swiping all those black stockings. The reason being she'd read in one of those British magazines that Mick Jagger fancied birds in black stockings.

Carol's mother found the note and gave it to Jimmy. The old lady was getting back at Virginia. The week before, Virginia had told Carol she thought her mom and Jimmy were jumping each other's bones and Carol had gone and repeated it to her old lady. Carol's mother denied it, but, of course, we found out later that Virginia was right.

After Jimmy got that note, he came barreling into the house. It was pretty late. Shirley had already left for work. I was in the top bunk, reading a Nancy Drew. Virginia was rolling her hair up in OJ cans. Sylvester was batting one of the cans around on the floor.

We knew by the pounding of Jimmy's footsteps on the stairs that something bad was about to happen. He charged into the room and lunged for Virginia. He yanked an OJ can out of her hair, taking some hair with it.

She screamed and Sylvester dove under the bed.

"You know who wears black stockings?" he bellowed at her. "Goddamn whores! Goddamn whores!"

He began to pull all our clothes out of the closet. Not just the stuff Virginia had stolen. Everything. He spat on the clothes. He ripped up the black stockings. He tore the magazines to shreds. He snapped the Rolling Stones albums like they were potato chips. He decapitated my Ringo doll.

"Daddy don't Daddy don't Daddy don't," I wailed. But he just kept destroying everything he could get his hands on.

The whole time Virginia didn't say a word and that enraged him even more.

He grabbed her hair and dragged her down the stairs.

I followed, whimpering.

"Daddy don't Daddy don't Daddy don't."

"What do you have to say for yourself?" he screamed at Virginia.

She was as silent as the Mummy. She didn't cry. She just glared at him. I was used to seeing her crumple when Jimmy got mad. But now she was sixteen going on seventeen and he could go to hell.

The more defiant Virginia got, the angrier Jimmy became.

"Say something, you little bitch!" he yelled.

She didn't say a word. She just kept staring at him like she wanted to stick a shank in his breadbasket.

Jimmy pushed her to the floor and grabbed her bare feet.

"Goddamn black stockings! Goddamn whore!" he kept shouting, and began to yank her around by her feet.

"Leave her alone! Leave her alone!" I begged him.

"Shut up! Your sister's a goddamn whore and a goddamn thief!"

He kept dragging her around, but she still didn't say a word.

Finally, he dropped her feet like they were napalm.

"Get on your knees," he told her. "Get on your goddamn knees."

She didn't move.

"Do what he says," I cried. "Just do what he says."

Virginia struggled to sit up and got on her knees like she was about to start praying.

He stood over her.

"Say you respect me."

She didn't say a word.

He slapped her face.

"Say it. Say you respect me."

She didn't say it.

He slapped her again.

"Say you respect me. Say it or I'll put a bullet through your goddamn head."

"Say it!" I screamed.

She glared up at him.

"I respect you," she said, her voice dripping with insincerity.

"Say it again."

"I respect you."

"Say it again."

"I respect you."

Each time she said it she sounded more disrespectful. I thought he was gonna plug her for sure. But just her saying it seemed to satisfy him.

"Now get your ass upstairs and clean up that mess. I want you to throw all that crap in the garbage."

Virginia got off her knees and we both went back upstairs.

"My own daughter's a goddamn whore," he called after us.

"He's the one who's fooling around, not me," Virginia said under her breath.

We salvaged what we could and threw out the rest. I kept Ringo's head. Virginia kept a pair of black stockings.

Free at Last

After that, Virginia became even more sullen.

"I'm just counting the days," she told me. "Counting the days till I'm eighteen and out of this hellhole."

"Where will you go?" I asked.

"England. Where else, dummkopf?"

"How will you get there, dummkopf? It costs a lotta dough."

"I'll take a bus to New York and then stow away on a boat," she said.

We knew where the boats to Europe left from because we'd gone there to see YaYa and Papou off. Every few years they went back to Greece to lord it over the relatives who still lived in the old country.

Virginia's plan got me to thinking. She had only one year and three months to go until she was eighteen, the age when kids were free to tell their parents to screw off. But I'd just turned twelve. I didn't think I could make it six years without ending up six feet under.

So I hatched a plan with Tina. We'd run away to England too. We'd become go-go dancers. I'd marry Ringo. She'd marry Paul.

I packed some supplies—Skippy peanut butter, Ritz crackers, Chuckles, and Lipton tea bags 'cause I'd heard English people guzzled tea like Pepsi.

One day after school I stole a double sawbuck from Shirley's purse while she was sleeping. Then I snuck out the back door with my suitcase.

Tina was waiting for me. She held a pillowcase filled with Fig Newtons, Twinkies, Lorna Doones, and a Bible. We began to trudge toward the downtown bus station a few miles away.

It was freezing cold and I was hungry and the suitcase was heavy. I kept shifting it from one hand to the other. Tina was dragging her pillowcase on the ground.

The truth was the whole thing was doomed from the start, but neither of us wanted to admit it.

After getting about halfway there, I turned to Tina.

"We started too late," I said. "It'll be dark by the time we get there."

Tina looked relieved.

"We shouldn't have left before dinner," she said.

"Maybe we should go back," I suggested.

Tina was already turning around.

The trip back seemed harder and longer. I could see my dream of freedom receding with every step.

Tina and I said good-bye, vowing to try another day.

I snuck the suitcase back into the house and the money back into Shirley's purse.

It would be a long time until I gained my freedom.

Hank, on the other hand, looked like he might be going free any day.

His lawyer, Stanley Brown, filed a motion for him to be released from the hospital. Brown presented reports from three headshrinkers saying Hank was now as sane as anybody and should be let out.

It had been less than two and a half years since the murders.

The newspaper was once again filled with stories about Hank and I pored over each one.

Dr. Harry Kozol, the big-shot headshrinker who had helped convince the grand jury that Hank was nuts, now said Hank was "a very sober man."

"I am certain that this man, out in society . . . will not do something weird or twisted or harmful," he testified.

In fact, the big shot had changed his mind about what had caused Hank to stab two people in the first place. He'd originally thought Hank was a paranoid schizophrenic—a term I had to get Jimmy to explain. But now he just felt Hank had had a lousy, rotten marriage.

"He reacted to a long stress, causing him to crack. I doubt very many men could stand this so long."

It didn't seem to matter that Hank was no longer under the homicide-inducing stress of being married to Doris when he killed her. Apparently just having been married to her all those years was enough. But now that she was out of the way he was hunky-dory.

When Hank appeared before the hospital staff to discuss his possible release he said the main thing he had been guilty of in the past was putting his wife on a pedestal. His manner was described as aggressive and hostile, and he even talked about the county attorney being out to get him.

Nobody seemed to hold any of that against him.

Of course there were still some people who didn't want Hank to go free. The assistant attorney general. The family of John Betley. And the do-gooders who thought Hank shoulda fried in the first place.

But the law was clear. If the headshrinkers said Hank was OK there was nothing anyone could do to keep him locked up.

On August 3, 1966, Hank was paroled from the nuthouse. He had to see a headshrinker and a probation officer for a little while, but that was it.

"Doris must be turning over in her goddamn grave," said Shirley, and I knew she was really PO'd 'cause usually she didn't curse.

"Am I gonna have to call Hank Uncle Hank now?" I sulked.

I was sitting crouched by the TV. We were watching the Red Sox and I was all set to switch the channel bingo bango if Jimmy came home.

"Over my dead body," Shirley said.

Before long, Hank came over to have a drink with Jimmy. I kept my distance and eavesdropped on them from the kitchen.

"You dodged a bullet, you sonofabitch," said Jimmy. "I hope you gave Stanley Brown a big frickin' tip."

"He got paid good. He didn't need a goddamn tip."

"You didn't throw him a little extra, you cheap Polack?"

"Don't start bugging me, Greek. I gotta keep my nose clean. I can't get into any goddamn fights."

"You're too old to fight me now, Polack. You're almost fifty. You're an old buck. Hell, my kid could take you. That's right, a skinny little girl could take you."

"Shut up. I'm warning you."

"I can ride you like crazy. I can ride you like goddamn Seabiscuit," Jimmy laughed, "and you can't do a goddamn thing about it."

"Screw you, Greek," Hank snapped, and walked out the door.

"Whatsa matter? They take away your sense of humor in the cracker factory?" Jimmy called after him.

Hank didn't answer. He didn't look back. He just drove away.

"Maybe he won't come back," I said hopefully.

"He'll be back. He's just gotta cool down like a racehorse," Jimmy said.

Jimmy was right. Hank cooled down and they were still buddies.

But for a guy used to getting into fights all the time, not being able to get into one was gonna be a tall order.

Not long after he walked out on Jimmy, Hank slipped into a bar called Cecille's. He sat by himself, drinking and minding his own business.

Three egghead college boys from out of town were yukking it up near him.

They didn't know who the hell Hank Piasecny was. All they saw was an old buck in a fedora hat. That hat cracked them up. They rode him about it like goddamn Seabiscuit.

Hank sat there steaming mad.

Fortunately, a guy Hank knew, Butch, was also in the bar. Butch came over and asked Hank why he didn't clock those punks. When Hank explained his predicament, Butch got mad too.

He clocked the punks for Hank. One. Two. Three.

"I wish I'd been there," said Jimmy when Hank gave him the blow-by-blow the next time he stopped by. "I woulda stuck my Nazi knife in them and dumped their bodies at sea. The world woulda had three less eggheads. Good riddance, fish bait."

Hank laughed pretty hard at that and they drank a toast to Butch.

If Hank couldn't defend his honor, there were still a lot of guys around who would do the job for him.

But not every social outing turned out so well for him.

Soon after, Jimmy invited Hank to go out clubbing with him and Shirley, just like in the old days. Hank was going stag, but Jimmy assured him there were lots of desperate broads at the joint they were going to who would go for an old buck like him.

As usual, Jimmy made Shirley try on a bunch of dresses before they left. I helped her zip and unzip them, getting the fabric caught in the zipper a few times 'cause Jimmy kept telling us to hurry the hell up. Hank was meeting them at the club and Jimmy didn't want to keep the big shot waiting.

When they got to the club, though, none of the desperate broads wanted to fox-trot with Hank. They didn't want those hands that had ventilated two people wrapped around their rib cage. One by one, they turned Hank down. Jimmy whispered to Shirley to get her ass up and dance with Hank so he didn't look like a palooka. Shirley did as she was told, praying that the song would be a short one. While they were dancing, the owner of the joint, a Greek guy, came over to Jimmy. He asked Jimmy to please, please not bring Hank in there again 'cause he was scaring all the women. He asked real nice 'cause he knew Jimmy had a temper. He promised Jimmy free drinks whenever he wanted and that got Jimmy to go along with the plan. When Hank and Shirley returned to the table, Jimmy was already standing up.

"Let's blow this joint," he said to Hank. "I shouldn't have taken you to such a dive. You couldn't pay me to sleep with these broads."

"Me neither," said Hank. "I wouldn't do 'em for free."

Susan Grows Up, Not Me

Around the time that Hank got out of the nuthouse, Susan finally returned to college. She'd gotten her head mostly straightened out and she still dreamed of going to medical school. She enrolled in the University of New Hampshire and planned to study real hard and graduate in a year.

I was excited to hear that Susan was back to being Susan, that her old man being a murderer hadn't totally messed up her life.

Jimmy gave himself some of the credit. He said he'd had a talk with her. He told her to get her ass back in the ring. He said she was ahead on points and it was no time to throw in the goddamn towel.

All that fall I kept pestering Jimmy about how Susan was doing. He said she was breezing through her classes and already applying to medical school.

I pictured her in her white coat saving dying pip-squeaks right and left.

But right before Christmas, at the end of Susan's first semester, I heard some startling news.

"Susan got herself hitched," Jimmy said.

I couldn't believe it. What about all the dying pip-squeaks?

"She's not dropping out," Jimmy assured me.

Still, I felt Susan had let me down. Maybe she was still messed up in the head? 'Cause who in their right mind would want a stupid husband—someone telling you where to go, what to do, what to wear?

I grilled Jimmy about the guy, but he didn't know much. He said he was a lot older than Susan and he'd been in the military.

"Did Hank make her get married?" I asked, immediately putting the blame on him.

"Nah. Hank doesn't even care for the joker."

"So why would Susan do it?"

"All girls need a husband. Otherwise everyone thinks they're a whore or a lesbian."

"Why do people think they're Lebanese?"

Jimmy cracked up.

"Not Lebanese, dum-dum, lesbian. It's when two girls wanna jump in the sack together."

Jimmy could tell I was confused. That amused him even more.

"Hell, I woulda thought you had put all this together by now. You're s'posed to be a brain. Didn't the kids at school tell you about fairies and dykes?"

"Sure," I said. "I know all about fairies."

"You're not as smart as you think you are, kiddo. You're not such an egghead. How much do you know about the birds and the bees?"

"I know all about that," I mumbled, feeling my face burning up and wishing I could turn into a fairy and fly away.

"I knew the score when I was way younger than you. Hell, I wasn't much older than you when I lost my cherry. I'll never forget it. I played hooky and went to Hampton Beach and met this woman, a real knockout. She took me under the boardwalk and made a man of me."

I just kept looking down at the kitchen floor, counting the squares of cracked linoleum, hoping Jimmy would shut up. But he didn't.

"I took right to it, like a duck to water. She didn't even know it was my first time."

"It's my bedtime," I finally blurted out. "Can I go to bed?"

"Yeah. Just remember one thing. It's different for boys and girls. Boys are s'posed to fool around. Girls gotta stay pure as the driven snow. Not ninety-nine percent Ivory Soap pure. One hundred percent pure. If I ever catch you fooling around, I'll put a bullet right here."

He put a finger right between my just-beginning-to-rise breasts.

I shot out of the kitchen and up the stairs and into my bedroom.

The room was icy cold. Virginia had the window cracked and was blowing cigarette smoke out the crack.

"Daddy's creepy," I said.

"Tell me about it," she said. "Five more months and I'm outta here."

"Susan went and got married."

"That's probably the only way she could get away from creepy Hank," said Virginia as she blew a perfect smoke ring out the window.

"Can you teach me how to do that?" I asked.

"You're too young to smoke," she said, but I begged her, knowing she'd give in.

I got the hang of it real fast.

As I blew smoke rings I kept thinking about Susan getting hitched and vowed never to follow in her footsteps. More and more, I was seeing the world in a new light. It was 1966, for cripes' sake! Things were changing. Didn't Susan know? I sure did. Virginia had given me some pot to try a few months back and life was full of possibilities. Marriage was for squares. Old fogies. Grown-ups. And grown-ups were the Enemy.

So I kinda wrote Susan off. Sayonara, Susan.

That Christmas, Shirley's Secret Present to me, the thing I wanted most of all in the world, was a pair of white go-go boots. I danced around my bedroom in them, planning to audition for *Hullabaloo* as soon as I turned eighteen.

Right after New Year's, a man named Albert DeSalvo, who had confessed to being the Boston Strangler, was locked up for life. Jimmy did his best to convince me that they'd nabbed the wrong guy. He insisted the Strangler was still out there ready to pounce. But I was twelve by then and didn't scare so easy. What bothered me more than what Jimmy said was that the Strangler didn't turn out to be a loner like Norman Bates. He was a dago who coulda passed for a Greek and he had a wife and two kids. Even scarier, he had the same head-shrinker, Dr. Harry Kozol, who had helped Hank beat the rap.

"Maybe that headshrinker will decide the Strangler is normal like Hank and the Strangler will get sprung one day too," I said to Jimmy.

"Don't be a dummkopf," he replied. "The Strangler was found guilty by a jury and Hank wasn't."

"How come?"

"Because they said Hank was nuts and the Strangler was sane."

"I don't get it."

"It's all a big song and dance, kiddo. Maybe if the Strangler had had Hank's lawyer instead of that palooka F. Lee Bailey he'd be knocking on our door right now."

That night, Jimmy scratched on my bedroom door, pretending to be the Strangler. I didn't cower in bed like I used to. I jumped down from the top bunk and threw open the door.

"Ha ha, you can't fool me anymore," I said, when Jimmy looked surprised.

"You're a little killjoy," he said. "You wait, I'll get you next time. I'll get you good."

I closed the door and went back to bed, trying not to think about what murder or mayhem he had in store for me.

I was tired of thinking about murder and mayhem. I was almost a teen-rager and what I cared about was peace and love.

Not that I could let on to Jimmy what a peacenik I had become. I still acted like the same pip-squeak who ate up *Blood Feast*. I pretended to be all gung ho to see *Frankenstein Created Woman* when Jimmy took me to it. But even he had to admit the movie was a real stinker.

"It's those bleeding hearts, they're ruining the movies," railed Jimmy on the way home. "There hasn't been a decent slice-and-dice since *Blood Feast*. The raggedy-ass do-gooders don't want us to see blood, not in the movies, not in Vietnam, not in a goddamn hamburger. They want us to live in a goddamn bloodless world and eat weeds. Well, I got news for them. Real life is bloody. It's a bloody horror movie."

I sat there feeling smug. Jimmy was wrong.

The darkness was lifting and he was blind.

Turn on, tune in, drop out, dummkopf.

Good Blood, Bad Blood

Not long after that, I started to bleed. I woke up one morning and there it was. Virginia had once told me that I would start bleeding Down There, but I thought she was trying to scare me.

I ran downstairs to Shirley, who was just home from work, nursing a high-ball and looking like she'd just set a new world's record in sunglass making.

"I'm bleeding to death," I blubbered.

Shirley assessed the situation and turned bright red.

"You're fine," she mumbled.

"I'm not fine. I'm dying," I cried.

"It's not bad blood, it's good blood," she said.

She quickly explained I'd have cramps and have to wear a napkin once a month from then on. She told me to hide the napkins in the garbage so Jimmy would never know they were there.

"He can't stand the sight of woman's blood."

"I hate blood. I don't wanna bleed."

"It's good blood," Shirley repeated. "It's so you can have a baby someday."

"I don't want a squalling brat."

"You sound just like your father."

"I do not."

"The blood means you're becoming a grown-up," she said, thinking that might cheer me up.

"I don't wanna be a grown-up. I hate grown-ups."

"You hate me?" she asked, sounding hurt.

"No, you're not a grown-up. You're my mother."

"I sure feel like a grown-up," she said. "I feel like an old lady. My baby's not a baby anymore."

It was true, we were all getting older.

Virginia finally turned eighteen, in May 1967. I thought she'd split for England right on her birthday, but she didn't. Shirley made her a cake and as she blew out the candles I asked what she was wishing for.

"To win the sweepstakes, dummkopf."

"The sweepstakes is gambling for dummkopfs," said Jimmy. "For Joe Blow too dumb to handicap a race."

"You wouldn't say that if we won," countered Shirley, who had taken to secretly buying sweepstakes tickets and hiding them in a Kotex box.

"No one from this family is gonna win, 'cause the odds are a billion to one and we're cursed with Norris Luck."

"It doesn't cost anything to dream," Virginia said.

A month later, she graduated from high school and got a job as a waitress at the restaurant in the Carpenter Hotel, where people drank tea just like they were in Merry Olde England. Jimmy made her turn over most of the money she made to pay for her room and board 'cause that's what Papou had made him do.

One Saturday morning after Shirley got home from work, she took me to the Carpenter so we could see where Virginia worked. We went for breakfast because that was the cheapest meal of the day. Shirley did her hair up like she was going out clubbing and we both got dressed up. I wore a minidress I had talked her into buying me. She let me wear it because Jimmy was out fishing on the *Aristotle Onassis*.

The dining room seemed grand, but Virginia looked miserable. She was dressed like a maid and her hair was pulled back instead of hanging in her kisser the way she liked it. She was small, barely 5'1"—I already towered over her—and she was dwarfed by the big plates of blueberry pancakes we had ordered.

"My wrists are killing me," she said when she awkwardly dropped the plates in front of us.

"You look nice," I lied.

"I do not, you little liar," she said.

"It's like Buckingham Palace in here," said Shirley. "You won't want to eat my cooking after working here."

"Those pancakes are as tough as a Frisbee compared to yours," Virginia said, and she was right.

We left her a big tip even though she wasn't the best waitress in the world.

"She'll get the hang of it," Shirley said. "It sure beats slaving away in a factory."

Meanwhile, Susan had also graduated. She was twenty-five and her big dream was coming true. She would be heading off to medical school at the University of Vermont in the fall, one of just a few girls there studying to be doctors.

Hank came over to share the good news.

"I always knew she'd go far," said Jimmy. "Maybe she'll find a cure for the Big C."

"For Chrissake, shut the hell up about the Big C."

"Hey, it don't matter how tough you are. Any one of us could get it. Even you."

"I'm not afraid of any goddamn cancer."

"Don't say that word in this house!" Jimmy barked, superstitious about saying the word *cancer* 'cause YaYa had made him superstitious about saying it.

"Jesus, you Greeks are all goddamn head cases."

"Yeah? Look who's talking, the guy who whacked his wife."

Jimmy burst out laughing and I thought Hank was gonna slug him for sure, but Hank just laughed too and they had a drink to celebrate Susan's success.

After that, Jimmy made me go and get my seventh-grade report card. He flashed it at Hank. I had gotten all As again that year.

"See that? You're not the only one with an egghead daughter," he said. "Maybe *my* kid will find the cure for the Big C, not yours."

"Susan don't wanna cure the Big C," Hank insisted. "She wants to study blood."

"Oh yeah? Hematology?" said Jimmy. "Hey, that's a damn good field. They say everything, and I mean everything, starts in the blood."

Good Goddamn Riddance

That summer the whole world moved to KooKooLand and Jimmy said they oughta drop a bomb on it. It was the Summer of Love.

I almost ran away but I didn't.

Virginia didn't get the hang of things at the restaurant like Shirley said and got canned. Jimmy told her she better find a husband quick, preferably one who didn't know she was a hopeless case in the kitchen department. He said he was gonna ask around and find a Greek boy just off the boat for her to marry.

That got Virginia to finally twenty-three skidoo. She'd been dragging her feet about it for several months. For one thing, it was taking her a long time to save up enough dough 'cause Jimmy was taking it all. For another, she was afraid Jimmy would kill her before he let her walk out the door.

She was almost right.

When she told him she was moving out, all hell broke loose.

"You're not leaving my goddamn house to go whoring around and ruin my good name!" Jimmy shouted at her, blocking the front door.

Virginia was lugging two shopping bags that I had helped her pack, both of us blubbering all the while.

"It's the law," Virginia sobbed. "You can't stop me."

I hovered right behind her, not wanting her to go either.

"She's gotta go sometime," Shirley choked out. "You were fifteen when you left YaYa and Papou's and—"

"I was going off to frickin' war, not to screw around," he shot back, which didn't make sense since he was always bragging about making it over there with a bunch of German dolls.

"I'm just saying, she's grown-up—"

Jimmy stuck his face right into Shirley's.

"Keep your snout out. She's not even your goddamn kid."

While Jimmy was distracted by Shirley, Virginia bobbed and weaved around him and made it out the front door.

Jimmy went tearing after her.

Sylvester shot out the front door like he wanted to jump in one of those shopping bags.

I stood frozen for a moment, then charged outside too, with Shirley right behind.

Jimmy was slapping and kicking Virginia all the way down the sidewalk as she tried to get away.

"Jim, don't!" cried Shirley.

"Don't hurt her!" I sobbed.

He didn't seem to hear us. He looked like he was in a trance. He kept slapping and kicking.

I was sure he was gonna kill her. I had to do something. So I jumped on his back and wrapped my scrawny arms around his broad chest like when he used to carry me through the Combat Zone.

"Leave her alone leave her alone leave her alone!" I screamed, my face scrunched up like a little fist.

He stumbled back like he was drunk as a skunk, which he was, and I held on for dear life.

"Get in the house or you'll be next," he bellowed.

My sneak attack gave Virginia an opening. She broke free and took off down the street, looking back once.

"I'm sorry," she moaned. I knew what she meant. Sorry to leave us. Sorry for what he might do to me now.

Jimmy finally shook me off. I landed on my keister and quickly scrambled back up.

Several neighbors were peering out their windows. The Greek girls across the street looked horrified. Their older brother, who was home from the service, stepped outside in his uniform.

"What's the trouble, Jimmy?" he called out.

"Trouble? My goddamn daughters, that's the goddamn trouble."

"If you don't calm down, somebody's gonna call the cops."

"Oh yeah? Who's gonna call the cops? You?"

"I didn't say me. But somebody—"

"You call yourself a Greek? Greeks mind their own business. Greeks keep family business within the family. They don't call any cops. You think you're some tough guy in a uniform? Well, come over here, tough guy. I'll fight you."

"I'm not going to fight you, Jimmy. I'd lose. We both know that."

"Goddamn right," Jimmy said.

The Greek boy came across the street and approached Jimmy like he was trying to tame a tiger. He talked to Jimmy in Greek. Jimmy eyed the guy suspiciously, then laughed a few times and started throwing the baloney. He asked the kid if he wanted to marry his oldest daughter and take her off his hands, but the kid said he wasn't in the market for a wife and Jimmy told him that was smart, told him to make it with a lot of women all over the world like he had done in the merchant marine. He lit a cancer stick and invited the kid in for a nightcap, but the kid said no thanks. Jimmy said it was too bad he didn't have a son like him who knew how to respect his elders, and told him to kill a few gooks for him. Then he turned to me and Shirley.

"Get your asses inside," he said. "You're causing a goddamn scene."

We scurried inside, not knowing what would happen once we got in there.

But Jimmy didn't do anything. He just told Shirley that he was starving and to make him a couple of fried egg sandwiches. Then he went in to watch *The Jackie Gleason Show*.

He said only one more thing that night about Virginia leaving.

Good goddamn riddance.

But Virginia didn't go very far.

She just moved in with her friend, Angela, who lived one street over in the projects. Angela was about Susan's age and already had three brats who Virginia sometimes babysat. I babysat them myself once. They hurled a dump truck at my noggin and dumped the Oscar Mayer wieners I was supposed to feed them in a puddle of mud.

Virginia said the brats weren't so bad once you got to know them, and insisted Angela was a great mother. For her, Angela could do no wrong. Angela was her Susan.

Jimmy disagreed. He said Angela was a goddamn whore and a goddamn idiot for having so many goddamn brats.

Virginia steered clear of our street for several weeks. But shortly after I began eighth grade, she started to sneak back home to see Shirley and me when Jimmy's car was gone. That's how I found out she had become crazy about a drummer named Dennis. One Friday night when Shirley was working and Jimmy was out clubbing, Virginia took me to see Dennis play. I put on a pink miniskirt and some white lipstick and we smoked a little pot on the way there. I didn't feel anything from the pot, but I pretended that I did. The gorilla guarding the front door winked at me and let us right in 'cause I looked old for my age. I was jittery with excitement. When we got inside, though, my excitement took a nosedive. The joint was a real dump. It smelled like Clorox and vomit, and the floor was sticky with crud. One corner had been turned into a makeshift stage illuminated by a few dim colored lights. Dennis's band was already playing. I could tell right away they stank. Dennis couldn't keep a beat, but I had to admit he was pretty cute. He had ropes of dirty-blond hair that whipped his eyeballs when he drummed.

"We're madly in love," said Virginia, as I watched Dennis flirting with a bunch of skanks between sets.

"Isn't he ever gonna come over here?" I asked.

"He's gotta say hi to his fans. That's how it is when you're dating a musician. It's kinda hard. I've gotta share him with the world."

Dennis never came over to say hi to us, so I never did get to meet him.

I thought I would down the road 'cause Virginia said they'd be getting married one day, possibly in Golden Gate Park.

But a few months later, Virginia showed up at our apartment crying her eyes out. Dennis had dumped her when she tried to pressure him into moving up the date of their nuptials. She looked like she'd put on some weight and confessed to being so heartbroken she was eating Angela out of house and home.

"Good goddamn riddance," I said, trying to make her feel better and glad that Dennis was out of the picture.

As the weeks passed, Virginia continued to show up crying and continued to get fatter. Finally she broke down and told Shirley and me that she might be in the family way.

"He only put it in a little ways," she sobbed. "He said I couldn't get pregnant that way. He says it must be someone else's, but it isn't. I only did it with him 'cause I thought we were getting married."

"Boys only care about one thing," moaned Shirley. "I told you that."

"No you didn't. You never told me anything about the birds and the bees."

"I—I thought I did," Shirley stammered.

"I don't want a brat," Virginia sobbed. "I threw myself down the stairs at Angela's but nothin' happened."

"I could kill that Dennis. I could shoot him dead," I blurted out.

"It's not his fault. It's my fault," Virginia insisted.

"We have to tell your father," Shirley finally said. "He's going to find out anyway when word gets around that you're big as a house."

"I might as well just kill myself," Virginia whimpered, "before he goes and does it himself."

For the next few weeks I could barely concentrate in school. I was afraid I'd come home one day and find Virginia with her brains blown out. I pictured

Jimmy tossing her bloated body off the *Aristotle Onassis* and telling people she must've gone to KooKooLand with all the other kooks. I racked my brain to figure a way out of the mess but couldn't come up with anything.

Then, one day, I came home from school and saw a note Shirley had left for Jimmy before she went to bed.

The rabbit died the note said. I had no idea what it meant, but I found out when Jimmy got home.

"The test came back positive. Your whore of a sister got herself knocked up. Virginia's no goddamn virgin. But don't tell anyone or I'll knock your teeth down your throat."

I acted like it was news and held my breath to see if he was going for his shotgun.

But Jimmy had another solution.

"I'm getting rid of that brat. I'll be damned if I'm gonna let her drag our name through the mud."

He got on the phone with Dr. C. Even though he was speaking in Greek, I could tell he was begging, and when that didn't work, threatening.

Finally, he hung up.

"I talked him into it," he said. "But we all have to keep our big traps shut or he could lose his license again—for good this time."

"I'll keep it on a stone wall, Daddy. Forever 'n' ever."

When Virginia found out Jimmy was saving her from the mess she had gotten in, she threw her arms around him, sobbing, and told him he was the best father in the whole world.

"Get one thing straight. I'm not doin' it for you, I'm doin' it for me," he said. "So I can show my face in front of Hank and my buddies. So they're not yuk-yuk-yukking behind my goddamn back."

Virginia nodded. She didn't care why he was doing it or who he was doing it for. She just didn't want the brat.

Dr. C said it was too dangerous to do the thing at his office. YaYa and Papou were away in Greece and Jimmy had a key to their place, so he took Virginia over there. Shirley and I went along to take care of her.

Virginia looked scared, but I told her everything would be groovy and then I spat on her.

But things weren't so groovy.

Virginia had waited too long to tell anyone that she was in the family way. It turned out Dr. C couldn't do what he usually did. He tried something else to make Virginia lose the baby. He told Jimmy he'd done the best he could and we'd just have to wait and see what happened and then he took off.

Jimmy took off too. He didn't want to be around any woman's blood and Shirley said there was bound to be a lot of it.

I suddenly felt dizzy.

Don't be a goddamn chicken, *pluck pluck pluck*, I scolded myself. Make believe it's Karo syrup.

Shirley offered to make Virginia and me some Greek food, but that was the last thing we wanted.

After an hour, Virginia got a stomachache. It got a little worse and a little worse. Finally she went into the bathroom and something came out of her. She took one look at it and flushed it away.

We were all relieved.

"That wasn't so bad," Virginia said.

Then she began to bleed. She turned white as a sheet, but the sheets weren't white. Her temperature shot up and she moaned she was dying and screamed to be taken to the hospital.

I started to blubber. Shirley sent me into the other room and called Jimmy.

When Jimmy showed up, he wouldn't take Virginia to the hospital. He'd made a pact with Dr. C not to do it.

"You made your bed, you'll lie in it," he yelled at Virginia through the closed door.

He called Dr. C and begged him to come over and see what he could do.

It seemed like forever before Dr. C got there, but maybe it wasn't.

Dr. C went into the bedroom with Virginia and closed the door.

Shirley sat there numb and Jimmy paced and I promised God I'd never do anything bad or wrong or stupid ever again if he'd just let my sister live.

God was awake and heard me.

The bleeding stopped and Virginia's temperature went down. She was so weak she could barely raise her head off the pillow. Jimmy force-fed her scrambled eggs like Papou did when she was a little girl.

She got better.

Shirley made Dr. C a farina cake to thank him.

Jimmy promised to trim his trees for nothing for the rest of his life.

Dr. C said he just wanted everyone to forget the whole thing. He insisted this was really and truly *the last time* he would bail out any Greek's misbehaving daughter.

"We dodged a bullet," Jimmy told him. "You and me, we dodged a goddamn bullet."

Ball and Chain

Virginia learned her lesson. She got married a few months later, in the summer of 1968, to the first guy who asked her. He wasn't a drummer or even a guy who pretended to be one. He was a budding marine named Wayne.

I begged her not to do it, but she said she owed it to Jimmy for bailing her out of a jam.

Wayne's parents weren't too thrilled about the wedding either. Since Jimmy had no dough and said he wouldn't blow a big wad on a shindig even if he was loaded, Wayne's parents had to spring for it.

I was a bridesmaid and wore a yellow gown that Jimmy said made me look like a banana. I didn't smile for the photos. Besides hiding my Dracula teeth, I was sad about Virginia marrying a guy who bad-mouthed hippies and was gung ho to go to Vietnam.

I didn't think it was a match made in heaven.

I wasn't even sure there was such a thing.

I wanted to believe there was. I really did. I wanted to believe you could meet a guy like Dustin Hoffman in *The Graduate* and run away with him from your miserable life. I wanted to believe you could love the guy and he would love you back until you both croaked. But everywhere I looked it just seemed like men and women, husbands and wives, fathers and mothers hated each other's guts. Everyone in the projects, sooner or later, got busted up. Everyone but Jimmy and Shirley, anyway. But if I knew one thing for sure already, it was that I didn't want a ball and chain like Jimmy.

I'd rather be a goddamn old maid, I thought. That wasn't the worst thing in the world to me anymore.

Now and then I wondered about Susan and how married life was treating her.

One day, I found out.

Jimmy and I had stopped off at the drugstore on our way home from a movie. Jimmy went through a fist-sized container of tranquilizers every month and was there to pick up a refill.

Susan was getting a prescription filled too. She was in her second year of medical school and looked pretty worn out.

"Jesus, Susan, you look like hell," said Jimmy, who never ceased to let a person know if they were not looking their best.

"Hi, Jimmy," Susan smiled weakly. Then she noticed me. "Wow, you're so grown up."

"Hi, Susan," I mumbled, feeling that familiar shyness come over me.

"She's the same old Dracula," Jimmy said, waving his fang fingers in front of his face.

"And you're the same old Jimmy," she said. She turned back to me. "So what grade are you in now?"

"Ninth. I'm finally in high school," I said, hoping that might impress her.

"She wanted to go where you went, Central," Jimmy piped up. "But those pencil pushers said it was out of our district. They didn't want a little project kid in their North End school. Well, nobody tells me where my kid goes. I checked around. My old lady's place made it into their goddamn district, just barely. So I told 'em my kid's living there, screw you."

Susan looked happy for me.

"So, you're living with your grandmother now?"

"Nah, she's still under my roof," said Jimmy.

"So she's supposed to lie and not get caught for four years?"

"Hey, she's my daughter." Jimmy laughed. "I taught her everything I know."

"I hope not," quipped Susan, and changed the subject. "So you been in the winner's circle lately, Jimmy?"

"Ah, I'm mostly outta the game. I had one great horse and there'll never be another like him, so they can keep all those other nags."

The truth was he was broke and couldn't afford another nag, but that was another story.

"Racing's gone to hell anyway," he added. "Did you hear Big Brother's forcing us to have girl jockeys?"

"Girl jockeys, girl doctors. What's the world coming to?" replied Susan.

"Don't get wise, kiddo," said Jimmy. "I know you're a damn good rider, but trotting down country lanes, la-dee-da-dee-da, is not racing. Racing's dangerous. And having dames out there is only gonna make it more dangerous."

"Danger, Will Robinson, danger," Susan intoned, imitating the robot in *Lost in Space*.

"You think it's funny? Those girls're gonna get some good men killed."

"Well, I hope not," said Susan, becoming more serious. "There're enough good men getting killed already."

"So you're still a bleeding heart? Your old lady musta drummed that into you, 'cause it sure as hell wasn't Hank."

Susan suddenly looked morose.

"I've got to get going," she finally said. "I've got a gazillion things to do."

Jimmy put his arm around her.

"You work yourself too hard. Don't let becoming a goddamn doctor make you sick. You don't wanna crack up again, do you?"

"I could use the rest," she joked.

Jimmy lowered his voice.

"Your old man told me that no-good husband of yours smacked you and threw you out of a car or something."

Susan looked away.

"I can't remember what happened exactly," she said. "When the police found me I was unconscious. I was bruised up pretty bad."

I was stunned. Jimmy hadn't said anything to me about Susan getting roughed up.

"I'll get somebody to teach that joker a lesson. Just say the word."

"Jimmy, no! We're getting a divorce, so—"

"I don't like him gettin' off scot-free."

"Well, two wrongs don't make a right."

"Hey, don't gimme that turn-the-other-cheek baloney. I've had it up to here with those suckers. I'd like to teach 'em all a lesson. Sucker Punch 101."

"Whoa, easy," said Susan, patting him like he was a skittish horse. "You don't want to crack up too."

"Yeah, well, there's enough jerkos out there to drive you crazy. Enough to fill the goddamn *Titanic* and take you down with them."

Susan looked like she'd had enough of the conversation.

"I've got to go," she said again. "You steer clear of the icebergs, Jimmy."

"Yeah, you do the same, kid," said Jimmy.

He opened the container of tranquilizers and slipped a few in her pocket.

"Just in case you need to take the edge off."

"Thanks," she said, surprised. "Thanks a gazillion."

"C'mon, Dracula, don't lollygag," he barked at me.

"Bye, Susan," I said quickly.

She surprised me by giving me a hug.

"Say hi to Central," she said, as if it was a person and she missed it.

"I will," I promised.

Not long after that, I heard Susan was back in the hospital. Not the loony bin, the normal kind. Something was wrong with one of her kidneys and they had to yank it out. Jimmy read up on her condition in his medical books and said she was gonna be OK, a person could get by just fine with one kidney.

Hank went to visit her after the operation. They were giving her morphine for the pain. He told her to just tough it out and have a drink instead. He offered her a slug of what he had in his pocket, but she didn't take him up on it.

After several days Susan got released from the hospital. She had to take a leave of absence from medical school to recuperate. She moved back in with Hank. I didn't think that was such a hot idea, but I reminded myself of what all those headshrinkers had said. Hank wasn't ever gonna murder anybody again.

And, anyway, I had my own life to worry about. I was determined to get good grades at Central and prove to Jimmy I was no dummkopf. I studied hard and didn't get too friendly with anyone. I didn't join any clubs or put myself in situations where kids or teachers would start nosing around my life. I didn't want to have to come up with excuses why I couldn't invite anyone over to my place. If anyone asked what my father did I said he was a doctor. It didn't seem like that much of a stretch.

Meanwhile, Jimmy and Hank found other clubs besides the Greek's joint to hang out at, places where the women weren't so picky and didn't mind a quickie with a guy who had ventilated his ex-wife. Hank played the field. He didn't want another ball and chain.

Hank had more free time now 'cause he wasn't running his own business. The state wanted to put an on-ramp to the highway smack in the middle of where his store was and made him shut the place down. Jimmy said he oughta fight the goddamn pencil pushers, but Hank insisted he didn't want the goddamn responsibility anymore.

Hank couldn't just live the life of Riley, though. He'd blown a lot of dough on the shyster. Not to mention his goddamn kids. So he took a job in another guy's boat shop. But that didn't mean he was gonna toe the line. If a customer rubbed him the wrong way, he'd still blow cigar smoke right in the numbskull's kisser. Sometimes, when his boss was out, he'd even have S-E-X right on the guy's desk.

At least that's what he told Jimmy and what Jimmy told me.

Virginia was having a lot of S-E-X of her own. But hers was married S-E-X, which she didn't think was as F-U-N.

By then, Virginia was living with Wayne in military housing in North Carolina. She called home whenever Shirley sent her a few extra bucks. If we were lucky, she called when Jimmy was gone.

"Wayne wants a bunch of brats," she groaned to me over the phone.

"It's 'cause he's Catholic," I said, being an expert on that subject.

"I keep tellin' him we oughta live a little first. I've never even seen the Stones, for cripes' sake."

"Wayne hates the Stones. He's never gonna take you to see 'em."

"I could go by myself."

"Fat chance."

"Well, I'm not havin' a kid. I'm just not."

She lowered her voice, even though Wayne wasn't there. He was off training to kill some gooks, or so he said.

"I'm on the pill. He doesn't know. Keep it on a stone wall. Don't tell Mom and Dad."

"I don't tell them anything, dummkopf."

But by the next phone call, a few months later, Virginia had totally changed her tune. She'd gone off the pill, and was learning to cook and was trying to be a better wife. If Wayne went to Vietnam and got killed, she said, she'd never forgive herself for not trying harder to make him happy.

"I owe him a kid. And, anyway, what else have I got to do?"

"You could do a lot of things."

"Like what. Waitressing? Whoopee-do."

"You could become a stewardess. That way, you could fly back here all the time."

"I'm too short. And my nose is too big."

"Your nose isn't big. Daddy's is."

"I got his stupid nose. You didn't. Thank your lucky stars."

I didn't know what to say about that, so I changed the subject.

"So what did you make Wayne for breakfast this morning?" I asked her.

Wayne ate like a horse and Virginia was always entertaining me with stories of his food consumption.

"A dozen eggs, a pound of bacon, and half a loaf of toast."

"You married Godzilla!" I squealed.

"No, I married a marine," she replied.

A short while later, in the summer of 1969, Virginia came to Old Orchard Beach to see the family. Wayne was still training to go to Vietnam and couldn't come with her. We were up in Maine for Shirley's two-week vacation from the sunglass factory and were staying in the same apartment where I'd had my first taste of lobster. Jimmy's declaration of love for the place was still written above the door, though by now it was pretty faded.

I was trying to talk Virginia into going back on the pill.

"A kid's a ball and chain," I said. "Like in that Janis Joplin song."

"I hate Janis Joplin," Virginia scowled. "She sounds like a hyena."

I couldn't believe my ears. We had always loved the same music.

"Wayne's brainwashing you!" I shouted. "Next thing I know you're gonna be bad-mouthing hippies."

"Well, somebody's gotta go fight for our freedoms and it sure ain't gonna be the hippies."

"I suppose you don't believe in smoking pot anymore either."

Her face lit up. "You got pot?"

Oh yeah, I had pot. Bruce, the lobster poacher who had put together our bunk beds while zonked out on glue had moved up in the world and was now a pot dealer. He had shown up a few days before with a stack of dough and a mountain of grass, both of which he had laid out on our kitchen table. He was trying to entice Jimmy into going into the pot business with him.

"All this could be yours," he said, waving his hand over the drugs and dough like he was Monty Hall on *Let's Make a Deal.*

"Forget it," Jimmy replied. "I don't want no part of nothing the goddamn hippies do. Besides, I tried that crap before those longhairs were in diapers and it don't give you a buzz like booze."

"Try this stuff," Bruce insisted. "It's strong, King Kong strong. They use a special, top-secret-type fertilizer."

"Don't tell me about goddamn fertilizer, OK? I know how to grow a lawn greener than you, greenhorn."

"Maybe you're too scared to get high," needled Bruce, lighting up a joint. "Maybe you're an old geezer now like your pal Hank and you're more chicken than rooster."

"I'll show you who's chicken. I'll bust your skull open and eat your Kentucky Fried brain on a spit."

"Take it easy, Jimmy," Bruce laughed. "I don't want to fight. I'm a lover, not a fighter."

"OK, lover boy, I'll show you. Gimme a goddamn puff," Jimmy barked.

Bruce passed the joint to Jimmy.

"Hold it in till your lungs feel like they're gonna explode," coached Bruce.

Jimmy had no trouble doing that since that's how he puffed cancer sticks, dragging deep, sucking down every wisp of smelly smoke.

Jimmy passed the joint to Shirley. I could tell she was scared. Scared that she'd do it wrong and scared Jimmy would yell at her for doing it wrong and scared of what it might do to her. She took a drag and had a coughing fit.

"What a greenhorn," Jimmy crowed. "Pass it back to Bruce. You're burning up dough. That wacky tobaccy ain't cheap."

"Can I try it?" I asked, pretending I was a greenhorn too.

"Are you kidding? You're still a pip-squeak."

"You got me drunk when I was ten."

"You got her drunk?" croaked Shirley.

"I gave her a taste. Is it my fault she can't hold her liquor? Besides, booze'll never hurt you. In Greece that's what they give babies for medicine."

"She's fifteen. Let her have a toke," said Bruce.

"Butt out, hophead," said Jimmy. "Her brain cells are still developing. You'd know that if you read a book once in a while."

"I don't have time to read," said Bruce, spitting a mouthful of Pepsi on the pot so it would look darker and sell for more dough. "I'm a businessman now. I got a complicated operation to run."

"Yeah, you're such a big shot I oughta give you a big shot in your big fat head," said Jimmy, getting up to make another highball.

Bruce winked at me and slipped me a big fat joint.

I saved it to share with Virginia when she came up.

Bruce was right. It was strong, King Kong strong.

Virginia and I laughed our heads off and got so hungry we could've outeaten Wayne. There wasn't much food in the fridge—no bologna, not even any bread. We made sandwiches using slices of American cheese as bread. We spread mustard on the cheese and used pickles as the filling. They were the best sandwiches we had ever eaten.

We turned on the TV and watched men walk on the moon and felt like we were flying high right up there with them.

The next day, Virginia had changed her mind about everything.

"I'm going back on that pill," she said. "I don't give a flying you-know-what what Wayne says."

"Thank God," I said. "I thought I'd lost you to the pod people."

"I wish we could go to Woodstock," she said.

"Let's do it. Let's run away," I squealed.

"Sure, dummkopf, we'd get about as far as you and Tina did," she said.

Virginia went back to Wayne. She went back on the pill, but not fast enough. She found out she had a bun in the oven right before she found out Wayne had his orders for Vietnam.

The day she told me, she cried like a baby.

I wasn't sure if she was crying because Wayne was going to Vietnam or because she had a bun in the oven. I don't think she was sure either.

Sickening

Virginia moved back to Manchester when Wayne went off to Vietnam. She rented an apartment with money YaYa gave her. The apartment was on the top floor of a dirty-white triple-decker. The floors sloped so bad that if you dropped a jawbreaker it would roll from one side of the room to the other. There was a porch that had been a big selling point before Virginia rented the place, but once she signed on the dotted line the landlord said he wouldn't use it if he were her and claimed no liability if she used it anyway and it collapsed.

But Virginia loved the place. It was the first time she'd ever lived on her own. She scrubbed every inch of the apartment and decorated it with stuff she found at a North End thrift shop. She made curtains out of somebody's old tablecloth, and tablecloths out of old curtains, and everything looked cool, like in a magazine. Once in a while, when she was puking her guts out, she remembered that a kid was growing inside her and that her private paradise wouldn't be private very long. But usually she just tried to forget about that part.

She got a black cat from an animal shelter even though black cats were supposed to be bad luck. She told Jimmy the people at the shelter had screwed up and said the cat was a boy when it was really a girl. She told Jimmy the cat's name was Cyn, short for Cynthia, but it was really Sin.

Jimmy hated Sin and Sin hated him.

Several times a week Jimmy would stop by the crooked apartment to check on Virginia and make sure she was dressing like a Greek crone, not like a hippie or a whore. Sin would hiss at him and Jimmy threatened to shoot her right between the eyes. Virginia said the cat was a sweetheart with everyone else, so it must be something about him. She said maybe he reminded Sin of someone who had once tortured her.

But it turned out Sin was temperamental because she was in the family way just like Virginia. She soon gave birth to a whole litter of little black girl kittens. Jimmy vowed to drown them all in the Merrimack River, but I didn't think he was serious. After all, he was crazy about cats. On the other hand, he was just plain crazy, so who could say? Fortunately, Virginia found homes for all the girl kittens so we never had to find out if Jimmy meant business.

Around this time, Susan also got herself a cat. She named him Hank 'cause he was a little wild and a little crazy. She returned to medical school with the cat, determined to become a doctor once and for all. But she still felt lousy and the doctors couldn't figure out what was wrong.

Finally, Susan figured it out herself.

"She's only half a doctor, but she knows more than those half-wits," Jimmy told me. He said Susan had something called lupus. I asked what it was and he said it was a disease where the body went berserk and attacked itself like in a horror movie.

"So, she's dying?" I blurted out, miserable.

"Nah, she's not kicking the bucket. They got stuff they can give her. But there ain't no cure."

"Could I catch it? Like if she hugs me?" I asked, feeling my chest constricting.

"Don't be a numbskull. It's not a goddamn virus. You get it or you don't and they don't know why. It's the luck of the draw."

Susan had gotten Norris Luck. Maybe she had caught it *from me?*

After that, she had to leave medical school again. She returned to New Hampshire to try to get better. I didn't see how being around mean ole Hank could make anybody feel better, but I knew better than to say that.

Jimmy started to think he was sick again, too. He got the Yankee doctor to check *him* out for lupus. Then, MS, Lou Gehrig's disease, and his old standby, the Big C.

Jimmy's headshrinker kept insisting Jimmy's aches and pains were all in his head, so Jimmy finally said "frick you" and quit seeing her. On the drive back home after his last visit, he was elated. He said the headshrinker was probably a dyke anyway, since she wasn't married, and a dyke couldn't tell him anything about being a man. He told me *I* could be his headshrinker from then on 'cause the only thing headshrinkers did was listen and nod while they were picking your goddamn pocket and I could do the listening and nodding just fine and save him some dough in the process.

"Hell, you know me a helluva lot better than that goddamn dyke. And you're a whole lot sharper too. I been wasting my time with that numbskull. So, whaddaya say, Doc?"

He laughed and threw his arm around me.

I can do it, I suddenly thought. I can make him better. *I'm* the only one who can. It's all up to me.

For the next few weeks, Jimmy acted like I was his best buddy. He told me his troubles, which I mostly knew already—everyone was out to get him and life sucked—and I told him he was smarter than Einstein, tougher than Dempsey, and the best duck hunter on the planet. I said he could even be a great trumpet player if he picked it up again.

I buttered him up like a piece of burnt toast.

"You're the best goddamn medicine," he said. "Better than goddamn Librium."

He said he only needed someone like me to believe in him to be the man he always wanted to be.

And I believed him.

Until the man he really was showed up again.

We were at the movies. It was a picture Jimmy had been dying to see, called *Take the Money and Run*. Jimmy had been crazy about Woody Allen for years. He was always corralling me to watch Woody do his comedy act on every talk show he was on.

"Pay attention," he said, half-joking, as the lights went down. "You might learn somethin.'"

The movie grabbed me right away. Woody played a guy who wanted to be a musician but stank at it and became a petty criminal instead. Jimmy and I both cracked up through the whole thing.

After it was over, I felt giddy. I threw my arms around Jimmy. It felt great that I had a father who took me to such a cool movie.

In the lobby, Jimmy puffed on a cancer stick and checked out the movie's poster.

"He's a goddamn genius, like Chaplin," he said.

"The part where he wrote 'gub' instead of gun on his holdup note, that was a riot," I added, still laughing about it.

"Woody Allen's a four-eyed Jew who couldn't fire a gun if his life depended on it," Jimmy said, so loud other people turned around and glared.

I stopped laughing.

"But mark my word, that little kike's goin' far."

I turned red and wished that I could go far—far away—or better yet, he could.

Lucky So-And-So

Virginia turned twenty-one and soon after gave birth to a boy. When she went into labor, Wayne was still in Vietnam and Shirley and YaYa had to work and everybody said I was too young to be there, so Virginia was all by herself at the hospital. But the kid popped out like nothing after only three hours. The doctor said he was surprised since Virginia was so petite. He thought he'd have trouble yanking it out. He said she was one lucky lady.

"Figures," sulked Virginia in her hospital bed. "It's the only thing in my stupid life that's ever come easy."

She named the kid Dustin, after Dustin Hoffman, because she had a crush on Hoffman like I did and because she'd never heard of anybody else with that name. She figured at least her kid would be special his whole life in some way.

They sent her home from the hospital with a baby blanket and a box of diapers.

"Well, you did it. You had a brat, you screwed up your life," said Jimmy when he saw his first grandchild. "Congratulations, dummkopf. At least it wasn't a girl."

He said Dustin was a stupid name and insisted on calling him Dunce-tin.

Virginia cried for weeks after having that baby.

Between crying jags she wrote Wayne ten-page letters telling him how happy she was and how coochie-coo cute his baby was because every day someone or something reminded her that Wayne could be blown up at any second and her last letter might be the last good thing he ever saw.

Like Virginia, Dustin cried all the time. After a few weeks of Dustin's blubbering, Virgina got so sick of it she gave his bassinet a shove. She didn't mean to do it so hard, she really didn't. The bassinet went sailing down that slanted floor like a bullet. I caught it right before it smashed into the wall. Virginia and I were horrified, but Dustin just started giggling. Virginia learned he had a little daredevil streak just like her and fell in love with him right then and there and vowed to try to be a good mother even though she wasn't sure what that meant or how to do it.

Before long Dustin was sleeping through the night, with Sin curled up next to him licking him like he was one of her long-lost kittens.

Virginia continued to write to Wayne all the time and noticed a big change in his letters. He no longer knew what he was doing over there or what he was fighting for. He'd sailed on a river of blood and now he wanted to jump ship. He finally decided war, all war, was wrong and asked to be reclassified as a conscientious objector. Wayne's change of heart didn't go over too well with his superiors. They didn't believe that people could change their hearts or their minds. They made him stick it out.

But he was a lucky so-and-so. He managed to finish his tour of duty and come back home.

Virginia acted like she was happy he was home, but really, she wasn't. She'd gotten used to living with a boy and liked it better than living with a man. The difference being she could tell a boy what to do instead of having men always telling her what to do.

Before long, Wayne had grown out his balding, stringy hair and sprouted a bushy mustache and was smoking pot all the time. He wasn't sure what he wanted to do with his life. He took up painting—not house painting, picture painting. The pictures didn't look so hot to me, but what did I know? I'd never been to a museum or done any artwork outside of a coloring book.

At first, Virginia dug the new Wayne. At least they were sort of on the same wavelength. At least he didn't want to kill people. But after a while it became clear he was on a frequency that none of us could tune into. He talked a mile a minute but always ended up at a dead end.

Against my better judgment I asked Wayne to teach me how to drive. Jimmy had refused to teach me—he said getting into a car with a female behind the wheel was a suicide mission. But Wayne said he'd been on plenty of suicide missions and it didn't faze him. He took me out in Virginia's clunker, a Pontiac she'd bought from a guy who knew a guy who knew Jimmy. The car broke down all the time and once caught on fire, but for the moment it was running OK. On my first lesson, I was scared but did pretty well. Wayne barked orders—left, right, left, right—and I followed them. At one point he asked what my biggest fear about driving was. Going on the highway, dummkopf, I answered. Before I knew it, he had directed me right onto the highway. Once I saw what he had done I screamed and begged him to take the wheel. He just grinned at me. I eased off the gas until we were only going ten miles an hour. Other drivers started blowing their horns at me.

"Faster! Step on it!" Wayne barked.

I didn't follow his order.

He stomped his foot down on mine on the accelerator. The car shot forward like a bullet.

"We're going to die!" I shrieked.

"So what?" Wayne replied. "We're all going to die someday."

"You're crazy!" I screeched.

"That's a relative term," he said, keeping my foot pinned to the gas.

I white-knuckled the steering wheel and did my best to swerve around any vehicle that came into my path. Somehow I managed to avoid hitting anything and barreled off at the next exit. Wayne finally lifted his foot off mine and I pulled over, shaking like Shirley's wringer washer with an unbalanced load.

"See? You faced your worst fear and lived," he said.

I punched him on the arm and made him drive the rest of the way home.

When we got back to the crooked apartment I told Virginia what had happened and we agreed Wayne had more than a few screws loose.

She tried to get him to see a headshrinker even though it hadn't done much for Jimmy, but he said there was nothing wrong with him. He said he was saner than when he first went into the Marine Corps.

In a sense, he was right.

How I managed not to crash that afternoon, I'll never know. Maybe those summers driving bumper cars at Old Orchard Beach had paid off. Or maybe God was looking out for me even though I had given up on being a good Catholic a long time ago. Or maybe, like Jimmy said, I was just a lucky so-and-so.

All I know is I passed my driving test with flying colors. And even Jimmy, when he was finally brave enough to get in a car with me, had to admit I was pretty good behind the wheel.

"You drive like a goddamn man," he said, beaming, as I took a corner fast enough to make the wheels squeal.

It was the biggest compliment he'd ever given me.

Easy Money

As I made my way through high school, I managed to keep up the sham that I was living with YaYa and Papou. When I finally started to make friends, I told them my grandparents were sickly and that's why nobody could come over to my place. My friends' parents took pity on me and invited me to their North End homes for family dinners where they used a separate fork to eat salad and no one sucked the eyes out of the fish.

One time at dinner I asked for a glass of milk. There was dead silence around the table.

"We don't mix dairy with meat," my new friend, Robin, said.

"Oh," I replied. "You're like on a diet?"

"We're Jewish," she said.

"Oh yeah," I said. "I just forgot."

"How about some juice? Grape? Orange? Apple?" asked Robin's mother. I couldn't believe there were so many choices, like in a restaurant.

"Apple, please," I replied. "If it's not too much trouble."

"It's no trouble. You're so polite," said Robin's mother.

"What religion are you, if you don't mind my asking?" asked Robin's father with a pleasant smile.

"Greek," I replied, starting to get anxious.

"You're Greek Orthodox? The ancient Greeks were brilliant, I'm sure you know that. They provided the foundation for philosophy. Have you read Sophocles or Plato?"

"Not yet," I said. "But I plan to."

"Do you know why we don't eat dairy with meat?"

I didn't have a clue.

"That's OK. A lot of Jews don't know either."

He proceeded to explain all sorts of things about Jews, but not in a boring way. He told stories that made me laugh and I didn't miss the glass of milk one bit. Finally, he toasted Robin and me for making the National Honor Society. He didn't call me a brownnoser like Jimmy had when he found out.

After a while, I didn't feel I had to hide stuff, at least not as much. Eventually, I confessed to Robin's family that I was living with my parents in the South End. I told them I had wanted to go to a better high school. I didn't mention the projects, but I was pretty sure they'd figured it out since they were all so goddamn smart. But they didn't rat me out or anything. They praised me for wanting to get a good education.

Before long most of my friends were Jewish. It wasn't like there were that many Jews in Manchester, but whatever ones there were I made friends with.

Their fathers were doctors and lawyers and businessmen. They had their own bedrooms, with window seats, and their own bathrooms. They played tennis and had summer houses on Cape Cod. Like the Greeks, they were crazy about food, but the food was different.

Bagels, lox, chopped liver, matzo balls. I devoured it all.

A girl named Ellen became my best friend. One day she brought me to her house for a special dinner—a seder. Ellen's father sat me beside him and explained the meaning of all the weird things on the table, like a bone with no meat on it. The only thing I didn't like was the gefilte fish, but Ellen told me nobody liked gefilte fish, nobody under sixty anyway.

I was intrigued by the whole Exodus story. I related to the ancient Jews' longing to get out from under a bully's thumb. It seemed that for centuries, some people were always trying to make other people's lives living hell. But the Jews had finally gotten free, so I figured maybe there was hope for me.

Of course, I didn't spill the beans to Jimmy about going to Ellen's seder. Like my visits to the Catholic church, I kept it on a stone wall.

When Jimmy finally realized I was befriending a bunch of Jews, I expected him to blow a gasket. But he just kidded me about being a Jew lover and that was that. He had a problem with "the Jews" but not with individual Jews. Individual Jews, like the ones he did landscaping for—some of whom were the parents of my new friends—were OK. The whole thing made no sense, but, like most things with Jimmy, you didn't question it if you knew what was good for you.

Jimmy grew especially fond of Ellen. Maybe it was because she swooned over Shirley's Greek food and would've eaten the eyes out of a fish if Jimmy dared her to. Or maybe it was because she'd read more books than Jimmy, including his favorite ones. Or maybe it was because she was so goddamn funny Jimmy said she belonged on Carson.

Probably it didn't hurt that she had breasts the size of cantaloupes. I caught him gawking at them more than once.

My own breasts were only the size of grapes, but Ellen's father couldn't take his eyes off them either. It seemed like fathers were just fascinated by breasts and, even though their ogling felt icky, there wasn't much you could do about it.

Pretty soon, Ellen invited me to spend the weekend with her family on Cape Cod.

"Maybe you'll meet the Kennedys," gushed my old pal Tina, who was still taken with the Kennedys even though one of them had drowned a girl in his car a while back.

"I'll get Caroline's autograph for you if I do," I promised.

Ellen drove over to the projects to pick me up. She was sporting a shiny BMW that her father had just given her for her birthday. It was the color of crisp new money and smelled like no car I'd ever been in since I'd never been in a new car.

As I slid onto the buttery leather seat, Ellen popped a few quaaludes.

"You want one?" she giggled, waving a prescription bottle. It was filled with what looked like a couple hundred quaaludes she had conned her family doctor into giving her for migraine headaches.

"Thanks but no thanks," I said. I'd smoke pot any day of the week, but pills were too frickin' scary. I'd felt that way ever since I'd swallowed too many Flintstones vitamins when I was stoned, forgetting they were medicine and downing them like candy. Too many Freds and Wilmas made me puke.

Ellen gulped down a few more quaaludes and drove ninety-five miles an hour all the way to the Cape. Except for swerving up onto the sidewalk at one point, she did OK. I was used to Jimmy driving fast and loaded, so I knew what to do. I closed my eyes.

Unfortunately, I didn't meet the Kennedys that weekend, but I had a blast anyway. I ate lobsters—bought, not stolen—but they tasted just as sweet. I went antiquing with Ellen and her mother and watched them pay a bundle for old junk like what was lying around Grammy's Nova Scotia barn. I drove that BMW, drove it like a man.

At one point, Ellen's mother sat me down and quizzed me about where I was planning to apply to college.

I got tongue-tied and lied and said I hadn't decided yet. Even though for years I'd dreamed about following Susan to medical school, I had no idea what it actually took to get into college. Ellen, who hated being put on the hot seat by her mother herself, came to my rescue. She offered to be my college guide.

"I'll be your Timothy Leary for higher education," she laughed, high as a kite.

Ellen, much to her parents' horror, wasn't applying to any colleges. In fact, she'd just dropped out of Central, the latest in a series of high schools and prep schools that she'd either left or gotten booted out of.

"I'll tell you all the schools my mother wants *me* to apply to and you can apply instead!" Ellen plotted.

"Cool!" I said, not letting on there was no frickin' way I could go to college unless Shirley won the sweepstakes and then managed to hide it from Jimmy before he snatched it away to buy a bunch of half-crippled racehorses.

"And don't worry about the tuition," Ellen assured me, like she was reading my mind. "You can apply for a scholarship and you'll get it 'cause you're such a brain."

Here's the thing—I didn't know what a scholarship was. But I was determined to find out.

I was in a great mood when I got back from the Cape, but that didn't last long. Jimmy was waiting with more bad news about Susan. She'd checked herself into the state loony bin, the same place Hank had been locked up in.

"I don't know what the hell's the matter with her," Jimmy ranted. "She should be a goddamn doctor, not a goddamn patient."

"Maybe she's still sad about Hank killing her mother."

"Baloney. That was six or seven years ago. Besides, he gave that kid everything—horseback lessons, ski lessons, golf lessons. She was treated like a princess, just like her goddamn mother. Maybe that's what's wrong—he spoiled them both. They were spoiled rotten."

"Can we go visit her like we visited Hank?"

"You think I can just take off and go places like you, my big-shot daughter who swans around Cape Cod with the Kennedys and the Jews? I gotta work for a living. You'll find out soon enough what that's like. The kiddie gravy train's ending pretty soon and you're gonna have to get a rat-race job in a rat-race maze like the rest of us."

So we put off going to visit Susan, and to be honest, I was relieved. I didn't really want to see her in that place, and besides, I had other things on my mind. I had become obsessed with learning about colleges and spent hours at a bookstore poring over the *College Handbook*. I didn't have the money to buy the book but nobody seemed to mind that I sat on the floor reading it from cover to cover. But the more I read, the further down on that floor I sank. There were *hundreds* of colleges—I had never dreamed so many existed—all filled with serious-but-carefree, brilliant-but-normal Leaders of Tomorrow. I didn't see how anybody could pick one college out of the bunch or how any one of them could pick me. I was feeling like a kid bound for a rat-race job in a rat-race maze when I came to the chapter on Radcliffe. I suddenly remembered Susan talking about it and Jimmy saying I'd never in a million years get in. That sealed the deal. *That's* where I wanted to go.

I met with the guidance counselor and relayed my grandiose plan. The counselor smirked and said that it was unlikely Radcliffe would take me and that I better apply to a few safety schools.

When I told Ellen I was set on Radcliffe, she wasn't encouraging either, but for a different reason.

"It's for squares and eggheads," she said, sounding a lot like Jimmy.

Ellen was more keen on colleges where artists and weirdos went. She suggested Bennington in Vermont, where a famous modern dancer, Martha Graham, had modern-danced on the front lawn.

"It's the most expensive school in the country, but don't worry about that," she said.

Yeah, right.

When Jimmy saw college applications arriving in the mail he had a conniption fit.

"People like us don't go to college! Who the hell do you think's gonna fork over the dough for it? Not me, that's for goddamn sure!"

"They have something called s-s-scholarships," I stammered.

"I know all about scholarships, dummkopf," he said. "But you're a little white girl. They only give those to the niggers."

"Ellen says they'll give me one."

"What does she know about it? She's a rich Jew who could buy her way into any college in the country. So don't get your goddamn hopes up."

I thought he was probably right. I tried not to get my goddamn hopes up.

While I was sweating over applying to colleges, things were getting worse over at Virginia's. Wayne was smoking more pot and getting even weirder. Virginia was reluctant to leave Dustin alone with him, but sometimes she just had to. One day they had no clean clothes and she needed to go to the Laundromat. It was raining cats and dogs and Dustin had a cold and she didn't want to get him any sicker.

She wasn't gone that long.

When she came home lugging a mountain of laundry, she found Wayne painting a weird picture but no sign of Dustin.

"Where's Dusty?" she asked, coming out of the bedroom where she'd expected to find him napping.

Wayne didn't answer. He just kept on painting the weird picture.

"Wayne, where's Dusty?" Virginia asked again, starting to get a queasy feeling.

"He's in the hospital," Wayne said matter-of-factly.

Virginia shrieked.

Wayne told her to chill out. He said Dustin was fine. He'd just drunk from a glass of turpentine Wayne was using to clean his paintbrushes.

"You numbskull!" Virginia yelled, and threw the closest thing to her—a frypan—at his head, missing him by a mile 'cause she had never had a good aim.

Then she ran out of the crooked apartment, down two creaky flights of stairs, through the rain turning to snow, into her crappy Pontiac. Drove to the hospital like a maniac over the slippery streets, stalling a few times on the way.

But she was a lucky so-and-so.

Dustin didn't die. He hadn't drunk very much of the turpentine. He just cried a lot and he was OK.

Kids are always getting into stuff, Wayne, shrugged. It could happen to anybody.

But Virginia didn't see it that way. After Dustin got out of the hospital, she packed up her stuff, took him, and moved in with a friend.

"Greek women don't leave their husbands!" YaYa screeched when she heard. "He didn't even beat you!"

"He almost killed Dustin!"

"That's what you get for leaving him with your husband! God was punishing you! A good Greek wife takes care of the children! Go back and tell him you're sorry. Get down on your knees."

But Virginia wouldn't do it. She wouldn't get down on her knees. She wouldn't live any longer in that crooked apartment with a man who felt like a stranger. Who'd always felt like a stranger. Wayne had served his purpose. He'd gotten her free of Jimmy. But now she saw an out and she took it.

"What're you gonna do for dough?" I asked Virginia, scared she'd end up panhandling in front of city hall.

"I dunno. I hate work," she said. "That's one thing Daddy's right about. It sucks."

"Maybe you can move to a commune. There's always a lotta kids running around those places. Maybe you'd meet, like, a cute farmer."

"Mummy didn't want to marry some smelly farmer and neither do I," she replied. "I got bigger plans than that."

The friend Virginia had moved in with had just started working at a massage parlor a few towns over and said there was easy money to be made there. So Virginia decided to give it a try.

She told Jimmy she was doing a little babysitting.

She bought a platinum-blond wig to wear as a disguise. She bought a jet-black bikini 'cause that was the uniform.

At first, she only gave massages. But it sure as hell wasn't easy money. It was harder on her wrists than carrying trays of leaden pancakes had been. On top of that, she had to fight off big, blubbery guys who wanted her to massage more than their blubber.

Before long, the money the blubbery guys offered her to massage their Down There was too tempting to resist. Pretty soon, she was only massaging their Down There. If some rube asked for a regular massage too, she told him she'd broken her hand in a car wreck and could only use it so much, doctor's orders. If the rube wanted a stupid body massage he couldn't have a Down There massage too.

He always chose the Down There.

After a while, she barely had to use her hands at all. She just lay on the massage table and let the guys squash her with their blubber and they paid her even more money. Of course, the scumbag who ran the joint took his cut, but it still left her with enough dough to rent a nice apartment, nicer than the crooked one. One with its own washer so she didn't have to go to the Laundromat and use a machine that some idiot had washed a bunch of shitty diapers in right before her.

Virginia also worked out a good arrangement for taking care of Dustin. The friend who had gotten her started at the massage parlor had a kid too and they staggered their shifts and babysat for each other.

"It's a perfect setup," Virginia assured me, when I expressed misgivings about her working at the massage parlor.

"What if Jimmy finds out? He'll kill you for sure."

"He's not gonna find out. I wear a wig, dummkopf. And sometimes I use a British accent. I tell them my name is Mary Quant."

"But what if somebody like Hank goes in there? What if you have to do it with Hank?"

"I wouldn't do it with Hank," Virginia snapped. "I'd draw the line at Hank."

Virginia had a little blue suitcase that she took to work. Once, while she was getting ready to leave, I peeked into it. In addition to wigs, bikinis, and makeup, she had toothpaste, handcuffs, and a rubber Down There. She also had several Hershey's bars. I was surprised to see them. Unlike me, Virginia never went in much for candy.

"Can I have a chocolate bar?" I asked.

"No," she said, startled. She closed the suitcase with a sharp click.

"Don't be stingy," I moaned.

"They're for work," she snapped.

"What do you mean?"

"Never mind," she replied. "What you don't know won't hurt you."

Sucker Punch

I had a big, fat problem.

To apply to Radcliffe I had to show up in person for an interview and Jimmy would be damned if he'd take me.

"Those tight asses just wanna give the Little Match Girl the once-over. Well, screw them. I'd like to light a little match up their tight asses."

"They make everybody who lives close by go there, not just me."

"If you believe that, I raised a gullible idiot and you belong at Dum-Dum University."

"What if Ellen takes me?"

"Oh, you think if you pull up in her kraut car instead of my jalopy they'll say open sesame? Well, think again, Einstein."

"I wasn't thinking about her car," I said, but the truth was I wasn't too keen on pulling up with the *Aristotle Onassis* strapped to Jimmy's roof.

"Don't gimme that. You're becoming a spoiled teen-rager with your spoiled Jew friend. Well, I'm not letting you go. What if you get lost and end up in the Combat Zone without your old man there to protect you?"

"Ellen knows her way around Boston," I argued. "She goes shopping there all the time."

"I bet she does. But one wrong turn from Saks Fifth Clip Joint and you end up in Chelsea. And you know who's from Chelsea?"

"The Boston Strangler," I said, "but he's locked up."

"Hey, there's a lot more like him where he came from."

"But if I don't show up for an interview, I won't have a chance."

"You never had a chance," he said. "I guess you still believe in Santa Claus too?"

He mimicked a bawling brat, rubbing his eyes with his hairy fists.

And I decided right then and there to shoot him.

I had nothing to lose. Nothing. If I couldn't go to Radcliffe, my stupid life was over.

So here was my plan:

I'd get him to take me hunting the next time he was going. I'd wait till he'd had a few stiff ones and wasn't feeling any pain. When he sent me out to retrieve a duck, I'd pretend I couldn't find it. He'd threaten to plug me and leap out of the *Aristotle Onassis* to go look for it. I'd grab his rifle and plug him instead—once in the back. With any luck, the bullet would lodge in his heart—assuming he still had one.

I'd make believe it was just a terrible accident.

I'd confess to being a nearsighted girl with no goddamn aim.

I'd cry, boo hoo hoo.

It'd make a damn good essay for a college application: "I'm a Little Match Girl with a Dead-as-a-Duck Father I Shot by Mistake." Maybe it would get me into Radcliffe after all.

And I'm pretty sure the plan would've worked, but I didn't get to try it out 'cause Jimmy sucker punched me. He reversed course like the *Aristotle Onassis* caught in a squall. He told me we could probably swing by Radcliffe on the way to Suffolk Downs racetrack, just as long as I didn't make him late for the goddamn daily double.

The morning of the interview he went hunting. Lucky for him, I stayed home. I spent hours getting ready. I'd borrowed an outfit from Ellen that was a little droopy on top, but otherwise I thought I looked like a million bucks. As usual, Jimmy was running late. He had no time to change, not that he would have changed anyway. He was wearing a red plaid shirt with the elbows worn through, pants caked with mud from tromping through the marshes, and shoes with broken shoelaces that had been tied back together.

"You look like crap," he said. "You got nothin' to fill that dress out. You're a beanpole like your Olive Oyl mother."

"I hope we're not gonna be late," I said, knowing my words would be a challenge to him.

"Hell, I'll get us there with time to kill," he vowed, and stepped on it.

More than once on the way there he suggested we blow Radcliffe off and go straight to the track.

"I got better odds of winning the trifecta than you got of getting into that blue-blood finishing school."

"I got good grades, I'm in the National Honor Society, I'm an editor of the school magazine. Like Susan, she—"

"Don't talk to me anymore about goddamn Susan. She's nothin' but a disappointment to poor Hank, always tryin' to squeeze dough from him since she got back out of the nuthouse. She didn't even have the moxie to finish medical school. She wasn't so smart after all."

"Well, I think I've got as much chance as anybody of getting into Radcliffe."

"Oh yeah? Well, think again, dummkopf. You're gonna get your little life-is-fair heart broken. And I hate to see that happen. I hate to let those bastards do that to you, string you along. 'Cause you don't need them, remember that. You got me and your mother and your stupid sister and your goddamn cat. Screw them. Screw those bastards. Let's go right to the track, whaddaya say?"

"It doesn't hurt to try," I insisted.

"Oh yeah it does," he replied, his voice hardening. "It does hurt."

All the way to Cambridge he proceeded to list all the reasons I wouldn't get in. I had a pimple on my nose. I had Dracula teeth. I had stringy hair. I was wearing a borrowed dress and they'd know it 'cause it didn't even fit me right. I had bitten-down fingernails. I hadn't read all the books he'd told me to read. I hadn't even read goddamn *Moby-Dick*. Hell, *he'd* have a better goddamn chance of getting in than I did. Maybe *he* oughta go in for the interview instead of me.

By the time we pulled up in front of the building, Jimmy had convinced me.

I didn't have a snowball's chance in hell of getting in.

When we finally sat down in the waiting room—ten minutes late—there was only one other prospective student sitting there. A gorgeous black girl with a giant Afro.

Jimmy kept elbowing me in the ribs and motioning to the girl.

"What did I tell ya? She's gettin' your goddamn spot," he hissed, loud enough that I was afraid the girl would hear.

I stared down at the plush Oriental rug. I tried to lean away from Jimmy in the hopes that people would think he was with somebody else. I pretended I had another father waiting in another car just outside. A car that smelled like a new cow, not an old fish. A car without *Aristotle Onassis* on the roof and Hitler in the glove box.

The beautiful black girl got called in before me.

"What did I tell ya?" Jimmy repeated louder. "They're takin' that Ubangi, not you."

The tears I had been holding back all day all week all year all my frickin' life came pouring out.

A woman called my name. I could barely see her through my tears. But I could feel her glaring at Jimmy. I was convinced she'd heard what he said.

I followed the woman into her office like I was heading to the guillotine. She guided me to a beautifully upholstered chair. I sat on the edge of it. I didn't see the point of getting too comfortable.

"Are you all right?" the woman asked, her voice as cold and brittle as an icicle.

"My mother's sick," I mumbled, the first thing that came into my mind.

"Oh, I'm sorry," the woman said, her voice melting a little.

My nose was running and I only had my sleeve or the beautiful upholstery to rub it on. The woman handed me a tissue like she was trying not to touch me.

"Maybe we should reschedule your appointment for another day?"

"No, I c-can't c-come back," I stammered. "This is my only chance."

"All right, well then . . . tell me why you'd like to attend Radcliffe," she said, like she was talking to the door I would soon be heading out of.

My mind went blank.

"My friend Susan told me to come here," I managed to blurt out.

"Oh, is she an alum?" the woman said, seeming to perk up a bit.

"No," I admitted. "She just told me about it."

"I see," the woman said.

The interview was over in ten minutes.

Jimmy shot up as soon as we appeared at the door.

"Let's blow this mausoleum," he said

At least he wasn't late for the daily double.

But it would've been better if he was.

"Don't quit on me! Don't quit on me!" Jimmy shouted to a tired horse falling into the back of the pack while the jockey lashed him with a whip.

As I watched that horse get splattered with mud, I had only one thought.

I give up.

Thick and Thin

The thin envelope came and Jimmy said I told you so. I hid it in the garbage like a stinky mackerel so I'd never have to see it again.

When the thick envelope arrived I didn't give a shit. Bennington, the most expensive school in the country, was giving me what Jimmy called a free ride on the gravy train.

"They must not be too picky if they picked you," he said before splitting for the track. He had landed a plum job in the spit box collecting piss from the horses after they raced to make sure they weren't being juiced. I didn't think he was the ideal person for that job, but I figured they must not know he'd been a juicer himself.

After he left, the telephone rang. It was Ellen's mother calling to find out about the thickness of my envelopes.

When she heard about Bennington giving me a scholarship she screamed so loud I thought my eardrum would explode.

"It's a school for weirdos," I sulked, fed up with being an outcast.

"I'd give my right arm to have a daughter going there," she said.

"I hate you, I hate you!" I heard Ellen shout, before she grabbed the phone to congratulate me.

After I said yes to Bennington, Jimmy said no to me. He said he wouldn't show up for my high school graduation no matter how much YaYa pleaded with him.

"What kind of man doesn't attend his own daughter's graduation?"

"A man who's gotta work for a living, unlike his big-shot daughter."

"Well, maybe if you hadn't quit school like a bum you'd have a decent job. You wouldn't have to stand around in the mud waiting for a racehorse to make wee-wee."

"Go ahead. Cut me down. Break my balls. That's all you've ever done. It's your goddamn fault I didn't amount to anything."

"Holy God, what did I do to deserve you?"

"I know what you goddamn did," he said darkly, still convinced she'd cheated on Papou.

I told myself I was glad Jimmy wasn't coming to my graduation, but it wasn't true. As Jimmy would say, it hurt like a bastard. As I stood in a sea of several hundred classmates, I kept looking for my father, convinced he'd pull a sneak attack and show up. I wanted him to kid me about being an egghead and dare me to go break a window. I wanted him to tell me I looked like a Greek priest in my cap and gown. I wanted him to ride me about only graduating fourth in my class and call me dum-dum.

But I really was a dum-dum for thinking he was gonna show.

Over the summer, I counted down the days until I could get the hell outta there. I got a job at a day-care center making jelly sandwiches and reading *See Spot Run!* to pip-squeaks. As my departure date got closer, Jimmy got madder. Once again he became convinced that Shirley was cheating on him. When he came home from the spit box, he put his hand on the couch to see if he could feel any heat where she might have been lying down with another man. Shirley begged him to call Dr. C to give him a shot, but he said he'd give her a shot— right in her cheating heart just like Hank had done to Doris. He said he'd dig a grave for her with his bare hands right next to Doris's. He said he'd plug me too like Hank shoulda done to Susan since she was a useless daughter too—a weak, useless daughter who was back in the nuthouse again.

Finally, Shirley had had enough.

I was almost gone and she wanted out.

One night when they were going at it like cats and dogs she told him to pack his bags.

"You're not kicking me out. I'm leaving," he said. "I won't live with a god-damn whore anymore."

Sayonara, baby.

He moved into a flophouse downtown.

Hallelujah! We were in heaven. Shirley cooked less and slept more and even looked happy when she came home from work. I wore minidresses and played the O'Jays on Jimmy's hi-fi.

We watched every Red Sox game.

Jimmy hung out with Hank. They got plastered and vowed never to have another ball and chain yank their chain.

One night Jimmy showed up at Virginia's massage parlor. Virginia's friend spotted him and tipped her off and Virginia hid in one of the rooms, her heart pounding, until the coast was clear.

Virginia quit her job that night. She got another job at a massage parlor in Massachusetts. It was a longer drive but she didn't mind 'cause she was driving a Jaguar now. She'd gotten the Jag—minus its ID numbers—as a birthday present from a guy she'd started dating, a car thief named Armie.

"He's a real gentleman," she insisted. "He always holds the car door open for me. So what if it's hot?"

Things were really going our way. I really started to believe it.

Then, one night, about a month after Jimmy left, I was home alone. It was after eleven and Shirley had already left for work. I was reading *Slaughterhouse-Five*. It was Jimmy's copy that he'd left behind. It had his comments in the margins, but I tried to ignore them.

I heard someone jiggling the front door, trying to get in.

Before I could make it to the closet where the nearest gun was, Jimmy was charging down the hall. He grabbed me and threw me onto the couch.

He hadn't shaved in days, his hair was even greasier than usual, and he was wearing the same clothes he'd had on his back when he left.

"You think you're pretty goddamn smart, don't you? Pretty goddamn smart."

I tried to speak, but my throat had closed up.

My eyes darted around, looking for anything I could use as a weapon. A big glass ashtray overflowing with lipstick-stained Luckies was just out of reach.

Jimmy leaned over me, smelling of sour whiskey.

"You got what you always wanted, didn't you, you little rat? You got your goddamn mother to yourself. You put her up to this, didn't you?"

"I didn't," I managed to choke out. The truth was I'd been as amazed as he was that she'd kicked him out.

"You're a lying little bitch. She did it because of you. And if you don't fix what you broke, I'll come back here and shoot her. Your mother's blood will be on your hands."

"Daddy, no!"

"Daddy, no!" he mimicked me.

"Leave us alone," I begged him.

"Leave you alone? This is *my* goddamn house. If you think you can kick me out of my own goddamn house you got another thing coming. You tell your mother to take me back. She always does what you want. You been pulling those strings since you were born. You tell her to take me back, or else. I ain't nothing without her. We been through thick and thin."

"I can't tell her what to do!"

"Oh yes you can. You do it, you hear me, or you'll end up like no-good Susan without a no-good mother."

And then he was gone.

I raced to the closet to get the gun.

I held on to the gun all night in case he came back.

I turned everything over and over and over in my mind.

If I begged her to take him back she'd have a miserable life.

If I didn't she'd have no life at all.

But there was a third choice. The one I kept coming back to like a song you don't like but can't get out of your head.

He had to go.

Carried Away

All the next day at work as I played hopscotch and ring-around-the-rosy I tried to find another way out, an angle that didn't involve a gun, a knife, or rat poison.

I thought about calling the cops but not for very long. I'd been trained my whole life to keep cops on a stone wall. And since they went and shot those kids at Kent State, who could trust them? Anyway, I figured they wouldn't be any harder on Jimmy than they'd been on Hank. Even if they did arrest him—which I wasn't convinced of since he'd talked his way out of more tickets than I could count—once they let him go he'd be madder than ever.

I stayed late at work that day, mopping up splotches of Welch's grape juice and sharpening Crayolas, trying to put off going home as long as I could.

I stopped at the Temple Market and bought some Marlboros and smoked a couple.

When I finally made the turn into the projects I saw Jimmy's car parked in front of our building.

I froze. Then I took off running.

I ran like Shirley's life depended on it.

I ran faster than I'd ever run—fast enough, I hoped, to finally beat Jimmy.

When I charged through the door I didn't see or hear anyone. The kitchen was empty.

I ran into the living room.

Shirley was sitting on the couch. Jimmy was kneeling on the floor, his head resting in her lap. She was stroking his greasy hair.

She looked up at me with dead, baby-doll eyes.

"Your father's coming home," she said.

Jimmy lifted his head from her lap and gave me a triumphant smile.

"I love your old lady and she loves me," he said.

Later, Shirley told me he had gotten Papou to come over and talk to her. Papou had said she had to take Jimmy back. He said that's what Greek wives

271

did and even though she wasn't technically speaking Greek she was married to a Greek and that made her a Greek wife.

At first, Shirley had held her ground.

I've had it, she told Papou. You and YaYa don't know how he is. He's nutty as a fruitcake.

Papou put his arm around Shirley, something she couldn't remember him ever doing before. He reeled her in like a half-dead mackerel.

I know he's crazy, Papou said. I know he gets carried away sometimes. But he's crazy about you. How many women can say they have a man who would go to the ends of the earth for them? A man who would kill for them? From now on, I'll keep him in line. I'll do that for you, for the family. Because my son's no good without you. You make him good. Without you, who knows what he could do? You want that on your conscience?"

Dirty fighter, dirty fighter.

Two against one.

TKO.

"Your father needs me. I can't ruin his life," she explained to me later.

"What about you? What about your life?"

"Oh, I'll make do."

I could have tried to argue her out of it, but I was afraid to say anything. My words were like bullets. One wrong word and she might be dead.

The following day Shirley was back to cooking up a storm, making all of Jimmy's favorite foods that he had missed in his absence.

As she cooked, she sang a James Taylor song we both loved, one that she said reminded her of Jimmy.

Goodnight you moonlight ladies
Rock-a-bye sweet baby James

Over the next few weeks she baked dozens of Greek pastries dripping with honey for me to take to college.

"So you'll have something sweet to remind you of home," she said.

I borrowed YaYa's suitcase, the same one I had taken to Old Orchard Beach every summer. I dug it out of a pile of junk Jimmy stored in YaYa's basement—broken lawn mowers he never got around to fixing, duck decoys so eaten away by salt water they'd only fool myopic birds, and half-empty bottles of horse liniment from Jimmy's long-gone days as a racehorse owner.

"You keep the suitcase as a going-away present," YaYa whispered to me. "Just don't tell Papou. What he doesn't know won't hurt him."

YaYa also made me a whole bunch of Greek pastries dripping with honey. The honey was soaking through the box already and made my hands sticky.

Shirley repacked the pastries when I got home. She examined them like she inspected sunglasses at work, having just been promoted from piecework to quality control.

"These can't hold a candle to mine," she announced.

When it came time to leave for college, Jimmy refused to drive me.

"Find your own way there, big shot," he said.

Virginia would have driven me except she'd broken up with the car thief and he'd stolen her stolen Jaguar back.

Ellen couldn't do it either. She was miserable about not going to college herself and couldn't get out of bed.

So, Ken, another of my North End friends, offered to take me.

I said good-bye to my dusty stuffed animals and the makeshift bunk beds and our cat, Sylvester, who was really old and slept through my good-bye.

Jimmy left early for the spit box so he wouldn't have to see Shirley blubbering over me, but Shirley said it was so he wouldn't start blubbering himself.

She slipped me an envelope with about two hundred dollars. It was in small bills and change, money she had saved up.

"Call when you get there. Ring once and hang up and that way we'll know you're OK but you won't have to pay for the call. If you really need to call, use the change."

"Promise you'll call the cops if he gets carried away."

"Oh, your father treats me good now," she insisted. "That time on his own taught him a thing or two. He's a changed man."

I don't know if she really believed that.

I sure as hell didn't.

As I drove away, she watched until I was clear out of sight. So nothing bad would happen to me.

I did the same for her.

Asylum U

I finally made it over the state line.

I crossed the border from New Hampshire to Vermont.

Five years earlier, Susan had headed off to Vermont, bound for medical school, full of promise. She couldn't make a go of it and now she was back in New Hampshire, back in the nuthouse. Literally. I vowed not to follow in her footsteps.

The first person I saw when I arrived on campus was Paul Newman.

I thought I must be hallucinating since I'd smoked a little pot on the way there, but no, it was really him.

A moment later Rita Hayworth strolled by. What was even weirder was that nobody else seemed to notice either one of them. It was as if everyone had grown up in a world where movie stars were as common as rats at the dump, and only I, the Little Match Girl, thought it was a big deal.

It turned out both movie stars had daughters going to Bennington. Just like me. Sort of.

The dorm I got assigned to was a beautiful old wooden building. I found my room and unpacked. I had only the one suitcase, so it didn't take long. My roommate had gotten there before me and dumped her stuff, but other than that, there was no sign of her. Several large stringed instruments took up most of our room.

Before long, my roommate, her older sister, and their cheerful dad appeared. The sister was a senior and both girls were classical musicians. The cheerful dad had driven them all the way from Delaware, stopping for a picnic on the way.

"I hope her viola da gamba is not in your way." the dad said.

I didn't know what language he was speaking. Spanish? Armenian?

"We're going to dinner at a French restaurant. Would you like to join us? They make a superb *soupe à l'oignon*."

I begged off. I said I had plans with the friend who drove me, the friend who was long gone.

After they left I ate a bunch of baklava and smoked a few Marlboros and tried to remember the name of that Armenian instrument.

I missed my mother my sister my cat my stuffed animals my room my rickety bunk beds.

I even missed Jimmy.

I took a bunch of change to the pay phone in the hallway and called home.

"I'm here safe and sound," I said when Shirley picked up.

I watched a cute boy with glasses carry a bunch of musical equipment into his room—keyboards, amplifiers, and some contraptions I later learned were called Moog synthesizers.

Maybe Bennington was really a music school and I had skipped over that part in the *College Handbook*?

"What's it like there? Is it all fancy like the North End?" Shirley quizzed me.

"The buildings are kind of old, like up in Canada. And one of them is a barn."

"They charge up the keister to go to school in a goddamn horse barn?" piped up Jimmy, and that's when I realized he was listening in on the extension.

"There's a nice big lawn," I said.

"Yeah, some poor sap like your old man has to mow that big frickin' lawn," he groused.

"Well, I better not use up all my change," I said.

"Next time, ring once and hang up. Don't waste your mother's hard-earned dough."

"I'm so proud of you," Shirley blurted out.

"Hang up before you start blubbering," Jimmy told her.

"I love you, Mom," I said, trying not to start blubbering myself.

"What about me, dum-dum?"

"I love you too," I mumbled.

"You better. 'Cause the only reason you're there is you take after me in the brains department. My genes got you there. And don't you forget it."

"I won't," I said, and my time ran out.

From then on, most Sunday nights I just rang once and hung up.

It was just as well since I didn't want them to know how miserable I was.

I'd found myself in a nuthouse like Susan. At least that's how it seemed to me.

Everywhere I looked, people were behaving strangely. Girls in nightgowns twirled by themselves on that big lawn, dancing to their own private music. Their mongrel dogs ran free and shat on the lawn and the twirlers twirled on it and didn't mind. Some people walked around stark naked. Others wore giant lobster costumes.

A guy told me he had the mark of the devil on his chest and asked if I wanted to see it.

I said no thanks, maybe another time.

Still, I tried to fit in. I took a beginning music class.

The first day we were told to compose something.

Here's what I knew about music up to that point:

Do Re Mi Fa So La Ti Do.

The professor assured me anyone could compose music. A baby composes when it cries, he said. Music is just sound, and sound is all around.

My fellow classmates didn't seem daunted by the assignment. One kid composed a piece that consisted of him dragging his chair across the floor, making scraping sounds.

The only sound I made in that class was *click*. The sound of the door closing as I transferred the hell out of there.

After that I decided to stick with what I knew, literature and science.

I vowed to go to medical school—and, unlike Susan, to make it through.

I got a job selling my body—in an art class, not at a massage parlor. I posed naked while rich kids in paint-spattered overalls that made them look poor created facsimiles of my tits. I was a virgin and had never been naked in front of strangers, but I was used to imagining myself elsewhere—in somebody else's car or house or city—so that's what I did. I pretended I was in a bikini on a beach in KooKooLand instead of stark naked and covered with goose bumps in Vermont.

I needed more money, so I got more jobs—washing peanut butter tofu off dishes in the cafeteria and assisting a writing teacher. The money I made paid for cancer sticks and thrift shop clothes. I wore cocktail dresses and antique underwear, men's baggy suits and a coat made of monkey fur.

I wasn't the weirdest dresser on campus.

Slowly, I made a few friends, including the cute guy with glasses who played his Moog synthesizers for me.

But sadness kept dragging me down.

I started seeing a campus shrink. It was free, and besides, all the kids at Bennington seemed to have one. One girl's shrink came all the way from New York to see her. And he always spent the night in her room.

But my headshrinker didn't help very much. It wasn't her fault. I was too ashamed to tell her what was really going on. Too ashamed to tell her the real story about my family. I couldn't even bring myself to spill the beans about what Jimmy really did. I said nothing about pancakes, hot TVs, or juiced-up nags. I kept all that on a stone wall. I told the shrink Jimmy was a landscape architect. I'd never even known such a job existed until a girl in my dorm asked what my father did after telling me hers worked on stupid Wall Street. I got all tongue-tied and mumbled something about landscaping. "Oh, he's a landscape architect," she said, like she knew him better than I did. From then on, that was my story. Jimmy Norris the con artist became Jimmy Norris the landscape architect.

After a few weeks, I stopped seeing the shrink altogether. I didn't feel much like going to classes either. I stayed in bed and smoked cigarettes. I didn't even eat the baklava that kept arriving from Shirley.

You'll never fit in here, I told myself. *Nevernevernever.*

There were just too many things I didn't know. Too many references I didn't get. Too many jokes that went over my head. Jokes I wouldn't have laughed at anyway 'cause I was too afraid to show my Dracula teeth.

Finally, I'd had my fill of feeling like a dummkopf. I was on the verge of packing up and leaving Bennington.

And then Jimmy showed up.

"What the hell're you doing, dum-dum?" he barked, after throwing open the door and finding me sleeping in the middle of the day.

"Daddy?" I said, groggily.

"I thought I'd come get a look at this clip joint," he joked. "Maybe I wanna go here myself."

He had stopped off on his way home from a nearby racetrack. He was hoping to get back into the racing game and had gone there to check out a couple of nags.

I looked down and saw horse manure on his worn-out shoes.

Those shitty shoes just broke my heart. I burst out crying.

Jimmy looked startled. He watched me blubbering for a moment, then yanked the door shut.

"What the hell's the matter with you? You're in the lap of luxury here and you're bawling like a brat. You could be out hustling for a goddamn living like me."

"I can't make it here, I can't," I blubbered. "I wanna leave."

Jimmy's eyes narrowed. He stormed over to the bed. I cringed. I didn't know what he was going to do.

But he just sat down on the bed next to me and lit a cancer stick. He stared at my overflowing ashtray on the floor.

"It's a goddamn lousy habit," he said. "You oughta quit."

"What difference does it make? We all die anyway," I blurted out between sobs.

He glared at me. Then he reached out and grabbed my arm with his Hairy Claw.

"Look, no kid of mine goes down in the first round, you hear me? You're as goddamn good as any of these tight-assed little rich kids. Hell, you're better. You got something they'll never have. You got street smarts. You got moxie. You got balls, OK? Even though you're a goddamn girl. So sit your ass up, go out and get some goddamn Greek penicillin, and show those sons-of-bitches what you're made of."

I blubbered a little more and then sat my ass up.

Jimmy didn't hang around much longer.

He went home.

But I stayed.

I dug in my heels. I studied hard. I tried to stay focused on where I was, not where I'd been.

I was grateful to Jimmy for showing up when he did. Grateful for the father-daughter lecture.

I even missed him a little.

Like always, though, my good feelings toward him didn't last.

When I called home a few weeks later, Jimmy was out and Shirley sounded awful. I could tell she had been crying.

"What happened? Did he go nuts again?"

"I'm just going through the change of life," she lied. "It's nothing. I'm just a little blue."

"I'm coming home! I'll get a bus in the morning."

I was lying too. I was already planning to hitchhike to save money.

"No! You stay there! You got away, you stay away!"

She said she was feeling better already from hearing from me and I should go and have fun.

"I live through you," she said before she blew me kisses and hung up.

Once again I found myself thinking about Susan. About how she must've felt when her college dean showed up and told her that her mother had died. I wondered if she'd been lounging in the library or laughing with friends or blissfully asleep. I wondered if she blamed herself for going off and leaving her mother at the mercy of a father who showed her no mercy.

The next day I hitchhiked into town. It had gotten bitterly cold and I pictured myself stranded on the border between Vermont and New Hampshire in my monkey fur coat that was bald in spots and not very warm. I bought a carton of cancer sticks 'cause it was cheaper to buy them that way, and smoked a few 'cause that was the only thing that seemed to calm me down.

I told myself Shirley was probably OK.

I told myself Jimmy wasn't as crazy as Hank.

I told myself Shirley was probably OK a bunch more times.

Finally, I crossed to the other side of road and stuck out my thumb.

I headed back to campus.

Why did the chicken cross the road?

Because she chickened out.

Pluck pluck pluck.

I didn't have balls after all. I didn't have the balls to save my own sweet mother 'cause I was a weak, stupid, selfish teen-rager.

I could hear Jimmy's voice in my head telling me that. I could hear him in my goddamn head all the goddamn time. I wished I could get him the hell out. I wished somebody would lobotomize me like that guy in *One Flew Over the Cuckoo's Nest*—a book that Jimmy—who else?—had told me to read.

Sign me up for a Jimmy lobotomy.

So what if it made me a dummkopf?

Happy Holidays

I didn't end up returning home until right before Christmas. I hitchhiked there and had no trouble getting rides 'cause old codgers always picked up eighteen-year-old girls. I carried a pair of scissors in case any of the codgers got fresh, but I was a lucky so-and-so and none of them did. I had the last guy drop me off near the projects and walked the rest of the way, lugging my suitcase. It was only about four thirty, but it was already pretty dark. I trudged along those familiar streets that didn't look so familiar anymore. Strings of half-lit Christmas bulbs drooped around iced-up windows and didn't make me feel merry. I was afraid of finding Jimmy half-lit himself. But, when I got closer to our apartment, I was relieved to see Jimmy's car wasn't even there. I walked up the icy, muddy path to the front door, took a deep breath, and walked inside. Shirley raced over to greet me. She'd put on a pretty new dress for my homecoming and a little face paint but not too much. None of that could disguise the fact that she looked exhausted. When I hugged her she felt thin and as fragile as phyllo dough.

"This place must look small after living in such grand style," she said, embarrassed.

"My dorm room is tiny," I assured her. "And this place looks great. I love those new curtains."

I could tell she'd gone all out decorating, shopping, and baking, even more than usual.

"I got 'em at the secondhand store. I get everything there now. Except your presents. Those are brand spankin' new. Don't tell your father, though."

"How's he been? He's always crappy around Christmas."

"Oh, he treats me good now. Go see how I fixed up your room."

I walked upstairs to my old bedroom, carrying my suitcase.

When I got to the top of the stairs I saw them.

Two bullet holes in the ceiling.

I dropped my suitcase. It went tumbling back down the stairs, splitting open and spilling its contents.

"What happened?" I screamed, running down the stairs, trampling on my stuff.

Shirley already had her story worked out.

"The gun went off by accident."

"You're covering for him!"

"No, he was horsing around. Just trying to scare me."

"This is it! You have to leave!"

"It was my fault. I opened my big mouth."

"Next time he'll kill you!"

"He'll kill me if I try to leave. Doris learned that the hard way. This is my cross to bear. Now, let's just try and have a nice Christmas."

I knew right then and there, I couldn't save her. I couldn't beat him. He was bigger, stronger, faster, meaner. He could charm a bird off a tree. And if not, he could shoot it off.

I repacked my suitcase and lugged it back upstairs. I felt empty inside. I saw my room had bright new curtains and matching rainbow bedspreads on the bunk beds.

I went to the bathroom and peed. As I sat on the toilet, I noticed a hunk of the bathroom door had been kicked out and superglued back in.

"I was stupid and locked myself in," Shirley explained when I went back downstairs and asked her about it. "Your father had to rescue me. I don't know what I would've done if he hadn't been here."

She needed to lie—to herself even more than to me. It was the only way she could keep going.

"How long were you stuck in there?" I asked, resigned to playing along.

"Oh, not too long. Anyway, it's in the past. It's all in the past."

We let it go. It was Christmas. Hark! Jimmy was the savior.

A short while later, the Savior came home from hunting. He'd bagged a Christmas goose and a trunkful of ducks. He'd outwitted the wardens once more and was jubilant.

"The prodigal daughter is home," he said, aiming his rifle at me. Ha ha. Just horsing around.

The next day, Shirley cooked his goose. Ha ha. If only.

I wasn't hungry, but I put on a good face, and goddamn, if that goose wasn't delicious.

I asked for seconds.

Jimmy took off to go hunting again, and it was the best Christmas gift he could have given us.

Virginia came over with Dustin and we opened some presents. Shirley gave Dustin lots of toys and said how nice it was to have a kid in the house again for Christmas.

Virginia told me she'd met a new guy at the massage parlor. He was married but he treated her like a queen.

We all had to make the best of things.

I knew I had to. I was going to be living there for three long months. Classes didn't start up again until March. During the winter, Bennington students were required to go off and get Life Experience. They were encouraged to pursue whatever arty thing caught their fancy. It was a total blast for the kids who studied mime with Marcel Marceau in Paris or worked for the *New York Times* in Cairo or photographed sea turtles in the Galápagos.

For me, it was pretty frickin' terrible.

I had to move back in with Jimmy and go back to wiping pip-squeaks' noses at the day care center I'd worked at the summer before.

At first, it wasn't so bad. Jimmy was off hunting a lot—sometimes alone, sometimes with Hank. The track was closed for the winter, so he didn't have to collect horse pee in the spit box for a while. In the meantime, he was making dough selling Percodans he had snowed his doctor pals into giving him for his bad back neck elbow wrist you-name-it. He was also selling Percodans that those same docs were prescribing to Shirley for her bad back neck elbow wrist you-name-it after Jimmy had coached her how to describe the ailment convincingly.

I tried to ignore the drug dealing and did my best not to get on Jimmy's bad side. I dressed like a Greek crone and learned from YaYa how to make baklava that Jimmy gobbled down and deemed "not too terrible."

I went food shopping with Jimmy—a day-long affair. We drove a half hour to a market owned by a Greek 'cause the prices were cheaper and 'cause Greeks had to stick together. We drove to a meat market where the butcher would let Jimmy go in the back and cut up his own lamb. We drove to a farm that had eggs that had just dropped out of a chicken's Shame.

Once we passed a kosher market and Jimmy pulled over on a whim. We went in and he asked the guy for a pound of bacon. Just for the fun of it, he said, when we were back in the car. Just to ride a Jew 'cause they didn't have a sense of humor. The guy in the market didn't have one. He'd ordered us off the premises.

As we drove away, I stared into the passing cars. I projected myself into one of them. I counted how many days I had left. Too goddamn many.

My only escape was going to the movies. At least once a week, Jimmy took me to one. He was glad to have me around again as a movie companion, since Hank and his other hunting buddies weren't movie buffs and wouldn't know Rossellini from Ronzoni. Usually, we snuck booze and baklava into the theater so he'd have something to drink and I'd have something to eat.

That winter, the film Jimmy was most looking forward to was *Last Tango in Paris*. He idolized Marlon Brando and saw himself in the characters Brando played. The tragic ex-boxer in *On the Waterfront*. The rebellious seaman in *Mutiny on the Bounty*. The soulful gangster in *The Godfather*. The sexy tough who knew how to keep a woman in line in *A Streetcar Named Desire*.

But watching *Last Tango* with Jimmy was torture. After the scene where Brando used a stick of butter on Maria Schneider—an actress not much older than me—Jimmy slipped away to the bathroom and didn't come back for a while. When he returned, he looked sweaty and disheveled, and from then on I kept my eyes glued to the screen, pretending I was absorbed in the movie, just like I had done years before at *Blood Feast*.

When the film was finally over, all I could think was I never wanted to see *any* movie with Jimmy again. Never wanted to sit beside him in the dark, feeling his breath rise and fall and having him squeeze my arm during the good parts.

I kept counting down the days until I could get out of Jimmy Jail.

But the days moved as slow as the horses Jimmy was betting on at the bookie joint.

I didn't have much to distract me. I didn't even see much of Virginia. Between working at the massage parlor, taking care of Dustin, and her new romance, she was pretty tied up.

I did get to see Hank a few times, though—not that I wanted to. One night, he came over for one of Shirley's home-cooked meals. Nearly a decade after he'd murdered Doris, Hank still didn't have a wife. He'd kept his word never to return to Marriage Jail and have another ball and chain. By then he was in his mid-fifties—ancient in my estimation—but he still seemed tough as nails. He still blamed Doris for her failings, chief of which was giving birth to a daughter who took after her. A female who popped pills like jelly beans to get through the day and who drained him dry. A female who was a quitter and couldn't tough things out. A no-account loser who checked herself in and out of the nuthouse.

"That kid's the biggest disappointment of my goddamn life," he said, as

Shirley dished up seconds of her meltingly tender lamb and orzo and then melted into the background.

Look who's talking, I could've screamed. You're a frickin' murderer.

I felt like pushing his face into that plate of food. Instead, I kept my eyes focused on my own plate even though I had lost my appetite.

"My kid won't quit in the homestretch like yours did, Polack," laughed Jimmy, half-lit and already gobbling down his second helping. "She's gonna be a rich goddamn doctor and write me all the prescriptions I want and buy me a stable full of racehorses. If she don't, I'll put a bullet through her goddamn egghead."

He poked me on the forehead, leaving a buttery fingerprint.

Hank sneered at Jimmy. Then he started in on his son. Hank wasn't happy with Terry either. He'd screwed up royally by leaving the Catholic church to become a follower of some TV evangelist.

"Goddamn kids. If I had it to do over I wouldn't have had any," said Jimmy, like I wasn't even there. "I'd be free as a goddamn bird."

I guess he was in Jimmy Jail too.

We were all in goddamn Jimmy Jail.

Only Shirley managed to find a way out.

She went to sleep.

At first, that's all I noticed. She started sleeping all the time. Sleeping more than Rip Van Frickin' Winkle. I told myself she worked too hard and I tried to be as quiet as a mouse.

Then, she began to waste away. She lost so much weight she was skin and bones. I tried to get her to eat, but she was never hungry.

She stopped cleaning the apartment. A pile of laundry grew like mold beside the wringer washer. Balls of dust, cat hair, and pinfeathers from Jimmy's plucked ducks drifted across the floor. Splotches of deer blood spattered the linoleum like a Jackson Pollock—by then I knew who he was. I tried to pick up some of the housekeeping slack, but Jimmy could dirty a room faster than you could ever clean it up.

The last straw for Jimmy was when Shirley's cooking went down the tubes. One day, she even burned a pan of spanakopita.

"What the hell's the matter with you?" he screamed.

Shirley just shrugged and said she was stupid and promised to eat every burnt morsel, nothing would go to waste.

I said I'd eat some too.

The next day, Jimmy dragged Shirley off to the Yankee doctor. I was worried sick what the doctor might find. I knew Jimmy was thinking the Big C, and I was too. But the doctor said Shirley was just run down. He told Jimmy to give her some vitamins to pep her up.

When I got home from work, I was happy to hear Shirley was probably OK. As Shirley changed back into her nightgown, Jimmy went rooting around in the medicine cabinet and unearthed an ancient bottle of One A Days. When he opened the bottle, we both got a big surprise. Instead of vitamins, he found booze.

Jimmy went ballistic. He knew what it meant. He'd found YaYa's booze hidden all over when he was a kid. He screamed at Shirley that she was a god-damn alkie.

Shirley barely reacted. I tried to talk to her, but she just wanted to go back to sleep. Jimmy told her to get her alkie ass back to bed—which she did, gladly.

I sat there, flabbergasted. I knew Shirley drank a lot, but relative to Jimmy, it hadn't seemed that bad.

Jimmy told me to give him a goddamn hand and we tore the house apart. We found booze hidden everywhere—inside empty bottles of Aunt Jemima pancake syrup and boxes of Tide detergent and jars of Pond's Vanishing Cream.

Jimmy sat down and had a drink. He told me to have one too, but that was the last thing I felt like.

The problem, Jimmy quickly concluded, was Shirley's goddamn hormones. Women just went batty around her age.

He picked up the phone and called a female cousin of his. She'd had a crack-up from her hormones not long before but was doing OK now. The cousin recommended a shrink near the Massachusetts town where she lived.

The next day, we drove Shirley there.

The doctor took one look at Shirley and put her right in the hospital.

Over the next few days, the doctor dried Shirley out. The nurses tried to get her to eat, but she just scrunched herself up and went back to sleep. When they finally coaxed her into nibbling something, she threw it up.

After several days, Shirley wasn't getting much better. The shrink trans-ferred her to a private nuthouse that looked like a country club. Jimmy and I met with him in his office and he told us she might be there for quite a while. I was worried about how we were going to pay for it, but the shrink said Shirley had pretty good insurance and he knew how to finesse it.

Jimmy said frick this. He missed the old Shirley's home cooking, before she went bonkers and started to burn things. He said he was losing weight himself without any decent food and was probably worse off than she was.

"Give her some goddamn happy pills and send her the hell home bingo bango!" he yelled at the shrink.

But the shrink held his ground. He'd seen Shirley tremble when Jimmy walked in the room. He refused to send her the hell home. In fact, he said he didn't think it was wise for Shirley to see Jimmy at all right now.

"Not wise? I'll show you what's wise! Me! I'm wise! I'm Mr. Wiseguy!" shouted Jimmy, looking like he was going to clock the guy or, worse, go get his gun from the car. "Nobody tells me what to do with my own goddamn wife! She's mine! Now sign her the hell outta here or *you'll* be headin' out—feet first!"

The shrink didn't flinch. He was from a Middle Eastern country and no doubt had seen his share of tough guys. He had Jimmy's number. He told Jimmy if he sent Shirley home she'd die in a few weeks and her heavenly spanakopita would go to heaven with her.

"You're this close to losing her," the shrink said, holding his fingers a millimeter apart. "Now, I'm an agnostic like you," he continued, having by then listened to his share of Jimmy's ranting about the sad and pointless state of human existence in a possibly godless universe. "But, on the off chance there is a God, I wouldn't want to offend him by depriving my wife of lifesaving medical attention. I don't think that would go down too well, do you?"

Jimmy started to tremble a little himself. He couldn't quite shake the fear of eternal damnation he had acquired sitting beside YaYa in the Greek church when he was a pip-squeak. Even if the odds of hell being real were a million-to-one, it didn't seem worth the risk. So Jimmy did what the shrink said. He agreed to let Shirley stay and not to visit her. He agreed to drive me there to see her and wait outside like a dog in a doghouse.

"Congratulations," he told me. "You did it. You got your goddamn mother to yourself."

The day after the shrink informed Shirley that Jimmy had been barred from seeing her, she started to eat. Within a week she was gaining weight, participating in activities, and looking forward to therapy. She developed a bit of a crush on the shrink.

By my second visit she told me she didn't miss the booze at all and felt like she was on a holiday.

"I better not seem too happy, though, or they'll make me leave," she whispered.

Eventually, we both knew, it would come to that. She'd have to leave.

And so would I.

I returned to my by then much-missed college nuthouse.

And, shortly after, Shirley returned to Jimmy.

She said she was done with booze and done with swallowing Jimmy's baloney.

"Things are gonna change around here," she said. "You wait and see."

Happy Together

Jimmy was so relieved to have Shirley back, he finally got her a new washing machine. Well, not new exactly—some guy he knew had salvaged it from an apartment building that was being torn down—but at least she didn't have to yank stuff through a wringer anymore.

I called home every Sunday to check up on her.

"He waits on me hand and foot," she said. I wasn't sure I could believe her, but then Jimmy confessed he'd even mopped the kitchen floor.

As spring arrived, he trekked deep, deep into the woods to find a rare trillium orchid for her for Mother's Day.

"We're like newlyweds," Shirley insisted.

Meanwhile, I developed a crush of my own. The boy with the Moog synthesizers and I hit it off even though he'd grown up in Locust Valley with a maid and his father ran a big corporation and had written a best seller.

That summer I moved to New York for a job at a museum. I crashed with a Bennington friend in her artist father's painting studio and lost my virginity to Moog Boy.

I'd already been on the pill for months. After what had happened to Virginia, I wasn't taking any chances.

One balmy night, Moog Boy and I drove all around Manhattan in his father's brand-new Fiat. We had the top down and a full moon was peeking out between the glittering skyscrapers.

Moog Boy was wearing sunglasses. We passed a joint back and forth and listened to jazzy, Moog-y music. Sun Ra.

We ate garlicky veal piccata in Little Italy.

I felt like I was living in a Fellini film. *La Dolce Vita.*

Moog Boy kissed me at every red light.

We ran out of gas in the middle of Fifty-Seventh Street and a doorman helped us push the car to the curb. We jumped in a cab, got more gas, and drove out to Locust Valley.

The sun was coming up on the big, beautiful houses with the big, frickin' lawns that somebody like Jimmy had to mow.

Quit thinking about goddamn Jimmy, I screamed at myself. This is your frickin' life.

Not really. It was Moog Boy's life.

We hung out in his room, smoked some more pot. We watched his home movies. There were no bleeding animals in them.

So what?, I thought. So what?

Moog Boy's mother came into the room. She had white-blond hair and white-blue eyes.

I jumped up to greet her. I smiled without showing my Dracula teeth.

I wanted her to like me so bad.

But right away I could tell she didn't. It wasn't just paranoia from the pot or me feeling like the Little Match Girl.

Something about her reminded me of Hank. She had a nose like a hunter. She could sniff out where someone was going and where someone had been.

I was right. She didn't like me.

But I can't say that I liked her much either. Not after she snapped at the black maid.

"Ellie! Go get me a stamp!"

Moog Boy was as embarrassed by her as I was by Jimmy.

We did have something in common.

So, we fell in love.

I didn't tell Jimmy and Shirley. I didn't want to hear Jimmy say Moog Boy must be as blind as Helen Keller. Or hear Shirley say invite him for a visit.

But all summer I still called home. Called every Sunday like a religious obligation.

One Sunday I heard from Jimmy that Susan had fallen in love too. She'd met a guy named Ed in the nuthouse and was crazy about him.

I didn't know whether to be happy about that or not.

I crossed my fingers for Susan. That was the best I could do.

Soon after, I went back to Bennington for my second year.

I studied hard and tried to figure out what the hell I wanted to be for the rest of my life. A doctor to fix Jimmy? A filmmaker to entertain him? At least I had eliminated stewardess.

Moog Boy and I stayed in love.

Virginia and the married guy stayed in love.

Jimmy and Shirley stayed in love. Or so Shirley said.

In the midst of all that, I still thought about Susan. I kept tabs on her new romance over the next several months.

Her relationship blossomed. Susan and her sweetheart got out of the nuthouse and got married. They had a nice little apartment and a cat. They went to church. Like her brother, Susan had given up the family religion to become a Christian, although she wasn't following a TV evangelist.

It seemed like Susan's second marriage was working out a whole lot better than her first. It seemed like things were finally turning around for her.

I wanted to think so, anyway.

But no such luck.

As I was finishing up my second year at Bennington and planning to move back to New York with Moog Boy, I got some terrible news from Jimmy.

Susan's husband had slit his throat in their bathroom and bled to death in her arms.

If there was a God, it seemed like he had it in for Susan.

If there was a God—and I was less convinced of it every day—he was a mean so-and-so like Jimmy.

If there was a God, he was not all-seeing like my childhood friend Tina had insisted—he was the evil eye.

Maybe somebody needed to spit on Susan to ward him off.

For years YaYa had spat on me, and look where it got me. My life was going pretty well. In fact, my life was soaring, while Susan's—despite her churchgoing—was plummeting.

After years of looking up to Susan all I could do now was look down.

Down, down, down.

Thinking about Susan just got me down.

I wanted to reach out to her before I left for New York, but I decided I wouldn't know what to say.

I convinced myself we'd never really had that much in common. We'd always been separated—either by age, by distance, or by tragedy.

I told myself she'd always been a bigger part of my life than I'd ever been of hers.

I told myself she probably wouldn't want to see me anyway.

I told myself that my good fortune would only make her feel bad.

And maybe all that was true.

But I was also superstitious.

I didn't want her bad luck—if that's what it was—to rub off on me.

She had inspired me for years, but now I was on my own.

I was free as a goddamn bird. And I didn't want anyone holding me back.

I moved out of miserable New England for good. I put miles between me and Jimmy and Hank and Susan.

Moog Boy had dropped out of college, and impulsively I decided to leave Bennington too. I wanted to live where the fun was. I wanted to live in glamorous New York.

Moog Boy's parents had a penthouse on Sutton Place they weren't using and we stayed there for a few months before getting an apartment with Moog Boy's trust fund. I told Jimmy I was living with a Greek girlfriend. That lie worked fine since Jimmy never called to check up on me 'cause he didn't want to spring for a phone call.

I applied to Sarah Lawrence, a school just outside the city that I could commute to. I got another scholarship and transferred there.

I said sayonara, baby, to becoming a doctor. I realized that was Susan's dream, not mine.

I wanted to make movies. Film was a risky racket compared to medicine, but I was from a family of gamblers, so I rolled the dice. I reminded myself I was a lucky so-and-so. I reminded myself of that a lot.

Moog Boy bought me a Super 8 camera for my birthday.

I spent Thanksgiving at the Locust Valley Country Club.

I spent Christmas in Bel Air—Moog Boy's family had another house there.

I smoked a spliff with the actress from *Last Tango in Paris*. She was dating Moog Boy's sister. We cruised around L.A. in a big black kraut car—a Mercedes-Benz. The actress stopped to give a handsome homeless man her espadrilles. The guy reminded me of Jimmy, but I tried not to think about that.

I did everything I could to fit in. I kept hiding my Dracula teeth. Got my hair cut where Moog Boy's sister got hers cut. Got my blackheads squeezed at Mario Badescu. Bought some espadrilles. I studied the quirks of Moog Boy's family. I laughed at jokes about Locust Valley lockjaw. Learned how to pronounce Perrier. Pretended I knew where the hell Antigua was. I passed—just barely—living in fear most of the time. Fear of sounding like a dummkopf. Fear of looking like a rube. Fear of making one wrong move and ending up back in Rubeville.

At night, in my dreams, I was still there.

I guess you could say they were nightmares.

During the day, I had a lot of stomachaches and went to a lot of doctors. I thought I might have the Big C, but nothing ever turned up.

I quit smoking, not wanting to push my luck—and not wanting to smell like Jimmy.

In school, I made short films and wrote scripts and watched movies till my eyes felt like glassy marbles. For my senior film project, I returned to New England to film Virginia. I was shooting a documentary about five women and how money determined their choices in life. I filmed Virginia getting ready to leave for the massage parlor. The film got shown in the city and people applauded, but it was still hard for me to watch Virginia put on that platinum-blond wig.

When I was finally about to graduate from Sarah Lawrence, Virginia made plans to drive Shirley down for my graduation. At the last minute, Jimmy surprised everybody and tagged along.

"The first egghead college graduate in the family. I guess I gotta see that with my own goddamn eyes," he said on the phone.

I was nervous about him coming, but sort of pleased, too. It still stung that he hadn't come to my high school graduation.

Shirley bought him a seersucker suit and, amazingly, he agreed to wear it—with a bright pink shirt and a pair of shades. He looked pretty sharp.

After I was given that hard-won piece of paper and the ceremony was over, I found my family in the crowd. Shirley and Virginia were blubbering with happiness. When I saw them, I started blubbering too. Jimmy made fun of us, three crying women. He rubbed his eyes with his hairy fists like a squalling brat.

"Well, you're officially an egghead," he said. "And I could use a drink."

So we grabbed some refreshments and Jimmy began to mingle. I wasn't surprised that he fit right in.

"*The Bicycle Thief* is De Sica's masterpiece," he told my film teacher. He described growing up poor and Greek before the war with one bicycle for three brothers—*his* bicycle thief story—and my teacher was riveted.

"Your life would make a great film," my teacher said.

"I'm writing a book about it," he bragged, which was news to me.

"What's this about you writing a book?" I asked after the teacher left.

"I'm talking it into a tape recorder. You're not the only writer in this family. My story will blow anything you could do outta the water."

A stoner with dreadlocks came over to say hi. Before long Jimmy was telling him about the crazy Jamaican, Alboy, with whom he'd smoked weed in the merchant marine.

"Gimme your number," Jimmy said, and winked. "I can get some for you."

"*Daddy*," I laughed. I turned to the stoner. "He's just kidding."

"Too bad," the stoner said.

After the stoner drifted away, I chastised Jimmy.

"You can't peddle drugs here."

"Hey, I'm just foolin' around. What're you scared of? You already graduated. They can't toss you out. Don't be such a Goody Two-shoes. No wonder you don't seem to have many friends. I guess you weren't that popular, huh?"

"*Jim*," said Shirley.

"*Daddy*," said Virginia.

"Your daughter's got lots of friends. Everybody likes her," said Moog Boy, timidly.

"Take it easy, Sir Galahad," Jimmy joked. "At least you're man enough to stick up for her."

He lit a cancer stick and guzzled some wine right out of the bottle.

A plump girl I was friendly with came over and bummed a Lucky off him. He lit her cigarette with the end of his. He told her she had eyes like Liz Taylor's.

"Your father's so cool," she whispered to me. "Like a character out of *Mean Streets*."

"He's a character all right," I said, as I watched Jimmy make a group of kids I didn't know laugh.

All day long, Jimmy stole my thunder at my own graduation. But I didn't care. I was the Girl with the Outlaw Father in a school that romanticized outlaws. I knew how to work that. And I knew, when all was said and done, my life was moving ahead without him.

As a graduation present Moog Boy had given me a trip for two to England. It almost made up for the fact that Jimmy gave me nothing at all—not even a "Congratulations, Dracula."

Toward the end of the summer, I took Virginia on the adventure we'd both dreamed of years before. She was still working at the massage parlor and by then really needed a break.

The Beatles had broken up. The mods and rockers were over. And Brian Jones was dead. But Carnaby Street was still there. And Virginia still knew how to get a five-finger discount.

Merry Olde England made New England feel like it was a million miles away. For once, I barely thought about Jimmy and Shirley. I know I didn't think about Hank or Susan.

But that was all about to change.

Jimmy had told me at graduation that Susan's life had been going from bad to worse.

After her second husband killed himself, she spiraled down. She went back to popping pills and bouncing checks.

Broke, desperate, her back to the wall, she begged Hank to let her move in with him until she could get on her feet.

It was not a good move.

From day one, Hank didn't want her there and they fought like cats and dogs.

Susan told people Hank had begun to call her by her mother's name when he got drunk.

She said she awoke one night to find him pointing a rifle at her.

She said it was only a matter of time before she ended up dead.

Something had to give.

Jimmy told Hank to kick Susan the hell out.

Susan, it seemed, had come to the same conclusion. She got the hell out.

She decided to leave New Hampshire once and for all. She was going to escape to California just like Doris had dreamed of doing. Her aunt Irene had answered Susan's prayers and told her to come stay with her.

But things never seemed to work out for Susan.

When Virginia and I returned from England, I called Jimmy and Shirley to tell them we were back in New York.

"Hi—" I said, and that's all I got out before Jimmy shouted into the phone.

"Hank blew his brains out!"

Sayonara, Hank

It happened early on a Saturday morning, just like the murders of Doris Piasecny and John Betley fourteen years before.

The Manchester police received a call from Susan around six a.m. She said she was concerned because she hadn't been able to reach Hank on the phone. She said she was leaving town and needed to retrieve some of her belongings that were still in his house.

The police sent a cruiser over to Hank's. They found him lying facedown in a pool of blood with his head blown off and his 12-gauge shotgun by his side.

It seemed pretty obvious what had happened.

But what had driven Hank to do it?

Had the guilt over killing two people—including the wife he had once been crazy about—finally caught up with him? That was my theory—or, more accurately, my hope.

Had Hank's disappointment with his no-account daughter pushed him over the edge? That was Jimmy's theory.

Had turning sixty—all alone and no longer the big shot he once was—been the last straw?

Or had it simply been a lethal combination of booze and the blues that had triggered him to pull the trigger?

Nobody could say for sure.

All I hoped was, with the man who had murdered her mother now dead, Susan might finally find a little peace.

But I should've known better.

On September 5, 1977, two days after Hank's body was found, Susan went to the funeral home for one final private viewing of her father—the grim routine of a person mourning a loved one. Or a not-so-loved one.

But Susan's visit didn't turn out to be routine. Far from it.

Susan said she saw something. Something no one else had noticed. Not the police. Not the medical examiner. Not the funeral home.

She said she saw a small hole in Hank's chest. She said she took a pencil, the only medical instrument she had at her disposal, and probed the hole to see what it was.

Susan, the almost-doctor, performed her own autopsy.

She examined her father's body and said she found a smaller-caliber bullet hole in Hank's chest.

She said her father hadn't committed suicide after all.

He'd been murdered.

Someone had killed him and made it look like suicide.

She went to the cops and told them they'd made a big mistake. She told them about the little hole.

The cops didn't buy it. They knew Susan had been in the nuthouse plenty of times. They knew she popped pills, forged prescriptions, and had been in trouble with the law.

The cops didn't give Susan the time of day.

Nobody did. Not her relatives. Not Hank's friends. Not his enemies. Not the medical examiner. Not the funeral parlor director.

Susan tried to convince anyone who would listen, but nobody would.

The family went ahead and buried Hank. There were no calling hours at the funeral home.

But even if there had been, Jimmy wouldn't have gone. He hated funerals and wouldn't be caught dead at one. He mourned his old merchant marine buddy in the way he thought Hank would appreciate.

He got good and loaded.

He vowed to shoot a few ducks in Hank's honor.

And that was that.

People needed to go on with their lives.

I sent Susan a card telling her I was sorry about Hank. I wasn't really, but I couldn't say that.

The card came back. It had an old address.

Jimmy got ready for hunting season. He bought a new rifle.

I landed my first job: adding sound effects to nature documentaries and soft-core porno flicks.

And Virginia went back to not giving massages at the massage parlor.

But Susan couldn't go on with her life.

She wouldn't let it rest.

She kept hounding the cops.

She kept hounding her relatives.

Finally, she filed a petition with the superior court that stated her suspicions.

She wanted Hank's body dug back up.

Nearly a month after Hank had been buried, Susan obtained a warrant to do just that. She didn't trust the medical examiner who had ruled Hank's death a suicide. She brought in a forensic pathologist from Massachusetts to perform the autopsy.

The news shocked everybody but Susan.

The guy found a .22-caliber bullet in Hank Piasecny's heart.

He didn't know whether it was the small-caliber bullet to the heart or the shotgun blast to the head that had actually killed Hank.

But one thing was certain. Just as Susan had claimed, Hank had been murdered.

Keystone Kops

"Some no-good bastard rubbed out Hank," Jimmy barked when I picked up the phone, surprised that he was calling me.

I thought he must be drunk.

He was, but he was also dead sober.

I grilled Jimmy for the details. When I found out Susan had been the one to discover the crime, I was even more stunned. I couldn't imagine how she was functioning, much less how she'd been sharp enough to notice something nobody else had. I couldn't see how she could survive this latest revelation. Both of her parents had been murdered years apart? What were the odds of that? A zillion-to-one?

And who killed Hank Piasecny?

Once again, everyone had a theory.

Did he piss off a customer at the boat shop where he still worked? One of those people who bugged him and got a kisser full of cigar smoke as a fuck you?

Did he get into a drunken argument at a bar like he had done so often in his salad days, and maybe his adversary had followed him home for some payback?

Was the killer a mental case Hank had had a few run-ins with at the nuthouse and who was now on the loose?

Or was the killer, as Jimmy suggested, "Just some nigger who couldn't take a joke when Hank called him a nigger"?

It was hard to say, almost a month after the murder, who had done it. With the crime scene cleaned up and potential clues washed away, the cops had a tough task ahead of them.

Everything had to be reexamined.

After learning of the new evidence, the first medical examiner and the funeral director both insisted they had seen the bullet hole but just hadn't realized it was a bullet hole. The funeral director said it just looked like "a break in the skin, as far as we were concerned."

The cops had missed a few glaring clues themselves. For one thing, it turned out there had been a trail of blood at least ten feet long at the crime scene, a trail leading from the kitchen to the hallway where the body was found. Given that one side of Hank's head had been blown off, it was highly unlikely he could have moved ten inches, much less ten feet.

Then there was the matter of the gun's positioning. It was found lying beside Hank's right arm, but it was the left side of his head that had taken the shot.

When you considered the whole picture you had to agree with Jimmy.

"The frickin' Keystone Kops woulda done a better job."

Home Free

E ven so, it took the cops only a month to find the killer.

It wasn't that hard.

She was right in front of them.

On Halloween Day, 1977, they arrested Susan.

Susan—who had tipped them off in the first place.

Susan—who had fought to have Hank's body exhumed.

Susan—who had been home free.

When the cops arrested her she didn't argue, clam up, or proclaim her innocence.

She agreed to confess to the murder.

She just asked that her brother and her lawyer be there when she did.

Perhaps, after all the years of suffering, she finally felt some relief.

During the month of the investigation, her behavior had become increasingly desperate as she tried to evade detection for the crime she herself had "uncovered."

She stole whatever she could get her hands on—golf clubs, ice skates, an alarm clock—presumably hoping to pawn them.

She returned to the scene of the crime and pocketed her father's eyeglasses, telling a friend the missing glasses would bolster a case of negligence she planned to file against the police.

She wrote a threatening message on her car in lipstick and tried to convince the police it was a warning from the killer that she was next on his hit list.

Finally, as the police were beginning to put the pieces together and zero in on Susan, she came up with a truly bizarre scheme. She enlisted the help of a young woman she knew named Mary. A young woman she must've thought was pretty naive. She asked Mary to go to the police and confess to the murder.

She seemed to think if the cops got sidetracked with investigating Mary, it would give her time to slip away.

Maybe she was still planning to escape to California.

Maybe she was trying to frame Mary for the crime.

Susan's true motives, I was beginning to realize, were not always easy to figure out.

But Mary was not as naive as Susan might have hoped. She did go to the police—behind Susan's back. She told the police that Susan was trying to get her to make a false confession.

The police, now convinced that Susan was the killer, enlisted Mary in a scheme of their own. They goaded Mary to pump Susan for details about what had happened the night of the murder. They told Mary to tell Susan she needed those details to make her "confession" more believable.

This is what Susan told Mary to say:

She, Mary, had been breaking into Hank's house when Hank suddenly appeared with his shotgun. She shot him in self-defense with a .22-caliber pistol. He was still alive, so she picked up the rifle and shot him in the head. She tried to drag his body into the bedroom, but he was too heavy. She left him where he was and wiped down her fingerprints.

The main question the cops were still hoping to answer was the whereabouts of the .22-caliber pistol. A cousin of Susan's had reported such a weapon missing from his home and the cops were convinced it was the murder weapon. They told Mary to ask Susan about the pistol.

Susan instructed Mary to tell the cops that she had tossed the gun into the Merrimack River.

When I thought about it later, I couldn't help but feel that the Merrimack was the perfect hiding place for Susan's murder weapon. The river embodied everything the city was and had been for more than a hundred years. It sliced through Manchester like a wet, oily knife. It ran beside the crumbling, long-abandoned mills. It lapped the ground contaminated with anthrax from the goatskins that immigrant factory workers had turned into the linings of fine wool coats. Coats those workers could never afford to buy. It took whatever garbage the angry people of a dying New England city threw into it and never gave anything back.

It was the river that ran beside Hank's Sports Center.

It was the river I feared swallowing me up in a Greek baptism.

It was the river I'd pictured leaping into in my darkest days of living in the shadow of it.

Divers searched that murky water, where Susan said the gun could be found, and turned up nothing. Maybe the gun had been carried away by the sludgy current. Maybe it had washed up onshore and been found by someone who liked to go rat shooting at the dump. Or maybe Susan never threw it in there in the first place and was just sending the Keystone Kops on a wild-goose chase to buy herself more time.

Even without the gun as evidence, the cops decided they had to move quickly and make an arrest.

Mary told them Susan was beginning to threaten her.

Susan was charged with first-degree murder and held without bail in the Hillsborough County jail. It was the same jail her father had been held in after murdering her mother.

The next day, Susan made her first court appearance. She didn't enjoy the same protection from being photographed that Hank had received when he was arrested. A front-page photo in the *Union Leader* showed her looking frail, hunched over, and wearing a neck brace from a fender bender she had supposedly gotten into the previous week. She didn't look like the person who could've taken down Hank Piasecny. Then again, maybe that neck brace was part of a new scheme.

Susan's attorney entered no plea on her behalf and she was held without bail.

I called Jimmy to find out the latest.

He said he hoped they'd throw the book at Susan. In his book she had committed the biggest sin of all.

"That kid never respected her old man. Even as a pip-squeak. She stole goddamn candy from Hank's first store. She's nothing but a conniving little con artist."

Takes one to know one, I thought.

"I felt like knocking off my old man plenty of times, but did I? No. 'Cause he's the king of the goddamn jungle. The king's the king. The king's always right—even when he's wrong."

You're wrong, I thought.

"Hank shoulda just wiped her out along with that whore of a mother!" he yelled, really building up a head of steam. "I mean it, they better keep that bitch locked up for the rest of her goddamn life, 'cause if they let her out, I'll go looking for her myself. I'll blow her goddamn brains out. *Kaboom!*"

When he said that, something in me just snapped. *Kaboom!* I was sick of listening to all the things Jimmy said that turned my stomach. Sick of either pretending to agree with him or being a silent accomplice. Sick of clamming

up out of fear that he would come after me like Fuad Ramses or the Boston
Strangler. Sick of being afraid he'd blow *my* goddamn brains out.

"Goddamn Hank got what he deserved!" I yelled back, and hung up on
him.

Sure, I was defending a murderer. But some part of me still admired Susan.
Maybe now more than ever.

Sorry but Not Sorry

wish I could say that was the last I ever spoke to Jimmy, but it wasn't. After all, I was a good Greek girl, raised to respect her parents.

Before long, Shirley called to broker a truce.

"I just want us all to get along. Is that asking too much?"

I held my ground, for a few minutes at least.

"I'm not speaking to him ever again. I'll talk to you, but not him."

"You're putting me in the middle. You're making me choose sides."

"Nobody's putting you in the middle."

"I can't go against him. I can't call you behind his back. He'll see it on the bill. I have to live with him, you don't. If you don't talk to him, I can't talk to you."

"You're making *me* choose sides! I can't listen to him say awful things anymore."

"Oh, he doesn't mean half of what he says. His bark is worse than his bite. And look what *you* said about Hank. That wasn't very nice either. No matter what you think, he was Daddy's friend and he's gone and you didn't show any sympathy. Now who's the mean one?"

Jimmy was still the mean one, but I called and apologized.

I didn't want to be cut off from my mother.

Jimmy continued to rant about Susan as if nothing had happened between us. He mailed me newspaper articles, dissected her case, and handicapped her chances of being strung up. New Hampshire hadn't hanged anyone in almost forty years, so the odds, he said, were "a million-to-goddamn-nothing."

Over the next few months I learned that the state had engaged Dr. Hans Standow to evaluate Susan's sanity. As fate would have it, he was one of the shrinks who had examined Hank.

But Susan had other ideas. She wanted Dr. Harry Kozol to examine her instead. Dr. Kozol was the Harvard hotshot who, in addition to examining Hank and the Boston Strangler, had gained fame the previous year for evaluating kidnap victim–turned–bank robber Patty Hearst. Susan felt Kozol had been sympathetic to her in the past. He'd even offered to put in a good word for her with Harvard when she was applying to medical schools.

Susan had her lawyer file a motion to have Kozol appointed as an independent expert. She refused to just sit back and let the shrinks evaluate her; she was going to evaluate them too.

But, unfortunately, the state turned Susan down. Kozol was expensive and, since the state was footing the bill, they preferred to go with a cheaper guy. Unlike Hank, Susan didn't have the money to pay for him herself.

Also unlike Hank, Susan didn't have a hotshot lawyer who could maneuver to keep her in the state hospital rather than in the much less comfortable county jail. After a few weeks at the nuthouse, Susan was shipped back to the slammer.

Dr. Standow came to the jail and examined Susan over the course of three afternoons. The doctor said Susan was able to provide him with an "extensive history of her life" and her "extremely traumatic upbringing."

She told him about Hank's heavy drinking.

She told him about Hank threatening the family with a shotgun.

She told him about Hank sexually abusing her from the age of four to eight.

Whether this last revelation was true, no one but Susan could know for sure.

About eight months after Hank's murder, Dr. Standow testified at Susan's court hearing before a judge.

The shrink contended Susan had had a "lifelong love-hate relationship" with her father—something I could certainly relate to. He said this tortured relationship had finally been "resolved by his death." However, he felt Susan's guilt over what she had done was far from resolved. He said that Susan's exhuming of Hank's body had been a manifestation of this guilt.

The shrink pronounced Susan, just like her father, mentally ill. In fact, he thought it was likely she had inherited her condition from Hank.

He thought Susan was more of a danger to herself than others. He recommended housing her in an open ward at the state hospital, where she could receive occupational therapy and other treatment.

Like Hank, Susan was found not guilty by reason of insanity. Like Hank, she was committed to New Hampshire Hospital for life, or until she was deemed no longer insane.

The hearing took thirty-five minutes.

Jimmy mailed me a clipping about it.

The article said that at the end of the hearing Susan stood before the judge, smiling, tears streaming down her cheeks.

Were they tears of relief? Sadness? Victory?

I wasn't sure, but I wanted to find out.

Reunion on
Pleasant Street

Four months later, I returned to New England to see Susan.

Jimmy and Shirley picked me up at the airport in Boston. I hadn't been home in a while and we all seemed nervous.

"I recognized you right away, Dracula," Jimmy said when I walked up, like he'd been afraid he wouldn't.

"What a fancy haircut!" squealed Shirley, who had given herself a perm for the occasion.

"I bet you paid some fairy a double sawbuck for that hack job," Jimmy needled me.

I had paid a lot more than twenty bucks, but I lied.

"It wasn't that expensive."

"You shoulda paid *me* the dough. I woulda cut it for you."

Remembering his drunken haircuts, I forced a smile.

"And you wouldn't have ended up looking like a sheepdog either."

"*Jim*," said Shirley.

"What? I can't even ride my own daughter anymore?"

Then he looked in the rearview mirror at me.

"You look pretty goddamn good, kiddo."

I beamed. I couldn't help it. His opinion still mattered.

We drove into the projects. The buildings had finally been repainted. I can't say it cheered the place up much.

Downstairs in the apartment, there were a few more stuffed ducks on the wall and a new TV.

Upstairs, Shirley had hung fresh curtains and bought new bedspreads for the bunk beds. Jimmy had piled a bunch of eight-track tape players in the corner.

The bullet holes were still in the ceiling.

The next morning, I anxiously got dressed to go see Susan. I put on jeans and a turtleneck. I blow-dried my sheepdog hair. I tried to look nice but not too nice. I wanted to seem like I was doing well but not too well.

307

Jimmy, of course, had no intention of going along and I was glad about that.

"The only way I'd visit that murdering bitch is with a loaded .22," he said.

Shirley insisted she had too much housework, maybe she'd go next time, but I knew she really just didn't want to go against Jimmy.

I didn't want to visit Susan alone. I was afraid that seeing my childhood idol locked up in the nuthouse might put me away. So I called up Virginia. Before I could even ask, she offered to go with me. She jumped in her jalopy and drove up from Massachusetts. She was living right over the New Hampshire border, but at least she'd made it out of the state. She'd also finally left the massage parlor and the married man. Dustin was getting older and she was trying to clean up her act. She was working at an appliance store and she'd become a vegetarian, which drove Jimmy crazy. She'd met a nice guy, a musician, and thought he might be Husband Number Two.

On the short drive up to Concord, I got more and more nervous. I hadn't let Susan know I was coming. I'd told myself it would be nice to surprise her, but I think I was just afraid she'd tell me not to come.

I had called the hospital the day before to make an appointment. But, unlike with Hank, none was necessary.

She doesn't get many visitors, the woman on the phone had said.

I'd hung up and felt depressed.

I still felt pretty depressed.

Virginia tried to distract me on the way with funny stories about working at the appliance store. She was the person you called if your new fridge was a lemon. She had to calm down angry people all day long. She said she felt right at home.

Before long, Virginia's jalopy made the familiar turn onto Pleasant Street.

The hospital looked like it hadn't changed much since we had visited Hank, although having now been to college, I no longer thought it resembled one.

Virginia and I waited in a drab, crowded recreation room, while an attendant went to fetch Susan. I was clutching a gift-wrapped box of my favorite local fudge. My hands were so sweaty they were ruining the wrapping.

Susan walked into the room, looking for a familiar face. I jumped up, hoping that she'd recognize me. I had no trouble spotting her. She looked amazingly well: trim, pretty, and neatly dressed.

She lit up with surprise when she saw us.

I hurried toward her and awkwardly gave her a hug. Virginia did too.

"Wow. I didn't expect to see you guys here," she said, smiling and shaking her head.

"I'm sorry I didn't call," I said. "I wanted to surprise you."

"I'm surprised all right," she said. "This is the best surprise I've had in ages."

I handed her the damp box of candy.

"Oooh, that's my favorite!" she said.

At least I knew we still had one thing in common.

"Are you home from college?" she asked. It seemed like she'd been keeping tabs on me too.

"I graduated last year," I told her.

"I always knew you'd make it. I knew you'd get there one way or the other. Jimmy must be proud of you."

"Oh, I don't know," I said.

"Yeah, I guess you can never really tell with him."

We all kind of laughed.

"Let's go over there where it's less crazy," she said, pointing to an empty table. "Although less crazy here is still pretty crazy," she joked.

She seemed pretty normal. At least she still had her sense of humor. I guess I thought murdering her old man might've taken that away. But maybe it had brought it back.

We sat down at the table and ate some fudge. Susan talked a blue streak. She was totally up on world events—the Camp David Accords, the new pope, the Red Sox getting creamed by the Yankees. I wasn't sure if her talkativeness was due to the meds she was on or her being starved for scintillating conversation.

"Can you believe I'm in here?" she asked at one point, with a wry shake of her head.

All around us, catatonic and delusional people shuffled about. One woman stuck her face in mine, speaking gibberish. Susan spoke to the woman like a doctor. She told the lady she needed to adjust her dose of something and gently shooed her away.

Susan wanted to know all about my life and Virginia's life. Virginia told her about Dustin and the appliance store. I told her about the low-budget Brian De Palma movie I'd cowritten that had been shot on the Sarah Lawrence campus that summer.

"It's like a student film," I said, trying to play it down so the gulf between us wouldn't seem so wide.

"Who's in it? Anyone famous?"

"Kirk Douglas," I mumbled.

"I once danced with Paul Newman at a political rally," she boasted, trying to one-up me a little.

I didn't mention I'd had a Paul Newman sighting of my own.

"You should write a movie about *me*," she insisted. "But you better hurry up 'cause lots of other writers, real big shots, are interested in my story."

"Your life would make quite a story," I said.

Of course that was part of the reason I was there. But I hadn't quite figured that out yet.

"Did you see that *New Yorker* piece on me?" she asked.

I looked surprised.

"The *New Yorker*? Wow—"

"Yeah, I always wanted to be in that magazine. I just thought it might be for one of my poems, but I guess I'll take what I can get."

She leaned a little closer to me.

"I didn't mean to kill him, you know."

I tensed. Out of the corner of my eye I saw Virginia do the same.

"I—I figured you probably didn't," I stammered.

"Me too," said Virginia, in barely a whisper.

With no hesitation, no self-consciousness, Susan launched into talking about the night she killed her father.

"It was self-defense," she said. "It was me or him. He was gonna kill me. You know he threatened to all the time."

I nodded. Virginia nodded. We hung on her every word.

"I went to his house that night to get my stuff. I left a bunch of things behind when I had to get my butt out of there in a hurry. I mean, jeez Louise, I woke up one night and he was pointing a gun at me! I wasn't going to stick around after that! I said, 'I'm *out of here*.' But, like I said, I still had some stuff there. Some paintings I'd made that I really liked. Some poems I wrote. Clothes I wanted to take to California. Did you know I was planning on moving there?'

"I think I read that."

"You can't imagine how many times I've said to myself, 'Susan, you idiot, you should've left that stupid stuff behind.' If I had, I wouldn't be in *this* stupid place."

"But . . . why did you bring a gun with you when you went over there?" I asked haltingly.

"Are you kidding? I was scared outta my wits. I was afraid he was going to kill me. So I took my cousin Mark's gun. I just borrowed it, really, from his house. I was going to put it back. I thought he wouldn't even notice. Wrong again, Susan. Anyhoo, I went there really late that night. I thought I could get in and get out without waking him up. I was hoping, anyway. But, just my luck, he woke up when I was climbing through the window. I looked up and there he was. Standing there in his undershorts, pointing his rifle right at me. You know what he said? 'Now I've got you just where I want you, you little bitch.' Those were his last words. I don't even know how I got the gun out of my purse so fast. I don't even remember pulling the trigger. I only fired once. Just to stop him."

"But what about the second shot?" Virginia blurted out.

"I'm getting to that part. He fell back on the floor and was just lying there, not moving or anything. I didn't see any blood. I thought maybe I didn't even hit him. I thought maybe he was playing dead. You know, playing possum. I thought he was going to jump up and get me, like in a scary movie or something, you know? But then when I got closer, I could see he wasn't breathing too good. I could tell he wasn't gonna make it."

She was silent for a moment.

"So I put him out of his misery. I took the rifle and shot him again. Shot him in the head."

It was chilling to hear her say it. Chilling to think about it.

I had thought about killing Jimmy many times, but Susan had actually pulled the trigger.

She had taken Hank's last breath. Obliterated whatever his last thought might have been. To kill her? Forgive her? Beg for his own forgiveness?

She had destroyed his personality. His sensibility. His awareness—or, more accurately, his lack of awareness.

"Why didn't you just shoot him again with the pistol?" I asked.

"I don't know. I don't know why."

"But why did you make it look like a suicide?"

"I don't know. It all happened so fast, like in a dream."

It was the same way Hank had described his murders. Maybe that's what murder felt like sometimes. Dreamy.

I suspected some of Susan's dreaminess could be attributed to her being hopped-up and asked her about that.

"Were you drinking that night? Or taking drugs or . . . ?"

"Oh, I don't want to talk about that," she said, dismissing my questions with a wave of her hand. "Anyway, I never thought the cops would really buy the whole thing was a suicide. But they're a bunch of idiots, those Manchester cops."

"Is that why you had Hank's body exhumed? To show up the police? That's what some people think—"

"No! Those people are stupid too! I did it for my *babcia.*"

Virginia and I looked confused.

"My grandmother," she explained, translating the Polish word. "I did it for her, not for the police. I didn't want her to think her son was damned forever. Anyway, I thought I could get away before the cops even suspected me. I thought I'd be out in California playing golf and they'd be chasing their tails. Wrong again, Susan."

She never admitted that guilt might have played a part in her getting caught.

She did admit feeling remorse.

"Every single day I regret what I did," she said.

I wasn't sure if she meant killing Hank or digging him up.

When I asked her to clarify, she assured me she was talking about the murder.

But I wasn't totally convinced.

I decided to leave it at that.

When we finally said good-bye, we promised to write. We promised not to lose touch again.

In the car Virginia said, "I don't know what to think. Did she kill him in self-defense or in cold blood?"

I thought about it and shook my head.

"Both, I think."

For the rest of the way home, Virginia and I were silent.

One thought kept running over and over in my head.

That could have been me.

Terry's Take on Things

Before returning to New York, I decided to pay a quick visit to Susan's brother, Terry. I wanted to express my sympathy and to see how he was holding up. Terry was now in his early thirties and living with his wife and kids in a rural town an hour north of Manchester. His glory days as a boxer were long over and he was working as an insurance salesman. According to Jimmy, he was still gung ho about that TV preacher.

Once again, Virginia offered to go with me.

"It's like the old days. Hanging out together," she said.

On the way up we listened to the Stones and talked about our boyfriends.

Finally, we arrived at the remote cabin in the woods where Terry was living.

He seemed glad to see us. He invited us into his living room and served us coffee and sugar cookies. I noticed that several copies of the *New Yorker* containing the story of the Piasecny family were displayed on the coffee table.

I started to tell Terry about my trip to see Susan, but he cut me right off.

"She's nothing to me. *Nothing*," he snapped.

I flinched. His words seemed so unfair. He'd turned against Susan for murdering their father in a way he'd never turned against Hank for killing their mother.

"But, she's been through so much, and—"

"I don't want to talk about her," he said, more sharply.

I clammed up. But he kept on ranting about Susan.

"She's always been no good. Always been violent. Women like her are drawn to violence like moths to a flame. They even love being beaten up. Look at her, both of her husbands beat her and she liked it."

His words hit me like a left hook.

"I can't imagine anyone likes being beaten," I managed to choke out.

"Then you don't know Susan. And you're not too swift."

Get me outta here, I thought. Get me the hell outta here or I'm really gonna punch him.

From the topic of violence-loving women, Terry jumped right into talking about violence-hating women.

He said most women, the ones who didn't love violence like Susan, had an "overexaggerated" reaction to it. As an example, he brought up his young daughter, who was playing nearby. He cruelly mimicked how she would cringe when he threatened to belt her one.

Virginia and I glanced at each other, horrified.

I wanted to grab that little girl and make a run for it.

Instead, I just said we had to be going.

Before we left, Terry insisted on reading us something from the Bible.

John 8:32: "And you shall know the truth, and the truth shall make you free."

I thought that was pretty ironic. Even though Terry's family secrets had been cracked open like a bottle of Jimmy's harsh whiskey and splashed all over the newspapers and in the *New Yorker* fucking magazine, Terry seemed anything but free.

Susan wasn't free either. Obviously. She was locked up.

It was dark by the time Virginia and I hightailed it out of there.

Virginia nearly plowed into a tree in her haste to get away.

On the drive back to Manchester, I made up my mind. I was going to write about Susan and Terry. About Jimmy and Hank. About Shirley and Doris.

I wasn't a violence lover. I was a violence hater.

I wasn't thinking that telling the truth would set me free.

I just hoped—somehow, someday—it might help that little girl.

Down but Not Out

Shortly after I saw Susan—a mere seven months after she had been committed for life—she petitioned the court to set her free. Dr. Standow, the psychiatrist whose assessment of Susan had been instrumental in her being found not guilty by reason of insanity, had examined her again. He found her to no longer be a danger to society or to herself and, stunningly, recommended that she be released.

On February 6, 1979, there was a court hearing to decide Susan's fate before the same judge who had committed her.

Several witnesses, including Susan, testified.

The state attorney general strongly objected to Susan's release. Dr. Standow, the state argued, had previously characterized Susan's mental illness as "long-standing." It was hard to imagine the illness had resolved itself in a few short months.

Some of the hospital staff had their own objections. The director of Susan's unit described her as disruptive and manipulative. He said if she didn't get her way she got angry. He said she bribed other patients to do things for her.

By his description, Susan sounded a lot like Hank.

Susan, in her own defense, painted a starkly different picture. She described the environment at the hospital as inhumane. She insisted she wasn't even getting privileges, like physical recreation, to which she was entitled.

Another staff member admitted this was true. He said Susan didn't have the same privileges as the male patients because the hospital didn't have a separate forensic unit for women. The hospital didn't have enough staff to monitor her if she went outside.

Because she was a rarity—a criminally insane woman—Susan was out of luck.

The next day, the judge denied Susan's petition.

Susan was disappointed, but she knew there'd be other chances. By law, she had to be reevaluated every two years.

Nevertheless, she did start to get a little depressed. I could tell when she wrote to me that her mood was pretty lousy. She said there was no one on her ward she could relate to, no one she could talk to intelligently about art and music and poetry.

She thought having an animal might cheer her up. She put in a request to get a cat on the ward. A couple of the other units had therapeutic animals. But her request was denied. "The environment wouldn't be good for the cat," she said she was told.

"Can you believe that logic?" she wrote. "It's OK for humans, though."

Most of all, she was starved for contact with the outside world. She tried to keep up her connection to it by watching the news and reading *Time* magazine.

She sent me a letter a few months after the mass suicide of Jim Jones's followers in Guyana.

"How can so many minds get so perverted at the same time?" she wondered.

It was a good question, one that I thought could be asked about our own hometown.

But I didn't push myself too hard to answer it. Not then, anyway.

It was a mental maze I was afraid of getting lost in.

I didn't want to get depressed myself.

I didn't want to pervert my own mind.

So, I tried to put it aside.

I got on with my life.

I got a cat of my own.

I got a new boyfriend, a cute young actor. Moog Boy and I had drifted apart but were still friends. Nobody stays with the first guy they sleep with, do they?

I got a great new job that Brian De Palma recommended me for. I started working on a boxing movie for Martin Scorsese and Robert De Niro. I flew with them to a tropical island to be their gal Friday for five weeks as they shaped the movie's screenplay. All day long I happily typed words like *cocksucker* and *motherfucker*. At night, Marty and I drank piña coladas and listened to Van Morrison while Bobby kept to his boxing regimen and went to bed early.

Three squares a day, I could have anything I wanted. Anything off the menu. Or anything the hotel had flown in from Paris especially for us. Foie gras, sweetbreads, filet mignon with béarnaise. Like a little heathen, I pointed to what I wanted until I learned how to pronounce it.

One night Marty and I went out to dinner. I ate boneless quail with grapes off a gold plate the size of a flying saucer while a white-turbaned waiter kept filling my glass with Cristal. I listened to Marty analyze Jimmy's favorite boxing movie, *Body and Soul*. I knew the movie inside out and could hold my own. We talked about films for hours. *City Lights*. *The Thief of Bagdad*. *White Heat*.

My head was spinning from the champagne and the whole shebang.

"Made it, Ma. Top of the world!" I felt like shouting like Jimmy Cagney in *White Heat*.

I just hoped I didn't get shot down in the end like him.

When we returned to New York, Marty and Bobby kept me on as their researcher. I spent my days talking to washed-up boxers and gruff old guys like Papou. I was right in my sweet spot. I was working on a story about an angry-but-soulful lug who beat his wife to a bloody pulp.

Shortly before the start of shooting, Jake LaMotta, the boxer the movie was about, got arrested for smacking his fifth wife. Suddenly, some of the people I was calling for research questioned why we were making a film about such a monster. I assured them the movie wouldn't glorify LaMotta, but, still, some people hung up on me. I had my own concerns about how the wife-beating incident might impact the movie. Primarily, it didn't gel with the movie LaMotta's redemption at the end. But then, who really wanted to see a movie about the real guy? Who wanted to be left with the message once a brute, always a brute? Who wanted a story with no hope? Where was the nuance in that?

Even if it was sort of true.

When the movie came out, it was so brilliant nobody remembered or cared what the real Jake LaMotta had done. I didn't care either. I made a quick trip to Manchester to take Jimmy to see it.

When the lights came up, Jimmy sat dazed and drained in his seat like he'd just gone twelve rounds.

He'd seen his life flashing in front of his eyes at twenty-four frames per second.

He'd had a psychic smackdown.

"I had a ringside seat to that slugfest," he blurted out—meaning the slugfest of boxing and wife beating and self-loathing—"and that movie didn't pull any goddamn punches."

Raging Bull rocked Jimmy's world almost as much as *Blood Feast* had rocked mine.

Maybe a part of me was looking for a little payback.

But I was also hoping to hold a mirror up to Jimmy. To get him to see the error of his ways. To lead him to his own possible redemption.

I didn't know if it had worked. For his sake, and even more for Shirley's, I hoped that it had.

Loaded

Two and half years after Susan was arrested for killing her father, she was released. With two shrinks saying she was no longer a danger to herself or anyone else, the state had to let her go. New Hampshire's quirky insanity law had freed Susan just like it had let Hank walk.

I found out about Susan's release when I called home one Sunday night. I'd been in the dark about her for a while. We hadn't had a falling out. She'd just stopped responding to my letters. I think it had become too hard for her to see the different paths our lives had taken.

"That conniving little scam artist conned those headshrinkers," snarled Jimmy. "Well, she better cross to the other side of the street if she sees me coming."

"Oh, *Jim*, you don't mean that," squeaked Shirley.

I sure hoped Shirley was right.

But I also hoped Susan stayed the hell out of Manchester.

I wanted her to live. I wanted her to succeed. I wanted her life to have a second act. I still believed that was possible.

When Susan left the hospital in the summer of 1980, she had a lot going for her. She was only thirty-eight. She was bright, attractive, and college-educated. She had meds, religion, and therapy to keep her going. She had an apartment—in Concord, *not* in Manchester.

I wish I could say she turned her life around. I wish I could say that once the man who had menaced her childhood and murdered her mother—the villain of the story—was out of the picture, Susan's life had a happy ending. I wish I could say, against all odds, she finished medical school and made it to California. That she met a nice Jewish doctor and I danced at their wedding. That she had a little girl with beautiful cheekbones and named her after Doris.

But stuff like that only happens in movies.

Within a week, Susan was arrested.

Not once. Not twice. Three times.

First some cops caught her smoking a joint in a parked car. Then she was arrested twice for trying to obtain controlled drugs with forged prescriptions.

That was two felonies, one misdemeanor, and counting.

"I told you that kid was a bad seed," crowed Jimmy, when he gleefully delivered the news.

I was overcome with sadness.

I got off the phone quickly. I didn't want Jimmy to hear me blubbering.

After that, I vowed to try to forget about Susan. I didn't need another criminal in my life.

And I had a brand-new job to keep me occupied.

My dream job.

Woody Allen had hired me as his assistant.

Jimmy—no surprise—took credit for it.

"Hey, I'm the one who took you to your first Woody Allen film. I deserve a cut of your big, fat paycheck," he said when I called to tell him, hoping he'd at least say "nice going, kiddo."

"I—I'm only making three hundred bucks a week," I stammered.

"That's good money for a dummkopf girl."

"Daddy's very proud of you," piped up Shirley. "We both are."

"Maybe I'll come down there one a these days," Jimmy said. "Even though Woody's a Jew and I'm a greaseball, I think we'd really hit it off."

I panicked.

He's not going to come, dummkopf, I told myself. He's just trying to get a rise out of you.

But I was wrong.

I came home from work one day and Jimmy was standing on the front steps of my building.

"Who do ya think you are, Annie Hall?" he cracked, giving me the once-over.

I was wearing an Annie Hall–ish getup. Floppy hat. Necktie. Men's shoes.

"Wow, what I surprise," I managed to choke out.

He had on a getup of his own. Bright turquoise shirt. Black polyester pants. Shades. He was dressed for a night out, Jimmy style.

"Get changed and let's hit the town," he said.

With trepidation, I brought him inside to meet Keith, the actor boyfriend.

Keith looked as startled as I was to see Jimmy.

"You're a Jew boy, right?" he said to Keith.

"Yup," gulped Keith, who had heard his share of Jimmy stories.

"You want a belt?" Jimmy asked. I thought for a second he meant a punch, but then he took a pint of whiskey out of his pocket.

"No thanks," said Keith. "I gotta go rehearse. Maybe another time. You guys have fun."

He squeezed my hand for moral support and took off, bingo bango.

After he was gone Jimmy said, "So, he wears contact lenses?"

"Not all Jews wear glasses!" I shouted, exasperated.

"Take it easy, Dracula. I'm just ridin' ya. He seems OK. Kinda short, though. Tell him he oughta dress like a jockey. Ya know, bright colors. It'll make him seem bigger."

I said I'd pass on the fashion tip.

He lit a cancer stick and offered me one.

"I quit, remember?"

He held out the whiskey.

I shook my head.

"You don't booze it up, either?"

"Not much," I admitted.

"Hard to believe you're my goddamn kid. Maybe your old lady was screwin' around on me. Just like you're screwin' around. You're shacked up with that Jew boy, aren't you?"

I edged away from him a little in case he lashed out.

"Yes," I finally croaked.

But he didn't slug me. He just took another slug.

"Well, at least nobody back home knows about it. At least you're keepin' it on a stone wall. Just don't get yourself knocked up like your dummkopf sister. Don't let no brat crimp your style."

"I won't," I said, relieved that he was cutting me slack like I was a son.

He punched me playfully.

"C'mon, let's go get into some trouble."

I changed my clothes. Jimmy said I looked like Annie Hall at a clown convention.

We headed to Times Square. Jimmy knew his way around. We checked out the dives he had gone to when he was in the merchant marine. Times Square was still seedy and a lot of the dives were still there.

Jimmy had a ball and I rolled with it.

It was like the old days, trolling around the Combat Zone.

Am I ever gonna grow up? I thought. Am I ever gonna be frickin' free of him?

Jimmy stayed the weekend, flopping on the couch in the living room. At night, he watched porn tapes he'd purchased in Times Square from a guy like Uncle Barney.

Keith rehearsed all weekend and I stayed out of the living room.

At one point, Jimmy asked when we were going to hook up with Woody, but I told him, aw shucks, Woody was out of town.

At the end of the weekend, Jimmy said he'd had a blast and we should do it again real soon.

I said I'd be working most weekends from then on, so he better call first the next time.

But he didn't end up coming back. He'd gotten too busy with work himself. Or so I found out the next time I saw him.

That was when I flew home for a surprise visit of my own. It was the day before Christmas. I hadn't seen Shirley in quite a while. She'd been sounding tired on the phone lately and I was worried about her. I was afraid she was going to end up drinking and sleeping again.

I got out of the cab and hastily paid the driver, feeling a familiar embarrassment at being dropped off in the projects. I gave the guy an extra-big tip to show him I didn't really belong there. And because it was goddamn Christmas and he was a working stiff.

Right away, as I approached the apartment, I got a bad feeling.

A picture of a gun had been glued to the front door. The barrel of the gun was pointed right at me and any other dummkopf dumb enough to show their kisser around there. On the picture were the words NEVER MIND THE DOG. BEWARE OF OWNER.

I tried to ignore the sign and walked in.

A couple around my age—a guy I'd had a crush on in grade school and a girl I'd played hopscotch with—were lolling about in the kitchen. Their eyes were glazed and I could tell they didn't recognize me.

"Well, look who's here! Annie Hall!" shouted Jimmy. He was sprawled in a new chair that kind of resembled a throne, drinking a highball, smoking a cancer stick.

Shirley came running into the room, holding a shoe box. She was thrilled to see me, but flustered.

She did look tired, but she wasn't skin and bones like I'd feared. In fact, she'd put on a lot of weight. My mother, who'd always been as skinny as Olive Oyl, was now as heavy as Bluto.

"Oh, my God, I look a fright," she said as she grabbed me and hugged me so hard I nearly fell over.

"You should've let me know you were coming! I didn't make any baklava!"

"I just wanted to surprise you. I missed you."

"How about me, big shot?" Jimmy grinned. "Didn't you miss me? Say yes, or I'll clock you one."

"Sure," I lied. "I missed you."

"You're lucky I didn't plug you. I thought you were the fuzz."

"She's back!" Shirley sang out. "It'll be just like old times!"

My stomach knotted up, just like old times.

Someone knocked on the door.

One knock. Two knocks. One knock.

Just like at the bookie joint.

A few more glazed-eyed hopheads came in. The first two got what they came for and scattered like cockroaches, never recognizing me.

If Susan knew about this place, I thought, she'd be next in line. Not that Jimmy would've sold to her. He would've drawn the line there.

I went up to my old bedroom.

It was now a drugstore.

Shoe boxes filled with pill bottles were piled on the top bunk. Back braces, neck braces, wrist braces, and a walker were scattered about the room.

It didn't take long for me to figure out that Jimmy's pill-pushing operation had really taken off. Percocet, Darvon, Valium. He was making money hand over fist.

Shirley, however, appeared to be doing the lion's share of the work. In addition to running back and forth to doctors to score the pills, she was answering the constantly ringing phone, taking the hopheads' dough, doling out the precious tablets from the shoe boxes, and keeping track of inventory.

I knew right away what Jimmy was doing. He was setting Shirley up to take the fall. He figured if they ever got pinched, she'd get off easy 'cause she was a goddamn woman.

But it turned out Shirley wasn't a total patsy. I discovered she had an operation of her own going on. Jimmy had taught her, by example, how to play the accordion, how to skim a little off the top. For every double sawbuck she took in, she was keeping a deuce. I found cash hidden all over just like I had found hidden booze. It was tucked under lamps. Stuffed into Kleenex boxes. Hidden inside my old board game, Candy Land. With the money, Shirley had been redecorating. I found stacks of curtains for every season—snowflake designs for winter, daffodils for spring, roses for summer, horns of plenty for fall—curtains to cover up the windows into Shirley's miserable life. In the living room there was a fake Christmas tree with expensive glass ornaments to replace the ones Jimmy had pawned a long time ago. Shirley told me that when he threw a fit about the decorations, she said she'd found them by the side of the road. Just the way *he'd* lied to me about our ornaments.

I had to give her credit. She was pretty clever.

And then it hit me like a ton of bricks. Some of Shirley's ill-gotten gains had also been flowing my way. Over the previous several months she had been mailing me quite a few money orders.

"Buy yourself something fancy so everyone thinks you're loaded," she'd whisper when I called home to thank her after Jimmy had gotten off the other line.

She'd told me lies about the money too. She said she'd gotten a big raise at the factory. Made a killing at the track. Found a C-note on the ground while walking home from the Temple Market. I believed her—or maybe I was just lying too. Lying to myself. I spent the money on beautiful shoes and nice haircuts. On records and movie tickets. On eating in Greek restaurants that were never as good as home.

But on that trip back for Christmas, I woke the fuck up.

When Jimmy left to go to the bookie joint, Shirley gave me one of her secret Christmas presents. An envelope with a thousand bucks.

I burst into tears.

"I can't accept this," I told her. "I can't take any more money."

Her eager smile vanished.

"Don't take away my only happiness. It's the only thing I'm living for, to make you happy."

"This won't make me happy. It's blood money."

"No, we're *helping* these people! They hurt like hell from lifting boxes and shoveling snow and mowing lawns and doing piecework like I used to do before I got promoted to quality control. You don't know what it's like. You went to college. You never had to dirty your pretty hands with anything but a typewriter."

They were the excuses Jimmy was feeding her so she wouldn't feel bad about what she was doing.

"I've got a clean conscience," Shirley insisted.

At least one of us did.

"You could go to jail," I moaned.

She expelled a bitter laugh like she was spitting out sour milk.

"Your father's too smart. He'll never get caught. He's done everything under the goddamn sun and never got caught."

"I can't take this money," I repeated.

"It won't change anything if you don't. Your father's never gonna stop doing this. He loves it. He's got more money than ever to blow on the horses. The only thing that'll happen if you don't take the money is I'll feel worse. Is that what you want? You want to make me feel bad?"

She cried and begged me some more to take the money.

I took it. She felt better, but now I felt worse.

"Buy yourself something fancy so everyone thinks you're loaded," she said again.

Me and the hopheads. We were all loaded.

And, the next day I found out, so was Shirley.

She had become a pothead.

I smelled it when she came out of the bathroom.

No doubt it was taking the edge off that guilty conscience she didn't have.

Like a parent confronting a teenager, I sat Shirley down and grilled her about the pot.

She said Jimmy—who else?—had gotten her started with it. He had gotten fed up with her being a teetotaler. He thought it made her a goddamn stick-in-the-mud. He was sick of getting half-lit alone. He wanted her to get half-lit too. He thought two halves made a whole lot of fun.

He made her a highball.

But Shirley had stood her ground. She flat out refused to drink it. The shrink at the rehab hospital had convinced her she'd be a dead duck if she started up again. He'd shown her pictures of her pancreas and liver, which looked like they'd been peppered with buckshot. Shirley reminded Jimmy that if she was a dead duck she wouldn't be able to get him any more pills.

He didn't like the sound of that. Maybe his dummkopf wife had a point for once in her stupid life.

So he talked her into smoking a little weed instead.

I could just hear his arguments.

For Chrissake, pot's safer than Luckies! Every goddamn longhair in the country is doing it! You're a big chicken—*pluck pluck pluck*—if you don't give it a try!

Finally she caved.

Light me up, she said.

Yabba dabba doo, Jimmy said.

He bought her a hash pipe.

And he got her the good stuff. Got it from Richie, a dealer in Boston he was supplying with pills. He gave Richie some extra pills and Richie gave him some extra pot. It was perfect. Nobody had to lay out any dough.

The pot explained Shirley's weight gain. Now instead of drinking booze and wasting away, she was smoking pot, getting the munchies, and ballooning up. After Christmas dinner, I watched her eat an entire coconut cream pie.

I told her that wasn't so good for her pancreas either.

She didn't like hearing that. I can't say as I blamed her. She was fed up with people telling her what the fuck to do.

"You're not a doctor," she snapped. "You just wanted to be one like that hophead Susan!"

It was time for me to leave.

I blubbered when I said good-bye and so did she.

As usual, Jimmy told us to quit our blubbering.

Then he told me to come back soon, he'd put me to work. He'd pay more than that cheapskate Woody Allen.

I didn't return home for a long time.

I threw myself into my job. I worked on three Woody Allen movies. I got a raise. I began writing my own screenplays. Screenplays about murderers and child killers.

I stopped calling home every Sunday. I skipped a few now and then.

I tried not to dwell on the bad things that were happening in Manchester. I was supposed to be the one who got away. I was supposed to be the goddamn success story.

But I didn't feel like a success story.

Thanks to Jimmy I was a glass-half-empty kind of gal.

Thanks to Jimmy I felt like throwing that half-empty glass against the frickin' wall.

I felt mad most of the time, but did my best to try to hide it. My best wasn't good enough.

I snapped at slowpoke cab drivers, was rude to rude people, yelled at my boyfriend for trying to make me feel better about my teeth.

"They're not frickin' 'cute'! I look like frickin' Dracula!" I screamed. Our relationship wasn't going very well.

One rainy night, I went out with a guy friend to pick up pizzas for us and a bunch of our friends. I'd already called in the order. When we got to the pizza joint, the lard-ass behind the counter had gotten the order wrong but wouldn't cop to it. He refused to make the pizzas over. I suddenly felt like killing him. "It was supposed to be sausage, not pepperoni, you dummkopf!" I screamed. I was not gonna pay for those goddamn pizzas. He could take those pizzas and shove 'em up his ass.

Then I threw every goddamn slice on the goddamn floor.

My friend was horrified.

I stood there, my heart pounding.

The lard-ass threatened to call the fuzz but finally made the pizzas over.

Waiting for the new pies to melt and blister felt like an eternity of shame.

When we got back to my apartment, our friends were ravenous.

"What took you so long?" somebody asked.

We didn't answer. Everyone else devoured the pizzas. We barely ate.

Later, after everyone had left, my friend said if I ever did something like that again our friendship would be over.

He said maybe I needed some help.

I could hardly look at him.

I felt like puking, but there was nothing inside me.

Nothing but that dull, mindless anger.

I waited until he left, and then burst out crying.

I cried until I finally told myself to quit my blubbering.

I found myself a headshrinker.

Unlike the one at Bennington, I told her the truth about Jimmy.

"I'd be mad as hell too if he was my father," she said.

After that I was still mad, but at least I didn't throw any more pizzas.

And I prayed I never would again.

God, if you exist—OK, you probably don't, but so what?—please don't let me be like Jimmy.

I was finally ready for that Jimmy lobotomy. It was a delicate operation and I hoped the patient wouldn't croak on the operating table.

Unfortunately, I was the only one with the experience and training to do it.

I was a goddamn doctor after all.

I put on my scrubs and got to work.

I tried to carve Jimmy out of my noggin—I mean, brain.

But of course there were complications.

One night, Shirley called me out of the blue.

I knew something was up.

"What's wrong?" I asked, trying not to imagine every bad scenario.

She said she had fallen down and broken her wrist. For real. No scam.

She sounded shaken up, but was trying to put a good face on it.

"How did it happen?" I pressed her, having my suspicions.

"Oh, you know I'm so clumsy. Your father always said I could trip over a leaf."

Maybe she was stoned. Or maybe Jimmy had pushed her.

I just couldn't pin her down.

Fortunately, there were a lot of Percocets around to ease her pain. Jimmy told her not to gobble down so many, she was depleting his goddamn inventory.

A couple of weeks later, when I called to check up on her, she had hurt the other wrist.

"Just a little sprain. I'm so clumsy."

"You know her, she could trip over a goddamn leaf," grumbled Jimmy on the other line.

I started to think seriously about kidnapping my mother.

I tried to get her on the phone to discuss a plan. But it wasn't easy. More and more, Jimmy wouldn't let her out of his sight. If he went to the racetrack, she went along. To the Greek market, she was riding shotgun. Rat shooting, same deal. He drove her to work and picked her up. She was still working the night shift even while drug dealing. She said it was the only time she felt a little free.

When I finally managed to get her alone on the phone, she wouldn't consider leaving.

"What am I going to do, move in with you? You've got your own life, and besides, I'd never find my way around New York. I can't even drive 'cause I got no sense of direction."

"You can't drive 'cause he never let you!"

"If I went down there, you know he'd come after me. He'd be fit to be tied and who knows what he'd do to both of us. I don't want him anywhere near you."

"If he showed up, I'd call the cops. The New York cops won't let him off the hook. They don't care if he's the best duck hunter in New England."

"If you call the cops, they'll go nosing around and find out what we've been doing. You want to put your own mother in jail?"

"I'm trying to save you!"

"Save me? I don't need to be saved. Your father's not the monster you make him out to be. He's not like Hank."

"He's *just* like Hank."

"Look, I know what I'm doing. I've got it figured out. He thinks *he's* the one keeping me in line, but I've got his number. If I just keep my mouth shut and do what he says, I can keep *him* in line."

That was it. She could control him by being controlled.

It wasn't much of a life, but it was better than ending up like Doris. Better than making your daughter a motherless child like Susan.

We were both out of options.

So she stayed. And I left her there.

I kept working for Woody and writing screenplays about violent men. Woody's producer read one of the scripts and offered to fly me out to Los Angeles—first class—to develop it.

It was good timing.

It was time to get away. Long past time.

So I picked up and moved to California.

"You belong in KooKooLand for leaving that cushy job with Woody Allen," Jimmy said, when I called to tell him the news. "That place is for numbskulls. It's for sissies who can't take the winter and who don't know how to shoot a goddamn gun. Just don't expect me to come out there to visit you."

"OK," I said, resisting the urge to shout yabba dabba doo. "But why don't you let Mom come out for a visit?"

"Are you nuts? She won't like it either."

"Those palm trees look pretty nice," Shirley said timidly. "I'd sure like to see one before I kick the bucket."

"We got plenty of goddamn trees around here. Better goddamn trees than those spindly-looking things that don't even give you any shade after you been mowin' a lawn for some rich Jew movie producer who's been bakin' himself like a nigger by his frickin' swimming pool. I'll tell you one thing. I hope that place has an earthquake and falls into the goddamn sea."

Never mind that I—his own daughter—would be drowning too.

Susan Being Susan

California didn't fall into the sea and neither did I.

All that sunshine really perked me up.

Being farther away from New Hampshire perked me up.

Writing about a murderer perked me up.

But sometimes it also made me think about Susan.

Just as Susan had been shadowed by Doris in that California sunshine, I was shadowed by Susan.

I thought about how many times I had fantasized about us hanging out on the beach together, free from the shadow of our fathers.

Once I saw a woman who looked like her and stopped in my tracks.

But it wasn't her.

I realized there was a good chance I might not even recognize Susan if she did walk by me.

I still tried to keep tabs on her through Jimmy and Shirley, but the news was never good.

She just couldn't stay out of trouble. I heard about her swindling people and forging prescriptions right and left. She was arrested more than twenty times. Some judges seemed to have sympathy for her and tried to cut her a break. But she'd end up right back in their courtroom. Finally, she was sentenced to a few years in prison.

And that's when she did something amazing.

Because New Hampshire was the only state in the country that couldn't be bothered to build a prison for women, Susan was forced to do her time in a county jail. Conditions at the jail were terrible. For five months of the year, when the weather was lousy, the women prisoners weren't even allowed outside to get a breath of fresh air. They were given yarn by their jailers and told to knit hats and mittens for the inmates at the men's prison so *they* could be more comfortable outdoors. All the perks offered to male inmates—rehab programs, a law library, prison jobs—were denied to the women. Worst of all, if a vacancy in a women's prison in another state opened up, a woman could be shipped there on a moment's notice, miles from her family and children.

Susan's bleeding heart bled for those women ripped from their children. It bled for the children, unfairly robbed of their mothers. She knew what that felt like. Every bone in her body told her the whole thing was wrong and that she had to do something about it.

But Susan being Susan, she didn't just write her congressman or send a letter to the local paper. She was Hank Piasecny's daughter and she aimed for the biggest target. She decided to sue the state. To force them to build a prison for women.

She convinced a legal aid group to take on the case. She enlisted a half dozen other women inmates to join her cause.

The class action lawsuit dragged on. Susan got paroled but didn't give up the fight. While she waited for her day in court, she stayed clean, worked menial jobs, and studied the law as intensely as she had once studied medicine. The legal battle brought out the parts of her that had always inspired me: her intelligence, her fearlessness, her compassion.

When the case finally came to trial, in November 1986, it had gotten even stronger. An additional seventeen female inmates added their names to it. Susan testified about what life had been like for her in the place she referred to as "the tomb."

The trial before a judge lasted eight days. When it was over, Susan's side scored a knockout. The judge, in an impassioned decision, agreed that the women prisoners were being treated like second-class citizens. He ordered the state to provide a temporary prison for them within a few months and to build a permanent one within two years.

Once again, Susan was in the news, but this time for a good reason.

Even Jimmy grudgingly had to give her credit for sticking it to the screws—and for outshining me.

"Ha ha. She's nosing you out in the backstretch," he said.

I was happy to let Susan have the limelight. I felt vindicated for all the years I'd kept rooting for her, long past when most people, Jimmy especially, had given up on her.

So much had been taken from Susan, but she'd still succeeded in her goal to give something back. And, no matter what happened to her from that point on, no matter where her life went from there, nobody could ever say she hadn't done something exceptional with it.

A Goner

After such a high point, there was probably nowhere for Susan to go but down.

Her demons came back to haunt her. Drug addiction, writing bad checks, stealing. At least when she got re-incarcerated, there was a better place for her to go.

Over the years, I continued to think about her, but it was impossible to keep track of her as she disappeared for stretches of time doing drugs and changing addresses. Occasionally, I sent letters that were never answered, until I finally stopped sending them.

I thought, once and for all, it was time to turn the page on a story that seemed destined to have a sad ending.

I didn't want to keep living in the past. Despite all of Jimmy's efforts to derail me, I had managed to make a great life for myself. I earned my living writing and producing small movies. I wasn't rich or a big shot, as Jimmy still loved to remind me, but I was doing what I loved.

I had also finally met the man I was going to marry. He was a writer, like me. His name was James. He didn't like being called Jimmy. That was fine by me. He was nothing like my father. He was gentle. Law-abiding. He'd never fired a gun. And he was Jewish. A rabbi was going to marry us.

Jimmy didn't come to the wedding—but not because of the rabbi. By then, he had gotten used to most of my boyfriends being Jewish. True, he still sometimes threatened to kidnap me and take me to Greece to marry me off to a guy like Papou. But I didn't think he was really serious about that. A trip to Greece would cost a bundle and he hadn't spent a red cent on me since I'd left home.

Still, he was willing to spring for a plane ticket to KooKooLand for my wedding.

"It'll be a day you'll never forget," he said, with a sly glee in his voice.

I hung up and got a familiar knot in my gut.

I pictured how things would go.

First, of course, he would get loaded.

Then, he would tell everyone I looked like the Bride of Frankenstein. He couldn't call me Dracula anymore since I'd gone and gotten braces a few years back and ruined all his fun.

He would call my husband four-eyes and announce all Jews were blind as a bat.

He would tell some woman she looked like Ava Gardner and try to grab her ass.

He would ask the rabbi if he liked pork chops. Hey, it was a joke. It wasn't his fault the guy had no goddamn sense of humor.

Imagining that whole scenario didn't make *me* feel like laughing. It made me feel like canceling my wedding and eloping.

Who needs a fancy shindig? I asked myself. Who needs to blow all that dough, anyway?

Suddenly, I froze. That's what he *wants*, I realized. He *wants* me to cancel it.

He was still putting ideas in my head.

Still putting words in my mouth like a ventriloquist.

But I was nobody's dummy anymore.

Nobody's goddamn dummkopf.

I didn't cancel my wedding.

I canceled Jimmy instead.

"I think it would be better if you don't come," I told him a few days later.

There was a seething silence on the other end of the phone.

"I wouldn't be caught dead at that shindig anyway," he finally barked, and hung up.

"How can you treat your father that way?" wailed Shirley, who had been listening in on the other line.

"I don't want to be miserable at my own wedding. Anyway, you heard him. He doesn't want to come."

"He's just saying that to save face. You insulted him. I think you just don't want your big-shot friends to meet your family."

"I want everyone to meet you. And Virginia too."

"Does your sister know you're doing this, not inviting your father?"

"I told her. She said she's still coming."

"Well, I can't say the same for myself," Shirley said, and hung up.

"My mother's probably not coming to the wedding," I wailed to my husband-to-be.

"I bet it'll work out. I bet she'll come around," said James, since, being the opposite of Jimmy, he was an optimist.

"But who will walk you down the aisle?" asked one of my girlfriends, when I told her about disinviting Jimmy.

"Me," I said. "I wouldn't put it past Jimmy to trip me on my way down the aisle."

"Oh, he can't be that bad," she said, laughing.

"Oh yes, he is. He really is."

I didn't regret my decision, even though Jimmy had stopped talking to me. That was kind of a blessing, actually.

And James was right. Shirley did end up coming.

Maybe one of us should go, she told Jimmy. We don't want the neighbors talking. We want to keep our problems on a stone wall, don't we?

She had his number. He grudgingly agreed to let her go.

Shirley lost a lot of weight to fit into a sexy black dress that she hid from Jimmy.

Virginia dyed her hair a fiery red, and painted her nails to match.

When they showed up, I thought they both looked great.

The night before the wedding, Jimmy sucker punched me.

He called and wished me a beautiful day. I wasn't sure if he really meant it, or if he was just trying to rock my boat. Trying to make me feel guilty.

But I didn't feel guilty. I shed a few tears and thanked him for calling.

Then I hung up and forgot all about him.

The next day, I had the best day of my life.

Shirley and Virginia had the time of their lives too.

They were both crazy about KooKooLand.

"I'd move out here if I was younger and had the guts to leave your father," Shirley sighed.

"I'd move if I didn't have a job, a husband, and a kid," said Virginia.

They both vowed to come back again soon.

I made Shirley a photo album of the wedding so she'd have a reminder of a good time in her life. Something to keep her going whenever things got rough with Jimmy.

And in the months after the wedding, things got really rough.

I didn't know how rough at the time. Shirley hid it. I found out later. More than I wanted to know.

Jimmy was going off the rails.

He was drinking even more than usual. Drinking morning, noon, and night. He was gambling more too. He blew all their drug dough on the horses. He berated Shirley nonstop. Once, he caught her watching a Red Sox game and went ballistic. He said she was drooling over those lard-ass players like an old whore.

He was determined to make Shirley pay for her good time in California. Every time he saw her looking at that photo album, he told her she was lording it over him. He felt like that goddamn photo album was proof of something he had suspected since the moment I was born: that she loved me more than him.

His jealousy festered like a boil. He became consumed with rage. Day after day he told Shirley she was stupid and worthless and ugly.

Finally, one August afternoon everything came to a head.

Jimmy had been boozing it up since breakfast. He cornered Shirley by the stove as she was making dinner. He told her flat out he wanted her dead. She saw the look in his eyes and grabbed for the closest weapon to defend herself—a hammer from the kitchen drawer. He wrenched the hammer away from her and began to smash the wall beside her head with it, threatening to smash her head in. She broke away from him and ran toward the bedroom. He threw the hammer at her. It landed on the floor in front of her and broke apart. A piece of it ricocheted into her ankle. She hobbled into the bedroom and locked herself in. He kicked the door down—he was still strong as an ox. He pushed her down on the bed, kneeled on top of her, and put his hands on her throat.

Shirley flailed underneath him, gasping for breath. His loveless eyes were deep, black pools trying to drown her.

She felt certain she was a goner.

But three things ended up saving her.

The mattress was old and saggy and didn't provide a stable surface for a sixty-eight-year-old drunk man.

All the booze that he had been consuming for most of the day finally kicked in.

And Shirley loved life—even if she was stuck sharing it with a murderous drunk—and wasn't ready for it to end.

She fought off her attacker, her husband of forty-five years.

She tattooed him with her fists like a boxer, until Jimmy lost his balance on that saggy mattress and fell over. She scrambled away from him and ran out of the room.

She did something she'd never done before. She called the cops down off that stone wall.

The cops came and arrested Jimmy, but not before he told them to go fuck themselves a whole bunch of times.

When the cops questioned Shirley, she told them the truth: It wasn't the first time Jimmy had attacked her.

Jimmy was put in jail for the night and then granted bail the next day. The bail conditions stipulated he couldn't go near Shirley, drink, or possess a firearm.

He left jail, promptly got plastered, and returned to the apartment, where he still had a few firearms squirreled away.

By now, Shirley had had enough time to assess her situation and she regretted calling the cops. She'd never lived alone in her entire life. She didn't drive. She'd never written a check or paid a bill. She didn't have a single friend she could call her own. She ate what Jimmy told her to eat. She wore what Jimmy told her to wear.

I'll die without him, she told herself.

He knew what he was doing all those years. He'd set her up.

When Jimmy stormed in the front door, Shirley didn't know whether to hide from him or hug him.

She tried to apologize, to smooth things over.

Jimmy was still mad as hell. He got out a suitcase and pretended to pack. He told her she wouldn't last two weeks without him. He told her it would get around that she was living there all alone. He told her one of the junkies they sold OxyContin to would break in and beat her skull in.

She begged him not to go.

The phone rang and Jimmy answered—hell, it was his goddamn phone.

A woman from the police department was checking up on Shirley. When the woman found out Jimmy was there, she hung up and sent a cruiser over to the apartment. One of the cops who arrived had handcuffed Jimmy the day before. He knew Jimmy wouldn't go without a fight, so he already had his handcuffs out.

This time, Shirley told the cops to beat it.

"Can't two people fight in peace?" she pleaded.

But it didn't matter what Shirley said or what she thought she wanted. The cops told Jimmy he was under arrest for violating his bail conditions.

"Go fuck yourself!" Jimmy yelled, and ran down the hall and into the bedroom. The cops took off after him. When they got to the doorway, Jimmy had already dropped to his knees and was reaching under that saggy mattress for his loaded pistol. The cops tackled Jimmy before he could get his hands on the gun. They struggled to handcuff him, Jimmy fighting all the way.

Outside, before they got him in the car, Jimmy told the cops if he could've gotten to that piece, he would've shot them both through the head.

Jimmy was rebooked into the Valley Street jail.

He was now facing two felony charges—resisting arrest and pulling a gun on a police officer. He was looking at a possible four years in prison.

When Shirley called to tell me what had happened, she left out a lot of the details. Most of those I learned down the road when I read the police report and when Shirley was a little more forthcoming.

Still, it sounded pretty terrible. I flew home to see her. She looked like a different person than the one who had come out to California. All the happiness had been wrung out of her like a dishrag.

She wasn't supposed to be in touch with Jimmy, but he was getting messages to her through his brothers, his friends, and sometimes Virginia, who he could still manipulate pretty good when he wanted to.

"He's sorry, he really is," said Virginia. "He can't stop crying."

"I don't give a damn how he feels. I want him locked up."

He called me on my cell phone, crying.

"I'm a palooka, but I love her," he said.

It sounded like a line from a boxing movie. But whether he was feeding me a line or he really meant it didn't matter.

"I don't want you anywhere near her," I said.

"You've never been on my side," he sobbed.

I hung up.

I told Shirley this was finally her chance and she should take it.

"Let them put him in prison and you'll be safe," I told her.

"I won't be safe," she cried. "I'll get my skull beat in. Those hopheads will all know he's not here to protect me."

"Then *move*. Just leave. Come out to California with me."

"I'm too scared to move. I'm not like you. You're the brave one in this family."

"Nothing could be as scary as living with him all these years."

"Your father's not all bad."

"Maybe not," I said. "But he's bad enough."

"I can't do it. I can't move out to KooKooLand."

I shook my head, resigned.

I returned to California, alone.

Before I left, Virginia and I made a plan. She'd spend some nights with Shirley. We'd both call her every day. I bought dowels to put in the windows so they couldn't be jimmied from the outside. I bought a phone with an answering machine so she could screen her calls. We did what we could.

"He's really sorry," Virginia repeated to me. "He's calling me every day. Maybe he deserves a second chance."

"He's had a million second chances. I don't think one more's going to make a difference."

"I can't abandon him like you," she burst out sobbing. "He didn't abandon *me* when my own mother didn't want me. I owe him something."

"He told you that, didn't he?"

"Yes, but it's true."

I hugged her and that was all I could do.

After I was gone, Virginia threw herself into caring for Jimmy and Shirley. She helped Jimmy move into an apartment near hers, cooked him Greek egg lemon soup, and did his laundry. She drove Shirley to the supermarket and to doctor appointments and did her laundry too on days when Shirley was too sad to do it herself.

Shirley took all of the money she had hidden away to pay for the best lawyer she could get for Jimmy.

The lawyer got Jimmy's friends to write letters on his behalf. Everyone attested to what an all-around great guy he was. Shirley wrote a statement saying Jimmy was a wonderful, loving husband who had made one terrible mistake. Jimmy went to AA and made a good show of sobering up.

Finally, Jimmy appeared in a trial before a judge. I stayed away, but Shirley and Jimmy gave me a full report later.

Jimmy was wearing a suit and tie and shiny new shoes. He'd had a haircut and a shave and there was no deer blood under his fingernails. He'd been sober for several weeks and his eyes were clear and contrite.

As Jimmy would say, he looked like John Q. Public.

The prosecutor didn't buy this new and improved Jimmy. He said the real Jimmy was a ticking time bomb. He compared him to a mass murderer named Carl Drega who had just terrorized New England. He wanted Jimmy locked up so he couldn't terrorize Shirley or anyone else in New England.

Jimmy was a ball of rage inside.

I'll show you a frickin' time bomb, he wanted to scream. Just let me out of this frickin' monkey suit and I'll show you, you punk.

But he just stood there, quietly remorseful.

The judge bought Jimmy's baloney, like people often did.

For the two felonies, including attempting to pull a gun on a police officer, Jimmy was given a one-year prison sentence, deferred—meaning he didn't even have to serve one day behind bars. He was also given two years' probation.

In a separate decision, for the hammer assault and attempted strangulation of Shirley, Jimmy paid a fine of about two hundred dollars.

I called home to find out what had happened and he picked up the phone. My heart sank.

I learned Jimmy, like his old buddy Hank, had beaten the rap.

Jimmy thought otherwise. He thought he'd gotten railroaded. Totally frickin' railroaded. Big Brother had taken away his guns. He couldn't own a firearm for seven frickin' years.

"Those bastards might as well have cut off my arms," he said. "They cut off my goddamn prick."

He vowed that when he got his hands on a weapon again, the cop who fingered him twice, that smart-ass with the handcuffs, was a goner. So was the loudmouth prosecutor.

Two shots, right to the noggin.

Bang bang.

The Last Round

A few months after Jimmy tried to kill Shirley, I began to look for Susan again. Maybe I was just looking for my next screenplay. Or maybe I was procrastinating about the screenplay I should've been writing. Or maybe I just felt she'd understand better than anyone what I'd been going through.

It was the beginning of 1998 and I hadn't been in touch with her for several years. I had no idea where she was or if she was even alive. But if she was, I was determined to find her.

I thought the most logical place to start looking for her, her most likely residence, was the women's prison. I called and tried to find out if she was incarcerated there. The pleasant woman who answered the phone turned unpleasant when I mentioned Susan's name. She put me on hold forever. When she finally came back, she said Susan wasn't in their system and hung up.

I tried a few more times, pretending to be other friends or relatives looking for Susan, but each time I got the same response. She wasn't there and nobody knew where she was.

I quickly discovered that Susan wasn't too popular with the folks in the criminal justice system. For one thing, she was a criminal, and a repeat offender at that. But, a bigger deal, I suspected, was that she had shown up the prison authorities with her lawsuit. They were supposed to be the good guys and she'd made them look bad.

And it wasn't just the jailers who weren't keen on Susan.

I ran into a roadblock at the Manchester library too. When the friendly librarian learned that I wanted to search the archives to find information about Susan, she became unfriendly. "You don't want to read about *her*," she insisted. I had to practically twist the old bat's arm to get her to show me the microfilm.

I didn't get any better reception at the local newspaper. I tried to place an ad to solicit information on Susan's whereabouts, but no amount of cajoling could get the paper to run it.

I reached out to some of Susan's relatives. I spoke to her uncle Ted, an ornery man who reminded me a lot of his younger brother, Hank. Ted had an additional reason to despise Susan. Susan had swiped the gun she'd used to kill Hank from Ted's son, Mark. Ted didn't know if his murderous, thieving niece was dead or alive, but the one thing he was one hundred percent certain of was that Susan had killed more people than she ever got caught for. In fact, she'd killed her own mother and made poor Hank take the fall for it.

"But she was away at college and Hank's truck was seen leaving the house," I said, incredulous.

Ted looked like he wanted to take a swing at me.

Clearly, he was not going to be of much help.

As a last resort, I turned to Jimmy. If anyone could get a line on where a druggie or thief was holed up, it was him.

Jimmy had settled right back into living with Shirley after his close brush with the law. I didn't talk to either of them very often. When I did, Shirley said Jimmy was a new man. I thought he sounded like the same old Jimmy. Dealing pills, gambling, boozing—but hey, in moderation so he wouldn't get caught by his probation officer.

When Jimmy heard about my search for Susan he told me he'd ask around, but take it from him, I was wasting my goddamn time.

"What is it with you and that hophead? Forget about her, will ya, once and for all! She's rotting in a ditch somewhere. Right where she belongs."

If anyone deserved to be rotting in a ditch, it was him, but I didn't tell him that. The last thing I wanted was to get him all riled up. He'd already purchased a few guns under the table to replace the ones he'd had to get rid of when he got pinched. A hunting buddy was keeping them for him so Jimmy's probation officer wouldn't find them during his periodic searches of the apartment.

At the time Jimmy bought those guns, he'd called and offered to hook me up with one of my own.

"You need a piece to defend yourself against those niggers in L.A. the next time some lowlife Rodney King fires them up."

If I needed a piece, it was to get peace from him.

But still, I said no. I didn't trust myself not to pull a Susan and use it on him.

Unable to talk me into getting a gun, Jimmy sent me a can of Mace instead. I stuck it in my underwear drawer and it leaked all over my lingerie.

No doubt he'd gotten it from Uncle Barney, who was still out there moving lousy merchandise.

Jimmy's efforts to find Susan were a dud too.

But he did turn up some upsetting information about her brother, Terry.

He had killed himself at the age of forty.

It seemed incredible. Every member of Susan's family had died violently.

"There's a curse on that family," said Jimmy, sounding like he wanted to spit. "Don't get yourself in the middle of it."

I asked him if he knew whether Terry had ever reconciled with Susan.

"Nah, he never had nothin' to do with her. That's what I heard, anyway. Look, I'm tellin' ya, just forget about that hophead. She's gotta be a goner by now."

But I refused to throw in the towel.

"Something tells me she's still out there. I just feel it."

"Ya know, you woulda got creamed in the ring," said Jimmy. "You won't even go down when you're beat."

He was right. If life was a boxing match—and that's what he'd always taught me it was—I wanted to be the last one standing.

I never, *never* wanted to give up.

So, I went back to where I started. I began calling people in the prison system again. I was convinced one of them must have a bead on Susan. One of them must know *something*.

And at long last, as Jimmy would say, *badoom*—I hit the target.

I got a parole officer on the phone, a guy I'd never spoken to before. He'd been on the job only a few months and I guess he didn't know enough to clam up like everyone else. He told me Susan was incarcerated, had been incarcerated the whole time I had been looking for her. She'd been in the women's prison for a while but they couldn't handle her there and had shipped her off to the men's prison in Concord. She was now in a mini prison within the men's prison, the secure psychiatric unit. SPU—pronounced *spew*—housed the most severely mentally ill criminals, men mostly and a few women. When I called back a prison official I had previously spoken to and told him I knew Susan was in SPU, he seemed surprised I knew and finally admitted that she was there. He grudgingly agreed to check with her treatment team and see if she was well enough to have a visit from me.

I waited and called and waited and called and waited and called. Finally, I got an answer. No visit. Sorry. Tough luck.

I asked if I could at least write to Susan. The prison official said I could try but he wasn't sure they'd pass on the letters. Over a few months I wrote to her several times. The letters were never returned, but I never heard anything back. My biggest fear was that Susan had gotten the letters and didn't want anything to do with me. Or maybe I'd stirred things up for her and made her worse. I pictured her getting a letter and freaking out and being put in a straitjacket. I didn't know if they still gave shock treatments in those places, but I pictured that too.

One day, with nothing to lose, I picked up the phone and called SPU directly. I was persistent and got the director of the unit on the phone. I told her I was an old family friend of Susan's. I told her I'd been searching for Susan for a long, long time. I told her Susan had been my inspiration to make something of my life.

There was a long pause.

The woman made no promises but said she'd see what she could do.

The next day, a sunny March morning in L.A., my phone rang early.

The caller's voice was throaty and playful, and I would've known it anywhere.

"This is Susan ... Piasecny ... Hughes ... Adair," she said, pausing between each word for maximum dramatic effect.

I leaned against the wall to hold myself up. I said her name over and over, like the mantra it had once been for me.

Susan. Susan. Susan.

I finally managed to ask how she was. She laughed and said she was pretty good—except for being locked up with a bunch of lunatics. I was relieved to see she still had that sense of humor. In fact, I thought she sounded pretty good.

She said she couldn't stay on the phone because she was on the director's line, but she gave me a number to call back on.

I hung up and let out a scream.

My husband hugged me.

"You found her," he said. "You finally found her."

I dialed Susan right back. We spoke for two hours that morning and another two that afternoon. There was so much to catch up on.

We talked about Susan's life over the past several years, her fight to get released from prison, her third marriage to a man who had died, her isolation from her family.

"There's just one thing I'd like to know—how's my brother doing?" she asked.

"I—I'll try to find out," I stammered.

I didn't know how to tell her about Terry.

Then she asked about Jimmy and Shirley.

I didn't dodge that question. I told her what Jimmy had done to Shirley.

She said Shirley should dump him and join me in California.

"That was my dream, remember, to move out there. Hey, maybe I can come visit you too when I get out?"

"Yeah, maybe," I said, trying not to sound too ambivalent. I wasn't sure Susan visiting me would be such a hot idea. After all, she was an addict, possibly crazy, and a bit of a con artist. I knew she'd crept into a man's house in the middle of the night and shot him dead, even if it was sort of justified.

I knew she wasn't the person I had imagined her to be when I was nine.

That person had never really existed.

After all these years, I was just getting to know her.

"Can you come visit me?" she asked shyly.

"I'm coming," I replied, with no hesitation.

Before I could visit, the prison authorities had to run a felony check on me. I assured them they wouldn't find anything. I was so squeaky clean I didn't even have a parking ticket.

"You turned out to be a real Dudley Do-Right," complained Jimmy, when I told him about the felony check. "Don't you ever just wanna go out and raise hell?"

"Nope."

I'd seen enough hell; I didn't need to raise any more.

While I waited to be approved for a visit, Susan called me constantly. My phone bills soared, but I couldn't refuse her calls. She had no one else to talk to.

All this time she kept asking about her brother. She told me she'd decorated her cell with images of men that reminded her of him—great athletes and handsome movie stars.

After clearing it with her doctor, I haltingly told her the truth.

She was pained to hear that Terry had died, but not surprised to learn he had killed himself. She said Terry, the strapping ex-boxer, had been pummeled by depression for years.

Hearing that, I was knocked for a loop. I'd spent so much of my childhood wishing I'd been born a boy—a big, strong, fighting boy like Terry. I thought my life would be better if I was a boy. I thought Jimmy would love me more if I could lace up some gloves, get in the ring, and beat someone silly until they tasted their own blood. But I could now see it wouldn't have made a difference.

Boy or girl, son or daughter, life as Hank or Jimmy's kid would've always been a fight. And, sometimes, like Terry, you just went down.

Blood Sisters

I left California and flew back to New Hampshire to see Susan. I rented a car and drove north from Manchester to Concord on a pleasant day in June. As I got close to the prison, the sky turned dark as if some numbskull up there had forgotten to pay the electric bill. The moment I pulled into the driveway, three shards of lightning sliced through the darkness and the clouds spilled their guts.

I shook my head. Too frickin' unbelievable.

I ran through the downpour and entered the main reception area, clammy from the rain and my anxiety. While I waited to get checked in, a guard, seeing my driver's license, began to kid me about California. Wasn't I afraid of getting buried in an earthquake? Or creamed on the freeway? Or frostbitten from those brutal winters?

Compared to this place, I joked back, fault lines, traffic, and perpetual sunshine suit me just fine.

After checking in, I was directed to a more remote area of the property, where the secure psychiatric unit was tucked away.

I was buzzed through several thick metal doors and took a filthy elevator up to SPU. I carried five bucks in change—all I was allowed to bring in—to buy Cheez Doodles and Kit Kats for Susan from the vending machines.

Although the main waiting room, where I'd checked in, had been jammed with visitors, the waiting room at SPU was totally empty. I figured the SPU patients were so far gone, most of their relatives had written them off.

I sat down on an orange plastic chair that was bolted to the floor, and nervously waited for someone to bring Susan. A noisy air conditioner blew cold air over my damp body. I wished I'd brought a sweater. I wished I wasn't so nervous. I wished Susan and I were meeting on a warm beach somewhere.

Five . . . ten . . . twenty . . . minutes went by, and still no Susan. I wondered if she was as anxious as I was. I wondered if she was going to stand me up.

Finally, the door buzzed open.

Susan walked through it, all spiffed up, like she was on a first date.

I jumped up to meet her.

She sauntered toward me with an impish smile. Though she had warned me that prison, Percodans, and poor health had taken their toll on her appearance, I would have recognized her anywhere. Now fifty-six, she was still quite attractive. Her dark hair was cut in a cool spiky-on-top, long-tail-in-the-back style. Her light olive skin was unlined and radiant. Her mink-brown eyes still seemed to have a hint of gold.

She turned to the guard and asked if she was allowed to give me a hug, or what. She'd never had a visitor and didn't know the drill. The guard nodded, bored.

We embraced and it wasn't awkward at all. My nervousness disappeared faster than those five bucks.

For three hours we ate piles of junk food and gossiped like old girlfriends. We talked about our fathers, of course, and about my life in the outside world.

She asked if I was going to have any pip-squeaks of my own. I told her I was scared I'd be a crummy parent. Scared of passing on Jimmy's genes. Just. Plain. Scared. I said it was miracle enough that I had a great marriage. I didn't want to push my luck.

She said she had a couple of stepkids from her third marriage but didn't see them anymore. She said she didn't see anyone from the outside anymore but tried not to get down about it.

Her Christianity got her through, she insisted. She took a stab at converting me, but I told her it was way too late for that. Jimmy had gotten to me first. I was an agnostic like him and didn't think that was going to change.

We moved on to talking about other things—Monica Lewinsky, the Oklahoma City bombers, cloning. She was still up on everything.

She kidded me to hurry up and write something about her already, she wasn't getting any younger. She reminded me she'd done some acting in high school and would be open to taking a part in the movie of her life.

She was a little crazy, a little delusional, but who isn't?

It was the kind of afternoon I'd dreamed of sharing with her years ago. Except, back then, I'd pictured us playing Candy Land in a bedroom with frilly curtains and stuffed animals on our laps. I never imagined it would be taking place in a prison with stale candy, barbed wire on the windows, and a guard breathing down our necks.

He told us our time was up.

I returned to the prison several more times that week. Not every visit was as delightful as the first. Sometimes Susan was lucid, sometimes not. She was friendly one moment, sullen the next. Whether she was schizophrenic or just medicated, I couldn't say. I had to roll with the punches. I had to accept her for who she was, not project on to her who I wanted her to be. Harsh though it might be, I wanted to live in the reality of Susan, not the fantasy.

The reality was pretty sad. I often sat in the car after I left her and cried.

On my last visit, I knew she was upset that I was leaving. She looked at me intently.

"Do you have any idea what it's meant to me to hear from you after all this time? You were the closest thing to a sister I ever had."

I nodded and hugged her.

The bored guard came to take her away. She followed him to the door. Then she turned and called out one last thing:

"I love you."

Her words startled me. They filled that sad, empty room with a kind of joy.

"I love you, too," I called back.

She stepped over the threshold and the door slammed behind her. I watched through the little window until she disappeared, the way Shirley had always done with me, so nothing bad would happen to her.

I stood there for several moments, still feeling her presence all around me.

I knew all those years of searching for Susan, of wanting something from her—approval, insight, love—had finally come to an end. I realized she had already given me everything I needed years ago—a road map for my life. Just because she hadn't followed the map herself didn't make it any less valuable.

KooKooLand

Susan completed her sentence in a few years, was paroled, and was never incarcerated again.

She lived the next several years in a small group home in Concord under the watchful eye of a court-appointed guardian, a nice woman who helped keep her on the straight and narrow. I visited her many times. One time, I even brought Shirley to see her. She hadn't had a mother's arms around her in a long time. I could see from her face how much it meant.

We stayed friends to the end—until her illnesses caught up with her and she passed away at sixty-five.

I flew back to the group home for a memorial service. I passed around a photo of Susan in her glory days, on her way to med school. I read a few poems she had published in her college paper.

"Wow, she was beautiful," said one person.

"And smart," added another.

"I loved her," said someone else.

"Me too," I said.

No one from her family was there. Just me. Her blood sister.

As for Jimmy, his worst fear came true. All those years of smoking and drinking finally caught up with him. He got lung cancer. The Big C.

He knew enough about medicine, and cancer in particular, to know his days were numbered. But he was a fighter, always a fighter, and he went down swinging. He got two-thirds of his lung chopped off. An hour out of surgery he yelled at the nurse to give him some goddamn scrambled eggs, then force-fed himself to get his strength back. He had a round of radiation and still hit the racetrack every day. He took an expensive drug that the VA paid for. He was, at long last, a veteran—the dummkopfs in Washington had finally reclassified the World War II merchant mariners as veterans.

"Now that most of us are kicking the bucket, those bastards are finally doing the right thing," he said, and on that score, I had to agree with him.

The whole time he had cancer, he never gave up cancer sticks.

"Rage, rage against the dying of the light," he said, quoting Dylan Thomas.

After fifteen months of raging, he was getting near the end. He said he was going to die like a man, in his own bed, and insisted Shirley take care of him. Shirley couldn't manage it alone. Virginia offered to move in with them, but I thought she'd done more than her share. So I moved back in with Jimmy and Shirley for the last month to help out.

I wish I could say knowing he was going to die made Jimmy nicer. I wish I could say it made him apologize for some of the awful things he'd done to us. I wish I could say it made him appreciate his family and the time we had left together.

But it didn't. It simply didn't.

It just made him madder.

He was mad at the raw deal of life, of his life in particular. He was mad at every single numbskull who was going to live on after him. He was mad that his big-shot daughter was going to be globe-trotting to film festivals while he was trapped six feet under like a palooka.

We tried—we *really* tried—to comfort him, but he just kept getting madder.

Here's how he spent those last few weeks:

He secretly threw out my wedding album, one of the things Shirley still treasured most in the world.

He compiled a list of all the wars he could remember, to prove that man was nothing but a killing machine.

He plotted how to become a killing machine himself and shoot the cop who had arrested him. He tried to enlist me in the plot, wanting me to drive the getaway car.

And, last but certainly not least, he tried to take Shirley and me with him into the great beyond.

This last act—whether spontaneous or planned, I can't really say—started out innocently enough.

He said he wanted to go for a Sunday drive.

"Great!" I said, pleased he was finally expressing something nice we could do together.

"I wanna drive my own goddamn car one last time."

He hadn't been behind the wheel for a few weeks and for good reason—he was too weak and medicated.

But I didn't say he was too weak. I knew better than to use that word to describe him.

And I didn't say he was too medicated. He was used to driving drunk.

"You can see the scenery better if I drive," I said.

"I don't care about that, dum-dum. I just want to feel like a goddamn man one last time in my life. Like I can go where I want, do what I want. I want to be King of the Road one more time. Can you at least give me that? I'm dying, for Chrissake."

I *was* a dum-dum. I fell for it.

Shirley and I proceeded to hook up his oxygen tank. His pants were falling off him. His eyes were a little yellow.

But he smiled at me and made a joke.

"Hop to it. I'm gonna croak before you two get me outta here."

We walked with him to the car. I held his oxygen tank. Shirley walked in front of him. I knew what she was thinking. If he toppled over, she'd cushion his fall.

It was almost April. Spring was in the air. New grass was poking up through the mud.

I helped Jimmy get behind the wheel of his big boat of a car. I was about to get in the passenger seat beside him, in case something went wrong. But he had other ideas.

"I want your mother sitting beside me. I want my beautiful doll beside me, just like old times."

I hesitated, and then climbed in the backseat.

And off we went. Just like old times.

At first, everything seemed fine. In fact, Jimmy's driving was better than before he got sick. At least he wasn't cutting people off. At least he wasn't flipping the bird and yelling *pluck pluck pluck*.

I began to relax. I told myself I was doing something nice for a dying man. So what if he was vengeful? I didn't have to be like him. I *wasn't* like him. I *wasn't*. That's what I told myself, as I sat in the backseat behind him.

Still, I couldn't help but notice how much, even in his debilitated state, I resembled him physically. In his sad, tired eyes, I could see the hue and shape of my own sad eyes. In the sag of his shoulders, I could feel the weight on my own shoulders. In his hand clenched on the steering wheel, I could see my own fist, lying in my lap like a knotted ball of roots that had outgrown its pot.

Like it or not, he was the man who made me.

I caught his eye in the rearview mirror and smiled.

I still held out a shred of hope for his redemption.

But it wasn't to be. Not in this life, anyway.

A young woman drove up beside him. She was singing along to a song: Madonna's "Like a Virgin."

Jimmy glared over at her, despising her carefree mood and the life she had in front of her.

"Goddamn women drivers!" he croaked in his cancer-wracked voice.

I felt my stomach start to tighten. Just like it had on that car ride to see *Blood Feast* decades before.

In Jimmy's car nothing had really changed. The car moved, but went nowhere. Time stood still like a deer in the headlights.

Jimmy yanked off his oxygen and defiantly lit a cancer stick. It was dangerous to smoke around oxygen, but when had danger ever stopped him?

At the next red light we came to, Jimmy sat there stone silent.

"This is a nice ride, isn't it?" chirped Shirley, hiding her real feelings.

All of sudden, he spat back two words: "Fuck it!"

He smashed his foot down on the accelerator and barreled into the path of oncoming traffic. Shirley and I screamed. I saw streaks of metallic color and heard rubber squealing as drivers slammed on their brakes.

Miraculously, nobody hit us.

Shirley, in her one act of driving, managed to jam her foot on the brake.

I don't know if somebody was watching out for us or if we were just a couple of lucky so-and-sos.

Whatever it was, the bad guy didn't win.

In Jimmy's race to end his life, a race he had tried to take us along on, he didn't prevail.

We finally beat him.

I took over the wheel and he never drove again.

He died a few weeks later.

I didn't feel as bad as I thought I would.

After several days, Shirley insisted she just wanted to be alone. She wasn't afraid of the hopheads anymore. Word had gotten around that she was out of the business. She told me to go home, and she told Virginia the same thing.

Virginia and I called her every day. She usually said she was OK, but we could tell she wasn't doing very well. Pretty soon, she fell into a deep depression. Virginia brought her food, but she wouldn't eat it. She stayed in bed and talked about how much she missed Jimmy.

I could only think of one thing that might cheer her up. A few months after Jimmy's death, I bought three tickets to a Red Sox game. All these years,

Shirley had remained a fan, despite every effort of Jimmy's to prevent her from being one. But she'd never been to an actual game.

I showed up unannounced and called Shirley from the front steps.

"Look out your window, Mom. I have a surprise for you."

All the shades to her apartment were down. She lifted the edge of one of them and her sad face peered out.

I held up the tickets.

The next day—on Shirley's eightieth birthday—Shirley, Virginia, and I made our way to Fenway Park. Virginia wasn't a baseball fan—she was just being a good sport. But even she stopped in her tracks when we entered that old ballpark and came upon that bright green field.

"It's beautiful," she said.

"Oh, my God," said Shirley.

Shirley watched every pitch as if it were the most important one in the history of the game.

Unfortunately, the Red Sox, being the Red Sox, lost.

But that was OK because it was the year they broke an eighty-six-year curse and won the World Series. And Shirley watched every game they played to do it.

After that, Shirley had eight fun, Jimmy-free years. She never learned to drive, but she learned how to write a check. She came to California several times. My husband always met her at the airport with yellow roses. She got to see a lot of palm trees.

As for Susan, she finally made it to California too.

When she died, there were no blood relatives to claim her ashes. Her guardian turned them over to me.

I scattered half of her ashes over her mother's frozen grave in New Hampshire.

And the other half I keep with me here in sunny California.

Sometimes I can't help it. I still call it KooKooLand.

Susan and Gloria, Concord, NH.

Acknowledgments

There are a number of people whose encouragement and early feedback meant so much to the writing of *KooKooLand*. I would especially like to thank:

Beth Atkin, for her deep love and support.

Kate Guinzburg, for spurring me on at a crucial moment and for her insightful notes.

Cheryl Hill, for suggesting I write the book in the first place and for being my *sistah*.

Lucinda Jenney, for always being in my corner and for giving me my wonderful goddaughter, Marion.

Janet Jones, for her love and kindness and for many delicious meals along the way.

Ellen Sherman, for showing me the way out of the projects.

Anne Spielberg, for our long friendship, our shared journey as writers, and our much-needed respites at the Milky Way with Leah.

My endless gratitude goes out to:

My film agent, Steve Fisher, who has been an ardent supporter of the book—and a dear friend—through all the years it took to write it.

My literary agent, Carol Mann, who also hung in there, and then made sure the book found the right home.

My publisher, Judith Regan, whose enthusiasm has been a writer's dream come true.

My editor, Alexis Gargagliano, who found just the right balance of encouragement and criticism to help make the book infinitely better.

I would also like to thank:

Jeffrey Ressner, for our way-too-brief friendship and for the role he played in helping the book find its perfect home.

Rina Echavez, for being a model of sweetness and strength and for facilitating Jeffrey's prediction.

Pablo Fenjves, for generously putting in a good word.

Johnny Rothman and Suzie Bolotin, for their longtime friendship and for convincing me to finally send the darn thing out.

Gary Emery, for his insights about life and writing and for helping me to leave the old KooKooLand behind.

The Greenbergs—Jennifer, Barry, Lauren, and Miranda—for being my incredible family-by-marriage.

Suzanne Joffe, Carol Joffe, and Nicole Holofcener, for being my incredible surrogate family.

Dan Opatoshu, Atma Wiseman, Amy Ness, Bonnie Palef, Henry Schipper, and Mitra Manesh, for their early reads of the manuscript and their unwavering support.

Cleo Damanis, for giving me a cushion to be creative.

Gordon Wood, for sharing the Wood family history and photos.

Peter Ansin, for being my early champion.

The Gordons—Keith, Barbara, and Mark—for loving me when I needed it most.

Jeffrey Townsend, for his love and generosity.

Michael Shedler, for always being a mensch.

Eight special friends, for injecting levity into my life.

Brian De Palma, for his tough-love lessons in writing and filmmaking.

Martin Scorsese and Robert De Niro, for giving me the opportunity to observe two great artists at work.

Woody Allen, for encouraging me as a writer and a filmmaker through the years.

Steve Friedman, for giving me my first writing job in KooKooLand.

And last, but most definitely not least, I am indebted to:

Susan Piasecny Hughes Adair, who inspired me.

My sister, Virginia, who bravely let me film and interview her, and who always wanted our story to be told.

My father, Jimmy, who taught me to appreciate books and movies, who sat for hours of interviews and who said, "Crucify me if you have to, to get the goddamn story right."

My mother, Shirley, who loved me unconditionally and gave me her blessing to jump off that stone wall.

My husband, James, who showed me just how wonderful a man can be.

GLORIA NORRIS grew up in a tight-knit Greek family. She attended Bennington College and graduated from Sarah Lawrence. She began her career in New York as an assistant to film directors Brian De Palma, Martin Scorsese, and Woody Allen. Since relocating to Los Angeles, she has worked as a screenwriter, with assignments that have taken her from Paris to the Amazon. As an independent producer, her films have premiered at the Sundance, Toronto International, and Tribeca Film Festivals.

4-13-16